Previous Years' Solved Papers

Sociology

For UGC-NET/SLET/JRF

Paper I, II and III

Atlantic Research Division

ATLANTIC
PUBLISHERS & DISTRIBUTORS (P) LTD

Published by
ATLANTIC
PUBLISHERS & DISTRIBUTORS (P) LTD
7/22, Ansari Road, Darya Ganj, New Delhi-110002
Phones : +91-11-40775252, 40775214, 23273880, 23275880
Fax : +91-11-23285873
Web : www.atlanticbooks.com
E-mail : orders@atlanticbooks.com

Disclaimer

- The author and the publisher have taken every effort to the maximum of their skill, expertise and knowledge to provide correct material in the book. Even then if some mistakes persist in the content of the book, the publisher does not take responsibility for the same. The publisher shall have no liability to any person or entity with respect to any loss or damage caused, or alleged to have been caused directly or indirectly, by the information contained in this book.
- The author has fully tried to follow the copyright law. However, if any work is found to be similar, it is unintentional and the same should not be used as defamatory or to file legal suit against the author.
- If the readers find any mistakes, we shall be grateful to them for pointing out those to us so that these can be corrected in the next edition.
- All disputes are subject to the jurisdiction of Delhi courts only.

Printed & bound in India by Atlantic Print Services

Preface

The University Grants Commission (UGC) conducts National Eligibility Test (NET) on various subjects twice every year, once each in June and December, to determine eligibility for college and university level lectureship and for award of Junior Research Fellowship (JRF), for Indian nationals in order to ensure minimum standards for the entrants in the teaching profession and research.

The book contains previous years' solved papers (objective type questions) on the subject of Sociology, from December 2005 to June 2014. It covers all three papers (Paper I, II wand III). In Paper I (General Paper on Teaching and Research Aptitude), and Paper II (Elective), solved papers have been included from December 2005. In Paper III (Core and Elective), solved papers of objective type questions have been included from June 2012, conforming to the existing UGC-NET pattern. In addition, five sets of Mock Tests for Paper I, II and III have been included in the book under Practice Papers. Answers have been given at the end of each set for self-check.

It will be useful for those preparing for UGC-NET/SLET/JRF in the subject of Sociology. It will give them a feel of the type of questions asked in NET in this subject, i.e. Multiple-choice, Matching type, True/False, Assertion-Reasoning type, etc. The papers included in this book will enable the students to judge their own level of competence besides adding to their knowledge. It will also help them revise the important questions in the entire syllabus and enhance their self-confidence. Suggestions for further improvement of the book are, however, welcome.

Atlantic Research Division

Contents

JUNE–2014

Note: This paper contains Sixty (60) multiple-choice questions, each question carrying two (2) marks. Candidate is expected to answer any Fifty (50) questions. In case more than Fifty (50) questions are attempted, only the first Fifty (50) questions will be evaluated.

PAPER–I

1. Break-down in verbal communication is described as
   (a) Short circuit
   (b) Contradiction
   (c) Unevenness
   (d) Entropy

2. The Telephone Model of Communication was first developed in the area of
   (a) Technological theory
   (b) Dispersion theory
   (c) Minimal effects theory
   (d) Information theory

3. The Dada Saheb Phalke Award for 2013 has been conferred on
   (a) Karan Johar (b) Amir Khan
   (c) Asha Bhonsle (d) Gulzar

4. Photographs are not easy to
   (a) publish (b) secure
   (c) decode (d) change

5. The grains that appear on a television set when operated are also referred to as
   (a) sparks (b) green dots
   (c) snow (d) rain drops

6. In circular communication, the encoder becomes a decoder when there is
   (a) noise (b) audience
   (c) criticality (d) feedback

7. In a post-office, stamps of three different denominations of ₹ 7, ₹ 8, ₹ 10 are available. The exact amount for which one cannot buy stamps is
   (a) 19 (b) 20
   (c) 23 (d) 29

8. In certain coding method, the word QUESTION is encoded as DOMESTIC. In this coding, what is the code word for the word RESPONSE?
   (a) OMESUCEM
   (b) OMESICSM
   (c) OMESICEM
   (d) OMESISCM

9. If the series 4, 5, 8, 13, 14, 17, 22, ... is continued in the same pattern, which one of the following is not a term of this series?
   (a) 31 (b) 32
   (c) 33 (d) 35

10. Complete the series BB, FE, II, ML, PP, ... by choosing one of the following option given.
   (a) TS (b) ST
   (c) RS (d) SR

11. A man started walking from his house towards south. After walking 6 km, he turned to his left and walked 5 km. Then he walked further 3 km after turning left. He then turned to his left and continued

his walk for 9 km. How far is he away from his house?

(a) 3 km (b) 4 km
(c) 5 km (d) 6 km

12. One writes all numbers from 50 to 99 without the digits 2 and 7. How many numbers have been written?

(a) 32 (b) 36
(c) 40 (d) 38

13. "If a large diamond is cut up into little bits, it will lose its value just as an army is divided up into small units of soldiers, it loses its strength."
The argument put above may be called as

(a) Analogical (b) Deductive
(c) Statistical (d) Causal

14. Given below are some characteristics of logical argument. Select the code which expresses a characteristic which is not of inductive in character.

(a) The conclusion is claimed to follow from its premises.
(b) The conclusion is based on causal relation.
(c) The conclusion conclusively follows from its premises.
(d) The conclusion is based on observation and experiment.

15. If two propositions having the same subject and predicate terms can both be true but cannot both be false, the relation between those two propositions is called

(a) contradictory (b) contrary
(c) subcontrary (d) subaltern

16. Given below are two premises and four conclusions drawn from those premises. Select the code that expresses conclusion drawn validly from the premises (separately or jointly).

Premises:
(a) All dogs are mammals.
(b) No cats are dogs.

Conclusions:
(i) No cats are mammals.
(ii) Some cats are mammals.
(iii) No dogs are cats.
(iv) No dogs are non-mammals.

Codes:
(a) (i) only (b) (i) and (ii)
(c) (iii) and (iv) (d) (ii) and (iii)

17. Given below is a diagram of three circles A, B and C inter-related with each other. The circle A represents the class of Indians, the circle B represents the class of scientists and circle C represents the class of politicians. p, q, r, s...represent different regions. Select the code containing the region that indicates the class of Indian scientists who are not politicians.

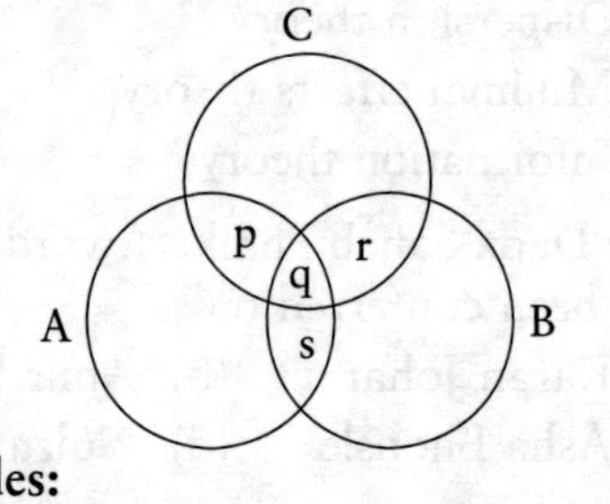

Codes:
(a) q and s (b) s only
(c) s and r (d) p, q and s

18. Read the following table carefully. Based upon this table answer questions from 18 to 22:

Net Area under Irrigation by sources in a country (Thousand Hectares)

Year	Government canals	Private canals	Tanks	Tube wells & other wells	Other sources	Total
1997-98	17117	211	2593	32090	3102	55173
1998-99	17093	212	2792	33988	3326	57411

1999-00	16842	194	2535	34623	2915	57109
2000-01	15748	203	2449	33796	2880	55076
2001-02	15031	209	2179	34906	4347	56672
2002-03	13863	206	1802	34250	3657	53778
2003-04	14444	206	1908	35779	4281	56618
2004-05	14696	206	1727	34785	7453	58867
2005-06	15268	207	2034	35372	7314	60196

18. Which of the following sources of irrigation has registered the largest percentage of decline in Net area under irrigation during 1997-98 and 2005-06?
(a) Government canals
(b) Private canals
(c) Tanks
(d) Other sources

19. Find out the source of irrigation that has registered the maximum improvement in terms of percentage of Net irrigated area during 2002-03 and 2003-04.
(a) Government canals
(b) Tanks
(c) Tube wells and other wells
(d) Other sources

20. In which of the following years, Net irrigation by tanks increased at the highest rate?
(a) 1998-99 (b) 2000-01
(c) 2003-04 (d) 2005-06

21. Identify the source of irrigation that has recorded the maximum incidence of negative growth in terms of Net irrigated area during the years given in the table.
(a) Government canals
(b) Private canals
(c) Tube wells and other wells
(d) Other sources

22. In which of the following years, share of the tube wells and other wells in the total net irrigated area was the highest?
(a) 1998-99 (b) 2000-01
(c) 2002-03 (d) 2004-05

23. The acronym FTP stands for
(a) File Transfer Protocol
(b) Fast Transfer Protocol
(c) File Tracking Protocol
(d) File Transfer Procedure

24. Which one of the following is not a/an image/graphic file format?
(a) PNG (b) GIF
(c) BMP (d) GUI

25. The first web browser is
(a) Internet Explorer
(b) Netscape
(c) World Wide Web
(d) Firefox

26. When a computer is booting, BIOS is loaded to the memory by
(a) RAM (b) ROM
(c) CD-ROM (d) TCP

27. Which one of the following is not the same as the other three?
(a) MAC address
(b) Hardware address
(c) Physical address
(d) IP address

28. Identify the IP address from the following:
(a) 300 · 215 · 317 · 3
(b) 302 · 215@ · 417 · 5
(c) 202 · 50 · 20 · 148
(d) 202 - 50 - 20 - 148

29. The population of India is about 1.2 billion. Take the average consumption of energy per person per year in India as 30 Mega Joules. If this consumption is met by carbon based fuels and the rate of carbon emissions per kilojoule is 15×10^6 kgs, the total carbon emissions per year from India will be
(a) 54 million metric tons
(b) 540 million metric tons

(c) 5400 million metric tons
(d) 2400 million metric tons

30. Which of the following cities has been worst affected by urban smog in recent times?
(a) Paris (b) London
(c) Los Angeles (d) Beijing

31. The primary source of organic pollution in fresh water bodies is
(a) run-off urban areas
(b) run-off from agricultural forms
(c) sewage effluents
(d) industrial effluents

32. 'Lahar' is a natural disaster involving
(a) eruption of large amount of material
(b) strong winds
(c) strong water waves
(d) strong winds and water waves

33. In order to avoid catastrophic consequences of climate change, there is general agreement among the countries of the world to limit the rise in average surface temperature of earth compared to that of pre-industrial times by
(a) 1.5°C to 2°C
(b) 2.0°C to 3.5°C
(c) 0.5°C to 1.0°C
(d) 0.25°C to 0.5°C

34. The National Disaster Management Authority functions under the Union Ministry of
(a) Environment
(b) Water Resources
(c) Home Affairs
(d) Defence

35. Match List-I and List-II and select the correct answer from the codes given below:

List I
A. Flood B. Drought
C. Earthquake D. Volcano

List II
1. Lack of rainfall of sufficient duration
2. Tremors produced by the passage of vibratory waves through the rocks of the earth
3. A vent through which molted substances come out
4. Excess rain and uneven distribution of water

Codes:	A	B	C	D
(a)	4	1	2	3
(b)	2	3	4	1
(c)	3	4	2	1
(d)	4	3	1	2

36. Which one of the following greenhouse gases has the shortest residence time in the atmosphere?
(a) Chlorofluorocarbon
(b) Carbon dioxide
(c) Methane
(d) Nitrous oxide

37. Consider the following statements and select the correct answer from the code given below:
i. Rajasthan receives the highest solar radiation in the country.
ii. India has the fifth largest installed wind power in the world.
iii. The maximum amount of wind power is contributed by Tamil Nadu.
iv. The primary source of uranium in India is Jaduguda.

Codes:
(a) i and ii
(b) i, ii and iii
(c) ii and iii
(d) i and iv

38. Who among the following is the de facto executive head of the Planning Commission?
(a) Chairman
(b) Deputy Chairman
(c) Minister of State for Planning
(d) Member Secretary

39. Education as a subject of legislation figures in the
(a) Union List
(b) State List
(c) Concurrent List
(d) Residuary Powers

40. Which of the following are Central Universities?
1. Pondicherry University
2. Vishwa Bharati
3. H.N.B. Garhwal University
4. Kurukshetra University
Select the correct answer from the codes given below:
Codes:
(a) 1, 2 and 3 (b) 1, 3 and 4
(c) 2, 3 and 4 (d) 1, 2 and 4

41. Consider the statement which is followed by two arguments (i) and (ii).
Statement: India should have a very strong and powerful Lokpal.
Arguments: (i) Yes, it will go a long in eliminating corruption in bureaucracy.
(ii) No, it will discourage honest officers from making quick decisions.
Codes:
(a) Only argument (i) is strong.
(b) Only argument (ii) is strong.
(c) Both the arguments are strong.
(d) Neither of the arguments is strong.

42. Which of the following universities has adopted the meta university concept?
(a) Assam University
(b) Delhi University
(c) Hyderabad University
(d) Pondicherry University

43. Which of the following statements are correct about a Central University?
1. Central University is established under an Act of Parliament.
2. The President of India acts as the visitor of the University.
3. The President has the power to nominate some members to the Executive Committee or the Board of Management of the University.
4. The President occasionally presides over the meetings of the Executive Committee or Court.
Select the correct answer from the codes given below:
Codes:
(a) 1, 2 and 4 (b) 1, 3 and 4
(c) 1, 2 and 3 (d) 1, 2, 3 and 4

44. Which one of the following is considered a sign of motivated teaching?
(a) Students asking questions
(b) Maximum attendance of the students
(c) Pin drop silence in the classroom
(d) Students taking notes

45. Which one of the following is the best method of teaching?
(a) Lecture (b) Discussion
(c) Demonstration (d) Narration

46. Dyslexia is associated with
(a) mental disorder
(b) behavioural disorder
(c) reading disorder
(d) writing disorder

47. The e-content generation for undergraduate courses has been assigned

by the Ministry of Human Resource Development to

(a) INFLIBNET
(b) Consortium for Educational Communication
(c) National Knowledge Commission
(d) Indira Gandhi National Open University

48. Classroom communication is normally considered as

(a) effective (b) cognitive
(c) affective (d) selective

49. Who among the following, propounded the concept of paradigm?

(a) Peter Haggett (b) Von Thunen
(c) Thomas Kuhn (d) John K. Wright

50. In a thesis, figures and tables are included in

(a) the appendix
(b) a separate chapter
(c) the concluding chapter
(d) the text itself

51. A thesis statement is

(a) an observation (b) a fact
(c) an assertion (d) a discussion

52. The research approach of Max Weber to understand how people create meanings in natural settings is identified as

(a) positive paradigm
(b) critical paradigm
(c) natural paradigm
(d) interpretative paradigm

53. Which one of the following is a non-probability sampling?

(a) Simple random
(b) Purposive
(c) Systematic
(d) Stratified

54. Identify the category of evaluation that assesses the learning progress to provide continuous feedback to the students during instruction.

(a) Placement (b) Diagnostic
(c) Formative (d) Summative

55. The research stream of immediate application is

(a) Conceptual research
(b) Action research
(c) Fundamental research
(d) Empirical research

Read the following passage carefully and answer questions 56 to 60:

Traditional Indian values must be viewed both from the angle of the individual and from that of the geographically delimited agglomeration of peoples or groups enjoying a common system of leadership which we call the 'State'. The Indian 'State's' special feature is the peaceful, or perhaps mostly peaceful, co-existence of social groups of various historical provenances which mutually adhere in a geographical, economic, and political sense, without ever assimilating to each other in social terms, in ways of thinking, or even in language. Modern Indian law will determine certain rules, especially in relation to the regime of the family, upon the basis of how the loin-cloth is tied, or how the turban is worn, for this may identify the litigants as members of a regional group, and therefore as participants in its traditional law, though their ancestors left the region three or four centuries earlier. The use of the word 'State' above must not mislead us. There was no such thing as a conflict between the individual and the State, atleast before foreign governments became established, just as there was no concept of state 'sovereignty' or of any church-and-state dichotomy.

Modern Indian 'secularism' has an admittedly peculiar feature: It requires the state to make a fair distribution of attention and support amongst all religions. These blessed aspects of India's famed tolerance (Indian kings so rarely persecuted religious groups that the exceptions prove the rule) at once struck Portuguese and other European visitors to the West Coast of India in the sixteenth century, and the impression made upon them in this and other ways gave rise, at one remove, to the basic constitution of Thomas More's Utopia. There is little about modern India that strikes one at once as Utopian: but the insistence upon the inculcation of norms, and the absence of bigotry and institutionalized exploitation of human or natural resources, are two very different features which link the realities of India and her tradition with the essence of all Utopians.

56. Which of the following is a special feature of the Indian State?
   (a) Peaceful co-existence of people under a common system of leadership
   (b) Peaceful co-existence of social groups of different historical provenances attached to each other in a geographical, economic and political sense
   (c) Social integration of all groups
   (d) Cultural assimilation of all social groups.

57. The author uses the word 'State' to highlight
   (a) Antagonistic relationship between the state and the individual throughout the period of history.
   (b) Absence of conflict between the state and the individuals upto a point in time.
   (c) The concept of state sovereignty.
   (d) Dependence on religion.

58. Which one is the peculiar feature of modern Indian 'Secularism'?
   (a) No discrimination on religious considerations
   (b) Total indifference to religion
   (c) No space for social identity
   (d) Disregard for social law

59. The basic construction of Thomas More's Utopia was inspired by
   (a) Indian tradition of religious tolerance.
   (b) Persecution of religious groups by Indian rulers.
   (c) Social inequality in India.
   (d) European perception of Indian State.

60. What is the striking feature of modern India?
   (a) A replica of Utopian State
   (b) Uniform laws
   (c) Adherence to traditional values
   (d) Absence of Bigotry

ANSWERS

1. (d)	2. (d)	3. (d)	4. (c)	5. (c)
6. (d)	7. (a)	8. (c)	9. (c)	10. (a)
11. (c)	12. (a)	13. (a)	14. (c)	15. (c)
16. (c)	17. (b)	18. (c)	19. (d)	20. (d)
21. (a)	22. (c)	23. (a)	24. (d)	25. (c)
26. (b)	27. (d)	28. (c)	29. (b)	30. (d)
31. (c)	32. (a)	33. (a)	34. (c)	35. (a)
36. (c)	37. (d)	38. (b)	39. (c)	40. (a)
41. (a)	42. (b)	43. (c)	44. (a)	45. (c)
46. (c)	47. (b)	48. (c)	49. (c)	50. (d)
51. (c)	52. (d)	53. (b)	54. (c)	55. (b)
56. (b)	57. (d)	58. (a)	59. (a)	60. (d)

PAPER–II

Note: This paper contains fifty (50) objective type questions of two (2) marks each. All questions are compulsory.

1. A statement of relationship between variables to be tested is known as
   (a) Research question
   (b) Hypothesis
   (c) Objective of the study
   (d) Problem of the study
2. For Marx, human potential is actualized
   (a) when democracy is institutionalized
   (b) in the objectification of products
   (c) during the capitalist stage
   (d) during the primitive stage
3. A relationship in which change in one variable always induce change in another variable is known as
   (a) positive correlation
   (b) linear correlation
   (c) unfounding relation
   (d) cause and effect relationship
4. Who among these theorist were the intellectual fountain heads of conflict theories?
   (a) G.H. Mead and Erving Goffman
   (b) Karl Marx and Max Weber
   (c) Emile Durkheim and Herbert Spencer
   (d) Edward Wilson and Charles Darwin
5. Given below are two statements, one labelled as Assertion (A) and the other labelled as Reason (R):
   Assertion (A): Both Lewis Coser and Randall Collins are grouped under the conflict school.
   Reason (R): Both of them highlight the function of conflict in maintaining the society.
   Codes:
   (a) Both (A) and (R) are true.
   (b) (A) is true, but (R) is false.
   (c) (A) is false, but (R) is true.
   (d) Both (A) and (R) are false.
6. The reasons for insurgency in the North Eastern region are
   (a) Ethnic conflicts and development deprivation
   (b) Land alienation and poverty
   (c) Criminalisation of politics and corruption
   (d) Religious fundamentalism and terrorism
7. **Assertion (A):** Townsend asserts that poverty can be defined objectively only in terms of the concept of relative deprivation.
   Reason (R): Society determines people's needs, patterns of food consumption.
   Codes:
   (a) Assertion (A) is true and Reason (R) is false.
   (b) Both Assertion (A) and Reason (R) are false.
   (c) Both Assertion (A) and Reason (R) are true and (R) is the correct explanation of (A).
   (d) Both Assertion (A) and Reason (R) are true, but (R) is not the correct explanation of (A).
8. Who suggested that God is society divinized?
   (a) Max Weber
   (b) E.E. Evans-Pritchard
   (c) Auguste Comte
   (d) Emile Durkheim
9. In an Indian family the parents prepare their daughters to be a good wife/daughter in her in-laws home, this is an example of

(a) Socialization
(b) Re-socialization
(c) Adult socialization
(d) Anticipatory socialization

10. Which theory among the following states that people are motivated by self-interest in the interactions with other people?
(a) Conflict (b) Exchange
(c) Interaction (d) Structural

11. Match item in List I with item in List II and choose the correct answer from the codes given below:

List I
A. Social class and stratification
B. The power Elite
C. Class, city and power
D. Class in modern society

List II
i. Bottomore, T.B.
ii. Castells, M.
iii. Mills, C.W.
iv. Saunders, P.

Codes:	A	B	C	D
(a)	i	iv	iii	ii
(b)	ii	i	iv	iii
(c)	iv	iii	ii	i
(d)	iii	ii	i	iv

12. "Sociology is the science of understanding of the meaning of social action." The proceeding statement was made by
(a) Max Weber
(b) Auguste Comte
(c) Herbert Spencer
(d) Emile Durkheim

13. The idea of 'imperatively coordinated associations' was given by
(a) Karl Marx
(b) Max Weber
(c) Lewis Coser
(d) Ralph Dahrendorf

14. According to Emile Durkheim religious practices are best understood as
(a) satisfying the spiritual interests of human beings.
(b) helping human beings to get relief from problems of mundane life.
(c) showing alternatives to the existing practices of collective life.
(d) contributing to the integration and stability of a society.

15. **Assertion (A):** Nepotism, favouritism and corruption have increased in Indian society.
Reason (R): The situation has risen due to lack of political will.
Codes:
(a) (A) is true and (R) is false.
(b) Both (A) and (R) are true.
(c) (A) is false and (R) is true.
(d) Both (A) and (R) are false.

16. The temporary form of marriage found among Muslims is called
(a) Nikah (b) Muta
(c) Mehr (d) Purdah

17. **Assertion (A):** Women empowerment resulted in rural India during the last two decade.
Reason (R): 73rd constitution amendment empowered rural Indian women.
Codes:
(a) Both (A) and (R) are false.
(b) Both (A) and (R) are true.
(c) (A) is false and (R) is true.
(d) (A) is true and (R) is false.

18. **Assertion (A):** Privatization of education in India is leading to commercialization of education.
Reason (R): Commercialization of education has deprived many poor deserving students from quality education.

Codes:
(a) (A) is true, but (R) is false.
(b) (A) is false and (R) is true.
(c) Both (A) and (R) are true, and (R) is the correct explanation of (A).
(d) Both (A) and (R) are true, but (R) is not the correct explanation of (A).

19. The statement "Organizations are arenas for struggle" was given by
(a) Randall Collins
(b) Karl Marx
(c) Ralph Dahrendorf
(d) Max Weber

20. Who suggested that conflict has a functional importance in society?
(a) Karl Marx
(b) Lewis Coser
(c) Ralph Dahrendorf
(d) Randall Collins

21. Match the List I with List II.
List I
A. Ralph Dahrendorf
B. G.H. Mead
C. Alfred Shultz
D. Lewis Coser
List II
i. Power Elite
ii. Phenomenology
iii. Functions of social conflict
iv. Symbolic Interactionism
v. Conflict and Authority

Codes:	A	B	C	D
(a)	iv	v	ii	iii
(b)	ii	iii	iv	i
(c)	v	iv	ii	iii
(d)	i	iii	iv	v

22. Which one of the following statement is not reflective of conflict perspective?
(a) Society as a struggle for resource and power.
(b) Change is inevitable, often beneficial and can be violent.
(c) Society is viewed as a complex system of parts that interact to perform various necessary functions.
(d) Conflict between classes determines social change.

23. Match the items in the List I with the items in the List II and select the correct answer from the codes given below:
List I
A. J.W.B. Douglous
B. D.H. Hargreaves
C. S. Bowles and H. Gintis
D. Ivan Illich
List II
i. The Home and the School
ii. Social relations in a secondary school
iii. Schooling in capitalist America
iv. Deschooling society

Codes:	A	B	C	D
(a)	i	ii	iii	iv
(b)	iv	iii	ii	i
(c)	ii	i	iii	iv
(d)	iii	iv	i	ii

24. Which theory advocates the view that the domain of sociology is the 'common sense world of everyday life'?
(a) Functionalism
(b) Structuralism
(c) Phenomenology
(d) Exchange theory

25. Which one of the following is not an element of symbolic interactionism?
(a) The self (b) The Ego
(c) Symbols (d) Role-Taking

26. **Assertion (A):** Sense of alienation is increasing among Dalits.
Reason (R): Atrocities have increased in recent years on Dalits.

Codes:
(a) (A) is true and (R) is false.
(b) (A) is false and (R) is true.
(c) Both (A) and (R) are false.
(d) Both (A) and (R) are true.

27. Match List I with List II and select the correct answer from the codes given below:

List I
A. G. Homans
B. Cart Wright
C. M.S. Olmsted
D. R.H. Turner

List II
i. The small group
ii. Collective behaviour
iii. Group Dynamics
iv. The Human group

Codes:	A	B	C	D
(a)	iii	iv	ii	i
(b)	ii	i	iv	iii
(c)	i	ii	iii	iv
(d)	iv	iii	i	ii

28. Rewards and punishment associated with role expectations are called
(a) Mores (b) Sanctions
(c) Norms (d) Values

29. Match items in List I with items in List II and select the correct code from codes given below:

List I
A. Primary group
B. Reference group
C. In-groups and Out-groups
D. Organised group

List II
i. Summer, W.G.
ii. Bierstedt, Robert
iii. Hyman, R.
iv. Charles Cooley

Codes:	A	B	C	D
(a)	i	ii	iii	iv
(b)	ii	i	iv	iii
(c)	iii	iv	ii	i
(d)	iv	iii	i	ii

30. Which one of the following is not an example of social action?
(a) Two persons exchanging blows after a collision of their bicycles.
(b) Two cyclists expressing regrets to each other after their bicycles collide.
(c) Two cyclists going their respective ways without taking note of each other.
(d) Two cyclists coming from opposite directions trying to give way to each other.

31. "An Outline of Social Psychology" is written by
(a) C.H. Cooley
(b) Sigmund Freud
(c) Muzafer Sherif
(d) G.H. Mead

32. The idea of 'culture of poverty' was introduced by whom?
(a) Oscar Lewis
(b) Abel Smith
(c) Somuel Mencher
(d) Peter Townsend

33. Match the items in List I with the items in List II and choose the correct answer from the codes given below:

List I
A. Culture is man made part of environment.
B. Culture is that complex whole which includes knowledge, belief, art, morals, law customs and other capabilities and habits acquired by man as a member of society.

C. The culture of a society is the way of life of its members; the collection of ideas and habits which they learn, share and transmit from generation to generation.

D. Culture is a 'design for living' held by members of a particular society.

List II

i. E.B. Taylor ii. M.J. Herkovits
iii. Ralph Linton iv. C. Kluckhohn

Codes:	**A**	**B**	**C**	**D**
(a)	ii	i	iii	iv
(b)	i	iii	iv	ii
(c)	iii	ii	i	iv
(d)	iv	iii	ii	i

34. The theory that views people as "Stage managers" managing impressions presented to the world is
(a) Role theory
(b) Dramaturgy
(c) Looking Glass Self
(d) Dialectual theory

35. Which of the following does not characterize Herbert Blumer's theory of symbolic interactionism?
(a) The essence of society is found in actors and action.
(b) Society is made up of macro structures.
(c) Large-scale structures emerge from micro processes.
(d) Collective action gives rise to joint action.

36. Definite procedures or rules which people are expected to observe are known as
(a) Norms
(b) Values
(c) Institutions
(d) Group behaviour

37. Religion, marriage, family, caste are example of
(a) social values
(b) social institutions
(c) social norms
(d) social segmental division of society

38. Who is most generally regarded as the founder of symbolic interactionism?
(a) Herbert Blumer
(b) George Herbert Mead
(c) Max Weber
(d) Anthony Giddens

39. Which is not a form of social stratification?
(a) Religion (b) Class
(c) Caste (d) Gender

40. Match the items in the List I with the items in the List II and select the correct answer from the codes given below:

List I

A. Dependence and exploitation in work and marriage
B. The future of marriage
C. The death of the family
D. The family and marriage in Britain

List II

i. D.L. Banker and S. Allen
ii. J. Bernard
iii. D. Cooper
iv. R. Fletcher

Codes:	**A**	**B**	**C**	**D**
(a)	i	ii	iii	iv
(b)	iv	iii	ii	i
(c)	ii	i	iv	iii
(d)	iii	iv	i	ii

41. The maintenance provided by the husband to the divorced wife is called
(a) Dower (b) Mehr
(c) Alimony (d) Bride price

42. Which of the following is not true in the context of culture?
(a) Culture is cultivated.
(b) Culture and Civilization are two faces of the same coin.
(c) Culture refers to non-material while civilization to material aspects.
(d) Culture is what we have while the civilization is what we are.

43. Who among the following criticized Marxian theory as "a monocausal explanation for a multicausal world"?
(a) Max Weber
(b) Ralf Dahrendorf
(c) Randall Collins
(d) Lewis Coser

44. Karl Marx did not mention class conflict between
(a) The Haves and Havenots
(b) The Rich and the Poor
(c) The Bourgeois and the Proletariat
(d) The capitalists and the working class

45. Which one of the following is not an agency of socialization?
(a) Family (b) School
(c) Peer-Group (d) Media

46. Match items in List I with items in List II and choose the correct answer from the codes given below:

List I
A. Evolutionary Theory
B. Cyclical Theory
C. Conflict Theory
D. Structural Functional Approach

List II
i. Kingsley Davis
ii. Auguste Comte
iii. A. Sorokin
iv. Karl Marx

Codes:	A	B	C	D
(a)	i	ii	iii	iv
(b)	i	iv	ii	iii
(c)	ii	iii	iv	i
(d)	iv	i	ii	iii

47. Which one of the following is not an element of community?
(a) Territory
(b) We-feeling
(c) Cultural diversity
(d) Self sufficiency

48. Who has propounded that "the primary groups are the nursery of human nature"?
(a) Charles H. Cooley
(b) George Herbert Mead
(c) Ralf Dahrendorf
(d) Karl Marx

49. Who has authored the book *Society in India*?
(a) A.P. Barnabas
(b) Andre Beteille
(c) Kingsley Davis
(d) David G. Mandelbaum

50. Who argues that families are factories which produce human personalities?
(a) M.G. Smith
(b) D.H.J. Morgon
(c) G.P. Murdock
(d) T. Parsons

ANSWERS

1. (b)	2. (b)	3. (d)	4. (b)	5. (b)
6. (a)	7. (d)	8. (d)	9. (d)	10. (c)
11. (c)	12. (a)	13. (d)	14. (d)	15. (b)
16. (b)	17. (b)	18. (c)	19. (a)	20. (b)
21. (c)	22. (c)	23. (a)	24. (c)	25. (b)
26. (d)	27. (d)	28. (b)	29. (d)	30. (c)

31. (c)	32. (a)	33. (a)	34. (b)	35. (b)
36. (a)	37. (b)	38. (b)	39. (a)	40. (a)
41. (c)	42. (d)	43. (c)	44. (b)	45. (d)
46. (c)	47. (c)	48. (a)	49. (d)	50. (d)

PAPER–III

Note: This paper contains seventy-five (75) objective type questions of two (2) marks each. All questions are compulsory.

1. Which of the following is right combination contributed to the displacement among the tribal communities in India?
   (i) Deforestation
   (ii) Development projects
   (iii) Debt trap
   (iv) Land acquisition
   (v) Land alienation
   (vi) Drought

   Choose the correct answer form the codes given below:
   Codes:
   (a) Development projects – Land alienation – Debt trap
   (b) Deforestation – Debt trap – Drought
   (c) Development projects – Land acquisition – Drought
   (d) Development projects – Deforestation – Land acquisition

2. According to Anthony Giddens, 'structure' is
   (a) itself the form and shape of human life
   (b) outside or external to human action
   (c) itself exists in time and space
   (d) constraining and enabling

3. Who described the phenomenon of globalization in today's world as 'globalization of nothing'?
   (a) George Ritzer
   (b) Jean Baudrillard
   (c) Anthony Giddens
   (d) Michel Foucault

4. Match the items of List I with the items of List II and select the correct answer from the codes given below:
   List I
   A. G.S. Ghurye
   B. McKim Marriot
   C. A.R. Desai
   D. N.K. Bose
   List II
   i. Village India
   ii. The social Background of Indian Nationalism
   iii. The structure of Hindu Society
   iv. Occidental civilization

Codes:	**A**	**B**	**C**	**D**
(a)	i	ii	iii	iv
(b)	iv	i	ii	iii
(c)	iv	ii	iii	i
(d)	iii	iv	i	ii

5. 'The Social Construction of Reality' was authored by
   (a) Peter Berger
   (b) Brigette Berger and Peter Berger
   (c) Peter Berger and T. Luckmann
   (d) Niklas Luhman

6. Who stated "Ethnicity and Ethnic grouping are 'primordial factors' in the sense that they are given in the very condition of human existence"?
   (a) Fredrick Barth
   (b) Clifford Geertz
   (c) Max Weber
   (d) Michael Garfield Smith

7. Who divided the Chicago city into five zones in order to explain the incidences of Juvenile delinquency?
(a) C.R. Shaw and H.D. McKay
(b) A. Cohen
(c) E.H. Sutherland
(d) G. Tarde

8. Who is the author of the book *The Ultimate Resource*?
(a) Paul Ehrlich
(b) Julian Linken Simon
(c) Frank Notestein
(d) Kingsley Davis

9. Match the List I with the List II given below:
List I
A. Ethnocentrism
B. Westernization
C. Sanskritization
D. Dominant caste
List II
i. People of lower castes collectively adopt upper caste, practices and belief to acquire higher status.
ii. Yields economic or political power and occupies a higher position in the hierarchy.
iii. Explains the changes brought about in our society through western contact.
iv. Tendency of each group to take for granted the superiority of its own culture.

Codes:	A	B	C	D
(a)	ii	iii	iv	i
(b)	i	iii	iv	ii
(c)	iv	iii	i	ii
(d)	iii	ii	i	iv

10. Which of the following approaches encompass the programmes drawn on poverty alleviation, welfare and equity?
(a) Women in Development
(b) Women and Development
(c) Gender and Development
(d) Women, Environment and Development

11. "Sampurnanand Ashram" is associated with which of the following?
(a) Borstal School (b) Open Jail
(c) Closed Jail (d) Remand Home

12. Match the items in the List I with the items in the List II and select the correct answer from the codes given below:
List I
A. Social organisation in which men enjoy the power and authority
B. Belief that one sex is innately superior to the other
C. Social system in which women inherit property rights
D. Genetically based programme which predisposes mankind to behave in certain ways
List II
i. Biogrammay ii. Matriarchy
iii. Patriarchy iv. Sexism

Codes:	A	B	C	D
(a)	i	ii	iii	iv
(b)	iii	i	ii	iv
(c)	iii	iv	ii	i
(d)	iv	ii	i	iii

13. Who coined the concept of Vote Bank?
(a) Rajani Kothari (b) M.N. Srinivas
(c) Yogendra Yadav (d) A.R. Desai

14. **Assertion (A):** Gender roles are culturally influenced rather than biologically determined.
Reason (R): Cultural conception of gender divides the full range of human qualities into two opposing sphere of masculinity and feminity and their appropriate behaviour.

Select the correct answer from the codes given below:

Codes:

(a) (A) is true, but (R) is false.
(b) Both (A) and (R) are true and (R) is the correct explanation of (A).
(c) (A) is false, but (R) is true and (R) is the correct explanation of (A).
(d) Both (A) and (R) are false.

15. Rural development programmes resulted into which one of the following most undesirable social situation in the Indian rural society?
(a) De-peasantisation and suicides
(b) De-peasantisation
(c) Richness of farmers
(d) Suicide among peasants

16. Higher child Dependency Ratio is consequence of
(a) Increasing life expectancy at birth.
(b) Higher proportion of child labour.
(c) High fertility rate.
(d) Migration of elderly people.

17. **Assertion (A):** 'Systematic Source Book in Rural Sociology' vol. 1 edited by Sorokin, Zimmerman and Galpin reveals basic features of rural society firstly at the international scene.
Reason (R): As it includes comprehensive survey of the views of eminent sociologists belonging to various countries in the past epochs.
Choose the correct answer from the given code:
Codes:
(a) Both (A) and (R) are true and (R) is the correct explanation of (A).
(b) Both (A) and (R) are true, but (R) is not the correct explanation of (A).
(c) (A) is true, but (R) is false.
(d) (A) is false, but (R) is true.

18. 'Incarceration' means
(a) Freedom (b) Punishment
(c) Furlough (d) Probation

19. A sociological analysis of gender entails that one must examine
(a) Gender Division
(b) Gender Dis-examination
(c) Gender Performance
(d) All of the above

20. Transformation of Human Societies from agrarian to industrial and to post-industrial has widely been shaped by
(a) Technological innovations
(b) Application of knowledge for productivity
(c) Both (a) and (b)
(d) Training for work

21. Who has given the concept of 'Born Criminal'?
(a) Sutherland (b) Lombroso
(c) Tarde (d) Gillin

22. Who used the term 'New International Division of Labour' (NIDL) to describe the substantial relocation of operations to Third World countries?
(a) F. Frobel
(b) E. Durkheim
(c) Auguste Comte
(d) Adam Smith

23. **Assertion (A):** Urbanization and Industrialization in the era of globalization led to displacement of peasantry in India.
Reason (R): Peasants eviction is due to land acquisition pursued by the state.
Codes:
(a) (A) is true, (R) is false.
(b) Both (A) and (R) are true.
(c) Both (A) and (R) are false.
(d) (A) is false, (R) is true.

24. Through which process the worker's benefits are derived in an Industry?
    (a) Arbitration
    (b) Conciliation
    (c) Collective Bargaining
    (d) Adjudication

25. Who mentioned Alienation as the consequence of division of labour?
    (a) Sorokin (b) Durkheim
    (c) Gillin (d) Marx

26. **Assertion (A):** Low child sex ratio in India is mainly due to female foeticide.
    Reason (R): Son Preference is quite strong in India due to patrilineal system.
    Codes:
    (a) Both (A) and (R) are true.
    (b) (A) is true, but (R) is false.
    (c) Both (A) and (R) are false.
    (d) (A) is false, but (R) is true.

27. Match List I with List II in the context of National Population Policy–2000 objectives.
    List I
    A. Immediate
    B. Medium-term
    C. Long-term
    List II
    i. To address the needs of contraception, health care infrastructure and child health care.
    ii. To achieve stable population by 2045 at level consistent with the requirement of sustainable economic growth, social development and environmental protection.
    iii. Bring TFR to replacement level by 2010 through vigorous implementation of operational strategies.

Codes:	A	B	C
(a)	iii	i	ii
(b)	i	iii	ii
(c)	ii	iii	i
(d)	i	ii	iii

28. Knowledge based development does not depend on
    (a) Knowledge Accumulation
    (b) Knowledge Dissemination
    (c) Knowledge for Assumption
    (d) Knowledge for Production

29. Which is not an attribute of rural society?
    (a) Joint family
    (b) Agrarian economy
    (c) Pre-dominance of natural environment
    (d) Rural differentiation

30. **Assertion (A):** Slums are the breeding grounds for Juvenile delinquency in urban and industrial centres.
    Reason (R): Juveniles migrate from the rural areas to industrial and urban centres for employment.
    Codes:
    (a) Both (A) and (R) are true, but (R) is not the correct explanation of (A).
    (b) Both (A) and (R) are true, and (R) is the correct explanation of (A).
    (c) (A) is true, but (R) is false.
    (d) (A) is false, but (R) is true.

31. By which constitutional amendment the words "Secularism, Socialism and Integrity" have been included in its preamble?
    (a) Fourth Amendment 1955
    (b) Seventh Amendment 1956
    (c) Fourteenth Amendment 1962
    (d) Forty-second Amendment 1976

32. 'Live-in relationship' is a recent phenomenon visible and accepted in which society?
    (a) Tribal (b) Rural
    (c) Urban (d) Cosmopolitan

33. Major focus of Environment Conference Rio-92 was on
(a) Human Development
(b) Sustainable Development
(c) Poverty Reduction
(d) Population Control

34. Who has authored the book on *Social Mobility in Industrial Society*?
(a) S.M. Lipset and R. Bendix
(b) R.K. Merton
(c) P.L. Berger
(d) R. Bendix

35. Match List I with List II.
List I
A. Delinquency and Opportunity
B. Sociology of Deviant Behaviour
C. Social Inequality
D. Deviance and Society
List II
i. Cloward and Ohlin
ii. Clinard
iii. Beteille
iv. Taylor
Choose the correct answer from the codes given below:

Codes:	A	B	C	D
(a)	i	ii	iii	iv
(b)	iv	iii	ii	i
(c)	iii	iv	i	ii
(d)	ii	iii	iv	i

36. Who has written the book *Class and Class Conflict in Industrial Society*?
(a) Karl Marx (b) R. Dahrendorf
(c) Max Weber (d) R.K. Merton

37. Which is not an Indicator of Globalization?
(a) Free movement of labour and manpower
(b) Free flow of foreign capital for investment
(c) Free flow of defence technology
(d) Free flow of foreign capital technology

38. Select one of the following set of processes leading to stable population structure.
(a) Constant birth and death rate
(b) Increasing birth rate and constant death rate
(c) Decreasing birth rate and increasing death rate
(d) Constant birth rate and decreasing death rate

39. Which of the following refers to gender equity?
(a) Economic empowerment
(b) Egalitarian relationship
(c) Women's freedom and liberty
(d) Equal access to power, and other resources

40. According to census of India 2011, which of the following is not correct?
(a) Decadal growth rate of rural population has declined in 2001-2011 over 1991-2001.
(b) For every 10 urban dwellers in million plus cities/urban agglomerations 4 live in 5 such largest cities.
(c) The state of Gujarat has the largest number of cities/urban agglomeration with a population of one million or more.
(d) Sex ratio has increases in 2011 over 2001 in million plus cities.

41. Match List I with List II.
List I
A. Andre Beteille
B. A.R. Desai
C. Anthony Giddens
D. Stiglitz E. Joseph

List II

i. India's path of development
ii. Antinomies of society
iii. Globalization and its discontent
iv. The consequences of modernity

Codes:	A	B	C	D
(a)	ii	iii	iv	i
(b)	ii	i	iii	iv
(c)	iv	iii	ii	i
(d)	ii	iv	iii	i

42. Those attitudes or behaviour that confirm to the norms of one's own sex are known as
(a) Gender Identity
(b) Gender Appropriate
(c) Gender System
(d) Gender Sensitisation

43. In a mature form, the modern 'Demographic Transition' model theory is associated with
(a) Kingsley Davis
(b) Frank Notestein
(c) Thomas Malthus
(d) W.W. Roskow

44. Higher fertility is associated with
(1) Lower age at marriage
(2) Lower level of household income
(3) Higher illiteracy rate
(4) Higher proportion of urban population
Codes:
(a) 1, 2, 4 (b) 2, 3, 4
(c) 1, 2, 3 (d) 1, 3, 4

45. Match List I with List II and find the correct answer from the codes given below:
List I
A. A person enumerated outside the place of normal residence
B. Spouse and children joining the person, who lives other the place of normal residence
C. Persons displaced by war/violence and camped in out on other place
D. Person/Group seeking work each year for a short time in another place, than their normal residence and coming back to place of origin

List II
i. Forced Migration
ii. Circular Migration
iii. Migrant
iv. Associative Migration

Codes:	A	B	C	D
(a)	iii	iv	i	ii
(b)	iii	ii	iv	i
(c)	i	ii	iv	iii
(d)	iv	iii	ii	i

46. 73rd Constitutional Amendment is responsible for incorporation of the following provisions in the Gram Panchayats. Choose the most correct combination according to code.
(i) Reservation of women
(ii) Reservation for dalits
(iii) Involvement of Gram Sabha in decision-making
(iv) People participation
Codes:
(a) (i) and (iv) (b) (ii) and (iii)
(c) (iv), (iii) and (i) (d) (i), (ii) and (iii)

47. Who has authored the book *Social Deviance in India*?
(a) Sushil Chandra
(b) M.Z. Khan
(c) S.P. Srivastava
(d) R. Ahuja

48. Which one of the following is not a focus in population education in India?
(a) Create awareness relating to urbanization and environment problems.
(b) Develop awareness on population dynamics.

(c) Make a major instrument to control population.
(d) Create knowledge of population policy.

49. Match the items in List I with the items in List II and select the correct answer from the codes given below:

List I

A. M.B. Clinard
B. R.A. Cloward and L.E. Ohlin
C. A.K. Cohen
D. J. Bowlby

List II

i. Sociology of Deviant Behaviour
ii. Delinquency and Opportunity
iii. Delinquent Boys
iv. Forty-four Juvenile Thieves.

Codes:	**A**	**B**	**C**	**D**
(a)	i	ii	iii	iv
(b)	iv	iii	ii	i
(c)	iii	iv	ii	i
(d)	ii	i	iii	iv

50. Who argued that Merton failed to account for 'non-utilitarian crime' such as vandalism and joy-riding which do not produce monetary reward?
(a) W.B. Miller
(b) Albert K. Cohen
(c) R.A. Cloward
(d) L.E. Ohlin

51. **Assertion (A):** Development often leads to upsurge of Ethnic movement.
Reason (R): Displacement of people takes place due to construction of big dams.
Codes:
(a) (A) is false, (R) is true.
(b) Both (A) and (R) are false.
(c) Both (A) and (R) are true.
(d) (A) is true, (R) is false.

52. Which of the following communicable diseases is yet to be completely eradicated in India?
(a) Tuberculosis
(b) Cholera
(c) Small Pox
(d) None of the above

53. By 'Hindu Method of Tribal absorption' N.K. Bose means
(a) Forcible absorption of the tribals into the Hindu social organization
(b) Imitation of the Hindu way of life by the tribals because of superior cultural system
(c) Acceptance of the caste-system by the tribals because economic security and cultural liberalism in it
(d) Exploitation of the tribals by the colonial power

54. Match the items in the List I with List II and choose the correct answer from the codes given below:

List I

A. Androcracy B. Androgyny
C. Gynarchy D. Gynocracy

List II

i. Government by females
ii. Women's rule
iii. Men's rule
iv. Presence of male and female characteristics in the same person

Codes:	**A**	**B**	**C**	**D**
(a)	i	iii	iv	ii
(b)	iv	i	iii	ii
(c)	iii	iv	i	ii
(d)	iv	i	ii	iii

55. Match List I with List II.

List I

A. Maternity Benefit Act
B. Industrial Dispute Act

C. Factory Act
D. Workmen's Compensation Act

List II

i. 1961 ii. 1947
iii. 1948 iv. 1923

Choose the correct answer from the codes given below:

Codes:	A	B	C	D
(a)	i	ii	iii	iv
(b)	iv	iii	ii	i
(c)	ii	i	iii	iv
(d)	i	ii	iv	iii

56. D.P. Mukherjee observes that in order to be an Indian Sociologist one must be Indian first in the sense that
(a) one must be born in India
(b) one must be an uncritical admirer of Indian society and culture
(c) one must be a Sanskritist
(d) one must be acquainted with the Indian tradition and culture

57. Which of the following institutions reinforce the cultural dominance of patriarchy encouraging violence against women by reducing women to bodies and objectifying?
(a) Family
(b) Media
(c) Educational Institution
(d) Religion

58. Match the items in the List I with the items in the List II and choose the correct answer from the codes given below:

List I

A. Equity B. Anti poverty
C. Efficiency D. Empowerment

List II

i. Effective use of all factors of production
ii. Rights based approach
iii. Fair distribution of benefits of development
iv. Income generation programmes

Codes:	A	B	C	D
(a)	1	4	3	2
(b)	3	4	1	2
(c)	4	1	2	3
(d)	2	4	3	1

59. Match an item in List I and List II and mark the correct answer from the following codes:

List I (Books)

A. *Castes and Race in India*
B. *Remembered Village*
C. *Rajasthan Village*
D. *Indian Village*

List II (Authors)

i. S.C. Dube
ii. M.N. Srinivas
iii. G.S. Ghurye
iv. B.R. Chauhan

Codes:	A	B	C	D
(a)	i	ii	iii	iv
(b)	ii	iii	iv	i
(c)	iv	ii	iii	i
(d)	iii	i	iv	ii

60. Who discussed about the 'techniques of Neutralization' among the Juvenile delinquency in America?
(a) A.K. Cohen
(b) E.H. Sutherland
(c) D. Matza and G. Sykes
(d) W.B. Miller

61. Who observed that knowledge and power coexist and mutually support one another?
(a) J. Derrida (b) A. Giddens
(c) J. Habermas (d) M. Foucault

62. What does Anthony Giddens suggests by 'reflexivity'?

(a) Reflexive theories are theories that refer to themselves
(b) Reflexive theory suggest that the world of ideas reflects the material conditions
(c) The way in which people constantly examine their own practices and in the light of that examination, alter them
(d) The way in which sociologists reflect the social conditions of a community

63. **Assertion (A):** Science and Technology policy in India need to be oriented in such a way, so that it can meet the challenges of globalisation.
Reason (R): Privatisation of education, opening of job opportunities in M.N.C.'s and liberal trade and business policies are necessary for India's all round development.
Codes:
(a) Both (A) and (R) are true and (R) is the correct explanation of (A).
(b) Both (A) and (R) are true but (R) is not the correct explanation of (A).
(c) (A) is true, but (R) is false.
(d) (A) is false, but (R) is true.

64. Which of the following are associated with the strategic gender concerns? Select the correct answer from the codes given below:
(i) Food security
(ii) Consciousness raising
(iii) Education
(iv) Income generation programmes
(v) Political empowerment
Codes:
(a) (i), (ii), (iv) (b) (ii), (iii), (v)
(c) (iii), (iv), (v) (d) (v), (i), (iv)

65. Match the items in List I with the items in List II and choose the correct answer from the codes given below:
List I
A. Michel Foucault
B. Jacques Derrida
C. Anthony Giddens
D. Harold Garfinkel
List II
i. Writing and Difference
ii. Discipline and Punish
iii. Studies in Ethnomethodology
iv. The Constitution of Society: The theory of Structuration

Codes:	A	B	C	D
(a)	i	ii	iii	iv
(b)	iv	iii	ii	i
(c)	ii	i	iii	iv
(d)	ii	i	iv	iii

66. Correctional Institutions help reforming the Juvenile delinquents, the process of reformation is otherwise called as
(a) Anticipatory Socialization
(b) Adult Socialization
(c) Re-socialization
(d) Rehabilitation

67. Who suggested to study Rural-urban continuum first, in sociological research?
(a) A. Sorokin and Zimmerman
(b) Robert Redfield
(c) Mckin Marriot
(d) G.S. Ghurye

68. Match List I with List II.
List I
A. Beyond globalization: shaping a sustainable global economy
B. Rethinking globalisation: critical issues and policy choices

C. Globalisation and India
D. Globalisation challenges in India
List II
i. Henderson Hazel
ii. Martin Khor
iii. Purushottam Bhattacharya and Ajitava Chowdhary
iv. Alok Roy

Choose the correct answer from the codes given below:

Codes:	**A**	**B**	**C**	**D**
(a)	i	ii	iii	iv
(b)	iv	iii	ii	i
(c)	ii	i	iii	iv
(d)	i	ii	iv	iii

69. Which of the following is not associated with the 'Absolute Poverty'?
(a) Poverty line
(b) Deprivation index
(c) Basic necessities of life
(d) Material deprivation

70. Which of the following is the essential component of 'social exclusion'?
(a) Denial of quality food
(b) Denial of employment
(c) Denial of social rights
(d) Denial of housing

71. Match List I with List II:
List I
A. Crime and Personality
B. Human Deviance, Social problems and Social control
C. Delinquency and Drift
D. Juvenile Delinquency and urban areas
List II
i. H. Eysenck
ii. E.M. Lemert
iii. D. Matza
iv. C.R. Shaw and H.D. McKay

Choose the correct answer from the codes given below:

Codes:	**A**	**B**	**C**	**D**
(a)	i	ii	iii	iv
(b)	iv	iii	ii	i
(c)	iii	ii	i	iv
(d)	ii	iv	iii	i

72. **Assertion (A):** Rural sociology is a well developed and oldest field of sociology discipline in India.
Reason (R): Many prominent Indian social anthropologists and sociologists studied Indian rural society from early 20th century.
Choose the correct answer from the given codes:
Codes:
(a) (A) is true, but (R) is false.
(b) (A) is false, but (R) is true.
(c) Both (A) and (R) are true.
(d) Both (A) and (R) are false.

73. Choose the correct stages in the evolution of human society.
(a) Hunting and food gathering, hoeculture and domestication of animals, agricultural economy based on plough and domesticated animals and modern industrial capitalistic production.
(b) Hunting and gathering, agricultural economy and domestication of animals and modern industrial capitalism.
(c) Gathering, hunting, pastoral, agrarian, mechanised agricultural production.
(d) Food gathering, hunting, pastoral, horticulture and agriculture.

74. The process of social change to which people attribute positive values is termed as

(a) Globalization
(b) Urbanization
(c) Development
(d) Economic Growth

75. Who authored the Book, "More Equality"?
(a) Herbert J. Gans (b) J.C. Kincaid
(c) A.K. Sen (d) A. Gorz

ANSWERS

1. (d)	2. (d)	3. (a)	4. (c)	5. (c)
6. (b)	7. (a)	8. (b)	9. (c)	10. (a)
11. (b)	12. (c)	13. (b)	14. (b)	15. (a)
16. (c)	17. (a)	18. (b)	19. (d)	20. (c)
21. (b)	22. (a)	23. (b)	24. (c)	25. (d)
26. (a)	27. (b)	28. (c)	29. (d)	30. (a)
31. (d)	32. (d)	33. (b)	34. (a)	35. (a)
36. (b)	37. (c)	38. (a)	39. (d)	40. (c)
41. (b)	42. (b)	43. (b)	44. (c)	45. (a)
46. (d)	47. (a)	48. (c)	49. (a)	50. (b)
51. (c)	52. (a)	53. (c)	54. (c)	55. (a)
56. (d)	57. (b)	58. (b)	59. (d)	60. (c)
61. (d)	62. (c)	63. (b)	64. (b)	65. (d)
66. (c)	67. (a)	68. (a)	69. (b)	70. (c)
71. (a)	72. (c)	73. (a)	74. (c)	75. (a)

DECEMBER–2013

Note: This paper contains Sixty (60) multiple-choice questions, each question carrying two (2) marks. Candidate is expected to answer any Fifty (50) questions. In case more than Fifty (50) questions are attempted, only the first Fifty (50) questions will be evaluated.

PAPER–I

1. The post-industrial society is designated as
   (a) Information society
   (b) Technology society
   (c) Mediated society
   (d) Non-agricultural society

2. The initial efforts for internet based communication was for
   (a) Commercial communication
   (b) Military purposes
   (c) Personal interaction
   (d) Political campaigns

3. Internal communication within institutions is done through
   (a) LAN (b) WAN
   (c) EBB (d) MMS

4. Virtual reality provides
   (a) Sharp pictures
   (b) Individual audio
   (c) Participatory experience
   (d) Preview of new films

5. The first virtual university of India came up in
   (a) Andhra Pradesh
   (b) Maharashtra
   (c) Uttar Pradesh
   (d) Tamil Nadu

6. Arrange the following books in chronological order in which they appeared. Use the codes given below:
   (i) Limits to Growth
   (ii) Silent Spring
   (iii) Our Common Future
   (iv) Resourceful Earth
   Codes:
   (a) (i), (iii), (iv), (ii)
   (b) (ii), (iii), (i), (iv)
   (c) (ii), (i), (iii), (iv)
   (d) (i), (ii), (iii), (iv)

7. Which one of the following continents is at a greater risk of desertification?
   (a) Africa (b) Asia
   (c) South America (d) North America

8. "Women are closer to nature than men." What kind of perspective is this?
   (a) Realist (b) Essentialist
   (c) Feminist (d) Deep ecology

9. Which one of the following is not a matter a global concern in the removal of tropical forests?
   (a) Their ability to absorb the chemicals that contribute to depletion of ozone layer.
   (b) Their role in maintaining the oxygen and carbon balance of the earth.
   (c) Their ability to regulate surface and air temperatures, moisture content and reflectivity.
   (d) Their contribution to the biological diversity of the planet.

10. The most comprehensive approach to address the problems of man-environment interaction is one of the following:

(a) Natural Resource Conservation Approach
(b) Urban-industrial Growth Oriented Approach
(c) Rural-agricultural Growth Oriented Approach
(d) Watershed Development Approach

11. The major source of the pollutant gas, carbon mono-oxide (CO), in urban areas is
(a) Thermal power sector
(b) Transport sector
(c) Industrial sector
(d) Domestic sector

12. In a fuel cell driven vehicle, the energy is obtained from the combustion of
(a) Methane (b) Hydrogen
(c) LPG (d) CNG

13. Which one of the following Councils has been disbanded in 2013?
(a) Distance Education Council (DEC)
(b) National Council for Teacher Education (NCTE)
(c) National Council of Educational Research and Training (NCERT)
(d) National Assessment and Accreditation Council (NAAC)

14. Which of the following statements are correct about the National Assessment and Accreditation Council?
1. It is an autonomous institution.
2. It is tasked with the responsibility of assessing and accrediting institutions of higher education.
3. It is located in Delhi.
4. It has regional offices.

Select the correct answer from the codes given below:

Codes:
(a) 1 and 3 (b) 1 and 2
(c) 1, 2 and 4 (d) 2, 3 and 4

15. The power of the Supreme Court of India to decide disputes between two or more States falls under its
(a) Ad' (c) Original Jurisdiction
(d) Writ Jurisdiction

16. Which of the following statements are correct?
1. There are seven Union Territories in India.
2. Two Union Territories have Legislative Assemblies.
3. One Union Territory has a High Court.
4. One Union Territory is the capital of two States.

Select the correct answer from the codes given below:
(a) 1 and 3 only
(b) 2 and 4 only
(c) 2, 3 and 4 only
(d) 1, 2, 3 and 4

17. Which of the following statements are correct about the Central Information Commission?
1. The Central Information Commission is a statutory body.
2. The Chief Information Commissioner and other Information Commissioners are appointed by the President of India.
3. The Commission can impose a penalty upto a maximum of 25,000.
4. It can punish an errant officer.

Select the correct answer from the codes given below:

Codes:
(a) 1 and 2 only
(b) 1, 2 and 4
(c) 1, 2 and 3
(d) 2, 3 and 4

18. Who among the following conducted the CNN-IBN-The Hindu 2013 Election Tracker Survey across 267 constituencies in 18 States?
(a) The Centre for the Study of Developing Societies (CSDS)
(b) The Association for Democratic Reforms (ADR)
(c) CNN and IBN
(d) CNN, IBN and The Hindu

19. In certain code TEACHER is written as VGCEJGT. The code of CHILDREN will be
(a) EKNJFTGP (b) EJKNFTGP
(c) KNJFGTP (d) None of these

20. A person has to buy both apples and mangoes. The cost of one apple is ₹ 7/- whereas that of a mango is ₹ 5/-. If the person has ₹ 38, the number of apples he can buy is
(a) 1 (b) 2
(c) 3 (d) 4

21. A man pointing to a lady said, "The son of her only brother is the brother of my wife". The lady is related to the man as
(a) Mother's sister
(b) Grandmother
(c) Mother-in-law
(d) Sister of Father-in-law

22. In this series
6, 4, 1, 2, 2, 8, 7, 4, 2, 1, 5, 3, 8, 6, 2, 2, 7, 1, 4, 1, 3, 5, 8, 6, how many pairs of successive numbers have a difference of 2 each?
(a) 4 (b) 5
(c) 6 (d) 8

23. The mean marks obtained by a class of 40 students is 65. The mean marks of half of the students is found to be 45. The mean marks of the remaining students is
(a) 85 (b) 60
(c) 70 (d) 65

24. Anil is twice as old as Sunita. Three years ago, he was three times as old as Sunita. The present age of Anil is
(a) 6 years (b) 8 years
(c) 12 years (d) 16 years

25. Which of the following is a social network?
(a) amazon.com (b) eBay
(c) gmail.com (d) Twitter

26. The population information is called parameter while the corresponding sample information is known as
(a) Universe
(b) Inference
(c) Sampling design
(d) Statistics

Read the following passage carefully and answer questions 27 to 32:

Heritage conservation practices improved worldwide after the International Centre for the Study of the Preservation and Restoration of Cultural Property (ICCROM) was established with UNESCO's assistance in 1959. The inter-governmental organisation with 126 member states has done a commendable job by training more than 4,000 professionals, providing practice standards, and sharing technical expertise. In this golden jubilee year, as we acknowledge its key role in global conservation, an assessment of international practices would be meaningful to the Indian conservation movement. Consistent investment, rigorous attention, and dedicated research and dissemination are some of the positive lessons to imbibe. Countries such as Italy have demonstrated that prioritising heritage with significant budget provision pays. On the other hand, India, which is no less endowed in terms of cultural capital, has a long way to go. Surveys indicate that in addition to the 6,600 protected monuments, there are over 60,000 equally valuable heritage structures that await attention. Besides the small group in the service of Archaeological Survey of India, there are only about 150 trained conservation professionals. In order to overcome this severe shortage the emphasis has been on setting up dedicated labs and training institutions. It would make much better sense for conservation to be made part of mainstream research and engineering institutes, as has been done in Europe.

Increasing funding and building institutions are the relatively easy part. The real challenge is to redefine international approaches to address local contexts. Conservation cannot limit itself to enhancing the art-historical value of the heritage structures, which international charters perhaps overemphasise. The effort has to be broad-based: It must also serve as a means to improving the quality of life in the area where the heritage structures are located. The first task therefore is to integrate conservation efforts with sound development plans that take care of people living in the heritage vicinity. Unlike in Western countries, many traditional building crafts survive in India, and conservation practices offer an avenue to support them. This has been acknowledged by the Indian National Trust for Art and Cultural Heritage charter for conservation but is yet to receive substantial state support. More strength for heritage conservation can be mobilised by aligning it with the green building movement. Heritage structures are essentially eco-friendly and conservation could become a vital part of the sustainable building practices campaign in future.

27. The outlook for conservation heritage changed
    (a) after the establishment of the International Centre for the Study of the Preservation and Restoration of Cultural Property.
    (b) after training the specialists in the field.
    (c) after extending UNESCO's assistance to the educational institutions.
    (d) after ASI's measures to protect the monuments.

28. The inter-government organization was appreciated because of
    (a) increasing number of members to 126.
    (b) imparting training to professionals and sharing technical expertise.
    (c) consistent investment in conservation.
    (d) its proactive role in renovation and restoration.

29. Indian conservation movement will be successful if there would be
    (a) Financial support from the Government of India.
    (b) Non-governmental organisations role and participation in the conservation movement.
    (c) consistent investment, rigorous attention, and dedicated research and dissemination of awareness for conservation.
    (d) Archaeological Survey of India's meaningful assistance.

30. As per the surveys of historical monuments in India, there is very small number of protected monuments. As per given the total number of monuments and enlisted number of protected monuments, percentage comes to
    (a) 10 per cent (b) 11 per cent
    (c) 12 per cent (d) 13 per cent

31. What should India learn from Europe to conserve our cultural heritage?
   (i) There should be significant budget provision to conserve our cultural heritage.
   (ii) Establish dedicated labs and training institutions.
   (iii) Force the government to provide sufficient funds.
   (iv) Conservation should be made part of mainstream research and engineering institutes.

   Choose correct answer from the codes given below:

   Codes:
   (a) (i), (ii), (iii), (iv)
   (b) (i), (ii), (iv)
   (c) (i), (ii)
   (d) (i), (iii), (iv)

32. INTACH is known for its contribution for conservation of our cultural heritage. The full form of INTACH is
   (a) International Trust for Art and Cultural Heritage
   (b) Intra-national Trust for Art and Cultural Heritage
   (c) Integrated Trust for Art and Cultural Heritage
   (d) Indian National Trust for Art and Cultural Heritage

33. While delivering lecture if there is some disturbance in the class, a teacher should
   (a) keep quiet for a while and then continue.
   (b) punish those causing disturbance.
   (c) motivate to teach those causing disturbance.
   (d) not bother of what is happening in the class.

34. Effective teaching is a function of
   (a) Teacher's satisfaction.
   (b) Teacher's honesty and commitment.
   (c) Teacher's making students learn and understand.
   (d) Teacher's liking for professional excellence.

35. The most appropriate meaning of learning is
   (a) Acquisition of skills
   (b) Modification of behaviour
   (c) Personal adjustment
   (d) Inculcation of knowledge

36. Arrange the following teaching process in order:
   (i) Relate the present knowledge with previous one
   (ii) Evaluation
   (iii) Reteaching
   (iv) Formulating instructional objectives
   (v) Presentation of instructional materials
   (a) (i), (ii), (iii), (iv), (v)
   (b) (ii), (i), (iii), (iv), (v)
   (c) (v), (iv), (iii), (i), (ii)
   (d) (iv), (i), (v), (ii), (iii)

37. CIET stands for
   (a) Centre for Integrated Education and Technology
   (b) Central Institute for Engineering and Technology
   (c) Central Institute for Education Technology
   (d) Centre for Integrated Evaluation Techniques

38. Teacher's role at higher education level is to
   (a) provide information to students.
   (b) promote self learning in students.
   (c) encourage healthy competition among students.
   (d) help students to solve their problems.

39. The Verstehen School of Understanding was popularised by
   (a) German Social Scientists
   (b) American Philosophers

(c) British Academicians
(d) Italian Political Analysts

40. The sequential operations in scientific research are
(a) Co-variation, Elimination of Spurious Relations, Generalisation, Theorisation
(b) Generalisation, Co-variation, Theorisation, Elimination of Spurious Relations
(c) Theorisation, Generalisation, Elimination of Spurious Relations, Co-variation
(d) Elimination of Spurious Relations, Theorisation, Generalisation, Co-variation.

41. In sampling, the lottery method is used for
(a) Interpretation
(b) Theorisation
(c) Conceptualisation
(d) Randomisation

42. Which is the main objective of research?
(a) To review the literature
(b) To summarize what is already known
(c) To get an academic degree
(d) To discover new facts or to make fresh interpretation of known facts

43. Sampling error decreases with the
(a) decrease in sample size
(b) increase in sample size
(c) process of randomization
(d) process of analysis

44. The principles of fundamental research are used in
(a) action research
(b) applied research
(c) philosophical research
(d) historical research

45. Users who use media for their own ends are identified as
(a) Passive audience
(b) Active audience
(c) Positive audience
(d) Negative audience

46. Classroom communication can be described as
(a) Exploration
(b) Institutionalisation
(c) Unsignified narration
(d) Discourse

47. Ideological codes shape our collective
(a) Productions
(b) Perceptions
(c) Consumptions
(d) Creations

48. In communication, myths have power, but are
(a) uncultural
(b) insignificant
(c) imprecise
(d) unpreferred

49. The first multi-lingual news agency of India was
(a) Samachar
(b) API
(c) Hindustan Samachar
(d) Samachar Bharati

50. Organisational communication can also be equated with
(a) intra-personal communication.
(b) inter-personal communication.
(c) group communication.
(d) mass communication.

51. If two propositions having the same subject and predicate terms are such that one is the denial of the other, the relationship between them is called
(a) Contradictory
(b) Contrary
(c) Sub-contrary
(d) Sub-alternation

52. Ananya and Krishna can speak and follow English. Bulbul can write and speak Hindi as Archana does.
Archana talks with Ananya also in Bengali. Krishna cannot follow Bengali. Bulbul talks with Ananya in Hindi. Who can speak and follow English, Hindi and Bengali?
(a) Archana
(b) Bulbul
(c) Ananya
(d) Krishna

53. A stipulative definition may be said to be
(a) Always true
(b) Always false
(c) Sometimes true, sometimes false
(d) Neither true nor false

54. When the conclusion of an argument follows from its premise/premises conclusively, the argument is called
(a) Circular argument
(b) Inductive argument
(c) Deductive argument
(d) Analogical argument

55. Saturn and Mars are planets like the earth. They borrow light from the Sun and moves around the Sun as the Earth does. So those planets are inhabited by various orders of creatures as the earth is. What type of argument is contained in the above passage?
(a) Deductive
(b) Astrological
(c) Analogical
(d) Mathematical

56. Given below are two premises. Four conclusions are drawn from those two premises in four codes. Select the code that states the conclusion validly drawn.

Premises:
(i) All saints are religious. (major)
(ii) Some honest persons are saints. (minor)

Codes:
(a) All saints are honest.
(b) Some saints are honest.
(c) Some honest persons are religious.
(d) All religious persons are honest.

Following table provides details about the Foreign Tourist Arrivals (FTAs) in India from different regions of the world in different years. Study the table carefully and answer questions from 57 to 60 based on this table.

Region	**Number of Foreign Tourist Arrivals**		
	2007	**2008**	**2009**
Western Europe	1686083	1799525	1610086
North America	1007276	1027297	1024469
South Asia	982428	1051846	982633
South East Asia	303475	332925	348495
East Asia	352037	355230	318292
West Asia	171661	215542	201110
Total FTAs in India	5081504	5282603	5108579

57. Find out the region that contributed around 20 per cent of the total foreign tourist arrivals in India in 2009.
(a) Western Europe
(b) North America
(c) South Asia
(d) South East Asia

58. Which of the following regions has recorded the highest negative growth rate of foreign tourist arrivals in India in 2009?
(a) Western Europe
(b) North America
(c) South Asia
(d) West Asia

59. Find out the region that has been showing declining trend in terms of share of foreign tourist arrivals in India in 2008 and 2009.
(a) Western Europe
(b) South East Asia
(c) East Asia
(d) West Asia

60. Identify the region that has shown hyper growth rate of foreign tourist arrivals than the growth rate of the total FTAs in India in 2008.
(a) Western Europe
(b) North America
(c) South Asia
(d) East Asia

ANSWERS

1. (a)	2. (b)	3. (a)	4. (c)	5. (d)
6. (c)	7. (a)	8. (b)	9. (a)	10. (d)
11. (b)	12. (b)	13. (a)	14. (b)	15. (c)
16. (d)	17. (c)	18. (a)	19. (b)	20. (d)
21. (d)	22. (c)	23. (a)	24. (c)	25. (d)
26. (d)	27. (a)	28. (b)	29. (c)	30. (b)
31. (b)	32. (d)	33. (c)	34. (c)	35. (b)
36. (d)	37. (c)	38. (b)	39. (a)	40. (a)
41. (d)	42. (d)	43. (b)	44. (b)	45. (b)
46. (d)	47. (b)	48. (c)	49. (c)	50. (c)
51. (a)	52. (c)	53. (d)	54. (c)	55. (c)
56. (c)	57. (b)	58. (d)	59. (a)	60. (c)

PAPER–II

Note: This paper contains Fifty (50) objective type questions, each question carrying two (2) marks. All questions are compulsory.

1. "Sociology is a Science which attempts an interpretative understanding of social action." Who defined Sociology in this manner?
(a) T. Parsons
(b) MacIver and Page
(c) E. Durkheim
(d) Max Weber

2. "Culture is man's guide, it liberates as well as enslaves him as all guides do." Which of the following school represents this view?
(a) Evolutionary School
(b) Marxian School
(c) Diffusionistic School
(d) Culture-personality School

3. The term 'Sociological Imagination' was coined by whom?
(a) P. Berger
(b) C.W. Mills
(c) A. Giddens
(d) J.S. Mill

4. Arrange the following books in chronological order by using the codes given below:
i. Das Kapital
ii. Protestant Ethic and the Spirit of Capitalism
iii. Patterns of Culture
iv. The Elementary Forms of Religious Life

Codes:
(a) i ii iii iv (b) ii i iii iv
(c) iv iii i ii (d) iii iv i ii

5. Every man in society occupies a number of statuses. Different statuses associated with a single person are known as
   (a) Status inconsistency
   (b) Status sequences
   (c) Status set
   (d) Status succession

6. Which of the following are the physical conditions of a primary group?
   i. Physical proximity
   ii. Attraction
   iii. Smallness
   iv. Endurance
   (a) i, ii, iii and iv
   (b) i, ii and iii
   (c) i, ii and iv
   (d) i, iii and iv

7. Which of the following is not a primary group?
   (a) Scouts
   (b) A peer group
   (c) A class of students
   (d) Family

8. Which of the following are fundamental features of a social group?
   i. Organisation
   ii. We-feeling
   iii. Self-sufficiency
   iv. Explicit cultural goals
   (a) i and ii (b) ii and iii
   (c) iii and iv (d) i and iii

9. Given below are two statements labelled as Assertion (A), and the other labelled as Reason (R):
   Assertion (A): According to Durkheim education perpetuates and reinforces homogeneity in society among its members.
   Reason (R): Schools inculcate society's norms and values providing link between individual and society.
   Codes:
   (a) Both (A) and (R) are true and (R) is the correct explanation of (A).
   (b) Both (A) and (R) are true, but (R) is not the correct explanation of (A).
   (c) (A) is true, but (R) is false.
   (d) (A) is false, but (R) is true.

10. Match List I with List II:
   List I (Books)
   A. *De-schooling Society*
   B. *The Politics of Family*
   C. *Anti-social Family*
   D. *Schooling in Capitalist America*
   List II (Authors)
   i. R.D. Laing
   ii. S. Bowles and H. Gintis
   iii. Ivan Illich
   iv. M. Barrett and M. MacIntosh

Codes:	A	B	C	D
(a)	i	ii	iii	iv
(b)	iv	i	ii	iii
(c)	iii	i	iv	ii
(d)	ii	i	iii	iv

11. Match List I with List II:
   List I (Terms)
   A. Church B. Sect
   C. Denomination D. Cult
   List II (Features)
   i. Usually more individualistic and lacks sharply defined belief system
   ii. Usually conservative but not closely related to State
   iii. Often closely related to State and claim promptly on religious truth
   iv. Less conservative and connected with lower class

Codes:	A	B	C	D
(a)	iv	iii	ii	i
(b)	iii	iv	ii	i
(c)	ii	i	iv	iii
(d)	i	ii	iii	iv

12. The variable sum concept of power is based on the assumption that
    (a) value consensus is essential for society.
    (b) value dissension is essential for society.
    (c) value neutrality is essential for society.
    (d) values are essential for society.
13. The State moderates between different groups ensuring that all of them have some influence on public policy, is best manifested in
    (a) Socialist democracy
    (b) Republic democracy
    (c) Pluralist democracy
    (d) Traditional democracy
14. Match List I with List II:

    List I (Authors)
    A. V. Pareto
    B. G. Mosca
    C. R. Mitchell
    D. S. Lukes

    List II (Terms)
    i. The Ruling Class
    ii. The Non-governing Elite
    iii. The Iron law of Oligarchy
    iv. The Three Dimensional View

Codes:	A	B	C	D
(a)	ii	iii	iv	i
(b)	ii	i	iii	iv
(c)	ii	iii	i	iv
(d)	ii	iv	i	iii

15. Which of the following is an appropriate example of a social institution?
    (a) Market
    (b) Trade Union
    (c) Political Party
    (d) N.G.O.
16. According to Dahrendorf, Marx's Theory of Class Conflict is
    (a) to be rejected universally
    (b) to be accepted universally
    (c) to be accepted and modified generally
    (d) to be rejected, accepted and modified contextually
17. The process whereby the helpless human infant gradually becomes a self-aware, knowledgeable person, skilled in the ways of the culture into which he or she was born is known as
    (a) Re-socialization
    (b) Social position
    (c) Socialization
    (d) Shared understanding
18. Stages of cognitive-development related socialization was proposed by
    (a) H. Mead
    (b) S. Freud
    (c) C.H. Cooley
    (d) J. Piaget
19. Match List I with List II and find out the correct answer from the codes given below:

    List I
    A. E. Durkheim B. M. Weber
    C. Z. Bauman D. T. Parsons

    List II
    i. *The Social System*
    ii. *The Liquid Love*
    iii. *The Division of Labour in Society*
    iv. *The Religion of India*

Codes:	A	B	C	D
(a)	i	ii	iii	iv
(b)	iii	iv	ii	i
(c)	ii	iii	iv	i
(d)	iv	iii	ii	i

20. In a system of social stratification social rankings are based on certain attributes which may

(a) either be inherited or socially constructed.
(b) either be ascribed or acquired.
(c) either be acquired or socially constructed.
(d) either be ascribed, acquired or constructed.

Which is the correct one?

21. The social positions of
(a) caste, gender and ethnic groups are biologically determined.
(b) caste biologically, but gender and ethnic groups are economically determined.
(c) gender is biologically, while the ethnic and caste groups are culturally determined.
(d) caste, gender and ethnic groups are culturally determined.

Which one of the above is correct?

22. According to Marx and Dehrendorf unequal class position of a social group is determined by which of the following forms and extent of one's control over
(a) economic and cultural resources respectively.
(b) cultural and economic resources respectively.
(c) economic and political resources respectively.
(d) political and cultural resources respectively.

23. Who among the following sociologists analysed social classes in terms of market and property situation?
(a) M. Weber
(b) J. Goldthorpe
(c) E. Durkheim
(d) T. Parsons

24. Some assumptions are given below:
The definitional assumption(s) about class and class conflict in the Marxian theory is (are)
(i) every society is based on a degree of economic equilibrium.
(ii) class inequality is due to inherent political and social injustice.
(iii) class conflict is inherent in society.
(iv) economic inequality lies at the core of class conflict.
(v) class conflict is resolved through class alliance.

Select correct assumptions from the following:
(a) (i) and (ii)
(b) (i), (ii) and (iii)
(c) (ii), (iii) and (v)
(d) (iii) and (iv)

25. Transmission of traits from one culture to another is sociologically termed as
(a) Acculturation
(b) Diffusion
(c) Assimilation
(d) Enculturation

26. Who among the following is a proponent of cyclical theory of evolution?
(a) T. Parsons
(b) E. Durkheim
(c) O. Spengler
(d) H. Spencer

27. Identify the social processes which are linked to change of social structure:
(i) Industrialisation
(ii) Sanskritization
(iii) Modernisation
(iv) Globalisation
(v) Intergenerational mobility
(vi) Intragenerational mobility

Select the correct option:
(a) (i) (ii) (iv)
(b) (i) (iii) (iv)
(c) (iv) (v) (vi)
(d) (i) (iii) (iv) (v)

28. According to R.K. Merton, those observed consequences which lessen the adaptation or adjustment of the system are
(a) Functions
(b) Non-functions
(c) Dysfunctions
(d) Functional alternatives

29. In which of the book has Mannheim propounded the idea of Sociology of Knowledge?
(a) *The End of Ideology*
(b) *The End of History*
(c) *Ideology and Utopia*
(d) *The German Ideology*

30. A statement of prediction that sets forth the basis for testing the relationship between variables in an attempt to link theory to reality is called
(a) Random sampling
(b) Questionnaire
(c) Hypothesis
(d) Assumption

31. Name the technique which is to be used before the actual fieldwork starts
(a) Pilot study
(b) Census study
(c) Case study
(d) Survey

32. There are two statements, one is Assertion (A) and the other is Reason (R). Select the correct answer from the codes given below:
Assertion (A): Research design is a kind of blue print that is prepared before actually carrying out a research.
Reason (R): Many research plans are unable to produce a concrete finding.
Codes:
(a) Both (A) and (R) are true and (R) is the correct explanation of (A).
(b) Both (A) and (R) are true, but (R) is not the correct explanation of (A).
(c) (A) is true, but (R) is false.
(d) (A) is false, but (R) is true.

33. Identify the correct logical order as explained by Karl Marx:
(a) Class-in-itself, class-for-itself, social transformation, class conflict
(b) Class-in-itself, class-for-itself, class conflict, social transformation
(c) Class-in-itself, class conflict, class-for-itself, social transformation
(d) Class-for-itself, class conflict, class-in-itself, social transformation

34. In the context of Randall Collin's analysis, identify the correct one:
(a) Moves from macro-level to Meso-level and to micro-level social processes
(b) Moves from micro-level to Meso-level and to micro-level social processes
(c) Moves from micro-level to macro-level social processes
(d) Moves from macro-level to micro-level processes

35. Match List I with List II:
List I (Contributions of)
A. R.K. Merton
B. T. Parsons
C. B. Malinowski
D. L. Coser

List II (Approach)
i. Conflict Functionalism
ii. Need Functionalism
iii. Analytical Functionalism
iv. Empirical Functionalism

Codes:	A	B	C	D
(a)	iii	iv	ii	i
(b)	iv	iii	ii	i

(c)	ii	iii	iv	i
(d)	iv	ii	iii	i

36. What is triangulation?
 (a) A type of qualitative method of research
 (b) A type of qualitative analysis
 (c) A combination of qualitative and quantitative methods
 (d) A type of non-participant observation

37. Who among the following used the method of concomitant variation?
 (a) M. Weber
 (b) R. Dahrendorf
 (c) E. Durkheim
 (d) T. Parsons

38. Reliability of data implies
 (a) The same methods of investigation on the same materials produce the same results.
 (b) The different methods of investigation on different materials produce the same results.
 (c) The same methods of investigation on the same materials produce different results.
 (d) The same methods of investigation on different materials produce the same result.

39. Radical Sociology sought to support which of the following sociological thought systems?
 (a) Marxian
 (b) Functional
 (c) Symbolic interactionist
 (d) Positivist

40. Match the items of List I with List II and select the correct answer from the codes given below:

List I (Concept)
A. False Consciousness
B. Magic
C. Rational Action
D. Moral Community

List II (Authors)
i. Malinowski
ii. Marx
iii. Durkheim
iv. Weber

Codes:	**A**	**B**	**C**	**D**
(a)	i	iii	iv	ii
(b)	ii	i	iv	iii
(c)	iii	i	ii	iv
(d)	iv	ii	iii	i

41. **Assertion (A):** Karl Marx thought of all capitalist societies to be founded on exploitation of the proletariat.
Reason (R): The proletariat has not become increasingly impoverished.
Codes:
 (a) (A) is true, but (R) is false.
 (b) (R) is true, but (A) is false.
 (c) (A) is true, but (R) is not correct explanation of (A).
 (d) Both (A) and (R) are true and (R) is the correct explanation of (A).

42. Which of the following acts are necessary to keep the social system intact? Select the correct codes given below:
 (i) Adaptation
 (ii) Social action
 (iii) Integration
 (iv) Goal attainment
 (v) Latency (pattern maintenance)
 (vi) Socialisation
Codes:
 (a) (i), (ii), (iii) and (iv)
 (b) (iv), (v), (i) and (vi)
 (c) (i), (iii), (iv) and (v)
 (d) (i), (ii), (iv) and (v)

43. The indepth investigation of a phenomena, or a process, or an event that focuses on its historicity and

contemporary interlinks with wider society is termed as
(a) Content study
(b) Participant observation
(c) Content analysis
(d) Case study

44. Which of the following is not an ethical consideration in social research?
(a) Protecting the subjects from physical and psychological harm while collecting data
(b) Protecting the subjects confidentiality and privacy
(c) Acquiring consent of the subject in collecting information
(d) Acquiring data through deception

45. Which one of the following is not a measure of correlation?
(a) Chi-square
(b) Student's t-test
(c) Mean dispersion
(d) Product-movement coefficient

46. Kamla teaches in a college, organizes a kitty party, takes care of her daughter and presides over a meeting of women's organization. Which of the following concepts is used to describe her role?
(a) Role conflict
(b) Role set
(c) Multiple roles
(d) Role making

47. Match the concepts (List I) with the authors (List II) and then select the correct answer from among the codes given below:

List I (Concepts)
A. Anticipatory socialization
B. Sensate culture
C. Residues
D. Little community

List II (Authors)
i. R.K. Merton
ii. P. Sorokin
iii. V. Pareto
iv. R. Redfield

Codes:	A	B	C	D
(a)	ii	iii	i	iv
(b)	iii	ii	iv	i
(c)	ii	iv	iii	i
(d)	i	ii	iii	iv

48. The concept of 'Wert-rational' is associated with whom?
(a) M. Weber
(b) P. Sorokin
(c) T. Parsons
(d) J. Habermas

49. Which of the following pairs is not correctly matched?
(a) Social Evolution – H. Spencer
(b) Verstehen – M. Weber
(c) Rentier Class – V. Pareto
(d) Sacred and Profane – A. Comte

50. Who among the following analysts of social change used the term 'rentiers and speculators'?
(a) T. Veblen
(b) K. Marx
(c) V. Pareto
(d) A.J. Toynbee

ANSWERS

1. (d)	2. (d)	3. (b)	4. (b)	5. (c)
6. (d)	7. (a)	8. (a)	9. (a)	10. (d)
11. (b)	12. (a)	13. (c)	14. (b)	15. (a)
16. (d)	17. (c)	18. (d)	19. (b)	20. (d)
21. (d)	22. (c)	23. (a)	24. (d)	25. (b)
26. (c)	27. (b)	28. (c)	29. (c)	30. (c)

31. (a)	32. (a)	33. (b)	34. (b)	35. (b)
36. (c)	37. (c)	38. (a)	39. (a)	40. (b)
41. (c)	42. (c)	43. (d)	44. (d)	45. (d)
46. (c)	47. (d)	48. (a)	49. (d)	50. (c)

PAPER–III

Note: This paper contains seventy five (75) objective type questions of two (2) marks each. All questions are compulsory.

1. Who among the following is not regarded as a post-modernist thinker?
   (a) J. Alexander
   (b) J. Derrida
   (c) F. Jameson
   (d) J.F. Lyotard

2. Match the items of List I with those of List II and give the correct answer from the codes given below:

   List I (Books)
   A. *The Post-Modern Condition*
   B. *Writing and Difference*
   C. *Post-Modernism, or the Cultural Logic of late Capitalism*
   D. *The Archaeology of Knowledge and the Discourse on Language*

   List II (Authors)
   i. J. Derrida
   ii. J.F. Lyotard
   iii. M. Foucault
   iv. F. Jameson

Codes:	A	B	C	D
(a)	ii	iii	i	iv
(b)	iii	i	ii	iv
(c)	ii	i	iv	iii
(d)	i	ii	iii	iv

3. Match List I with List II and give the correct answer from the codes given below:

   List I (Dams)
   A. Sardar Sarovar
   B. Koel-Karo
   C. Machkunda
   D. Tehri

   List II (States)
   i. Orissa
   ii. Uttarakhand
   iii. Gujarat
   iv. Jharkhand

Codes:	A	B	C	D
(a)	iii	iv	i	ii
(b)	ii	i	iii	iv
(c)	i	ii	iii	iv
(d)	iv	ii	i	iii

4. Match List I with List II and give the correct answer from the codes given below:

   List I (Books)
   A. *The Coming of Post-Industrial Society*
   B. *The Post-Capitalist Society*
   C. *The Third Wave*
   D. *The Information Age*

   List II (Authors)
   i. A. Toffler
   ii. D. Bell
   iii. M. Castells
   iv. P. Drucker

Codes:	A	B	C	D
(a)	i	iii	iv	ii
(b)	ii	i	iii	iv
(c)	iii	ii	iv	i
(d)	ii	iv	i	iii

5. Match List I with List II and find out the correct answer from the codes given below:

   List I (Books)
   A. *Who were the Shudras?*
   B. *Social Background of Indian Nationalism*

C. *Homo Hierarchicus*
D. *Class, Caste and Occupation*

List II (Authors)
i. L. Dumont
ii. G.S. Ghurye
iii. A.R. Desai
iv. B.R. Ambedkar

Codes:	**A**	**B**	**C**	**D**
(a)	iv	iii	ii	i
(b)	iii	iv	ii	i
(c)	ii	i	iii	iv
(d)	iv	iii	i	ii

6. Match List I with List II and then find out the correct answer from the codes given below:

List I
A. Cultural Diversity
B. Social Justice
C. Purity and Pollution
D. Freedom Movement

List II
i. B.R. Ambedkar
ii. L. Dumont
iii. A.R. Desai
iv. D.P. Mukherjee

Codes:	**A**	**B**	**C**	**D**
(a)	iv	i	ii	iii
(b)	i	ii	iv	iii
(c)	iii	i	ii	iv
(d)	ii	iii	i	iv

7. **Assertion (A):** Graduates will be increasingly expected to return periodically to tertiary education institutions to acquire, learn and use knowledge and skills needed throughout their professional lives.

Reason (R): Even though higher education has always been formally designed as a structure for the production and organisation of advanced knowledge, the emergence of a knowledge economy and the importance of globalisation place new demands on higher education.

Find out the correct answer from the codes given below:

Codes:
(a) (A) and (R) both are correct, but (R) is not the correct reason of (A).
(b) (A) and (R) both are correct, and (R) is the correct explanation of (A).
(c) (A) is correct, but (R) is not true.
(d) (R) is true, but (A) is false.

8. Who among the following used the word 'Anomie'?
(i) M. Weber
(ii) K. Marx
(iii) E. Durkheim
(iv) R.K. Merton

Find out the correct combination:
(a) (ii) and (iii)
(b) (i) and (ii)
(c) (iv) and (i)
(d) (iii) and (iv)

9. **Assertion (A):** Displacement is one of the indicators of development.

Reason (R): Displacement brings hardship, miseries and other problems to the people.

Choose the right codes:

Codes:
(a) Both (A) and (R) are true and (R) is the correct explanation of (A).
(b) Both (A) and (R) are true, but (R) is not the correct explanation of (A).
(c) (A) is true, but (R) is false.
(d) (A) is false, but (R) is true.

10. **Assertion (A):** A society that is tolerant to some degree of deviant behaviour need not suffer from social disruption.

Reason (R): Deviant behaviour is result of lack of moral regulation within society.

Select the correct answer from the codes given below:

Codes:

(a) Both (A) and (R) are true and (R) is the correct explanation of (A).

(b) Both (A) and (R) are true, but (R) is not the correct explanation of (A).

(c) (A) is true, but (R) is false.

(d) (A) is false, but (R) is true.

11. E. Sutherland founded the theory of
(a) Blue collar crime
(b) Crime by dacoits
(c) White collar crime
(d) Cyber-crime

12. All countries pass through various stages of demographic transition. Which one of the following is not such a stage?
(a) Population explosion
(b) Stationary state
(c) Population stabilization
(d) Optimum stage

13. India recognized the population problem and adopted an official national programme in family planning in
(a) 1950 (b) 1952
(c) 1955 (d) 1975

14. Match the items in List I with the items in List II and choose the correct answer from the codes given below:

List I
A. Higher fertility-high mortality
B. High fertility-low mortality
C. Low fertility-low mortality
D. Low fertility-negligible mortality

List II
i. Developed society
ii. Primitive society
iii. Developing society
iv. Highly developed society

Codes:	A	B	C	D
(a)	i	iv	ii	iii
(b)	iv	ii	iii	i
(c)	iii	ii	iv	i
(d)	ii	iii	i	iv

15. In which of the following decade has there been an absolute decline of population size in India?
(a) 1971-1981
(b) 2001-2011
(c) 1931-1941
(d) 1901-1911

16. Which of the following are the factors associated with Infant mortality?
(i) Low Birth Weight
(ii) Lack of Institutional Deliveries
(iii) Nutritional status of Expectant Mother
(iv) Use of contraceptives

Codes:
(a) (i), (iii), (iv)
(b) (i), (ii), (iv)
(c) (ii), (iii), (iv)
(d) (i), (ii), (iii)

17. Match the items in List I with the items in List II, using correct codes given below:

List I (Major Thought)
A. 'Resources set the limits of population growth'
B. 'Human beings are the ultimate resource'
C. 'Contraceptive is best development'
D. 'Population regulations are essential for improving people's life'

List II (Person)
i. Julian L. Simon
ii. T.R. Malthus
iii. Plato
iv. Karna Singh

Codes:	A	B	C	D
(a)	i	iv	iii	ii
(b)	ii	i	iv	iii
(c)	iv	ii	i	iii
(d)	iii	i	ii	iv

18. According to A.R. Desai, the second phase of the development of nationalism (from 1885 to 1905) is characterized by
(a) the development of industry.
(b) the influence of socialism.
(c) the participation of peasants.
(d) the home rule.

19. A.R. Desai has pointed out many factors of the rise of Indian Nationalism. Identify the correct set of the factors:
(i) Agricultural and Industrial policies by the Britishers.
(ii) Means of Communication
(iii) National Reform Movements
(iv) Print Media
(v) Modern Secular Education
(vi) Electronic Media
Select the correct answer from the codes given below:
Codes:
(a) (i), (ii), (iii) and (vi)
(b) (i), (ii), (iii), (iv) and (v)
(c) (i), (iii), (iv) and (vi)
(d) (i), (ii), (iii), (iv), (v) and (vi)

20. Which of the following are the types of action as elucidated by J. Habermas?
(i) Rational
(ii) Emotional
(iii) Teleological
(iv) Normative
(v) Dramaturgical
(vi) Communicative
Select the correct answer from the codes given below:
Codes:
(a) (i), (ii), (iv) and (vi)
(b) (ii), (iii), (v) and (vi)
(c) (iii), (iv), (v) and (vi)
(d) (i), (iv), (v) and (vi)

21. A. Giddens has explained three types of rules and resources and corresponding processes. Identify the correct match from the following:

Rules & Resources	**Process**
A. Normative	i. Signification
B. Allocative & Authoritative	ii. Legitimation
C. Interpretative	iii. Domination

Select the correct answer from the given codes:

Codes:	**A**	**B**	**C**
(a)	i	ii	iii
(b)	i	iii	ii
(c)	iii	ii	i
(d)	ii	iii	i

22. What is structure according to A. Giddens?
(a) Patterns and standards of behaviour of actors.
(b) Rules and resources that actors use in interaction contexts.
(c) Values and ideals that regulate the conducts of human beings.
(d) Groups and collectivists that are formed in the course of social interaction.

23. Which of the following statements correctly describes the ethno methodology's view-point?
(a) "For full causal explanation it is necessary to determine what has given rise to the motives of social action."
(b) "Social life appears orderly to members of society only because members actively engage in making sense of social life."
(c) "Diversity is the order of the day. We have entered an era in which anything goes."
(d) "The effects of a social institution may be illustrated in terms of the analogy between society and an organism."

24. Which two of the following primary frames have been used by E. Goffman?
   (i) Natural frame
   (ii) Cultural frame
   (iii) Social frame
   (iv) Real frame

   Select the correct answer from the codes given below:

   Codes:
   (a) (i) and (iv)
   (b) (i) and (ii)
   (c) (i) and (iii)
   (d) (ii) and (iii)

25. By the colonization of life world J. Habermas meant
   (a) subjugation of the developing nations by the developed nations.
   (b) subjugation of society and culture by Economy and Polity systems.
   (c) subjugation of culture of a society by globalization.
   (d) subjugation of cultural view by the global capitalist class.

26. L. Althussar classifies Karl Marx's writings on the basis of the epistemological break. Identify the epistemological phases of Marx's writings.
   (i) Young Marx
   (ii) Mature Marx
   (iii) Traditional Marx
   (iv) Immature Marx
   (v) Orthodox Marx
   (vi) Revolutionary Marx

   Select the correct answer from the codes given below:

   Codes:
   (a) (i) and (ii)
   (b) (ii) and (iii)
   (c) (v) and (vi)
   (d) (ii) and (iv)

27. Which of the following concepts have been used by E. Goffman in his works?
   (i) Unfocussed interaction
   (ii) Focussed interaction
   (iii) Encounter
   (iv) Front region
   (v) Back region
   (vi) Impression management
   (a) (ii), (iii), (iv) and (v)
   (b) (i), (ii), (iii), (iv), (v) and (vi)
   (c) (ii), (iii), (iv), (v) and (vi)
   (d) (iii), (iv), (v) and (vi)

28. Choose an appropriate combination of the following statements which explains phenomenology:
   (i) Phenomenology deals with every day social life.
   (ii) Phenomenology focuses on the shared common-sense knowledge.
   (iii) Phenomenology is concerned with the causal explanation of human behaviour in the same way as other perspectives.
   (iv) Phenomenology attempts to search for the structural principles of social life.

   Select the correct answer from the codes given below:

   Codes:
   (a) (i) and (iv)
   (b) (ii) and (iii)
   (c) (iii) and (iv)
   (d) (i) and (ii)

29. Which of the following sets include the structural levels as mentioned by L. Althussar?
   (i) Economic
   (ii) Political
   (iii) Cultural
   (iv) Ideological

Select the correct answer from the codes given below:

Codes:

(a) (i), (ii) and (iii)
(b) (i), (ii) and (iv)
(c) (ii), (iii) and (iv)
(d) (i), (iii) and (iv)

30. Which of the following sets of specific concepts is used by A. Schutz?
(a) Typification, recipe, class, revolution
(b) Typification, stock knowledge, recipe, revolution
(c) Typification, life world, stock knowledge, class
(d) Typification, life world, stock knowledge, recipe

31. Which one of the following statements correctly identify 'subaltern perspective'?
(a) An approach to study society from Elite's point of view.
(b) Describe changes in society of the developed countries.
(c) Approach history from below, focused more on what happens among masses at the base level of society.
(d) An approach to study the postmodern societies.

32. The interpretative approaches' that, try to understand social action from the point of view of the social actors are
(a) Social philosophy and Phenomenology
(b) Culturology and Ethnomethodology
(c) Phenomenology and Ethnomethodology
(d) Neo-Marxism and Phenomenology

33. Who among the following sociologists used dramaturgy to explain the presentation of self in everyday life?
(a) Blumer (b) E. Goffman
(c) Luckmann (d) A. Schutz

34. According to A. Schutz, the phenomenologist
(a) deny the existence of the outer world.
(b) accept the regular bondage between the inner and outer world for social analysis.
(c) the outer world should influence the social world to construct the real social image.
(d) 'suspends' the belief in the existence of outer world for the construction of social reality.

35. Match the following:

List I (Authors)

A. P. Berger and T. Luckmann
B. A. Schutz
C. H. Garfinkel
D. P. Berger

List II (Books)

i. *The Problem of Social Reality*
ii. *Studies in Ethnomethodology*
iii. *The Sacred Canopy*
iv. *Social Construction of Reality*

Codes:	**A**	**B**	**C**	**D**
(a)	iv	i	ii	iii
(b)	i	ii	iii	iv
(c)	iv	i	iii	ii
(d)	i	iii	ii	iv

36. Which one of the following is not correct about A. Schutz's understanding of a social situation?
(a) Meaning that an individual attaches to situation in every day life is of crucial significance.
(b) Meaning that an individual attaches to a situation may be shared by persons with whom he interacts.
(c) The sharing of meaning through interaction with others in a social situation forms the basis of his 'reciprocity of perspectives'.
(d) Sharing of meaning that contributes to social disharmony forms the basis of his anti-'reciprocity of perspective'.

37. Which one of the following is not a type of capitalism according to Habermas?
(a) Informational Capitalism
(b) Liberal Capitalism
(c) Organised Capitalism
(d) Post Capitalism

38. Which one of the following is not a reason for declining female sex ratio in India?
(a) Gender role stereotyping and traditional role expectations
(b) Practice of Dowry and prevalence of illiteracy
(c) Migration of female work force from rural to urban areas
(d) Sex selective abortion

39. 'Gender difference' denotes an analytical framework in which
(a) biological differences between sexes are explained.
(b) political and economic differences among women are explained.
(c) social and ideological differences between white and non-white women are explained.
(d) social and ideological differences between sexes are explained.

40. Which of the following is correct about L. Althussar's theory of structuralism?
(a) Economy is the dominant arrangement and it controls political and ideological structure.
(b) Economy may be the dominant system, but the political and ideological structures have certain autonomy.
(c) History reshuffles all these structure to ensure economic determinism.
(d) Economy, political and ideological structure are autonomous of each other.

41. The human development perspective of development recognizes economic growth as
(a) an end in itself.
(b) a means to ensure economic prosperity.
(c) a means to ensure educational, health, employment of largest segments of population.
(d) a means to manage human relations in multinational corporate bodies.

42. Which brand of Feminists accept the view that 'State is a system of structures and institutions created by man in order to recreate male domination and female subordination'?
(a) Liberal Feminists
(b) Radical Feminists
(c) Marxist Feminists
(d) Eco Feminists

43. Which one of the following is not a part of Gandhian path of development?
(a) Social Trusteeship
(b) Non-violence
(c) Cooperative conflict
(d) Constructive work

44. What proportion of India's population live in urban areas according to 2011 Census?
(a) Around one fourth
(b) Around one third
(c) Around one half
(d) Around one fifth

45. Which sector of India's economy contribute the most in its GDP?
(a) Agriculture
(b) Service
(c) Industry
(d) All contributes equally

46. Who among the following agencies asserted that 'If development is not engendered, it is endangered'?

(a) UNDP
(b) World Bank
(c) IMF
(d) WTO

47. In recent decades India's contribution to the total CO_2 emission of the world has
(a) remained stagnant.
(b) increased significantly.
(c) declined substantially.
(d) declined in the agriculturally developed areas while increased in the industrialised areas.

48. 'India has missed the Industrial Revolution, but can't afford to miss the knowledge Revolution.'—suggested by
(a) Women's Commission of India
(b) Ministry of Human Resources Development
(c) Education Commission 1986
(d) Knowledge Commission of India

49. Match the List I with the List II:

List I (Authors)
A. J. Darrida
B. M. Foucault
C. H. Garfinkel
D. L. Althussar

List II (Concepts)
i. Episteme
ii. Indexcality
iii. Overdetermination
iv. Logo-centrism

Codes:	A	B	C	D
(a)	i	ii	iii	iv
(b)	ii	iii	iv	i
(c)	iii	iv	i	ii
(d)	iv	i	ii	iii

50. Who among the following scholars has not discussed the social aspects of automation?
(a) R. Blauner
(b) S. Mallet
(c) T. Bottomore
(d) D. Gallie

51. Which one of the following features is not a feature of industrial strike?
(a) A collective act involving certain amount of solidarity
(b) A collective act to express grievances
(c) The stoppage of work by a worker
(d) A regulated form of industrial conflict

52. Who is the author of the book *The Consequences of Modernity*?
(a) Y. Singh
(b) A. Giddens
(c) F. Fukuyama
(d) D. Harvey

53. Match the List I with the List II and select the correct answers from among the codes given below:

List I (Books)
A. *Social Change in Modern India*
B. *India's Changing Villages*
C. *Caste, Class and Power*
D. *Hindu Social Organization*

List II (Authors)
i. S.C. Dube
ii. M.N. Srinivas
iii. A. Beteille
iv. P.N. Prabhu

Codes:	A	B	C	D
(a)	i	ii	iii	iv
(b)	ii	i	iii	iv
(c)	iii	ii	i	iv
(d)	iv	ii	i	iii

54. Who among the following did not belong to what is known as the Frankfurt School of Sociology?
(a) H. Marcuse
(b) J. Habermas

(c) M. Horkheimer
(d) J. Alexander

55. "Productivity could be immensely increased by breaking down industrial tasks into a series of simple operations that could be precisely timed and optimally coordinated." This statement is related with
(a) Taylorism
(b) Fordism
(c) Marxism
(d) Post-Fordism

56. Which one of the following is not a work of E. Goffman?
(a) Self and Society
(b) Presentation of self in everyday life
(c) Asylums
(d) Interaction Ritual

57. Who among the following introduced the term 'Post Industrial Society'?
(a) J. Burnham
(b) G.K. Galbraith
(c) Daniel Bell
(d) R. Dahrendorf

58. Which one of the following conditions has not been discussed by Karl Marx in his analysis of class as conflict groups?
(a) Super imposition of authority
(b) Absence of mobility, property and general social status
(c) Super imposition of industrial and political conflict
(d) Absence of effective conflict regulation

59. There are two statements, one is an Assertion (A) and the other is Reason (R). Select the correct answer from the codes given below:
Assertion (A): Divorce Rate in India has increased over time.
Reason (R): Women have become more independent.
Codes:
(a) Both (A) and (R) are true and (R) is the correct explanation of (A).
(b) (A) is true, but (R) is not the correct explanation of (A).
(c) Both (A) and (R) are false.
(d) (A) is false, but (R) is true.

60. Which one of the following statements is true to describe 'Domestic Violence'?
(a) In 'Domestic Violence', the only victims are 'married women'.
(b) Girl chid are only vulnerable to Domestic violence.
(c) 'Domestic violence' include physical, sexual, mental and verbal abuse of a person in household setting.
(d) 'Domestic violence' is an indication of progressive society.

61. Which of the following are indicators of regional inequalities?
(i) Natural Resources
(ii) Skilled Manpower
(iii) Size of population
(iv) Political Party in power
Choose the combination for correct answer:
(a) (i), (ii) and (iv)
(b) (i), (ii) and (iii)
(c) (ii), (iii) and (iv)
(d) (iii), (iv) and (ii)

62. "The Clash of Civilizations' proposes that people's cultural and religious identities will be the primary source of conflict in the post cold-war world." Who proposed this view?
(a) J.S. Mills
(b) Max Weber
(c) Samuel P. Huntington
(d) Emile Durkheim

63. The following are the features. Identify the correct set of features of the little community as stated by R. Redfield:
   (i) Homogeneity
   (ii) Heterogeneity
   (iii) Self-sufficiency
   (iv) Distinctiveness
   (v) Primary relations
   Select the correct answer from the given codes:
   Codes:
   (a) (i), (iii), (iv) and (v)
   (b) (i), (iii) and (iv)
   (c) (ii), (iii) and (v)
   (d) (iii), (iv) and (v)

64. Which one of the following has not been included by D. Thorner in his classification?
   (a) Malik (b) Jamindar
   (c) Kissan (d) Majdoor

65. The 'Muria' tribes in India is found mostly in the State of
   (a) Chhattisgarh (b) Rajasthan
   (c) Odisha (d) Andhra Pradesh

66. Which one of the following is not predominantly associated with tribal economy in India?
   (a) Collection of forest produce and agricultural wage work
   (b) Wage work in agriculture and Animal husbandry
   (c) Animal husbandry and collection of forest produce
   (d) Household industry and industrial wage work

67. The Tebhaga and Telangana movements took place in the State of
   (a) Andhra Pradesh and Bihar respectively
   (b) West Bengal and Andhra Pradesh respectively
   (c) Andhra Pradesh and West Bengal respectively
   (d) West Bengal and Bihar respectively

68. Which one of the following is not a demand of farmers movements in India?
   (a) Fair price of Agricultural produce
   (b) Fertilizer subsidy
   (c) Distribution of land
   (d) Electricity subsidy

69. Who among the following tribes is matrilineal in India?
   (a) Khasi (b) Munda
   (c) Santhal (d) Ongi

70. According to R.W. Connel the term 'Gender order' refers to
   (a) The patterns of power relations between masculinities and feminities
   (b) The configuration of gender relations within a particular settings
   (c) The difference in status and prestige of women and men have in groups
   (d) The socially patterned interactions between men and women

71. "Economic growth should proceed only in so far as natural resources are recycled rather than depleted, biodiversity is maintained and clean air, water and land are protected." This statement is related with the concept of
   (a) Economic development
   (b) Social development
   (c) Sustainable development
   (d) Ethno-development

72. In Tebhaga movement, what is meant by Tebhaga?
   (a) $\frac{2}{3}$ (b) $\frac{1}{3}$
   (c) $\frac{3}{4}$ (d) 3

73. Who among the following explained for the first time in sociological literature Jajmani system as patterned interaction among the caste groups?
   (a) William Wiser
   (b) Oscar Lewis

(c) A.R. Desai
(d) Yogendra Singh

74. Naxalbari Peasant Movement was launched in the year
(a) 1967 (b) 1970
(c) 1977 (d) 1956

75. Green Revolution is related to
(a) Agricultural growth
(b) Industrial growth
(c) Milk production
(d) All of the above

ANSWERS

1. (a)	2. (c)	3. (a)	4. (d)	5. (d)
6. (a)	7. (a)	8. (d)	9. (d)	10. (b)
11. (c)	12. (d)	13. (b)	14. (d)	15. (d)
16. (d)	17. (a)	18. (a)	19. (b)	20. (c)
21. (d)	22. (b)	23. (b)	24. (c)	25. (b)
26. (a)	27. (b)	28. (d)	29. (b)	30. (d)
31. (c)	32. (c)	33. (b)	34. (d)	35. (a)
36. (d)	37. (a)	38. (c)	39. (d)	40. (b)
41. (c)	42. (a)	43. (c)	44. (b)	45. (b)
46. (a)	47. (b)	48. (d)	49. (d)	50. (c)
51. (c)	52. (b)	53. (b)	54. (d)	55. (c)
56. (a)	57. (c)	58. (c)	59. (b)	60. (c)
61. (b)	62. (c)	63. (b)	64. (b)	65. (a)
66. (d)	67. (b)	68. (c)	69. (a)	70. (a)
71. (c)	72. (b)	73. (a)	74. (a)	75. (a)

JUNE–2013

Note: This paper contains Sixty (60) multiple-choice questions, each question carrying two (2) marks. Candidate is expected to answer any Fifty (50) questions. In case more than Fifty (50) questions are attempted, only the first Fifty (50) questions will be evaluated.

PAPER–I

1. Which one of the following references is written as per Modern Language Association (MLA) format?
   (a) Hall, Donald. Fundamentals of Electronics,
   New Delhi: Prentice Hall of India, 2005
   (b) Hall, Donald, Fundamentals of Electronics,
   New Delhi: Prentice Hall of India, 2005
   (c) Hall, Donald, Fundamentals of Electronics,
   New Delhi: Prentice Hall of India, 2005
   (d) Hall, Donald. Fundamentals of Electronics.
   New Delhi: Prentice Hall of India, 2005

2. A workshop is
   (a) a conference for discussion on a topic.
   (b) a meeting for discussion on a topic.
   (c) a class at a college or a university in which a teacher and the students discuss a topic.
   (d) a brief intensive course for a small group emphasizing the development of a skill or technique for solving a specific problem.

3. A working hypothesis is
   (a) a proven hypothesis for an argument.
   (b) not required to be tested.
   (c) a provisionally accepted hypothesis for further research.
   (d) a scientific theory.

Read the following passage carefully and answer the questions 4 to 9:

The Taj Mahal has become one of the world's best known monuments. This domed white marble structure is situated on a high plinth at the southern end of a four-quartered garden, evoking the gardens of paradise, enclosed within walls measuring 305 by 549 metres. Outside the walls, in an area known as Mumtazabad, were living quarters for attendants, markets, serais and other structures built by local merchants and nobles. The tomb complex and the other imperial structures of Mumtazabad were maintained by the income of thirty villages given specifically for the tomb's support. The name Taj Mahal is unknown in Mughal chronicles, but it is used by contemporary Europeans in India, suggesting that this was the tomb's popular name. In contemporary texts, it is generally called simply the Illuminated Tomb (Rauza-i-Munavvara).

Mumtaz Mahal died shortly after delivering her fourteenth child in 1631. The Mughal court was then residing in Burhanpur. Her remains were temporarily buried by the griefstricken emperor in a spacious garden known as Zainabad on the bank of the river Tapti. Six months later her body was transported to Agra, where it was interred in land chosen for the mausoleum. This land, situated south of the Mughal city on the bank of the Jamuna, had belonged to the Kachhwaha rajas since the time of Raja Man Singh and was purchased from the then current raja, Jai Singh. Although contemporary chronicles indicate Jai Singh's willing cooperation in this exchange, extant *farmans* (imperial commands) indicate that the final price was not settled until almost two years after the mausoleum's commencement. Jai Singh's further cooperation was insured by imperial orders issued between 1632 and 1637 demanding that he provide stone masons and carts to transport marble from the mines at Makrana, within his "ancestral domain", to Agra where both the Taj Mahal and Shah Jahan's additions to the Agra Fort were constructed concurrently.

Work on the mausoleum was commenced early in 1632. Inscriptional evidence indicates much of the tomb was completed by 1636. By 1643, when Shah Jahan most lavishly celebrated the 'Urs ceremony for Mumtaz Mahal', the entire complex was virtually complete.

4. Marble stone used for the construction of the Taj Mahal was brought from the ancestral domain of Raja Jai Singh. The name of the place where mines of marble is
   (a) Burhanpur (b) Makrana
   (c) Amber (d) Jaipur
5. The popular name Taj Mahal was given by
   (a) Shah Jahan
   (b) Tourists
   (c) Public
   (d) European travellers
6. Point out the true statement from the following.
   (a) Marble was not used for the construction of the Taj Mahal.
   (b) Red sand stone is non-visible in the Taj Mahal complex.
   (c) The Taj Mahal is surrounded by a four-quartered garden known as Char Bagh.
   (d) The Taj Mahal was constructed to celebrate the 'Urs ceremony for Mumtaz Mahal'.
7. In the contemporary texts the Taj Mahal is known
   (a) Mumtazabad
   (b) Mumtaz Mahal
   (c) Zainabad
   (d) Rauza-i-Munavvara
8. The construction of the Taj Mahal was completed between the period
   (a) 1632-1636 A.D.
   (b) 1630-1643 A.D.
   (c) 1632-1643 A.D.
   (d) 1636-1643 A.D.
9. The documents indicating the ownership of land, where the Taj Mahal was built, known as
   (a) Farman
   (b) Sale Deed
   (c) Sale-Purchase Deed
   (d) None of the above
10. In the process of communication, which one of the following is in the chronological order?
    (a) Communicator, Medium, Receiver, Effect, Message
    (b) Medium, Communicator, Message, Receiver, Effect
    (c) Communicator, Message, Medium, Receiver, Effect
    (d) Message, Communicator, Medium, Receiver, Effect
11. Bengal Gazette, the first Newspaper in India was started in 1780 by
    (a) Dr. Annie Besant
    (b) James Augustus Hicky
    (c) Lord Cripson
    (d) A.O. Hume

12. Press censorship in India was imposed during the tenure of the Prime Minister
(a) Rajeev Gandhi
(b) Narasimha Rao
(c) Indira Gandhi
(d) Deve Gowda

13. Communication via New media such as computers, teleshopping, internet and mobile telephony is termed as
(a) Entertainment
(b) Interactive communication
(c) Developmental communication
(d) Communitarian

14. Classroom communication of a teacher rests on the principle of
(a) Infotainment
(b) Edutainment
(c) Entertainment
(d) Enlightenment

15. ________ is important when a teacher communicates with his/her student.
(a) Sympathy (b) Empathy
(c) Apathy (d) Antipathy

16. In a certain code GALIB is represented by HBMJC. TIGER will be represented by
(a) UJHFS (b) UHJSF
(c) JHUSF (d) HUJSF

17. In a certain cricket tournament 45 matches were played. Each team played once against each of the other teams. The number of teams participated in the tournament is
(a) 8 (b) 10
(c) 12 (d) 14

18. The missing number in the series 40, 120, 60, 180, 90, ?, 135 is
(a) 110 (b) 270
(c) 105 (d) 210

19. The odd numbers from 1 to 45 which are exactly divisible by 3 are arranged in an ascending order. The number at 6th position is
(a) 18 (b) 24
(c) 33 (d) 36

20. The mean of four numbers a, b, c, d is 100. If c = 70, then the mean of the remaining numbers is
(a) 30 (b) $\frac{85}{2}$
(c) $\frac{170}{3}$ (d) 110

21. If the radius of a circle is increased by 50%, the perimeter of the circle will increase by
(a) 20% (b) 30%
(c) 40% (d) 50%

22. If the statement 'some men are honest' is false, which among the following statements will be true. Choose the correct codes given below:
(i) All men are honest.
(ii) No men are honest.
(iii) Some men are not honest.
(iv) All men are dishonest.

Codes:
(a) (i), (ii) and (iii)
(b) (ii), (iii) and (iv)
(c) (i), (iii) and (iv)
(d) (ii), (i) and (iv)

23. Choose the proper alternative given in the codes to replace the question mark.
Bee – Honey, Cow – Milk, Teacher –?
(a) Intelligence (b) Marks
(c) Lessons (d) Wisdom

24. P is the father of R and S is the son of Q and T is the brother of P. If R is the sister of S, how is Q related to T?
(a) Wife
(b) Sister-in-law
(c) Brother-in-law
(d) Daughter-in-law

25. A definition put forward to resolve a dispute by influencing attitudes or stirring emotions is called
(a) Lexical (b) Persuasive
(c) Stipulative (d) Precisions

26. Which of the codes given below contains only the correct statements?
Statements:
(i) Venn diagram is a clear method of notation.
(ii) Venn diagram is the most direct method of testing the validity of categorical syllogisms.
(iii) In Venn diagram method the premises and the conclusion of a categorical syllogism is diagrammed.
(iv) In Venn diagram method the three overlapping circles are drawn for testing a categorical syllogism.

Codes:
(a) (i), (ii) and (iii)
(b) (i), (ii) and (iv)
(c) (ii), (iii) and (iv)
(d) (i), (iii) and (iv)

27. Inductive reasoning presupposes
(a) unity in human nature
(b) integrity in human nature
(c) uniformity in human nature
(d) harmony in human nature

Read the table below and based on this table answer questions from 28 to 33:

Area under Major Horticulture Crops
(in lakh hectares)

Year	Fruits	Vegetables	Flowers	Total Horti-culture Area
2005-06	53	72	1	187
2006-07	56	75	1	194
2007-08	58	78	2	202
2008-09	61	79	2	207
2009-10	63	79	2	209

28. Which of the following two years have recorded the highest rate of increase in area under the total horticulture?
(a) 2005-06 and 2006-07
(b) 2006-07 and 2008-09
(c) 2007-08 and 2008-09
(d) 2006-07 and 2007-08

29. Shares of the area under flowers, vegetables and fruits in the area under total horticulture are respectively:
(a) 1, 38 and 30 per cent
(b) 30, 38 and 1 per cent
(c) 38, 30 and 1 per cent
(d) 35, 36 and 2 per cent

30. Which of the following has recorded the highest rate of increase in area during 2005-06 to 2009-10?
(a) Fruits
(b) Vegetables
(c) Flowers
(d) Total horticulture

31. Find out the horticultural crop that has recorded an increase of area by around 10 per cent from 2005-06 to 2009-10?
(a) Fruits
(b) Vegetables
(c) Flowers
(d) Total horticulture

32. What has been the share of area under fruits, vegetables and flowers in the area under total horticulture in 2007-08?
(a) 53 per cent (b) 68 per cent
(c) 79 per cent (d) 100 per cent

33. In which year, area under fruits has recorded the highest rate of increase?
(a) 2006-07 (b) 2007-08
(c) 2008-09 (d) 2009-10

34. 'www' stands for
(a) work with web
(b) word wide web
(c) world wide web
(d) worth while web

35. A hard disk is divided into tracks which is further subdivided into
(a) Clusters (b) Sectors
(c) Vectors (d) Heads

36. A computer program that translates a program statement by statement into machine language is called a/an
(a) Compiler (b) Simulator
(c) Translator (d) Interpreter

37. A Gigabyte is equal to
(a) 1024 Megabytes
(b) 1024 Kilobytes
(c) 1024 Terabytes
(d) 1024 Bytes

38. A Compiler is a software which converts
(a) characters to bits
(b) high level language to machine language
(c) machine language to high level language
(d) words to bits

39. Virtual memory is
(a) an extremely large main memory.
(b) an extremely large secondary memory.
(c) an illusion of extremely large main memory.
(d) a type of memory used in super computers.

40. The phrase 'tragedy of commons' is in the context of
(a) tragic event related to damage caused by release of poisonous gases.
(b) tragic conditions of poor people.
(c) degradation of renewable free access resources.
(d) climate change.

41. Kyoto Protocol is related to
(a) Ozone depletion
(b) Hazardous waste
(c) Climate change
(d) Nuclear energy

42. Which of the following is a source of emissions leading to the eventual formation of surface ozone as a pollutant?
(a) Transport sector
(b) Refrigeration and Airconditioning
(c) Wetlands
(d) Fertilizers

43. The smog in cities in India mainly consists of
(a) Oxides of sulphur
(b) Oxides of nitrogen and unburnt hydrocarbons
(c) Carbon monoxide and SPM
(d) Oxides of sulphur and ozone

44. Which of the following types of natural hazards have the highest potential to cause damage to humans?
(a) Earthquakes
(b) Forest fires
(c) Volcanic eruptions
(d) Droughts and Floods

45. The percentage share of renewable energy sources in the power production in India is around
(a) 2-3% (b) 22-25%
(c) 10-12% (d) < 1%

46. In which of the following categories the enrolment of students in higher education in 2010-11 was beyond the percentage of seats reserved?
(a) OBC students
(b) SC students
(c) ST students
(d) Woman students

47. Which one of the following statements is not correct about the University Grants Commission (UGC)?
(a) It was established in 1956 by an Act of Parliament.

(b) It is tasked with promoting and coordinating higher education.
(c) It receives Plan and Non-Plan funds from the Central Government.
(d) It receives funds from State Governments in respect of State Universities.

48. Consider the statement which is followed by two arguments (I) and (II):
Statement: Should India switch over to a two party system?
Arguments: (I) Yes, it will lead to stability of Government.
(II) No, it will limit the choice of voters.
(a) Only argument (I) is strong.
(b) Only argument (II) is strong.
(c) Both the arguments are strong.
(d) Neither of the arguments is strong.

49. Consider the statement which is followed by two arguments (I) and (II):
Statement: Should persons with criminal background be banned from contesting elections?
Arguments: (I) Yes, it will decriminalise politics.
(II) No, it will encourage the ruling party to file frivolous cases against their political opponents.
(a) Only argument (I) is strong.
(b) Only argument (II) is strong.
(c) Both the arguments are strong.
(d) Neither of the arguments is strong.

50. Which of the following statement(s) is/are correct about a Judge of the Supreme Court of India?
1. A Judge of the Supreme Court is appointed by the President of India.
2. He holds office during the pleasure of the President.
3. He can be suspended, pending an inquiry.
4. He can be removed for proven misbehaviour or incapacity.

Select the correct answer from the codes given below:
Codes:
(a) 1, 2 and 3 (b) 1, 3 and 4
(c) 1 and 3 (d) 1 and 4

51. In the warrant of precedence, the Speaker of the Lok Sabha comes next only to
(a) The President
(b) The Vice-President
(c) The Prime Minister
(d) The Cabinet Ministers

52. The blackboard can be utilised best by a teacher for
(a) putting the matter of teaching in black and white
(b) making the students attentive
(c) writing the important and notable points
(d) highlighting the teacher himself

53. Nowadays the most effective mode of learning is
(a) self study
(b) face-to-face learning
(c) e-learning
(d) blended learning

54. At the primary school stage, most of the teachers should be women because they
(a) can teach children better than men.
(b) know basic content better than men.
(c) are available on lower salaries.
(d) can deal with children with love and affection.

55. Which one is the highest order of learning?
(a) Chain learning
(b) Problem-solving learning

(c) Stimulus-response learning
(d) Conditioned-reflex learning

56. A person can enjoy teaching as a profession when he
(a) has control over students.
(b) commands respect from students.
(c) is more qualified than his colleagues.
(d) is very close to higher authorities.

57. "A diagram speaks more than 1000 words." The statement means that the teacher should
(a) use diagrams in teaching.
(b) speak more and more in the class.
(c) use teaching aids in the class.
(d) not speak too much in the class.

58. A research paper
(a) is a compilation of information on a topic.
(b) contains original research as deemed by the author.
(c) contains peer-reviewed original research or evaluation of research conducted by others.
(d) can be published in more than one journal.

59. Which one of the following belongs to the category of good 'research ethics'?
(a) Publishing the same paper in two research journals without telling the editors.
(b) Conducting a review of the literature that acknowledges the contributions of other people in the relevant field or relevant prior work.
(c) Trimming outliers from a data set without discussing your reasons in a research paper.
(d) Including a colleague as an author on a research paper in return for a favour even though the colleague did not make a serious contribution to the paper.

60. Which of the following sampling methods is not based on probability?
(a) Simple Random Sampling
(b) Stratified Sampling
(c) Quota Sampling
(d) Cluster Sampling

ANSWERS

1. (d)	2. (d)	3. (c)	4. (b)	5. (d)
6. (c)	7. (d)	8. (c)	9. (a)	10. (c)
11. (b)	12. (c)	13. (b)	14. (b)	15. (b)
16. (a)	17. (b)	18. (b)	19. (c)	20. (d)
21. (d)	22. (b)	23. (d)	24. (b)	25. (b)
26. (b)	27. (c)	28. (d)	29. (a)	30. (c)
31. (b)	32. (b)	33. (a)	34. (c)	35. (b)
36. (d)	37. (a)	38. (b)	39. (c)	40. (c)
41. (c)	42. (a)	43. (b)	44. (d)	45. (c)
46. (a)	47. (d)	48. (c)	49. (a)	50. (d)
51. (c)	52. (c)	53. (d)	54. (d)	55. (d)
56. (b)	57. (c)	58. (c)	59. (b)	60. (c)

PAPER–II

Note: This paper contains Fifty (50) objective type questions, each question carrying two (2) marks. All questions are compulsory.

1. Match the followings:

List I (Concepts)
A. Cultural Lag
B. False Consciousness
C. Law of Similarity and Contact
D. Institutionalization of Class Conflict

List II (Authors)
i. K. Marx
ii. Ogburn

iii. J. Frazer
iv. R. Dahrendorf

Codes:	A	B	C	D
(a)	ii	i	iii	iv
(b)	iv	iii	i	ii
(c)	iii	ii	iv	i
(d)	i	iv	ii	iii

2. Fill in the blanks:
An institution is composed of _______.
(a) Actors and Groups
(b) Rules and procedures
(c) Values and norms
(d) All of the above

3. George Simmel's classification of group as 'Monad', 'Dyad', 'Triad' is based on
(a) Physical proximity
(b) Nature of membership
(c) Social relations
(d) Size of the group

4. An area of social living which is marked by some degree of social coherence and similarity is called
(a) Social group
(b) Society
(c) Community
(d) Association

5. C.W. Mills' perspective takes into account
i. Biography
ii. Sociography
iii. History
iv. Geography
v. Ethnography
Select the correct alternatives:
(a) ii only
(b) ii and iii only
(c) i and iii only
(d) i, ii, iv and v only

6. Which of the following instances may not be considered as a reference-group behaviour?
(a) Proletarianization
(b) Embourgeoisment
(c) Sanskritization
(d) Modernization

7. Which of the following is a set of informal groups?
(a) Clique, faction, caucus
(b) Gang, union, dacoits
(c) Slum, village, NGO
(d) Neighbourhood, Peer group, Panchayat

8. Who argued that the school prepares children to move towards universalistic standards and achieved status of adult society?
(a) E. Durkheim
(b) T. Parsons
(c) R.K. Merton
(d) K. Davis

9. Who defined religion in terms of a distinction between the sacred and the profone?
(a) B. Malinowski
(b) C. LeviStrauss
(c) A.R. Radcliffe Brown
(d) E. Durkheim

10. The capacity of any person, group or institution to issue commands is called
(a) Power
(b) Authority
(c) Influence
(d) Right

11. According to C.W. Mills, the power elite in America comprises those who hold "command posts" in
i. The major business corporations
ii. The military
iii. The Federal Government
iv. The State bureaucracy

Select the correct alternative:
(a) (i), (ii), (iii), (iv)
(b) (i), (ii) and (iii)
(c) (i), (iii) and (iv)
(d) (ii), (iii) and (iv)

12. Who argues that 'classes should be defined as imperatively coordinated associations'?
(a) M. Weber
(b) K. Marx
(c) R. Dahrendorf
(d) R. Collins

13. For R. Dahrendorf a post-capitalist society is characterised by
i. Decomposition of capital
ii. Differentiation of labour
iii. Diamond like class structure
iv. Regulations and institutionalization of conflicts
Select the correct alternative:
(a) (i), (ii), (iii) and (iv)
(b) (i), (ii) and (iii)
(c) (i), (ii) and (iv)
(d) (i), (iii) and (iv)

14. The concept of 'I' and 'Me' with reference to development of 'self' was used by
(a) S. Freud
(b) C.H. Cooley
(c) H.M. Johnson
(d) G.H. Mead

15. Given below are two statements, one labelled as Assertion (A) and the other as Reason (R):
Assertion (A): Personality system gets integrated into the social system through socialization.
Reason (R): Socialization helps actors to develop skills to play roles in society.
Select the correct answer from the codes given below:
Codes:
(a) Both (A) and (R) are true and (R) is the correct explanation of (A).
(b) Both (A) and (R) are true, but (R) is not the correct explanation of (A).
(c) (A) is true, but (R) is false.
(d) (A) is false, but (R) is true.

16. A status group, according to Max Weber, is characterised by
(a) Occupation
(b) Educational background
(c) Lifestyle
(d) Family background

17. Who among the following is regarded as the technological determinist of social change?
(a) E. Durkheim
(b) G. Simmel
(c) T. Veblen
(d) T. Malthus

18. The theoretical perspective that asserts that there are discernible stages which the society goes through more than once or even repeatedly is termed as
(a) Repeated Evolutionary Theory
(b) Unilinear Evolutionary Theory
(c) Cyclical Evolutionary Theory
(d) Reflexive Evolutionary Theory

19. Who among the following describes society as 'sui-generis'?
(a) Radcliffe Brown
(b) Malinowski
(c) E. Durkheim
(d) R. Benedict

20. Which of the following pairs are not included in Parsonian Scheme of 'Pattern-Variables'?
i. Affectivity Vs Affective neutrality
ii. Self-orientation Vs Collectivity orientation
iii. Particularism Vs Universalism
iv. Localism Vs Globalism
v. Quality Vs Performance
vi. Diffusion Vs Specificity
vii. Evolution Vs Revolution

Select the correct alternative:
(a) (i), (ii), (iii), (v) and (vi)
(b) (ii), (iii), (i), (vi) and (v)
(c) (ii), (iii), (v)
(d) (i), (v) and (vi)

21. Given below are two statements, one is labelled as Assertion (A) and the other as Reason (R):

Assertion (A): The postulate of functional unity of society maintains that all standardised social and cultural beliefs and practices are functional for society as a whole as well as for individuals in society.

Reason (R): The above said standardised items are indispensable parts of the working whole.

Codes:
(a) Both (A) and (R) are true, but (R) is not the correct explanation of (A).
(b) (A) is true, but (R) is false.
(c) (R) is true, but (A) is false.
(d) Both (A) and (R) are false.

22. Who among the following does not adopt the functional approach to the understanding of social phenomena?
(a) J. Alexander
(b) K. Davis
(c) R.K. Merton
(d) J. Habermas

23. The view that authority relations are the main cause of social conflict was held by whom?
(a) M. Weber
(b) K. Marx
(c) R. Collins
(d) R. Dahrendorf

24. Who among the following has classified status in terms of salient status, dominant status and controlling status?
(a) T. Parsons
(b) R.K. Merton
(c) W.E. Moore
(d) H.M. Johnson

25. What is common to magic, religion and science?
(a) Observation and experimentation
(b) Equal influence on human beings
(c) Orientation towards the unknown
(d) Orientation towards the supernatural

26. Who among the following is a proponent of dialectical approach to the study of Indian society?
(a) M.N. Srinivas
(b) D.P. Mukherjee
(c) A. Beteille
(d) Y.B. Damle

27. Which type of research aims to describe a social situation, social event, social system, social structure, etc.?
(a) Basic research
(b) Descriptive research
(c) Empirical research
(d) Explanatory research

28. A university has 7530 students and a researcher draws 10 per cent sample from it amounting to a total of 753. This is called
(a) Sample size
(b) Sample ratio
(c) Sample element
(d) Purposive sampling

29. Which technique of qualitative data collection is followed by researcher to understand people and their behaviour through direct, focused and non-verbal interaction in their natural setting?
(a) Interview
(b) Observation
(c) Case study
(d) Above all

30. According to Karl Marx, which of the following are elements of the forces of production?
   (a) Technology and capital
   (b) Capital, labour and technology
   (c) Science and technology
   (d) Capital, labour, science and technology

31. Who among the following used the concept of 'interaction ritual' in his theory?
   (a) R. Collins
   (b) L. Coser
   (c) E. Durkheim
   (d) H. Blumer

32. Who among the following argues that the withdrawal of legitimacy from an existing system of inequality is a critical precondition for conflict?
   (a) R. Dahrendorf
   (b) L. Coser
   (c) R. Collins
   (d) J. Habermas

33. Themetic and text analyses are used in
   (a) Path analysis
   (b) Data analysis
   (c) Form analysis
   (d) Content analysis

34. The study of recorded human statement based on newspaper, magazines, songs, poems, speeches, etc. are known as
   (a) Statistical analysis
   (b) Content analysis
   (c) Historical analysis
   (d) Comparative analysis

35. Which one of the following is not a type of reliability according to Kirk and Miller?
   (a) Quixotic: Circumstances in which single method of observation yields the same measurement repeatedly.
   (b) Dialectical: Observation between two conflicting situation.
   (c) Diachronic: Stability of an observation over a period of time.
   (d) Synchronic: Similarity of observation within same period of time.

36. Which one of the following is not a measure of central tendency?
   (a) Mean
   (b) Median
   (c) Mode
   (d) Standard deviation

37. "Men make history, but they do not make it just as they please; they do not make it under circumstances chosen by themselves, but under circumstances directly encountered, given and transmitted from the past." With whom is this statement related?
   (a) Karl Mannheim
   (b) Karl Marx
   (c) Karl Popper
   (d) Ralf Dahrendorf

38. "Thinking is simply an internalised or implicit conversation of the individual with himself by means of significant gestures." Who said so?
   (a) L. Althusser
   (b) H. Blumer
   (c) P. Blau
   (d) G.H. Mead

39. Which of the following is not a feature of association?
   (a) A collectivity of people
   (b) Having certain objectives
   (c) Voluntary membership
   (d) Pursuing ideal norms

40. Which of the following statements on the nature of social role is not correct?
   (a) It is a set of expectations.
   (b) It is impossible to define one's role without referring to another.

(c) It includes a series of rights and duties.
(d) It has no association with status.

41. According to Coser which of the following type of conflict may not be functional for the system?
(a) Conflict over core value
(b) Conflict over explicit realistic issues
(c) Frequent conflict over small issues
(d) Repetitive conflict of low intensity

42. Which of the following scales has real zero origin?
(a) Nominal
(b) Ordinal
(c) Interval
(d) Ratio

43. Who had applied the reference group theory to analyse mobility within the caste system?
(a) M.S.A. Rao
(b) G.S. Ghurye
(c) M.N. Srinivas
(d) Yogendra Singh

44. The concept of structural visibility was contributed by whom?
(a) T. Parsons
(b) R.K. Merton
(c) Radcliffe-Brown
(d) S.F. Nadel

45. Which one of the following pairs is not correctly matched?
(a) Organic solidarity – E. Durkheim
(b) Pattern variable – T. Parsons
(c) Looking-glass self – C.H. Cooley
(d) Individualistic functionalism – R.K. Merton

46. Triangulation is a method of assessing validity of one's research by
(a) Collecting three generational data.
(b) Analysing three generational data.
(c) Using different methods and theoretical analysis of different subject of study by one or more researchers.
(d) Mixing of different methods and theoretical analysis of same subject of study by one or more researchers.

47. The book *Street Corner Society* based on the following technique of research:
(a) Interview schedule
(b) Participant observation
(c) Content analysis
(d) Questionnaire

48. Identify the correct sequence in social research:
i. Report writing
ii. Data analysis
iii. Pilot study
iv. Formation of hypothesis
v. Null hypothesis
vi. Observation
(a) iv, v, iii, vi, ii, i
(b) iii, iv, i, ii, vi, v
(c) i, ii, iii, iv, v, vi
(d) vi, v, iv, iii, ii, i

49. Who among the following attempted micro-integrative conflict theory?
(a) Dahrendorf
(b) Coser
(c) Collins
(d) Marx

50. In the major conceptualizations of class, which of the following are not a basis of class situation?
i. Property
ii. Income
iii. Authority
iv. Caste

Select the correct answer from the codes given below:

Codes:

(a) i, ii, and iii (b) i and ii
(c) i and iii (d) ii and iv

ANSWERS

1. (a)	2. (b)	3. (d)	4. (c)	5. (c)
6. (d)	7. (a)	8. (b)	9. (d)	10. (b)
11. (b)	12. (c)	13. (a)	14. (d)	15. (a)
16. (c)	17. (c)	18. (c)	19. (c)	20. (a)
21. (a)	22. (d)	23. (d)	24. (b)	25. (c)
26. (b)	27. (b)	28. (b)	29. (b)	30. (c)
31. (a)	32. (b)	33. (d)	34. (b)	35. (b)
36. (d)	37. (b)	38. (d)	39. (d)	40. (d)
41. (a)	42. (d)	43. (c)	44. (b)	45. (d)
46. (d)	47. (b)	48. (a)	49. (c)	50. (d)

PAPER–III

Note: This paper contains seventy-five (75) objective type questions of two (2) marks each. All questions are compulsory.

1. Arrange in the logical order in which P. Berger has explained.
   (a) Habitualization, institutionalization, legitimation, externalization
   (b) Institutionalization, legitimation, externalization, habitualization
   (c) Habitualization, legitimation, externalization, institutionalization
   (d) Legitimation, institutionalization, habitualization, externalization

2. Which of the following categories can be placed in Althusser's concept of ideological state apparatus?
   i. Education
   ii. Family
   iii. Religion
   iv. State bureaucracy

   Select the correct answer from the codes given below:

   Codes:
   (a) i, ii and iv
   (b) i, iii and iv
   (c) i, ii and iii
   (d) ii, iii and iv

3. Which of the following methods used by H. Garfinkel in his exposition of ethnomethodology?
   i. The Documentary Method
   ii. The Breaching Experiments
   iii. The Reciprocity of Perspectives
   iv. The Etcetera Principle

   Select the correct answer from the codes given below:

   Codes:
   (a) i, ii and iii
   (b) ii, iii and iv
   (c) i, iii and iv
   (d) i, ii, iii and iv

4. Which of the following crises are stated by J. Habermas?
   i. Economic crisis
   ii. Political crisis
   iii. Legitimation crisis
   iv. Rationality crisis
   (a) Economic crisis, political crisis and rationality crisis
   (b) Economic crisis, legitimation crisis and rationality crisis
   (c) Political crisis, legitimation crisis and rationality crisis
   (d) Economic crisis, political crisis and legitimation crisis

5. Which of the following books are not written by F. Goffman?
   i. *Relations in Public*
   ii. *Behaviour in Public Places*
   iii. *Forms of Talk*
   iv. *Social Behaviour: Its Elementary Forms*

Select the correct answer from the codes given below:

Codes:

(a) i, ii and iii
(b) i, ii and iv
(c) i, iii and iv
(d) ii, iii and iv

6. To A. Giddens social theorizing involves
(a) Single hermeneutic
(b) Double hermeneutic
(c) Dialectical hermeneutic
(d) Historical hermeneutic

7. Who among the following distinguishes three components of the life world—culture, society and personality?
(a) A. Shutz
(b) E. Husserl
(c) P. Berger
(d) J. Habermas

8. Giddens' concept of regionalization implies that
(a) the reproduction of relations not only across time but also space.
(b) the process of social change is limited by regions.
(c) a regional society starts influencing other societies.
(d) the mainstream society acquires the features of regional societies.

9. In defining nationalism A.R. Desai is influenced by
(a) S.M. Lipset
(b) E.H. Carr
(c) M. Weber
(d) L. Althussar

10. Match the List I with the List II:

List I (Contributors)

A. D. Learner
B. B. Hoselitz
C. A.G. Frank
D. I. Wallerstein

List II (Approaches)

i. Development of Underdevelop
ii. Ideal typical
iii. World System
iv. Diffusion

Mark the correct answer from the codes given below:

Codes:	A	B	C	D
(a)	i	ii	iii	iv
(b)	i	iii	ii	iv
(c)	iv	ii	iii	i
(d)	iv	iii	ii	i

11. Which of the following statements is incorrect with regard to D.P. Mukherjee?
(a) He uses the dialectical approach.
(b) He combines Marx's, Dilthey's and Vedanta's approaches.
(c) Traditions can be distinguished between primary, secondary and tertiary.
(d) Modernity can be understood independent of tradition.

12. In which of the following sequences are 'Demographic Transitions' traditionally associated?
(a) High fertility, low mortality, high population growth
(b) Low mortality, low mortality to high fertility
(c) High fertility, high mortality to low mortality and low fertility, the later lagging behind
(d) Low fertility, high mortality to low fertility and low mortality with mortality lagging behind

13. Which of the following concept does not figure in Malthusian Theory of Population?
(a) Arithmetic progression
(b) Positive checks
(c) 'Stable population'
(d) Preventive checks

14. Match the items in List I with the items in List II and choose the right answer from the codes given below:

List I

A. Crude Rate
B. General Fertility Rate
C. Infant Mortality Rate
D. Birth Rate

List II

i. The number of live births per 1000 population in a given year
ii. The number of deaths of babies under age 1 year per 1000 live births in a given year
iii. The number of live births per 1000 women in 15-44 or 15-49 years in a given year
iv. Rate of any demographic event computed for an entire population

Codes:	A	B	C	D
(a)	iv	iii	ii	i
(b)	iii	i	iv	ii
(c)	ii	iv	iii	i
(d)	i	iii	ii	iv

15. 'Population pyramids' reveals the following information:

(i) Dependency burden
(ii) Birth and Death rate
(iii) Sex ratios of different ages
(iv) Approximate life expectancy of birth

From the above, find the combination for correct answer:

(a) (i) and (ii) but not (iii) and (iv).
(b) All (i), (ii), (iii) and (iv).
(c) (i) only but not (ii), (iii) and (iv).
(d) (iii) and (iv) but not (i) and (ii).

16. Match the items in List I with the items in List II and choose the right answer from the codes given below:

List I (Books)

A. *From Population to People*
B. *Gender Inequalities and Demographic Behaviour*
C. *Essay on Principle of Population*
D. *Regulatory Reproduction in India's Population*

List II (Authors)

i. K. Srinivasan
ii. T. Malthus
iii. S. Desai
iv. A. Bose

Codes:	A	B	C	D
(a)	iv	iii	ii	i
(b)	i	ii	iii	iv
(c)	ii	iv	i	iii
(d)	iii	i	iv	ii

17. Match Item I with Item II:

Item I (Concept)

A. Deviance
B. Crime
C. Anomie
D. Alienation

Item II (Explanation)

i. Lack of social norms
ii. Non-conformity
iii. Act that contravenes the law
iv. Self estrangement

Codes:	A	B	C	D
(a)	i	ii	iii	iv
(b)	iii	ii	iv	i
(c)	ii	iii	i	iv
(d)	iv	ii	iii	i

18. Who among the following is associated with the idea of 'Risk Society'?

(a) H.S. Becker
(b) Ulrich Beck
(c) Denial Bell
(d) Susan Baker

19. **Assertion (A):** Ecology movement are emerging from conflict over natural resources and people's right to survival.
Reason (R): Population increase is responsible for depletion of natural resources and environmental degradation.
Tick the right codes given below:
Codes:
(a) Both (A) and (R) are true and (R) is the correct explanation of (A).
(b) Both (A) and (R) are true, but (R) is not the correct explanation of (A).
(c) (A) is true, but (R) is false.
(d) (A) is false, but (R) is true.

20. Talcott Parsons have mentioned pillars of the sick role for the patient: Find out the correct combination.
i. Sick person is not personally responsible for being sick.
ii. Person is responsible for his/her sickness.
iii. The sick person is entitled to certain rights and privileges.
iv. The sick person must work to regain health by consulting a doctor.
Codes:
(a) i, ii and iii
(b) ii, iii and iv
(c) i, iii and iv
(d) iii, i and ii

21. **Assertion (A):** Technological advances have been taking place rapidly.
Reason (R): It has been due to the convergence of telecommunications and computing technology known as information and communication technologies.
Answer by using the correct codes from the following:
Codes:
(a) (A) is correct and (R) is its reason.
(b) Both (A) and (R) are false.
(c) (A) is true, but (R) is not its correct reason.
(d) (A) is false, but (R) is true.

22. Who among the following did not favour hierarchization of knowledge?
(a) E. Durkheim
(b) A. Comte
(c) M. Weber
(d) M. Foucault

23. Match List I with List II and find out the correct answer from the codes given below:
List I (Concepts)
A. Sexuality
B. Risk society
C. Communicative action
D. Hyper reality
List II (Authors)
i. U. Beck
ii. M. Foucault
iii. J. Baudrillard
iv. J. Habermas

Codes:	A	B	C	D
(a)	ii	i	iv	iii
(b)	i	ii	iii	iv
(c)	iii	ii	i	iv
(d)	iv	iii	ii	i

24. Who among the following theorists sees contemporary society as a death culture, with death being the "paradigm of all social exclusion and discrimination"?
(a) J. Baudrillard
(b) U. Beck
(c) M. Foucault
(d) J.F. Lyotard

25. Which one of the following was not specified as an objective of social development by the World Development Summit (1995)?
(a) Economic protectionism
(b) People empowerment

(c) People's initiatives
(d) Strengthening the capacities of the people

26. Match the items of List I with those of List II and find out the correct answer from codes given below:

List I (Scheme/Programme)

A. National Education Policy
B. National Literacy Mission
C. National Health Policy
D. National Perspective Plan for Women's Development

List II (Year)

i. 2002 ii. 1988
iii. 1986 iv. 2001

Codes:	A	B	C	D
(a)	iii	i	ii	iv
(b)	iii	ii	i	iv
(c)	iv	iii	ii	i
(d)	ii	i	iv	iii

27. Match List I with List II and give the correct answer from the codes given below:

List I

A. 73rd Constitutional Amendment
B. The Gyandoot Project
C. Human Development Reports
D. Sale or purchase of goods or services through the internet

List II

i. e-governance
ii. Women's empowerment
iii. e-commerce
iv. U.N.D.P.

Codes:	A	B	C	D
(a)	i	ii	iv	iii
(b)	iii	ii	i	iv
(c)	ii	i	iv	iii
(d)	iv	iii	ii	i

28. Intersubjective consciousness in everyday life is the core area of focus of the
(a) Phenomenologist
(b) Behaviouralist
(c) Cultural pluralist
(d) Human ecologist

29. Which one of the following is not correct about P. Berger and T. Luckman's understanding of knowledge?
(a) They are unconnected with validity of knowledge.
(b) They are deeply concerned about the validity of knowledge.
(c) They are concerned with the processes through which any body of knowledge get recognized as reality.
(d) They focus not upon social facts, but upon the creation of social meaning in human interaction.

30. Which of the following is considered to be the 'Tripartite Pillars of Schutz Theory of Phenomenological Sociology'?
(a) Life-world, other world and natural attitude
(b) Artificiality, other world and Intra-subjectivity
(c) Intra-subjectivity, life world and cultural world
(d) Life-world, inter subjectivity and natural attitude

31. Who among the following is considered to the founder of phenomenological sociology?
(a) J. Habermas
(b) A. Schutz
(c) H.R. Wagner
(d) K. Mannheim

32. Select the correct alternative about Habermas' reconstruction of Marxism:
i. Purposive rational action instead of superstructure
ii. Symbolic interaction instead of superstructure

iii. Societal modes of self-reflection instead of class consciousness
iv. Class competition instead of class conflict

Select the correct alternative:
(a) i, ii, iii (b) i, ii, iv
(c) ii, iii, iv (d) i, ii, iii, iv

33. The ethnomethodology as an approach to study society is concerned with
(a) the fundamental bases of social order
(b) issue of unequal distribution of power and authority in society
(c) distribution of resources in society
(d) shape up the social institutions from historical perspective

34. **Assertion (A):** Women's work participation has substantially increased in the informal sector of economy in India.
Reason (R): Education and skill development opportunities have expanded among rural women.
Select the correct answer:
(a) (A) is correct and (R) is the reason for (A).
(b) (A) is correct, but (R) is not the correct reason for (A).
(c) Both (A) and (R) are correct.
(d) Neither (A) nor (R) is correct.

35. 'Women's Rights are human rights' as an international policy for women's empowerment was accepted in an International Conference of Women held in
(a) Beijing
(b) Mexico
(c) Nairobi
(d) Copenhagen

36. Select the correct statements:
On the issue of low status of women in family the socialist feminists argue that gender inequality is
i. ideologically linked to their predominant engagement with household responsibility
ii. due their predominant engagement with unpaid household activities
iii. due to the low income of household
iv. politically linked to their political passivity

Select the correct alternative:
(a) i and ii (b) ii and iii
(c) ii and iv (d) iii and iv

37. Which one of the following is not correct with regard to the Liberal Feminists view on the State?
(a) The State is potentially a neutral arbiter and lack any ideology of its own.
(b) Men have captured the State.
(c) Men are pressure group, women are observers.
(d) Women should embrace strategies for meaningfully access the state and influence it.

38. The proportion of the aged (60+) population to the total population of India shows a trend of
(a) Stagnation
(b) Decline
(c) Increase
(d) Increase in urban but decline rural areas

39. What proportion of India's urban population live in slums?
(a) Around one-fifth
(b) Around one-fourth
(c) Around one-third
(d) Around one-half

40. What proportion of India's population does not get safe drinking water as per WHO?
(a) 15% (b) 25%
(c) 35% (d) 45%

41. Who held the view that Indian tribals were backward Hindus?
(a) G.S. Ghurye
(b) Y.B. Damle
(c) A.R. Desai
(d) N.K. Bose

42. Who among the following has used the dialectical approach to the study of Indian Society?
(a) M.N. Srinivas
(b) D.P. Mukherjee
(c) A. Beteille
(d) Y.B. Damle

43. Individuals, families and groups in the population can be said to be in poverty when they lack the resources to obtain the types of diet, participate in activities and have the living conditions and amenities which are customary, or at least widely encouraged or approved, in the societies to which they belong. Their resources are so seriously below those commanded by average individual or family that they are, in effect, excluded from the ordinary living patterns, customs and activities.
(Townsend, 1979, cf Harlambos and Hoborn: Sociology, p. 297).
From the above paragraph in which of the following way 'poverty' is defined?
(a) Poverty is absolute term.
(b) Poverty as 'Relative deprivation'.
(c) Poverty as 'absence of resources'.
(d) Poverty as 'exclusion of activities'.

44. From the statements given below choose the code depicting correct answer to describe the 'socially constructed gender inequalities'.
(i) Hormonal and chromosomes differences between male and female.
(ii) For similarly qualified persons, men favoured over women.
(iii) Men and women are thought to possess different physical, emotional and mental capabilities.
(iv) Practice of dowry has increased among the educated middle class in India.

Codes:
(a) All statements (i), (ii), (iii) and (iv).
(b) (ii) and (iii) but not (i) and (iv).
(c) (i), (ii) and (iv) but not (iii).
(d) (ii), (iii) and (iv) but not (i).

45. Given below are two statements—Assertion (A) and Reason (R). Pick the right answer from the codes:
Assertion (A): The problem of 'dowry deaths' is typically prevalent among the 'emergent urban middle class' in India.
Reason (R): The law of inheritance is discriminatory against women in India.
Codes:
(a) Both (A) and (R) are false.
(b) (A) is true, but (R) is false.
(c) Both (A) and (R) are true and (R) is not correct explanation of (A).
(d) (A) is true and (R) is correct explanation of (A).

46. The value of an individual's labour power which is 'left over' when an employer has repaid the cost involved in hiring a worker is called in Marxian term
(a) Use value
(b) Surplus value
(c) Exchange value
(d) Left-over value

47. The 'collective bargaining' usually centres around
(a) share in profit, job security and good working conditions
(b) job satisfaction, job security and new technology
(c) exploitation, profit generation and reinvestment
(d) corporate responsibility, global networking and profit sharing

48. "Integrate the working class into capitalist societies, making them less likely to become a radical or revolutionary force." This statement is related to
   (a) Political Parties
   (b) Interest Groups
   (c) Trade Unions
   (d) Peer Group

49. The average number of live-born children produced by women of childbearing age in a particular society, called
   (a) Morbidity Rate
   (b) Mortality Rate
   (c) Fertility Rate
   (d) Fecundity Rate

50. "The economic perspective that believes that free market forces, achieved by minimizing Government restrictions on business, provides the only route to economic growth." This statement explains the concept of
   (a) Post modernity
   (b) Neo-liberalization
   (c) Neo-Marxism
   (d) Neo-Fordism

51. Which of the following does not cause 'global warming'?
   (a) Greenhouses effects
   (b) Rise in the earth's temperature
   (c) Nanotechnology
   (d) Industrial development

52. The Domestic Violence Act was passed in which of the following years?
   (a) 1988 (b) 2001
   (c) 2004 (d) 2005

53. Who among the following is associated with 'Human Development Index (HDI) for measuring the level of development among various countries?
   (a) Raymond Firth
   (b) Mahabub-ul-Haque
   (c) M.N. Srinivas
   (d) A.R. Desai

54. The General Agreement on Trade in Services (GATS) suggests
   (a) cross border trade in education
   (b) localization of education
   (c) only state funding in education
   (d) Corporate funding in primary and state funding in professional education

55. Who is the author of the book *Tribal Movements in India*?
   (a) M.S.A. Rao
   (b) Ghanshyam Shah
   (c) K.S. Singh
   (d) S. Fuchs

56. Who among the following is not a Scheduled Tribe of India?
   (a) Bhils
   (b) Santhals
   (c) Gurjars
   (d) Ho

57. Which one of the following is not correct with regard to peasant?
   (a) The peasant represents little tradition.
   (b) The peasants in India are predominantly represented by the middle strata of caste hierarchy.
   (c) The peasants are dependants on land for the mainstay of their livelihood.
   (d) Though the peasants are dependent on land for the mainstay of their livelihood, they resort to several other activities for their livelihood security.

58. Which one of the social movements in rural India can be termed as an example of 'old' social movements?
   (a) Environment movements
   (b) Peasant movements
   (c) Ethnic movements
   (d) Regional autonomy movements

59. Which one of the following concepts are not replaced by Sanskritization by M.N. Srinivas?
(a) Brahminization and Sudraisation
(b) Brahminization and Kshatriyaization
(c) Kshatriyaization and Sudraisation
(d) Brahminization and Westernization

60. Which one of the following is not a features of caste system?
(a) Endogamy, purity and pollution, ritual hierarchy and ascribed occupation.
(b) Exogamy, purity and pollution, ritual hierarchy and ascribed occupation.
(c) Endogamy, purity and pollution, ritual hierarchy and achieved occupation.
(d) Monogamy, purity and pollution, secular hierarchy and ascribed occupation.

61. Match List I with List II and mark the correct codes given below:
List I (Authors)
A. Mekim Marriot
B. M.N. Srinivas
C. B.R. Chauhan
D. S.C. Dube
List II (Books)
i. *India's Village*
ii. *Indian Village*
iii. *Village India*
iv. *A Rajasthan Village*

Codes:	A	B	C	D
(a)	i	ii	iii	iv
(b)	ii	iii	i	iv
(c)	iii	i	iv	ii
(d)	iv	iii	ii	i

62. Match List I with List II and mark the correct codes given below:
List I (Authors)
A. M.N. Srinivas
B. B.R. Ambedkar
C. G.S. Ghurye
D. D.P. Mukherjee
List II (Book)
i. *Caste in India: Their Mechanism, Genesis and Development*
ii. *Diversities*
iii. *Dominant Caste and Other Essays*
iv. *Caste and Race in India*

Codes:	A	B	C	D
(a)	ii	iii	i	iv
(b)	iii	i	ii	iv
(c)	iv	ii	iii	i
(d)	i	ii	iii	iv

63. Match the items in List I with the items in List II and choose the correct answer from the codes given below:
List I
A. Social evolution
B. Positivism
C. Mode of Production
D. Cultural Lag
List II
i. Karl Marx
ii. William Ogburn
iii. Auguste Comte
iv. Herbert Spencer

Codes:	A	B	C	D
(a)	ii	i	iii	iv
(b)	i	iv	ii	iii
(c)	iv	iii	i	ii
(d)	iii	ii	iv	i

64. Which one of the following is not a demand of peasant movements in India?
(a) Land Distribution
(b) Fertilizer Subsidy
(c) Tenancy Rights
(d) Higher wage for agricultural labour

65. Who defined peasants as 'small agricultural producers, who, with the help of simple equipment and the labour of their families, produce mostly for their own consumption, direct or indirect, and for the fulfilment of obligations to holders of political and economic power'?

(a) A. Beteille
(b) T. Shanin
(c) A.R. Desai
(d) A.V. Chayanor

66. In Indian context increase in slum population depicts
(a) an extension of rural poverty
(b) an extension of rural prosperity
(c) an extension of urban prosperity
(d) a process of urbanization

67. Which one of the following is not a push factor of rural to urban migration?
(a) Rural unemployment
(b) Increasing practice of dowry in rural areas
(c) Rural poverty
(d) Decline of cottage and household industry in rural areas

68. Ethnicity is defined with reference to
(a) inherited and achieved socio-cultural attributes
(b) inherited political positions and achieved economic attributes
(c) inherited socio-cultural attributes
(d) achieved socio-cultural attributes

69. Which one of the following is not a feature of informal sector?
(a) Absence of effective legal protection
(b) Absence of employment security
(c) Absence of effective trade unionism
(d) Absence of gender segregation

70. Bonded labour is a
(a) cause of rural poverty and illiteracy.
(b) cause of prevailing hegemony of upper castes.
(c) product of rural poverty but cause of illiteracy and hegemony of the upper caste over the lower castes.
(d) Product of rural poverty, illiteracy and hegemony of upper castes over the lower castes.

71. The Juvenile delinquents in India belong to the age group of
(a) Below 12 years
(b) Below 14 years
(c) Below 18 years
(d) Below 20 years

72. The average size of landholding of Scheduled Tribes is
(a) higher than the Scheduled Castes
(b) lower than the Scheduled Castes
(c) similar to those of the Scheduled Castes
(d) higher than the Other Backward Classes

73. The social development strategy aims to ensure that
(a) economic development is achieved by integrating national economy with multinational corporations and their corporate social responsibility.
(b) collective voice of trade unions is protected and their concerns are addressed properly.
(c) each section of society is recognized as resource who needs to be benefited from economic development to ensure that their educational, employment, health, other basic necessities of lives are fulfilled and opportunities be provided for the realization of their full potential.
(d) Development process should protect the balance between tradition and modernity.

74. In the wake of globalization Indian economy has
(a) reassorted its commitment to socialist path of development.
(b) reoriented to mixed economic path.
(c) rejuvenated the Gandhian models of self sufficiency.
(d) opened up to economic neo-liberalism.

75. Gary Slapper and Steve Tombs have studied
(a) White-Collar Crime
(b) Cyber Crime
(c) Corporate Crime
(d) Organized Crime

ANSWERS

1. (a)	2. (c)	3. (d)	4. (b)	5. (a)
6. (b)	7. (d)	8. (a)	9. (b)	10. (c)
11. (d)	12. (c)	13. (c)	14. (a)	15. (b)
16. (a)	17. (c)	18. (b)	19. (d)	20. (c)
21. (a)	22. (d)	23. (a)	24. (a)	25. (a)
26. (b)	27. (c)	28. (a)	29. (b)	30. (d)
31. (b)	32. (a)	33. (a)	34. (b)	35. (a)
36. (a)	37. (c)	38. (c)	39. (a)	40. (a)
41. (a)	42. (b)	43. (b)	44. (d)	45. (c)
46. (b)	47. (a)	48. (c)	49. (c)	50. (b)
51. (c)	52. (d)	53. (b)	54. (a)	55. (c)
56. (c)	57. (b)	58. (b)	59. (b)	60. (a)
61. (c)	62. (b)	63. (c)	64. (b)	65. (b)
66. (a)	67. (b)	68. (c)	69. (d)	70. (d)
71. (b)	72. (a)	73. (c)	74. (d)	75. (c)

DECEMBER–2012

Note: This paper contains Sixty (60) multiple-choice questions, each question carrying two (2) marks. Candidate is expected to answer any Fifty (50) questions. In case more than Fifty (50) questions are attempted, only the first Fifty (50) questions will be evaluated.

PAPER–I

1. The English word 'Communication' is derived from the words
   (a) Communis and Communicare
   (b) Communist and Commune
   (c) Communism and Communalism
   (d) Communion and Common sense
2. Chinese Cultural Revolution leader Mao Zedong used a type of communication to talk to the masses is known as
   (a) Mass line communication
   (b) Group communication
   (c) Participatory communication
   (d) Dialogue communication
3. Conversing with the spirits and ancestors is termed as
   (a) Transpersonal communication
   (b) Intrapersonal communication
   (c) Interpersonal communication
   (d) Face-to-face communication
4. The largest circulated daily newspaper among the following is
   (a) *The Times of India*
   (b) *The Indian Express*
   (c) *The Hindu*
   (d) *The Deccan Herald*
5. The pioneer of the silent feature film in India was
   (a) K.A. Abbas
   (b) Satyajit Ray
   (c) B.R. Chopra
   (d) Dada Sahib Phalke
6. Classroom communication of a teacher rests on the principle of
   (a) Infotainment (b) Edutainment
   (c) Entertainment (d) Power equation
7. The missing number in the series:
   0, 6, 24, 60, 120, ?, 336, is
   (a) 240 (b) 220
   (c) 280 (d) 210
8. A group of 7 members having a majority of boys is to be formed out of 6 boys and 4 girls. The number of ways the group can be formed is
   (a) 80 (b) 100
   (c) 90 (d) 110
9. The number of observations in a group is 40. The average of the first 10 members is 4.5 and the average of the remaining 30 members is 3.5. The average of the whole group is
   (a) 4 (b) 15/2
   (c) 15/4 (d) 6
10. If MOHAN is represented by the code KMFYL, then COUNT will be represented by
    (a) AMSLR (b) MSLAR
    (c) MASRL (d) SAMLR

11. The sum of the ages of two persons A and B is 50. Five years ago, the ratio of their ages was 5/3. The present age of A and B are
(a) 30, 20 (b) 35, 15
(c) 38, 12 (d) 40, 10

12. Let *a* means minus (–), *b* means multiplied by (×), C means divided by (÷) and D means plus (+). The value of 90 D 9 *a* 29 C 10 *b* 2 is
(a) 8 (b) 10
(c) 12 (d) 14

13. Consider the Assertion I and Assertion II and select the right codes given below:
Assertion I: Even Bank-lockers are not safe. Thieves can break them and take away your wealth. But thieves cannot go to heaven. So you should keep your wealth in heaven.
Assertion II: The difference of skin-colour of beings is because of the distance from the sun and not because of some permanent traits. Skin-colour is the result of body's reaction to the sun and its rays.
Codes:
(a) Both the Assertions I and II are forms of argument.
(b) The Assertion I is an argument but the Assertion II is not.
(c) The Assertion II is an argument but the Assertion I is not.
(d) Both the Assertions are explanations of facts.

14. By which of the following proposition, the proposition 'some men are not honest' is contradicted?
(a) All men are honest.
(b) Some men are honest.
(c) No men are honest.
(d) All of the above.

15. A stipulative definition is
(a) always true
(b) always false
(c) sometimes true sometimes false
(d) neither true nor false

16. Choose the appropriate alternative given in the codes to replace the question mark.
Examiner – Examinee, Pleader – Client, Preceptor – ?
(a) Customer (b) Path-finder
(c) Perceiver (d) Disciple

17. If the statement 'most of the students are obedient' is taken to be true, which one of the following pair of statements can be claimed to be true?
I. All obedient persons are students.
II. All students are obedient.
III. Some students are obedient.
IV. Some students are not disobedient.
Codes:
(a) I and II (b) II and III
(c) III and IV (d) II and IV

18. Choose the right code:
A deductive argument claims that:
I. The conclusion does not claim something more than that which is contained in the premises.
II. The conclusion is supported by the premise/premises conclusively.
III. If the conclusion is false, then premise/premises may be either true or false.
IV. If premise/combination of premises is true, then conclusion must be true.
Codes:
(a) I and II (b) I and III
(c) II and III (d) All of the above

On the basis of the data given in the following table, give answers to questions from 19 to 24:

Government Expenditures on Social Services
(As per cent of total expenditure)

Sl. No.	Items	2007-08	2008-09	2009-10	2010-11
	Social Services	11.06	12.94	13.06	14.02
(a)	Education, sports and youth affairs	4.02	4.04	3.96	4.46
(b)	Health and family welfare	2.05	1.91	1.90	2.03
(c)	Water supply, housing, etc.	2.02	2.31	2.20	2.27
(d)	Information and broadcasting	0.22	0.22	0.20	0.22
(e)	Welfare to SC/ST and OBC	0.36	0.35	0.41	0.63
(f)	Labour and employment	0.27	0.27	0.22	0.25
(g)	Social welfare and nutrition	0.82	0.72	0.79	1.06
(h)	North-eastern areas	0.00	1.56	1.50	1.75
(i)	Other social services	1.29	1.55	1.87	1.34
	Total Government expenditure	100.00	100.00	100.00	100.00

19. How many activities in the social services are there where the expenditure has been less than 5 per cent of the total expenditures incurred on the social services in 2008-09?
(a) One (b) Three
(c) Five (d) All of the above

20. In which year, the expenditures on the social services have increased at the highest rate?
(a) 2007-08 (b) 2008-09
(c) 2009-10 (d) 2010-11

21. Which of the following activities remains almost stagnant in terms of share of expenditures?
(a) North-eastern areas
(b) Welfare to SC/ST and OBC
(c) Information and broadcasting
(d) Social welfare and nutrition

22. Which of the following item's expenditure share is almost equal to the remaining three items in the given years?
(a) Information and broadcasting
(b) Welfare to SC/ST and OBC
(c) Labour and employment
(d) Social welfare and nutrition

23. Which of the following items of social services has registered the highest rate of increase in expenditures during 2007-08 to 2010-11?
(a) Education, sports and youth affairs
(b) Welfare to SC/ST and OBC
(c) Social welfare and nutrition
(d) Overall social services

24. Which of the following items has registered the highest rate of decline in terms of expenditure during 2007-08 to 2009-10?
(a) Labour and employment
(b) Health and family welfare
(c) Social welfare and nutrition
(d) Education, sports and youth affairs

25. ALU stands for
(a) American Logic Unit
(b) Alternate Local Unit
(c) Alternating Logic Unit
(d) Arithmetic Logic Unit

26. A Personal Computer uses a number of chips mounted on a circuit board called
(a) Microprocessor
(b) System Board

(c) Daughter Board
(d) Mother Board

27. Computer Virus is a
(a) Hardware
(b) Bacteria
(c) Software
(d) None of these

28. Which one of the following is correct?
(a) $(17)_{10} = (17)_{16}$
(b) $(17)_{10} = (17)_{8}$
(c) $(17)_{10} = (10111)_{2}$
(d) $(17)_{10} = (10001)_{2}$

29. The file extension of MS-Word document in Office 2007 is ______.
(a) .pdf (b) .doc
(c) .docx (d) .txt

30. ______ is a protocol used by e-mail clients to download e-mails to your computer.
(a) TCP (b) FTP
(c) SMTP (d) POP

31. Which of the following is a source of methane?
(a) Wetlands
(b) Foam Industry
(c) Thermal Power Plants
(d) Cement Industry

32. 'Minamata disaster' in Japan was caused by pollution due to
(a) Lead (b) Mercury
(c) Cadmium (d) Zinc

33. Biomagnification means increase in the
(a) concentration of pollutants in living organisms
(b) number of species
(c) size of living organisms
(d) biomass

34. Nagoya Protocol is related to
(a) Climate change
(b) Ozone depletion
(c) Hazardous waste
(d) Biodiversity

35. The second most important source after fossil fuels contributing to India's energy needs is
(a) Solar energy
(b) Nuclear energy
(c) Hydropower
(d) Wind energy

36. In case of earthquakes, an increase of magnitude 1 on Richter Scale implies
(a) a ten-fold increase in the amplitude of seismic waves.
(b) a ten-fold increase in the energy of the seismic waves.
(c) two-fold increase in the amplitude of seismic waves.
(d) two-fold increase in the energy of seismic waves.

37. Which of the following is not a measure of Human Development Index?
(a) Literacy Rate
(b) Gross Enrolment
(c) Sex Ratio
(d) Life Expectancy

38. India has the highest number of students in colleges after
(a) the U.K. (b) the U.S.A.
(c) Australia (d) Canada

39. Which of the following statement(s) is/are not correct about the Attorney General of India?
1. The President appoints a person, who is qualified to be a Judge of a High Court, to be the Attorney General of India.
2. He has the right of audience in all the Courts of the country.
3. He has the right to take part in the proceedings of the Lok Sabha and the Rajya Sabha.
4. He has a fixed tenure.

Select the correct answer from the codes given below:

Codes:

(a) 1 and 4 (b) 2, 3 and 4
(c) 3 and 4 (d) 3 only

40. Which of the following prefix President Pranab Mukherjee desires to be discontinued while interacting with Indian dignitaries as well as in official notings?
    1. His Excellency
    2. Mahamahim
    3. Hon'ble
    4. Shri/Smt.

Select the correct answer from the codes given below:

Codes:

(a) 1 and 3 (b) 2 and 3
(c) 1 and 2 (d) 1, 2 and 3

41. Which of the following can be done under conditions of financial emergency?
    1. State Legislative Assemblies can be abolished.
    2. Central Government can acquire control over the budget and expenditure of States.
    3. Salaries of the Judges of the High Courts and the Supreme Court can be reduced.
    4. Right to Constitutional Remedies can be suspended.

Select the correct answer from the codes given below:

Codes:

(a) 1, 2 and 3 (b) 2, 3 and 4
(c) 1 and 2 (d) 2 and 3

42. Match List I with List II and select the correct answer from the codes given below:

List I

(A) Poverty Reduction Programme
(B) Human Development Scheme
(C) Social Assistance Scheme
(D) Minimum Need Scheme

List II

(i) Mid-day Meals
(ii) Indira Awas Yojana (IAY)
(iii) National Old Age Pension (NOAP)
(iv) MNREGA

Codes:	A	B	C	D
(a)	(iv)	(i)	(iii)	(ii)
(b)	(ii)	(iii)	(iv)	(i)
(c)	(iii)	(iv)	(i)	(ii)
(d)	(iv)	(iii)	(ii)	(i)

43. For an efficient and durable learning, learner should have
    (a) ability to learn only
    (b) requisite level of motivation only
    (c) opportunities to learn only
    (d) desired level of ability and motivation

44. Classroom communication must be
    (a) Teacher centric
    (b) Student centric
    (c) General centric
    (d) Textbook centric

45. The best method of teaching is to
    (a) impart information
    (b) ask students to read books
    (c) suggest good reference material
    (d) initiate a discussion and participate in it

46. Interaction inside the classroom should generate
    (a) Argument (b) Information
    (c) Ideas (d) Controversy

47. "Spare the rod and spoil the child", gives the message that
    (a) punishment in the class should be banned.
    (b) corporal punishment is not acceptable.
    (c) undesirable behaviour must be punished.
    (d) children should be beaten with rods.

48. The type of communication that the teacher has in the classroom, is termed as

(a) Interpersonal
(b) Mass communication
(c) Group communication
(d) Face-to-face communication

49. Which one of the following is an indication of the quality of a research journal?
(a) Impact factor (b) h-index
(c) g-index (d) i10-index

50. Good 'research ethics' means
(a) Not disclosing the holdings of shares/stocks in a company that sponsors your research.
(b) Assigning a particular research problem to one Ph.D./research student only.
(c) Discussing with your colleagues confidential data from a research paper that you are reviewing for an academic journal.
(d) Submitting the same research manuscript for publishing in more than one journal.

51. Which of the following sampling methods is based on probability?
(a) Convenience sampling
(b) Quota sampling
(c) Judgement sampling
(d) Stratified sampling

52. Which one of the following references is written according to American Psychological Association (APA) format?
(a) Sharma, V. (2010). Fundamentals of Computer Science.
New Delhi: Tata McGraw Hill
(b) Sharma, V. 2010. Fundamentals of Computer Science.
New Delhi: Tata McGraw Hill
(c) Sharma. V. 2010. Fundamentals of Computer Science,
New Delhi: Tata McGraw Hill
(d) Sharma, V. (2010), Fundamentals of Computer Science,
New Delhi: Tata McGraw Hill

53. Arrange the following steps of research in correct sequence:
1. Identification of research problem
2. Listing of research objectives
3. Collection of data
4. Methodology
5. Data analysis
6. Results and discussion
(a) 1, 2, 3, 4, 5, 6
(b) 1, 2, 4, 3, 5, 6
(c) 2, 1, 3, 4, 5, 6
(d) 2, 1, 4, 3, 5, 6

54. Identify the incorrect statement:
(a) A hypothesis is made on the basis of limited evidence as a starting point for further investigations.
(b) A hypothesis is a basis for reasoning without any assumption of its truth.
(c) Hypothesis is a proposed explanation for a phenomenon.
(d) Scientific hypothesis is a scientific theory.

Read the following passage carefully and answer the questions (55 to 60):

The popular view of towns and cities in developing countries and of urbanization process is that despite the benefits and comforts it brings, the emergence of such cities connotes environmental degradation, generation of slums and squatters, urban poverty, unemployment, crimes, lawlessness, traffic chaos, etc. But what is the reality? Given the unprecedental increase in urban population over the last 50 years from 300 million in 1950 to 2 billion in 2000 in developing countries, the wonder really is how well the world has coped, and not how badly.

In general, the urban quality of life has improved in terms of availability of water and sanitation, power, health and education, communication and transport. By way of illustration, a large number of urban residents have been provided with improved water in urban areas in Asia's largest countries such as China, India, Indonesia and Philippines. Despite that, the access to improved water in terms of percentage of total urban population seems to have declined during the last decade of 20th century, though in absolute numbers, millions of additional urbanites, have been provided improved services. These countries have made significant progress in the provision of sanitation services too, together, providing for an additional population of more than 293 million citizens within a decade (1990-2000). These improvements must be viewed against the backdrop of rapidly increasing urban population, fiscal crunch and strained human resources and efficient and quality-oriented public management.

55. The popular view about the process of urbanization in developing countries is
(a) Positive
(b) Negative
(c) Neutral
(d) Unspecified

56. The average annual increase in the number of urbanites in developing countries, from 1950 to 2000 A.D. was close to
(a) 30 million (b) 40 million
(c) 50 million (d) 60 million

57. The reality of urbanization is reflected in
(a) How well the situation has been managed.
(b) How badly the situation has gone out of control.
(c) How fast has been the tempo of urbanization.
(d) How fast the environment has degraded.

58. Which one of the following is not considered as an indicator of urban quality of life?
(a) Tempo of urbanization
(b) Provision of basic services
(c) Access to social amenities
(d) All of the above

59. The author in this passage has tried to focus on
(a) Extension of Knowledge
(b) Generation of Environmental Consciousness
(c) Analytical Reasoning
(d) Descriptive Statement

60. In the above passage, the author intends to state
(a) The hazards of the urban life
(b) The sufferings of the urban life
(c) The awareness of human progress
(d) The limits to growth

ANSWERS

1. (a)	2. (d)	3. (a)	4. (a)	5. (d)
6. (b)	7. (d)	8. (b)	9. (c)	10. (a)
11. (a)	12. (d)	13. (a)	14. (a)	15. (d)
16. (c)	17. (c)	18. (d)	19. (d)	20. (d)
21. (c)	22. (d)	23. (d)	24. (b)	25. (d)
26. (d)	27. (c)	28. (d)	29. (b)	30. (d)
31. (a)	32. (b)	33. (a)	34. (d)	35. (c)
36. (a)	37. (c)	38. (b)	39. (d)	40. (c)
41. (c)	42. (a)	43. (d)	44. (b)	45. (d)
46. (c)	47. (c)	48. (c)	49. (a)	50. (a)
51. (d)	52. (a)	53. (b)	54. (d)	55. (b)
56. (a)	57. (a)	58. (a)	59. (d)	60. (d)

PAPER–II

Note: This paper contains Fifty (50) objective type questions, each question carrying two (2) marks. All questions are compulsory.

1. Which one of the following is not a characteristic of a primary group?
   (a) Personal orientation
   (b) Long-term orientation
   (c) Relations are end in themselves
   (d) Relations are means to an end
2. Who, of the following, is the author of the book *Economy and Society*?
   (a) Max Weber
   (b) Anthony Giddens
   (c) E. Durkheim
   (d) A. Comte
3. Which one of the following is not an element of rural community?
   (a) We-feeling
   (b) Cultural diversity
   (c) Territory
   (d) Self-sufficiency
4. Choose the correct sequence of following in order of increasing complexity:
   (a) Hunting, Gathering, Agrarian, Pastoral, Industrial and Postindustrial societies
   (b) Gathering, Pastoral, Hunting, Industrial and Post-industrial societies
   (c) Hunting, Pastoral, Agrarian, Industrial and Post-industrial societies
   (d) Agricultural, Gathering, Hunting, Horticultural, Industrial and Post-industrial societies
5. Sociology is characterised by a perspective that places _______ in the foreground.
   (a) Individual
   (b) Unique social events
   (c) Social interaction
   (d) Culture
6. When two people interact with each other, they form
   (a) a society
   (b) an institution
   (c) an association
   (d) a dyadic group
7. Which one of the following Max Muller believed to be the earliest form of religion?
   (a) Naturism
   (b) Monoism
   (c) Animism
   (d) Fetishism
8. Ridicule is a
   (a) Social sanction
   (b) Social norm
   (c) Mores
   (d) Folkway
9. The term 'Reference group' was first introduced by
   (a) Hyman
   (b) Merton
   (c) Srinivas
   (d) Cooley
10. Match List I with List II and mark the correct answer from the codes given below the lists:

List I (Author)
A. Sorokin
B. Dahrendorf
C. Spencer
D. Durkhiem

List II (Change Perspective)
i. Structural functional
ii. Cyclical
iii. Dialectical
iv. Evolutionary

Codes:	A	B	C	D
(a)	ii	iii	iv	i
(b)	i	iii	ii	iv
(c)	ii	iv	i	iii
(d)	iii	i	ii	iv

11. The pivotal methodology of functionalist is
(a) Conjectural history
(b) Library work
(c) Fieldwork
(d) Content analysis

12. To Mead the 'generalised others' and 'significant others' are the creators of
(a) I (b) Me
(c) Ego (d) Super ego

13. The collection of roles that goes with a given status is termed as
(a) Multiple roles
(b) Conflict of roles
(c) Role set
(d) Summation of roles

14. **Assertion (A):** The situation in which a person is faced with demands from two or more roles that do not match is called role conflict.
Reason (R): Role conflict is not common in traditional societies where each person plays a limited number of roles.
Choose the correct answer from the given codes:
Codes:
(a) (A) is true, but (R) is false.
(b) Both (A) and (R) are true and (R) is the correct explanation of (A).
(c) (A) is false, but (R) is true.
(d) Both (A) and (R) are true, but (R) is not the correct explanation of (A).

15. Who has written the book *Urbanisation and Family Change*?
(a) Iravati Karve
(b) M.S. Gore
(c) Leela Dube
(d) I.P. Desai

16. Who studied the structural and functional unity of joint family in 'Mahua'?
(a) K.M. Kapadia
(b) Neera Desai
(c) I.P. Desai
(d) A.M. Shah

17. Match List I with List II and select the correct answer from the codes given below:
List I
A. Marriage and Family in India
B. Kinship organisation in India
C. Kinship and Marriage
D. Family in India

List II
i. A.M. Shah
ii. Robin Fox
iii. K.M. Kapadia
iv. Iravati Karve

Codes:	A	B	C	D
(a)	i	ii	iv	iii
(b)	iii	iv	ii	i
(c)	i	iii	iv	ii
(d)	ii	iii	iv	i

18. Who said that the social stratification in India is based on 'purity and pollution'?
(a) M.N. Srinivas
(b) A.R. Desai
(c) Louis Dumont
(d) Yogendra Singh

19. Who has given functional theory of social stratification?
(a) T.B. Bottomore
(b) K. Davis
(c) W.E. Moore
(d) Karl Marx

20. Match List I with List II and select the correct answer from the codes given below:
List I
A. Homeohierchicus
B. Human society
C. Modernisation of Indian Tradition
D. Caste, Class and Occupation

List II
i. G.S. Ghurye
ii. Yogendra Singh
iii. Louis Dumont
iv. Kingsley Davis

Codes:	A	B	C	D
(a)	i	ii	iii	iv
(b)	ii	iii	iv	i
(c)	iii	iv	ii	i
(d)	iv	ii	i	iii

21. Marxian theory of change, 'that change comes through revolution' indicates
(a) change in the existing structure.
(b) change of the whole structure.
(c) a partial change in the existing structure.
(d) a nominal change of the structural elements.

22. Match List I with List II and select the correct answer from the codes given below the lists:
List I (Theory of Change)
A. Cyclica
B. Linear-Evolutionary
C. Dialectic
D. Functional
List II (Author)
i. Karl Marx and Dahrendorf
ii. Toynbee
iii. K. Davis and W.E. Moore
iv. Auguste Comte

Codes:	A	B	C	D
(a)	iii	iv	i	ii
(b)	ii	iv	i	iii
(c)	iv	i	iii	ii
(d)	i	ii	iii	iv

23. The basic difference between classical and modern sociological perspectives is visible in the
(a) Silent shift from macro to micro-theoretical perspective
(b) Radical shift from micro to macro perspective
(c) Development of middle range theories
(d) None of the above

24. Who was Comte's Mentor?
(a) Montesquieu
(b) Morgan
(c) Saint Simon
(d) Robert Redfield

25. From among the following who believed in Social Darwinism?
(a) Diffusionists
(b) Evolutionists
(c) Functionalists
(d) All of the above

26. Parsons' analysis of social system is based on the principle of
(a) Manifest function
(b) Division of labour
(c) Homeostasis
(d) Functional unity

27. Who started his book *The Structure of Social Action* with the rhetorical question "who now reads Spencer"?
(a) Durkheim
(b) Parsons
(c) Weber
(d) Pareto

28. Phenomenology is a radical alternative to
(a) Positivism
(b) Evolutionism
(c) Functionalism
(d) Diffusionism

29. Durkheim's study of suicide helps us to understand
(a) Society's hold over the Individual
(b) Individual's hold on the society
(c) Suicide rates of various societies
(d) Degree of social integration of a society

Codes:
(a) (b) and (c)
(b) (a) and (b)
(c) (a) and (d)
(d) (b) and (d)

30. In Merton's functional analysis of society which of the following concepts are central?
(a) Functions and Dysfunctions
(b) Structural elements and functional pre-requisites
(c) Subjective and objective manifestation
(d) Manifest and latent functions
Codes:
(a) (b) and (c)
(b) (b) and (d)
(c) (a) and (c)
(d) (a) and (d)

31. "Kula" was associated with
(a) Trobriand Islanders
(b) Malinowski
(c) Andaman Islanders
(d) Frazer
Codes:
(a) (b) and (c) (b) (b) and (d)
(c) (a) and (b) (d) (a) and (c)

32. Durkheim considered animism as:
(1) Soul worship
(2) The belief that events in the world are mobilized by the activities of spirit.
(3) The belief in worshipping the animals.
(4) The belief in worshipping the natural objects.
Codes:
(a) (1) and (2) (b) (1) and (4)
(c) (2) and (3) (d) (2) and (4)

33. In his evolutionary framework Marx arranged societies in the order of
(1) Primitive Communism
(2) Feudalism
(3) Capitalism
(4) Socialism
The correct order is
Codes:
(a) (3), (2), (1), (4)
(b) (2), (3), (4), (1)
(c) (1), (4), (3), (2)
(d) (1), (2), (3), (4)

34. **Assertion (A):** For the emergence of capitalism, a particular motivation was required with regard to profit and work.
Reason (R): Capitalism was developed in the west because such a motivation was provided by Calvinism.
Select your answer from:
Codes:
(a) Both (A) and (R) are true and (R) is correct explanation of (A).
(b) Both (A) and (R) are true, but (R) is not the correct explanation of (A).
(c) (A) is true, (R) is false.
(d) Both (A) and (R) are false.

35. **Assertion (A):** Functionalism considers human society as a social system, as a set of interconnected parts which together form as a whole.
Reason (R): Social Institutions such as education and religion are viewed as a part of the social system rather than as isolated units.
Codes:
(a) (A) is true and (R) is false.
(b) (A) is false, but (R) is true.
(c) Both (A) and (R) are true, but (R) is not the correct explanation of (A).
(d) Both (A) and (R) are true and (R) is the correct explanation of (A).

36. Match the following:
List I (Thinker)
A. Max Weber
B. R.K. Merton
C. B. Malinowski
D. V. Pareto

List II (Concept)

i. Circulation of Elites
ii. Self fulfilling prophesy
iii. Ideal types
iv. Kula exchange

Codes:	A	B	C	D
(a)	iii	ii	iv	i
(b)	i	iv	ii	iii
(c)	ii	i	iii	iv
(d)	iv	iii	i	ii

37. Match the following:

List I (Authors)

a. A.R. Radcliff-Brown
b. H. Spencer
c. R. Dahrendorf
d. E. Durkheim

List II (Books)

i. *Rules of Sociological Method*
ii. *Structure and Function in Primitive Society*
iii. *Class and Class Conflict in Industrial Society*
iv. *Principles of Sociology*

Codes:	A	B	C	D
(a)	ii	iv	iii	i
(b)	iv	iii	ii	i
(c)	ii	iii	i	iv
(d)	i	iii	ii	iv

38. The book *Street Corner Society* was authored by
(a) L.A. Coser
(b) Max Weber
(c) William F. Whyte
(d) B. Malinowski

39. The figure that most frequently occurs in a given set of data is known as
(a) Mode (b) Median
(c) Mean (d) Average

40. Range is a measure of
(a) Central Tendency
(b) Dispersion
(c) Association
(d) Correlation

41. Who has given the formula for calculating rank correlation?
(a) Spearman
(b) Pearson
(c) Yules
(d) Garrett

42. An idea about a given state of affairs put forward in exact terms to provide basis for empirical testing is known as
(a) Ideal type
(b) Hypothesis
(c) Sociological imagination
(d) Empirical Research

43. Match List I with List II and select the correct answer from the codes given below the lists:

List I

A. Oral History
B. Survey
C. Sampling
D. Case study

List II

i. Quantitative Data
ii. People's Knowledge
iii. Indepth Study of a Unit
iv. Representative of a Whole

Codes:	A	B	C	D
(a)	i	ii	iii	iv
(b)	ii	i	iv	iii
(c)	iii	iv	i	ii
(d)	iv	iii	ii	i

44. Attribute is related to
(a) Qualitative variable
(b) Quantitative variable
(c) Constant
(d) None of the above

45. Match List I with List II and select the correct answer from the codes given below the lists:

List I
A. Empirical Research
B. Objectivity
C. Fact
D. Subjectivity

List II
i. Knowledge free from bias
ii. Personal assertion
iii. Field based data
iv. Empirical evidence

Codes:	A	B	C	D
(a)	i	ii	iii	iv
(b)	iii	i	iv	ii
(c)	ii	iii	iv	i
(d)	iv	i	ii	iii

46. Match List I with List II and select the correct answer from the codes given below:

List I (Type of research design)
A. Exploratory
B. Experimental
C. Descriptive
D. Diagnostic

List II (Nature of research question)
i. Why is it?
ii. What is it?
iii. How to treat it?
iv. How is it?

Codes:	A	B	C	D
(a)	iv	iii	ii	i
(b)	i	iv	iii	ii
(c)	ii	i	iv	iii
(d)	i	ii	iii	iv

47. What is the correct sequence of understanding research methodology?
(a) Nature of phenomena, methods of data collection, nature of social science, methods of data analysis.
(b) Nature of phenomena, nature of social science, method of data collection, methods of data analysis.
(c) Methods of data analysis, methods of data collection, nature of social science, nature of phenomena.
(d) Methods of data collection, nature of phenomena, nature of social science, methods of data analysis.

48. In case of doing a research which is the correct sequence?
(a) Formulation of the problem, data collection, hypothesis, analysis of data
(b) Data collection, hypothesis, formulation of the problem, analysis of data
(c) Formulation of problem, hypothesis, data collection, analysis of data
(d) Hypothesis, analysis of data, formulation of the problem, data collection

49. After data collection which is the correct sequence of the following steps?
(a) Editing of filled in tool, coding, report writing, tabulation
(b) Coding, report writing, editing the filled in tool, tabulation
(c) Report writing, editing filled in tool, tabulation, coding
(d) Editing filled in tool, coding, tabulation

50. Coefficient of correlation (r) indicates the extend of relationship between
(a) two qualitative variables
(b) two quantitative variables
(c) one qualitative variable and other quantitative variable
(d) All of the above

ANSWERS

1. (d)	2. (a)	3. (b)	4. (c)	5. (c)
6. (d)	7. (a)	8. (a)	9. (a)	10. (a)
11. (c)	12. (b)	13. (c)	14. (d)	15. (b)
16. (c)	17. (b)	18. (c)	19. (b)	20. (c)
21. (b)	22. (b)	23. (a)	24. (c)	25. (b)
26. (c)	27. (b)	28. (a)	29. (c)	30. (d)
31. (c)	32. (a)	33. (d)	34. (a)	35. (d)
36. (a)	37. (a)	38. (c)	39. (a)	40. (b)
41. (a)	42. (b)	43. (b)	44. (a)	45. (b)
46. (c)	47. (b)	48. (c)	49. (d)	50. (b)

PAPER–III

Note: This paper contains seventy-five (75) objective type questions of two (2) marks each. All questions are compulsory.

1. Which one of the following is correct about Ethno methodology?
   (a) Macro Sociology
   (b) Micro Sociology
   (c) Certainly not Macro Sociology
   (d) Certainly not Micro Sociology
2. Who has considered that 'most often action is routine and relatively unreflexive'?
   (a) Alfred Schultz
   (b) H. Garfinkel
   (c) Max Weber
   (d) John Heritage
3. Who has argued that ethno methods are 'reflexively accountable'?
   (a) Orbuch (b) Garfinkel
   (c) Schultz (d) Hilbert
4. Who was concerned with the composition of 'self' at the 'micro' level of social action and interaction?
   (a) Mead
   (b) Goffman
   (c) Berger
   (d) Luckman
5. Match the following List I and List II.
   List I
   A. The Structure of Social Action
   B. The Phenomenology of the Social World
   C. Presentation of Self in Everyday Life
   D. Studies in Ethnomethodology
   List II
   i. A. Schultz
   ii. Harold Garfinkel
   iii. T. Parsons
   iv. I. Goffman
   Mark the correct answer from the codes given below:

Codes:	**A**	**B**	**C**	**D**
(a)	i	ii	iii	iv
(b)	iii	i	iv	ii
(c)	i	iv	ii	iii
(d)	ii	iii	iv	i

6. Who has stated that neofunctionalism devotes roughly equal attention to 'action and order'?
   (a) J. Alexander
   (b) P. Colomy
   (c) G. Rhoades
   (d) All of the above
7. Who has defined neofunctionalism as "a self-critical strand of functional theory"?
   (a) Alexander and Giesen
   (b) Colomy and Rhoades
   (c) Rhoades and Giesen
   (d) Alexander and Colomy
8. Who has criticized the economic determinism to be implicit in parts of Marx's original work?
   (a) Habermas
   (b) Bottomore

(c) Morrow
(d) Althusser

9. What do the critical theorists state?
(a) Economic determinism was wrong.
(b) Economic determinism was not wrong.
(c) Economic determinism was not wrong but should be concerned with other aspects of social life as well.
(d) Economic determinism was wrong and should be concerned with other aspects of social life.

10. Who has contended, among the neo-Marxists, that mature Marx did not believe in any human nature?
(a) Habermas
(b) Harvey
(c) Dahrendorf
(d) Althusser

11. Who has observed a link between the structures of the mind and the structures of society?
(a) Lemert
(b) Radcliffe-Brown
(c) Levi-Strauss
(d) Foucault

12. Among the post structuralists who has focussed on the 'linkage between knowledge and power'?
(a) Lemert
(b) Miller
(c) Levi-Strauss
(d) Foucault

13. Who is said to have deconstructed language and social institutions?
(a) Derrida
(b) Godelier
(c) Foucault
(d) Smith

14. Who has envisioned an alternative stage (an alternative society) in which "speech will cease to govern the stage"?
(a) Foucault
(b) Derrida
(c) Lemert
(d) None of the above

15. According to post modernists which ideas of modernity are considered gone by or dead?
(a) Reason, rationality and progress.
(b) Rationality, progress and objectivity.
(c) Legality, rationality and objectivity.
(d) Objectivity, rationality and reason.

16. Who considers modernity as 'an unfinished project'?
(a) Derrida
(b) Giddens
(c) Althusser
(d) Habermas

17. Who had initiated the work on the total communities of India namely *People of India Project*?
(a) N.K. Bose (b) K.S. Singh
(c) Yogendra Singh (d) M.N. Srinivas

18. According to G.S. Ghurye, which are the features of society which is characterized by caste system?
I. Segmental Division of Society.
II. Civil and Religious abilities.
III. Hierarchy and Restrictions on feeding and social intercause.
IV. Choice of occupation and marriage.

Codes:
(a) I, II, III, IV (b) I, III
(c) I, II (d) I, III, IV

19. Match List I with List II and select the correct answer from the codes given below:

List I (Authors)
A. G.S. Ghurye
B. N.K. Bose
C. Surajit Sinha (ed)
D. D.N. Majumdar

List II (Books)

i. *Races and Cultures of India*
ii. *Scheduled Tribes*
iii. *Tribal Life in India*
iv. *Field Studies on the People of India: Methods and Perspectives*

Codes:	**A**	**B**	**C**	**D**
(a)	ii	iii	iv	i
(b)	iii	ii	iv	i
(c)	ii	iv	i	iii
(d)	i	iii	iv	ii

20. Who has stated that the entire course of Indian History shows tribal elements being fused into a general society?
(a) A.R. Radcliffe-Brown
(b) D.D. Kosambi
(c) S.S. Sarkar
(d) M. Marriott

21. According to N.K. Bose, the development of Indian Civilization is the result of
I. the repeated experiences of war leading to the spirit of nationalism.
II. a pattern of cultural pluralism under relatively peaceful conditions.
III. the communities in India do not constitute their distinct entities.
IV. diversity of culture but encouraging the economic organization for interdependence of all communities.

Select the correct answer from the codes given below:

Codes:
(a) II only (b) II, III, IV
(c) I, III (d) II, IV

22. Who is of the opinion that the notion of fundamental opposition between the pure and the impure is the hallmark of the caste system?
(a) M.N. Srinivas
(b) Louis Dumont
(c) Surajit Sinha
(d) B.R. Ambedkar

23. **Assertion (A):** D.P. Mukherjee preferred to call himself 'Marxologist' rather than Marxist.
Reason (R): He attempted a dialectical interpretation of the encounter between the Indian tradition and modernity which was characterized more by value assimilation and cultural synthesis and less by 'class struggle'.

Select the correct answer from the codes given below:

Codes:
(a) (A) is true, but (R) is false.
(b) Both (A) and (R) are true and (R) is the correct explanation of (A).
(c) (A) is false, but (R) is true and (R) is the incorrect explanation of (A).
(d) (A) is false and (R) is true.

24. Which are the characteristics of 'Dominant Caste' as given by M.N. Srinivas?
I. Numerical strength and Political power.
II. Economic power through ownership of land.
III. Western education and jobs in administration.
IV. Urban source of income.

Codes:
(a) I, II, IV (b) I, II, III, IV
(c) I, II only (d) II, III, IV

25. Which perspective is based on the assumption that Indian society is unique and the Indian social institutions can be better studied through the texts?
(a) Subaltern
(b) Indological
(c) Civilizational
(d) Structural/Functional

26. Which type of poverty refers to a lack of basic resources needed to maintain health and bodily functioning?

(a) Absolute poverty
(b) Relative poverty
(c) Culture of poverty
(d) Enforced poverty

27. Match the Authors in List I with books in List II and choose the correct answer from the codes given below:

List I (Authors)
A. A. Cohen
B. R.E. Dobash and R.P. Dobash
C. C.B. Gardner
D. F. Heidensohn

List II (Books)
i. *Women and Crime*
ii. *Gender and Public Harassment*
iii. *Women, Violence and Social Change*
iv. *Delinquent Boys*

Codes:	**A**	**B**	**C**	**D**
(a)	iv	iii	ii	i
(b)	i	ii	iii	iv
(c)	iv	iii	i	ii
(d)	iii	ii	iv	i

28. Prof. S.C. Dube's study on village compost pit and its failure is due to
(a) Inequality of caste and gender
(b) Religious disharmonies
(c) Intergenerational conflict
(d) None of the above

29. Who in developing the theory of deviance utilized explanatory factors that are typical of functional analysis, namely, cultural goals and institutionalized norms?
(a) Durkheim (b) Merton
(c) Parsons (d) Weber

30. **Assertion (A):** High birth rate is due to child marriage.
Reason (R): The practice of child marriage is due to customs, traditions and illiteracy in the society.
In the context of the above two statements, which one of the following is correct?
Codes:
(a) Both (A) and (R) are true and (R) is the correct explanation of (A).
(b) Both (A) and (R) are true, but (R) is not the correct explanation of (A).
(c) (A) is true, but (R) is false.
(d) (A) is false, but (R) is true.

31. **Assertion (A):** Ecological degradation leads to environmental pollution.
Reason (R): Deforestation, construction of big dams and other developmental activities are responsible for Ecological degradation.
In the context of the above two statements, which one of the following is correct?
Codes:
(a) Both (A) and (R) are true, but (R) is not the correct explanation of (A).
(b) Both (A) and (R) are true and (R) is the correct explanation of (A).
(c) (A) is true, but (R) is false.
(d) (A) is false, but (R) is true.

32. Match the items in List I with the items in List II and choose the correct codes given below:

List I (Books)
A. *Sociology of Environment*
B. *Staying Alive: Women, Ecology and Survival in India*
C. *The Third Wave*
D. *Modernization, Protest and Change*

List II (Authors)
i. S.N. Pawar and R.B. Patil
ii. Alvin Toffler
iii. Vandana Shiva
iv. S.N. Eisenstadt

Codes:	A	B	C	D
(a)	ii	i	iii	iv
(b)	iv	i	ii	iii
(c)	i	iii	ii	iv
(d)	iii	ii	i	iv

33. Who has propounded the "Theory of Differential Association"?
(a) R.K. Merton
(b) R.H. Burke
(c) G. Tarde
(d) E.H. Sutherland

34. Death resulting out of failure in love affair is an example of
(a) Fatalistic suicide
(b) Egoistic suicide
(c) Altruistic suicide
(d) Anomic suicide

35. 'Community Policing System' aims at prevention and control of Crime through
(a) Public
(b) Police
(c) Police and Public
(d) Army

36. Drug de-addiction centres provide which of the following facility/facilities?
(a) Counselling
(b) Medical assistance
(c) Yogic exercise
(d) All of the above

37. Judicial separation for a conflicting couple is granted for a maximum period of
(a) 7 years (b) 3 years
(c) 2 years (d) 5 years

38. Which type of intoxicant is taken by the use of Cigarette, Bidi, Tobaco, Cigar, etc.?
(a) Narcotics (b) Nicotine
(c) Sedatives (d) Hallucinogens

39. Probation and Parole are which form of punishment?
(a) Deterrent punishment
(b) Retributive punishment
(c) Extra-mural treatment
(d) None of the above

40. Borstal Schools are meant for the reformation of
(a) Juvenile delinquents
(b) Women Offenders
(c) Convicts
(d) None of the above

41. Match the Authors in List I with the title of Books in List II and choose the correct codes given below:

List I
A. P. Carlen
B. P. Walton and J. Young
C. D. Clark
D. R. Cloward and L. Ohlin

List II
i. *Women's Imprisonment: A Study in Social Control*
ii. *The New Criminology Revisited*
iii. *The Sociology of Death: Theory, Culture, Practice*
iv. *Delinquency and Opportunity*

Codes:	A	B	C	D
(a)	i	ii	iii	iv
(b)	iv	iii	ii	i
(c)	ii	i	iii	iv
(d)	iii	ii	iv	i

42. Who among the following has argued for bureaucracy contributing to nation building in India?
(a) A.R. Desai
(b) G.S. Ghurye
(c) R. Bendix
(d) S.C. Dube

43. 'Secularism curbs divisiveness that springs from religious differences and

also clears way for rapid development and nation building processes'. Which one of the following is not an element of secularism as per the statement given above?

(a) Integration of socio-economic and political system that can interlink and interpenetrate various sub-groups.
(b) Non-acceptance to the prejudice and parochialism.
(c) Visible demonstrated gains of interdependence and cooperation.
(d) Primordial loyalities as a part of social engineering in a society.

44. **Assertion (A):** The concept of 'secularization' as used in Indian Constitution implies that State does not provide patronage to any religion.
Reason (R): Religion does not hold significance in modern society.
Codes:
(a) (A) is true and (R) is false and (R) is the correct explanation of (A).
(b) (A) is false and (R) is true.
(c) (A) is true and (R) is false and (R) is not the correct explanation of (A).
(d) Both (A) and (R) are true and (R) is the correct explanation of (A).

45. Match an item in List I with an item in List II:
List I (Books)
A. *Modernisation of Indian Tradition*
B. *When a Great Tradition Modernises*
C. *Caste in Modern India*
D. *Caste, Class and Power*

List II (Thinkers)
i. Y. Singh
ii. M. Singer
iii. M.N. Srinivas
iv. Andre Betille

Codes:	A	B	C	D
(a)	i	ii	iii	iv
(b)	iv	iii	ii	i
(c)	iii	ii	i	iv
(d)	ii	i	iv	iii

46. Who has stated that in India, direction of change is represented in a linear evolutionary form from 'traditionalization' towards 'modernization'?
(a) M.N. Srinivas
(b) S.C. Dube
(c) Milton Singer
(d) Yogendra Singh

47. **Assertion (A):** Some scholars say, in countries which have recently introduced Sociology, indigenization of the subject is required.
Reason (R): This can be helpful in the growth of native scholarship and will contribute to the nation building process.
Codes:
(a) (A) is false, but (R) is true.
(b) (A) is true, but (R) is false.
(c) Both (A) and (R) are true and (R) is the correct explanation of (A).
(d) Both (A) and (R) are true, but (R) is not the correct explanation of (A).

48. **Assertion (A):** The purpose of privatization of Education was to improve the quality of Education.
Reason (R): Privatization of education has resulted into Mushroom growth of Educational Institution.
Codes:
(a) Both (A) and (R) are true and (R) is the correct explanation of (A).
(b) Both (A) and (R) are true, but (R) is not the correct explanation of (A).
(c) (A) is true, but (R) is false.
(d) (A) is false, but (R) is true.

49. Right to Education was introduced as Fundamental Rights under which of the following Article of the Indian Constitution?
Codes:
(a) Article – 14
(b) Article – 21
(c) Article – 21 – A
(d) Article – 16

50. **Assertion (A):** North-Eastern States are not facing any crisis with regard to female child sex-ratio.
Reason (R): There is increase of education among women in these States.
Codes:
(a) Both (A) and (R) are true, but (R) is not the correct explanation of (A).
(b) (A) is false, but (R) is true and (R) is the correct explanation of (A).
(c) Both (A) and (R) are false.
(d) (A) is true, but (R) is false.

51. Which Committee recommended three tier system for Panchayati Raj?
(a) Balwant Rai Mehta Committee
(b) Ashok Mehta Committee
(c) Sangama Committee
(d) Parliamentary Committee

52. Urban oriented development programmes generated urban centred employment which resulted into
(a) Rural to Rural Migration
(b) Urban to Rural Migration
(c) Rural to Urban Migration
(d) Urban to Urban Migration

53. Agrarian social structure is characterized by which of the following?
I. Land owner and landless labourers.
II. Land owning and businessmen.
III. Peasants and village moneylenders.
IV. Peasants and crop-sharers
Mark the correct answer from the codes given below:
Codes:
(a) I, II, III (b) II, III, IV
(c) I, III, IV (d) IV, II, III

54. Peasants movements failed in India because of
(a) trade unions were non-existent.
(b) trade unions were disinterested.
(c) no land reforms have been done.
(d) partial land reforms have been done.

55. Panchayats in modern India are characterized as
I. Participation of people at grassroot level.
II. Self-reliance.
III. Empowering of women.
IV. Bureaucratic control.
Mark the correct answer from the codes given below:
Codes:
(a) IV, II, III (b) I, II, III, IV
(c) IV, III, I (d) II, III, IV

56. Mark out the correct answer about Human Relations Approach to work place behaviour from the codes given below:
I. It is against those approaches which give individualistic and over-rational emphasis to explain workers' behaviour in material terms.
II. It emphasizes the importance of informal groups in industry.
III. It has set the beginning of a model of the factory as a social system and the worker as a social man.
IV. It considers the industrial man as a rational and economic man.

Codes:
(a) I, II (b) I, III, IV
(c) I, IV (d) I, II, III

57. What does cause alienation according to Karl Marx?
(a) The division of labour.
(b) The institution of private property.
(c) 'Cash nexus' of commercial relationships.
(d) All of the above.

58. During 1956, which were the countries visited by the study group comprising representatives from the Government, trade unions and the employers from India to study the experiences of workers' participation in management?
Codes:
(a) Poland, Sweden, U.K., France, East Germany, Russia.
(b) Holland, Sweden, France, Yugoslavia, Belgium, Czechoslovakia.
(c) U.K., Sweden, France, Belgium, West Germany, Yugoslavia.
(d) U.K., Sweden, Poland, Germany, Belgium, France.

59. Which model of workers' participation in Management is working in India?
(a) Quality circles
(b) Joint consultation
(c) Co-determination
(d) Self-management

60. What is incorrect about SEWA?
(a) It has unionized women workers in the unorganized sector.
(b) It combines three movements: labour, co-operative and development.
(c) It has organized many women co-operatives.
(d) It is restricted to Ahmedabad only.

61. Which is not an indicator of social development?
(a) Improvement in health
(b) Improvement in quality of life
(c) Improvement in education
(d) Increase in per capita income

62. "Structural adjustment programmes" introduced in 1980 were forced upon the Third World Countries with a view to
(a) recover debt
(b) check nepotism
(c) weed out corruption
(d) All of the above

63. India followed a mixed model of economic development since its independence from the foreign rule but was compelled to adopt LPG Policy. In which year the LPG Policy was adopted in India as a model of economic growth?
(a) 1980 (b) 1989
(c) 1990 (d) 1993

64. Who is of the view that social unrest is rooted in the capitalist path of development?
(a) A.R. Desai
(b) G.S. Ghurye
(c) D.P. Mukerji
(d) Surajit Sinha

65. "World System Theory" of development explains the relationships between the 'developed' and 'developing' countries. Who among the following gave 'World System Theory' of development?
(a) Gunnar Myrdal
(b) Wallersteins
(c) M.K. Gandhi
(d) A. Sen

66. Who is the Author of the Book *Essay on the Principle of Population*?
(a) G. Marshall
(b) M.K. Premi
(c) T. Malthus
(d) Peter R. Cox

67. The concept of social capillarity in studying population was used by
(a) Thomas Malthus
(b) Herbert Spencer
(c) David Herdiman
(d) D. Dumount

68. The determinants of fertility were explained in detail by
(a) Karl Marx
(b) Kingsley Davis and Judiath Black
(c) Double day
(d) Peter Berger

69. Which of the following is/are related to Demographic processes?
I. Fertility II. Mortality
III. Migration IV. Morbidity
Answer the correct combination:
(a) I and IV are correct.
(b) IV and II are correct.
(c) II and III are correct.
(d) III and IV are correct.

70. Match the items in List I with the items in List II and choose the correct codes given below:
List I
A. The death of a child below the age of one year.
B. The death of woman at the time of delivery.
C. The rate of falling ill due to diseases.
D. Killing of girls after birth.
List II
i. Morbidity
ii. Infant mortality
iii. Female infanticide
iv. Maternal mortality
v. Female foeticide

Codes:	A	B	C	D
(a)	i	iv	ii	v
(b)	ii	iv	i	iii
(c)	iv	iii	v	ii
(d)	v	iv	i	iii

71. **Assertion (A):** Women and Child Development Policy is called 'Protective discrimination.'
Reason (R): This is beneficial only for women.
Codes:
(a) (A) is true and (R) is false.
(b) Both (A) and (R) are false.
(c) (A) is true and (R) is false and (R) is not the correct explanation of (A).
(d) Both (A) and (R) are true.

72. Mark out the correct sequence of perspectives on gender and development in India:
(a) Welfare, Empowerment, Development.
(b) Empowerment, Development, Welfare.
(c) Development, Welfare, Empowerment.
(d) Welfare, Development, Empowerment.

73. Several International Meetings made declaration about feminist visions of development from a global perspective. Arrange these international meetings in order in which they were held. Use the codes given below:
I. Asian and Pacific Centre for Women Development (APCWD).
II. Workshop on Developing Strategies for the Future: Feminist Perspectives.
III. Dakar Declaration on Another Development with Women.
IV. Nairobi End of the UN Decade World Conference.
Codes:
(a) I, III, IV, II (b) II, I, III, IV
(c) III, I, IV, II (d) I, II, III, IV

74. Which is the main basis for the growth of eco-feminism?
(a) Deforestation in industrial society.
(b) Women's lives and their relation with the nature.

(c) Pollution and environmental degradation.
(d) Global warming.

75. Match the List I with List II given below:

List I (Feminists)
A. Simone de Beauvoir
B. Mary Wollstonecraft
C. Sulamith Firestone
D. Juliet Mitchell

List II (Books)
i. *The Dialectics of Sex*
ii. *Women's Estate*
iii. *The Second Sex*
iv. *The Vindication of the Rights of Women*

Codes:	**A**	**B**	**C**	**D**
(a)	iii	iv	i	ii
(b)	iii	i	iv	ii
(c)	i	iii	ii	iv
(d)	ii	i	iii	iv

ANSWERS

1. (c)	2. (a)	3. (b)	4. (b)	5. (b)
6. (a)	7. (d)	8. (a)	9. (c)	10. (d)
11. (c)	12. (d)	13. (a)	14. (b)	15. (a)
16. (d)	17. (b)	18. (b)	19. (a)	20. (b)
21. (d)	22. (b)	23. (b)	24. (b)	25. (b)
26. (a)	27. (a)	28. (a)	29. (b)	30. (a)
31. (b)	32. (c)	33. (d)	34. (a)	35. (c)
36. (d)	37. (c)	38. (b)	39. (c)	40. (a)
41. (a)	42. (c)	43. (d)	44. (c)	45. (a)
46. (d)	47. (c)	48. (a)	49. (c)	50. (a)
51. (a)	52. (c)	53. (c)	54. (d)	55. (b)
56. (d)	57. (d)	58. (c)	59. (b)	60. (d)
61. (d)	62. (d)	63. (c)	64. (a)	65. (b)
66. (c)	67. (d)	68. (b)	69. (c)	70. (b)
71. (b)	72. (d)	73. (d)	74. (b)	75. (a)

JUNE–2012

Note: This paper contains Sixty (60) multiple-choice questions, each question carrying two (2) marks. Candidate is expected to answer any Fifty (50) questions. In case more than Fifty (50) questions are attempted, only the first Fifty (50) questions will be evaluated.

PAPER–I

1. Video-Conferencing can be classified as one of the following types of communication:
   (a) Visual one way
   (b) Audio-Visual one way
   (c) Audio-Visual two way
   (d) Visual two way
2. MC National University of Journalism and Communication is located at
   (a) Lucknow (b) Bhopal
   (c) Chennai (d) Mumbai
3. All India Radio (A.I.R.) for broadcasting was named in the year
   (a) 1926 (b) 1936
   (c) 1946 (d) 1956
4. In India for broadcasting TV programmes which system is followed?
   (a) NTCS (b) PAL
   (c) NTSE (d) SECAM
5. The term 'DAVP' stands for
   (a) Directorate of Advertising & Vocal Publicity
   (b) Division of Audio-Visual Publicity
   (c) Department of Audio-Visual Publicity
   (d) Directorate of Advertising and Visual Publicity
6. The term "TRP" is associated with TV shows stands for
   (a) Total Rating Points
   (b) Time Rating Points
   (c) Thematic Rating Points
   (d) Television Rating Points
7. Which is the number that comes next in the following sequence?
   2, 6, 12, 20, 30, 42, 56, ______
   (a) 60 (b) 64
   (c) 72 (d) 70
8. Find the next letter for the series YVSP ______.
   (a) N (b) M
   (c) O (d) L
9. Given that in a code language, '645' means 'day is warm'; '42' means 'warm spring' and '634' means 'spring is sunny'; which digit represents 'sunny'?
   (a) 3 (b) 2
   (c) 4 (d) 5
10. The basis of the following classification is:
    'first President of India' 'author of *Godan*' 'books in my library', 'blue things' and 'students who work hard'
    (a) Common names
    (b) Proper names
    (c) Descriptive phrases
    (d) Indefinite description
11. In the expression 'Nothing is larger than itself' the relation 'is larger than' is
    (a) antisymmetric (b) asymmetrical
    (c) intransitive (d) irreflexive
12. **Assertion (A):** There are more laws on the books today than ever before, and

more crimes being committed than ever before.

Reason (R): Because to reduce crime we must eliminate the laws.

Choose the correct answer from below:

(a) (A) is true, (R) is doubtful and (R) is not the correct explanation of (A).
(b) (A) is false, (R) is true and (R) is the correct explanation of (A).
(c) (A) is doubtful, (R) is doubtful and (R) is not the correct explanation of (A).
(d) (A) is doubtful, (R) is true and (R) is not the correct explanation of (A).

13. If the proposition "All men are not mortal" is true then which of the following inferences is correct? Choose from the codes given below:
   1. "All men are mortal" is true.
   2. "Some men are mortal" is false.
   3. "No men are mortal" is doubtful.
   4. "All men are mortal" is false.

   Codes:
   (a) 1, 2 and 3 (b) 2, 3 and 4
   (c) 1, 3 and 4 (d) 1 and 3

14. Determine the nature of the following definition: "Abortion" means the ruthless murdering of innocent beings.
   (a) Lexical (b) Persuasive
   (c) Stipulative (d) Theoretical

15. Which one of the following is not an argument?
   (a) Devadutt does not eat in the day so he must be eating at night.
   (b) If Devadutt is growing fat and if he does not eat during the day, he will be eating at night.
   (c) Devadutt eats in the night so he does not eat during the day.
   (d) Since Devadutt does not eat in the day, he must be eating in the night.

16. Venn diagram is a kind of diagram to
   (a) represent and assess the validity of elementary inferences of syllogistic form.
   (b) represent but not assess the validity of elementary inferences of syllogistic form.
   (c) represent and assess the truth of elementary inferences of syllogistic form.
   (d) assess but not represent the truth of elementary inferences of syllogistic form.

17. Reasoning by analogy leads to
   (a) certainty
   (b) definite conclusion
   (c) predictive conjecture
   (d) surety

18. Which of the following statements are false? Choose from the codes given below:
   1. Inductive arguments always proceed from the particular to the general.
   2. A cogent argument must be inductively strong.
   3. A valid argument may have a false premise and a false conclusion.
   4. An argument may legitimately be spoken of as 'true' or 'false'.

   Codes:
   (a) 2, 3 and 4 (b) 1 and 3
   (c) 2 and 4 (d) 1 and 2

19. Six persons A, B, C, D, E and F are standing in a circle. B is between F and C, A is between E and D, F is to the left of D. Who is between A and F?
   (a) B (b) C
   (c) D (d) E

20. The price of petrol increases by 25%. By what percentage must a customer reduce the consumption so that the earlier bill on the petrol does not alter?

(a) 20% (b) 25%
(c) 30% (d) 33.33%

21. If Ram knows that y is an integer greater than 2 and less than 7 and Hari knows that y is an integer greater than 5 and less than 10, then they may correctly conclude that
(a) y can be exactly determined
(b) y may be either of two values
(c) y may be any of three values
(d) there is no value of y satisfying these conditions

22. Four pipes can fill a reservoir in 15, 20, 30 and 60 hours respectively. The first one was opened at 6 AM, second at 7 AM, third at 8 AM and the fourth at 9 AM. When will the reservoir be filled?
(a) 11 AM (b) 12 Noon
(c) 1 PM (d) 1:30 PM

The total electricity generation in a country is 97 GW. The contribution of various energy sources is indicated in percentage terms in the Pie Chart given below:

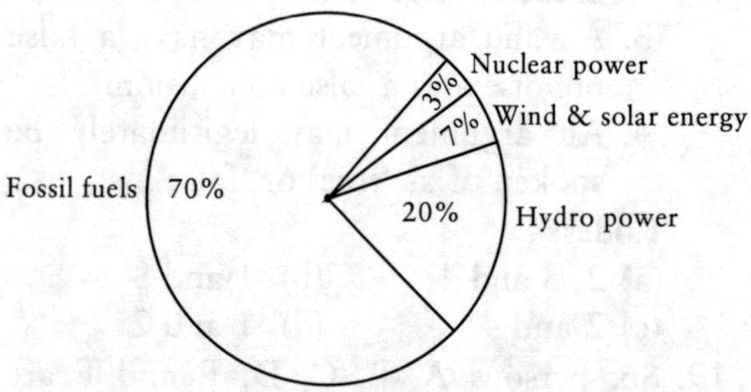

23. What is the contribution of wind and solar power in absolute terms in the electricity generation?
(a) 6.79 GW (b) 19.4 GW
(c) 9.7 GW (d) 29.1 GW

24. What is the contribution of renewable energy sources in absolute terms in the electricity generation?
(a) 29.1 GW (b) 26.19 GW
(c) 67.9 GW (d) 97 GW

25. TCP/IP is necessary if one is to connect to the
(a) Phone lines (b) LAN
(c) Internet (d) a Server

26. Each character on the keyboard of computer has an ASCII value which stands for
(a) American Stock Code for Information Interchange
(b) American Standard Code for Information Interchange
(c) African Standard Code for Information Interchange
(d) Adaptable Standard Code for Information Change

27. Which of the following is not a programming language?
(a) Pascal
(b) Microsoft Office
(c) Java
(d) C++

28. Minimum number of bits required to store any 3 digit decimal number is equal to
(a) 3 (b) 5
(c) 8 (d) 10

29. Internet explorer is a type of
(a) Operating System (b) Compiler
(c) Browser (d) IP address

30. POP3 and IMAP are e-mail accounts in which
(a) One automatically gets one's mail everyday
(b) One has to be connected to the server to read or write one's mail
(c) One only has to be connected to the server to send and receive email
(d) One does not need any telephone lines

31. Irritation in eyes is caused by the pollutant
(a) Sulphur dioxide (b) Ozone
(c) PAN (d) Nitrous oxide

32. Which is the source of chlorofluorocarbons?
(a) Thermal power plants
(b) Automobiles
(c) Refrigeration and Airconditioning
(d) Fertilizers

33. Which of the following is not a renewable natural resource?
(a) Clean air (b) Fertile soil
(c) Fresh water (d) Salt

34. Which of the following parameters is not used as a pollution indicator in water?
(a) Total dissolved solids
(b) Coliform count
(c) Dissolved oxygen
(d) Density

35. S and P waves are associated with
(a) floods (b) wind energy
(c) earthquakes (d) tidal energy

36. Match List I and List II and select the correct answer from the codes given below:

List I	List II
(A) Ozone hole	(i) Tsunami
(B) Greenhouse effect	(ii) UV radiations
(C) Natural hazards	(iii) Methane
(D) Sustainable development	(iv) Eco-centrism

Codes:	A	B	C	D
(a)	(ii)	(iii)	(i)	(iv)
(b)	(iii)	(ii)	(i)	(iv)
(c)	(iv)	(iii)	(i)	(ii)
(d)	(iv)	(ii)	(iii)	(i)

37. Indian Institute of Advanced Study is located at
(a) Dharmshala (b) Shimla
(c) Solan (d) Chandigarh

38. Indicate the number of Regional Offices of National Council of Teacher Education.
(a) 04 (b) 05
(c) 06 (d) 08

39. Which of the following rights was considered the "Heart and Soul" of the Indian Constitution by Dr. B.R. Ambedkar?
(a) Freedom of Speech
(b) Right to Equality
(c) Right to Freedom of Religion
(d) Right to Constitutional Remedies

40. Who among the following created the office of the District Collector in India?
(a) Lord Cornwallis
(b) Warren Hastings
(c) The Royal Commission on Decentralisation
(d) Sir Charles Metcalfe

41. The Fundamental Duties of a citizen include:
1. Respect for the Constitution, the National Flag and the National Anthem
2. To develop the scientific temper.
3. Respect for the Government.
4. To protect Wildlife.

Choose the correct answer from the codes given below:

Codes:
(a) 1, 2 and 3 (b) 1, 2 and 4
(c) 2, 3 and 4 (d) 1, 3, 4 and 2

42. The President of India takes oath
(a) to uphold the sovereignty and integrity of India.
(b) to bear true faith and allegiance to the Constitution of India.
(c) to uphold the Constitution and Laws of the country.
(d) to preserve, protect and defend the Constitution and the law of the country.

43. If you get an opportunity to teach a visually challenged student along with normal students, what type of treatment would you like to give him in the class?
   (a) Not giving extra attention because majority may suffer.
   (b) Take care of him sympathetically in the classroom.
   (c) You will think that blindness is his destiny and hence you cannot do anything.
   (d) Arrange a seat in the front row and try to teach at a pace convenient to him.

44. Which of the following is not a characteristic of a good achievement test?
   (a) Reliability
   (b) Objectivity
   (c) Ambiguity
   (d) Validity

45. Which of the following does not belong to a projected aid?
   (a) Overhead projector
   (b) Blackboard
   (c) Epidiascope
   (d) Slide projector

46. For a teacher, which of the following methods would be correct for writing on the blackboard?
   (a) Writing fast and as clearly as possible.
   (b) Writing the matter first and then asking students to read it.
   (c) Asking a question to students and then writing the answer as stated by them.
   (d) Writing the important points as clearly as possible.

47. A teacher can be successful if he/she
   (a) helps students in becoming better citizens
   (b) imparts subject knowledge to students
   (c) prepares students to pass the examination
   (d) presents the subject matter in a well organized manner

48. Dynamic approach to teaching means
   (a) Teaching should be forceful and effective
   (b) Teachers should be energetic and dynamic
   (c) The topics of teaching should not be static, but dynamic
   (d) The students should be required to learn through activities

49. The research that aims at immediate application is
   (a) Action Research
   (b) Empirical Research
   (c) Conceptual Research
   (d) Fundamental Research

50. When two or more successive footnotes refer to the same work which one of the following expressions is used?
   (a) ibid. (b) et al.
   (c) op. cit. (d) loc. cit.

51. Nine year olds are taller than seven year olds. This is an example of a reference drawn from
   (a) Vertical study
   (b) Cross-sectional study
   (c) Time series study
   (d) Experimental study

52. Conferences are meant for
   (a) Multiple target groups
   (b) Group discussions
   (c) Show-casing new Research
   (d) All of the above

53. Ex Post Facto research means
   (a) The research is carried out after the incident
   (b) The research is carried out prior to the incident

(c) The research is carried out along with the happening of an incident
(d) The research is carried out keeping in mind the possibilities of an incident

54. Research ethics do not include
(a) Honesty (b) Subjectivity
(c) Integrity (d) Objectivity

Read the following passage carefully and answer the questions from 55 to 60:

James Madison said, "A people who mean to be their own governors must arm themselves with power that knowledge gives." In India, the Official Secrets Act, 1923 was a convenient smokescreen to deny members of the public access to information. Public functioning has traditionally been shrouded in secrecy. But in a democracy in which people govern themselves, it is necessary to have more openness. In the maturing of our democracy, right to information is a major step forward; it enables citizens to participate fully in the decision-making process that affects their lives so profoundly. It is in this context that the address of the Prime Minister in the Lok Sabha is significant. He said, "I would only like to see that everyone, particularly our civil servants, should see the Bill in a positive spirit; not as a draconian law for paralyzing Government, but as an instrument for improving Government-Citizen interface resulting in a friendly, caring and effective Government functioning for the good of our People." He further said, "This is an innovative Bill, where there will be scope to review its functioning as we gain experience. Therefore, this is a piece of legislation, whose working will be kept under constant reviews."

The Commission, in its Report, has dealt with the application of the Right to Information in Executive, Legislature and Judiciary. The judiciary could be a pioneer in implementing the Act in letter and spirit because much of the work that the Judiciary does is open to public scrutiny, Government of India has sanctioned an e-governance project in the Judiciary for about ₹ 700 crores which would bring about systematic classification, standardization and categorization of records. This would help the judiciary to fulfil its mandate under the Act. Similar capacity building would be required in all other public authorities. The transformation from non-transparency to transparency and public accountability is the responsibility of all three organs of State.

55. A person gets power
(a) by acquiring knowledge
(b) from the Official Secrets Act, 1923
(c) through openings
(d) by denying public information

56. Right to Information is a major step forward to
(a) enable citizens to participate fully in the decision-making process
(b) to make the people aware of the Act
(c) to gain knowledge of administration
(d) to make the people Government friendly

57. The Prime Minister considered the Bill
(a) to provide power to the civil servants
(b) as an instrument for improving Government-citizen interface resulting in a friendly, caring and effective Government
(c) a draconian law against the officials
(d) to check the harassment of the people

58. The Commission made the Bill effective by
(a) extending power to the executive authorities
(b) combining the executive and legislative power
(c) recognizing Judiciary a pioneer in implementing the act in letter and spirit
(d) educating the people before its implementation

59. The Prime Minister considered the Bill innovative and hoped that
    (a) It could be reviewed based on the experience gained on its functioning.
    (b) The civil servants would see the Bill in a positive spirit.
    (c) It would not be considered as a draconian law for paralyzing Government.
    (d) All of the above.

60. The transparency and public accountability is the responsibility of three organs of the State. These three organs are
    (a) Lok Sabha, Rajya Sabha and Judiciary
    (b) Lok Sabha, Rajya Sabha and Executive
    (c) Judiciary, Legislature and the Commission
    (d) Legislature, Executive and Judiciary

ANSWERS

1. (c)	2. (b)	3. (b)	4. (b)	5. (d)
6. (a)	7. (c)	8. (b)	9. (a)	10. (c)
11. (d)	12. (a)	13. (b)	14. (b)	15. (b)
16. (a)	17. (c)	18. (c)	19. (c)	20. (a)
21. (a)	22. (c)	23. (a)	24. (b)	25. (c)
26. (b)	27. (b)	28. (d)	29. (c)	30. (c)
31. (c)	32. (c)	33. (d)	34. (d)	35. (c)
36. (a)	37. (b)	38. (a)	39. (d)	40. (b)
41. (b)	42. (d)	43. (d)	44. (c)	45. (b)
46. (d)	47. (a)	48. (d)	49. (a)	50. (a)
51. (b)	52. (d)	53. (a)	54. (b)	55. (a)
56. (a)	57. (b)	58. (c)	59. (d)	60. (d)

PAPER–II

Note: This paper contains Fifty (50) objective type questions, each question carrying two (2) marks. Attempt all the questions.

1. Sociological perspective is primarily related to an attempt to
    (a) change the social order
    (b) understand the social order
    (c) reform the social order
    (d) adjust to the social order

2. Match the items in List I with the items in List II and select the correct answer from the codes given below:

    List I (Concepts)
    (A) The poverty of Philosophy
    (B) Symbolic interactionism
    (C) Manifest and latent function
    (D) The social construction of reality

    List II (Social Scientists)
    (i) Peter Berger and T. Luckman
    (ii) Karl Marx
    (iii) Herbert Blumer
    (iv) R.K. Merton

Codes:	A	B	C	D
(a)	(i)	(iv)	(ii)	(iii)
(b)	(ii)	(iii)	(iv)	(i)
(c)	(iii)	(ii)	(i)	(iv)
(d)	(iv)	(iii)	(ii)	(i)

3. Which among the following is an example of a community?
    (a) Family (b) Marriage
    (c) Village (d) Refugee Camp

4. Emile Durkhiem defines society as
    (a) Community of ideas
    (b) Homogeneous community
    (c) Moral community
    (d) Ethical community

5. **Assertion (A):** According to Karl Marx class exploitation can be brought to an end only when the means of production is communally owned.
   Reason (R): The ruling class derives its power from the ownership and control of the means of production.
   Codes:
   (a) Both (A) and (R) are true and (R) is the correct explanation of (A).
   (b) Both (A) and (R) are true, but (R) is not the correct explanation of (A).
   (c) (A) is true, but (R) is false.
   (d) (A) is false, but (R) is true.

6. Which one among the following is an instance of social action according to Max Weber?
   (a) To cyclists colliding with each other.
   (b) Persons travelling in a train.
   (c) Two cyclists exchanging blows after they collide.
   (d) Persons opening umbrellas when it starts raining.

7. Which among the following is not, in Marxian terminology component of mode of production:
   (a) Means of production
   (b) Instruments of production
   (c) Forces of production
   (d) Relations of production

8. The Weberian model of social stratification has been used in the study of caste by
   (a) S.C. Dube
   (b) M.N. Srinivas
   (c) T.N. Madan
   (d) Andre Beteille

9. Which one among the following concepts is, according to Merton, capable of theoretically dealing with change?
   (a) Eufunction
   (b) Non-function
   (c) Quasifunction
   (d) Dysfunction

10. Sanskritization implies
    (a) Change in caste structure
    (b) Change of caste structure
    (c) Change for caste structure
    (d) None of the above

11. A teacher in carrying out his duties has to respond to the expectations of his colleagues, students and guardians of the students. These people constitute for the teachers.
    (a) Status set
    (b) Multiple roles
    (c) Role-set
    (d) None of the above

12. Which one of the following is not an institution?
    (a) Marriage
    (b) Education
    (c) Policing
    (d) Pick-pocketing

13. The prohibition of sagotra marriage among the Hindus is an example of marriage
    (a) Taboo
    (b) Clan exogamy
    (c) The rules of caste endogamy
    (d) The incest taboo

14. Which one of the following is known as the process by which cultural traits spread from one culturally distinct group to another?
    (a) Evolution
    (b) Assimilation
    (c) Accommodation
    (d) Diffusion

15. The movement of a person from the position of clerk in Calcutta headquarters of L.I.C. to that position in Delhi headquarters of L.I.C. is an example of

(a) Horizontal mobility
(b) Upward mobility
(c) Vertical mobility
(d) Downward mobility

16. When an Indian couple prepares its daughters so that she is accepted in her husband's family after her marriage, it is a case of
(a) Socialization
(b) Resocialization
(c) Anticipatory socialization
(d) Adult socialization

17. According to Durkheim, religion consists in the distinction between
(a) the sacred and the secular
(b) the pure and the impure
(c) the sacred and the profane
(d) the gods and the ghosts

18. Resocialization is clearly evident when a
(a) girl's marriage just takes place
(b) child is born
(c) person works as a member of a revolutionary party
(d) child starts going to school

19. Match the items in List I with the items in List II and choose the correct answer from the codes given below:

List I
(A) Looking-glass self
(B) Alienation
(C) Cultural lag
(D) Positivism

List II
(i) Karl Marx
(ii) William Ogburn
(iii) G.H. Mead
(iv) Auguste Comte
(v) C.H. Cooley

Codes:	A	B	C	D
(a)	(v)	(i)	(ii)	(iv)
(b)	(i)	(ii)	(iii)	(v)
(c)	(iv)	(iii)	(ii)	(i)
(d)	(iii)	(iv)	(i)	(ii)

20. Sociology in India was introduced at the institutional level after it was well-established in Europe and U.S.A. Which one among the following is the year of introduction of sociology at the formal/institutional level?
(a) 1894 (b) 1895
(c) 1939 (d) 1919

21. Match the items in List I with items in List II and select the right answer from the codes indicated below:

List I (Concept)
(A) Organic solidarity
(B) Religious Ethic
(C) Mode of Production
(D) Social evolution

List II (Sociologist)
(i) Herbert Spencer
(ii) Emile Durkheim
(iii) Vifredo Pareto
(iv) Karl Marx
(v) Max Weber

Codes:	A	B	C	D
(a)	(i)	(iii)	(iv)	(ii)
(b)	(ii)	(i)	(v)	(iii)
(c)	(v)	(iii)	(iv)	(i)
(d)	(ii)	(v)	(iv)	(i)

22. Match the items in the List I with the items in List II and select the correct answer from the codes given below:

List I
(A) Acculturation (B) Assimilation
(C) Accommodation (D) Integration

List II
(i) A condition in which people may work together even though there are differences which separate them
(ii) A process of adaptation in which elements of a culture form a composite whole

(iii) A condition in which people of a culture tend to acquire some elements of other culture and leave some elements of their own
(iv) A process wherein a minority group gradually gives up its own cultural patterns and acquire those of the dominant

Codes:	A	B	C	D
(a)	(i)	(ii)	(iii)	(iv)
(b)	(iii)	(iv)	(i)	(ii)
(c)	(ii)	(iii)	(iv)	(i)
(d)	(iii)	(iv)	(ii)	(i)

23. Which one of the following is an example of ascribed status?
(a) Teacher
(b) Student
(c) Brahmin
(d) Doctor

24. Tertiary sector is also known as
(a) Processing sector
(b) Forestry sector
(c) Mining sector
(d) Services sector

25. Match the items in List I with the items in List II and select the correct answer from the codes given below:

List I
(A) *Homo Hierarchicus*
(B) *The Savage Mind*
(C) *Caste, Class and Power*
(D) *Caste in Modern India and other Essays*

List II
(i) Claude Levi-Strauss
(ii) Andre Beteille
(iii) M.N. Srinivas
(iv) Louis Dumont

Codes:	A	B	C	D
(a)	(iii)	(ii)	(i)	(iv)
(b)	(ii)	(iii)	(iv)	(i)
(c)	(iv)	(i)	(ii)	(iii)
(d)	(i)	(ii)	(iii)	(iv)

26. Rise of new technologies in the sphere of information and communication leading to greater globalization is a future of
(a) Agrarian Society
(b) Industrial Society
(c) Post-Industrial Society
(d) Rural Society

27. Which of the following thinkers used a system of binary opposition in structural approach to social phenomena?
(a) Nadel
(b) Radcliffe-Brown
(c) Levi-Strauss
(d) Malinowski

28. Which of the following is correct according to Mead:
(a) Self can also emerge in the absence of social experience.
(b) Self does not allow people to take part in conversation with others.
(c) Body becomes a self only when a mind has developed.
(d) Mind and self can be separated from each other.

29. Which of the following does not represent the Dahrendorf's theory of conflict?
(a) Social change is ubiquitous in human society
(b) Conflict can be both latent and manifest
(c) Every society experiences social conflict
(d) Economic and social inequalities are the sole sources of conflict

30. Which of the following statements represents the functional theory of Emile Durkhiem?

(a) Society does not necessarily go through the fixed stages of development
(b) A whole is not identical to the sum of its parts
(c) Social phenomena can be reduced to individuals phenomena
(d) Collective will emanate from human will

31. Functionalism constitutes an important element in the social theories of
(a) E. Durkheim and C. Levi-Strauss
(b) E. Durkheim and Max Weber
(c) Talcott Parsons and Karl Marx
(d) A.R. Radcliffe-Brown and R.K. Merton

32. Choose the correct sequence of Parsons' schema of social action and social system
(a) Social system, cultural system, personality system and biological organism
(b) Personality system, cultural system, social system and biological system
(c) Biological organism, personality system, social system and cultural system
(d) Cultural system, biological system, personality system and social system

33. Match the items in List I with the items in List II and choose the right answer from the codes given below:

List I
(A) Malinowski (B) Durkheim
(C) Parsons (D) Merton

List II
(i) Pattern variables
(ii) Postulates of functional analysis
(iii) Collective consciousness
(iv) Biological need-based functionality

Codes:	**A**	**B**	**C**	**D**
(a)	(i)	(ii)	(iii)	(iv)
(b)	(ii)	(iii)	(i)	(iv)
(c)	(iii)	(iv)	(ii)	(i)
(d)	(iv)	(iii)	(i)	(ii)

34. Basic principles of symbolic interactionism include
(a) Human capacity for thought
(b) Social institutions and social interactions
(c) Mind and social consciousness
(d) Meanings and symbols that facilitate action and interaction

Select the correct answer from the codes given below:

Codes:
(a) (a) and (b)
(b) (b) and (c)
(c) (c) and (d)
(d) (a) and (d)

35. There are two statements, one is Assertion (A) and the other is Reason (R). Select the correct answer from the codes given below:

Assertion (A): People are able to order a world that otherwise would be confusing.

Reason (R): Symbols enable people to deal with the material and social world by allowing them to name, categorise and remember what they encounter.

Select the correct answer from the codes given below:

Codes:
(a) Both (A) and (R) are true and (R) is the correct explanation of (A).
(b) Both (A) and (R) are true, but (R) is not the correct explanation of (A).
(c) (A) is true, but (R) is false.
(d) (A) is false, but (R) is true.

36. Which one of the following, thinkers observed that conflict is likely to occur in social relations because violent coercion can always be used by people in an interaction setting?
(a) Collins
(b) Simmel
(c) Dohrendorf
(d) Coser

37. Who, among the following, has emphasized the positive functions of the conflict in society?
(a) Lewis A. Coser
(b) Karl Marx
(c) Max Weber
(d) Emile Durkheim

38. According to Durkheim, the nature of Modern law is
(a) Repressive
(b) Restitutive
(c) Normative
(d) Formal

39. Which of the following is not regarded as the characteristic feature of scientific method?
(a) Reliability
(b) Validity
(c) Replicability
(d) Common sense observation

40. The purpose of the survey is
(a) In depth study of social phenomena
(b) Extensive coverage of population
(c) Testing of a theory
(d) Establishing causal linkage

41. Which of the following is associated with Descriptive Design?
(a) Analysis of Demographic Trends
(b) Impact assessment of development intervention
(c) Causal explanation of violence against women
(d) Cross-cultural study

42. In which of the following types of research, hypothesis is a pre-requisite?
(a) Biographical study
(b) Experimental study
(c) Interpretative research
(d) Critical research

43. Which type of sampling method is ideally suited, where there is no knowledge about population?
(a) Convenient sampling method
(b) Purposive sampling method
(c) Quota sampling method
(d) Snowball sampling method

44. Participant observation method is ideally suited for the study of
(i) Tribal Culture
(ii) National Culture
(iii) Ethnographic study
(iv) Phenomenon of Globalisation
Select the correct answer from the codes given below:
(a) (i) and (ii)
(b) (i) and (iii)
(c) (i) and (iv)
(d) (iii) and (ii)

45. There are two statements, one is Assertion (A) and the other is Reason (R). Select the correct answer from the codes given below:
Assertion (A): Qualitative methods are often criticized for failing to meet the same standards of reliability.
Reason (R): The procedures used to collect data in qualitative studies are precise and accurate.
Codes:
(a) Both (A) and (R) are true and (R) is the correct explanation of (A).
(b) Both (A) and (R) are true, but (R) is not the correct explanation of (A).
(c) (A) is true, but (R) is false.
(d) (A) is false, but (R) is true.

46. There are two statements, one is Assertion (A) and the other is Reason (R). Select the correct answer from the codes given below:

Assertion (A): Life history research can help to raise people's consciousness and awareness of their exploitation.

Reason (R): Life history research encourages people to reflect upon the factors that have shaped thin life experiences.

Codes:

(a) Both (A) and (R) are true and (R) is the correct explanation of (A).
(b) Both (A) and (R) are true, but (R) is not the correct explanation of (A).
(c) (A) is true, but (R) is false.
(d) (A) is false, but (R) is true.

47. Match List I with the List II and mark the correct answer from the codes given below the lists:

List I

(A) Central Tendency
(B) Dispersion
(C) Correlation
(D) Test of Significance

List II

(i) Mean Deviation
(ii) Pearson's coefficient
(iii) Mean
(iv) 't'-test

Codes:	**A**	**B**	**C**	**D**
(a)	(i)	(ii)	(iv)	(iii)
(b)	(ii)	(iii)	(iv)	(i)
(c)	(iii)	(i)	(ii)	(iv)
(d)	(iv)	(iii)	(ii)	(i)

48. When a particular technique applied repeatedly to the same object producing the same result each time, it is said to have

(a) Validity (b) Reliability
(c) Probability (d) Subjectivity

49. Observe the following Table and answer the question given below:

Age Group	Frequency
20 – 29	04
30 – 39	06
40 – 49	09
50 – 59	12
60 – 69	15
70 – 79	09
80 – 89	04

In the distribution shown above the median falls in the interval between:

(a) 40 – 49 (b) 50 – 59
(c) 60 – 69 (d) 70 – 79

50. Calculation of number of deaths per thousand people falls under the measure of

(a) Nominal scale
(b) Ordinal scale
(c) Ratio scale
(d) Interval scale

ANSWERS

1. (b)	2. (b)	3. (c)	4. (c)	5. (a)
6. (c)	7. (b)	8. (d)	9. (d)	10. (a)
11. (c)	12. (d)	13. (b)	14. (d)	15. (a)
16. (c)	17. (c)	18. (c)	19. (a)	20. (d)
21. (d)	22. (b)	23. (c)	24. (d)	25. (c)
26. (c)	27. (c)	28. (c)	29. (d)	30. (b)
31. (d)	32. (c)	33. (d)	34. (d)	35. (a)
36. (a)	37. (a)	38. (b)	39. (d)	40. (b)
41. (a)	42. (b)	43. (d)	44. (b)	45. (c)
46. (a)	47. (c)	48. (b)	49. (b)	50. (c)

PAPER–III

Note: This paper contains seventy-five (75) objective type questions, each question carrying two (2) marks. All questions are compulsory.

1. According to Ethnomethodologists, which type of reasoning is used by the people?
   (a) Inductive Reasoning
   (b) Deductive Reasoning
   (c) Practical Reasoning
   (d) No Reasoning

2. 'Conversational analysis' is a part of which of the following methodologies?
   (a) Phenomenology
   (b) Verstehen
   (c) Ethnomethodology
   (d) Structuralism

3. When was 'Ethnomethodology' used for the first time?
   (a) 1940's
   (b) 1950's
   (c) 1960's
   (d) 1970's

4. "The 'self' in modern society becomes a sacred object in the same way that the collective symbols of primitive societies." Who has propounded this view?
   (a) Weber
   (b) Durkheim
   (c) Mead
   (d) Goffman

5. Who has written the work, *The Social Construction of Reality*?
   (a) Peter L. Berger
   (b) Thomas Luckmann
   (c) Both Berger and Luckmann
   (d) None of the above

6. Match List I with List II:

   List I
   (A) *Social Construction of Reality*
   (B) *Phenomenology of Social World*
   (C) *Presentation of Self in Every Day Life*
   (D) *Studies in Ethnomethodology*

   List II
   (i) Harold Garfinkel
   (ii) Irwin Goffman
   (iii) Berger and Luckmann
   (iv) Alfred Schutz

   Mark the correct answer from the codes given below:

Codes:	**A**	**B**	**C**	**D**
(a)	(i)	(ii)	(iii)	(iv)
(b)	(ii)	(iii)	(iv)	(i)
(c)	(iii)	(iv)	(ii)	(i)
(d)	(iv)	(ii)	(i)	(iii)

7. "Neo-functionalism operates with descriptive model of society that sees society as composed of elements which form a pattern." Who has stated this view?
   (a) P. Colomy
   (b) J. Alexander
   (c) T. Parsons
   (d) R.K. Merton

8. Who has written the book *Theoretical Logic in Sociology*?
   (a) N.J. Smelser
   (b) J.C. Alexander
   (c) Paul Colomy
   (d) Bernhard Giesen

9. Which problems neo-functionalism needed to surmount?
   (a) Anti individualism and idealism
   (b) Antagonism to change and anti-empirical bias
   (c) Both (a) and (b)
   (d) None of the above

10. How does critical school of theorists rectify the imbalance of economic determinism and other aspects of social life?
    (a) By focusing on economic and social realm.
    (b) By focusing on economic and historical realm.
    (c) By focusing on economic and cultural realm.
    (d) By focusing on economic and productive realm.
11. According to neo-Marxists, which of the ideas about human nature have often been used to argue against any social change?
    (a) Our natural greed and our natural gender differences
    (b) Our natural tendency to violence.
    (c) Both (a) and (b)
    (d) None of the above
12. Who considers 'structure as a model' of social world and 'not a reality' among the structuralists?
    (a) Levi-Strauss
    (b) Freud
    (c) Marx
    (d) Lemert
13. Who considers 'language as disorderly and unstable' in his concept of "Deconstruction"?
    (a) Derrida
    (b) Godelier
    (c) Foucault
    (d) Lemer
14. In the context of post-structuralism who has argued that 'what takes place on the stage "represents" what takes place in "real life" ...'?
    (a) Foucault
    (b) Giddens
    (c) Derrida
    (d) Dean
15. Who said to have articulated integration of 'agency and structure' in structuration theory?
    (a) Michael Foucault
    (b) J. Derrida
    (c) Anthony Giddens
    (d) J.M. Bernstein
16. Who has named 'juggernaut' to describe an advance stage of modernity?
    (a) Michael Foucault
    (b) Anthony Giddens
    (c) Max Weber
    (d) David Frisby
17. Which one of the following is not an indicator of cultural diversity in India?
    (a) Race (b) Caste
    (c) Class (d) Religion
18. Who has indicated diversities of Indian culture and contributed a book *Diversities*?
    (a) R.K. Mukherjee
    (b) D.P. Mukherjee
    (c) G.S. Ghurye
    (d) S.C. Dube
19. Who has edited the voluminous work *People of India*?
    (a) G.S. Ghurye
    (b) S.C. Dube
    (c) Yogendra Singh
    (d) K.S. Singh
20. Which are the works of G.S. Ghurye?
    I. *Tribal Heritage of India*
    II. *Cities and Civilization*
    III. *Culture and Society*
    IV. *Indian Sadhus*

    Select the correct answer from the codes given below:

    Codes:
    (a) IV only
    (b) I, III, IV
    (c) II, III, IV
    (d) I, II, III, IV

21. Match List I with List II:

List I (Authors)

(A) S.C. Dube
(B) M.N. Srinivas
(C) G.S. Ghurye
(D) B.R. Ambedkar

List II (Books)

(i) *India's Village*
(ii) *Caste and Race in India*
(iii) *Castes in India: Their Mechanism, Genesis and Development*
(iv) *Indian Village*

Select the correct answer from the codes given below:

Codes:	**A**	**B**	**C**	**D**
(a)	(i)	(ii)	(iii)	(iv)
(b)	(iv)	(i)	(ii)	(iii)
(c)	(iv)	(i)	(iii)	(ii)
(d)	(i)	(iv)	(ii)	(iii)

22. Who has opined that...Indian civilization has a specific ideology whose components are in a binary opposition to that of the West: modern against traditional, holism against individualism, hierarchy against equality, purity against pollution, status against power, etc.?
(a) Louis Dumont
(b) David Hardiman
(c) N.K. Bose
(d) G.S. Ghurye

23. Who is of the view that caste and untouchability do not let Hindus act as a community?
(a) David Hardiman
(b) Louis Dumont
(c) B.R. Ambedkar
(d) M.N. Srinivas

24. Which theoretical perspective is based on the view that liberty is neither received as a gift; it has to be fought for. Self-elevation is not achieved by the blessings of others but by self-struggle?
(a) Marxian
(b) Structural
(c) Subaltern
(d) Civilizational

25. Provisions for divorce among Hindus are provided under Hindu Marriage Act of which year?
(a) 1955 (b) 1956
(c) 1961 (d) 1973

26. The concept of 'Symmetrical Family' has been propounded by
(a) Young and Willmott
(b) Oakley
(c) Bauman and Smart
(d) Smart

27. The Dowry Prohibition (Amendment) Act was passed in which of the following years?
(a) 1963 (b) 1965
(c) 1984 (d) 1961

28. Which type of poverty involves assessing the gaps between the living conditions of some groups and those enjoyed by the majority of a population?
(a) Enforced poverty
(b) Culture of poverty
(c) Relative poverty
(d) Absolute poverty

29. According to whose argument "some conflict is functional because it serves as a safety valve, without which social hostility would eventually erupt violently"?
(a) Coser
(b) Marx
(c) Dahrendorf
(d) Gluckman

30. Given below are two statements, one labelled as Assertion (A) and the other labelled as Reason (R):

Assertion (A): Metropolitan cities are dominated by large size slums.

Reason (R): There has been large-scale migration of rural population to urban centres with the growth of industries and job opportunities.

In the context of the above statement, which one of the following is correct?

Codes:

(a) Both (A) and (R) are true, but (R) is not the correct explanation of (A).
(b) Both (A) and (R) are true and (R) is the correct explanation of (A).
(c) (A) is true, but (R) is false.
(d) (A) is false, but (R) is true.

31. Given below are two statements, one labelled as Assertion (A) and the other labelled as Reason (R):

Assertion (A): High growth of population is an indicator of low level of development in the society.

Reason (R): High birth rate is related to illiteracy and poverty in the society.

In the context of the above statements, which one of the following is correct?

Codes:

(a) Both (A) and (R) are true, but (R) is not the correct explanation of (A).
(b) Both (A) and (R) are true and (R) is the correct explanation of (A).
(c) (A) is true, but (R) is false.
(d) (A) is false, but (R) is true.

32. Given below are two statements one is labelled as Assertion (A) and the other labelled as Reason (R):

Assertion (A): Economic regional disparities exist in India.

Reason (R): Economic regional disparity is an outcome of allocation of budget by the Government.

In the context of the above statement, which one of the following is correct?

Codes:

(a) Both (A) and (R) are true and (R) is the correct explanation of (A).
(b) Both (A) and (R) are true, but (R) is not the correct explanation of (A).
(c) (A) is true, but (R) is false.
(d) (A) is false, but (R) is true.

33. Match the item in List I with the items in List II.

List I

(A) Chipko Movement
(B) Naxalbari Movement
(C) Narmada Bachao Andolan
(D) Ganga Bachao Andolan

List II

(i) Charu Mazumdar
(ii) Medha Patekar
(iii) Sunder Lal Bahuguna
(iv) G.D. Aggarwal

Choose the correct answer from the codes given below:

Codes:	A	B	C	D
(a)	(i)	(ii)	(iii)	(iv)
(b)	(iii)	(i)	(ii)	(iv)
(c)	(ii)	(iii)	(i)	(iv)
(d)	(iv)	(ii)	(i)	(iii)

34. "Imprisonment promotes the process of prisonisation." Which theory is against this view?

(a) Retributive Theory of Punishment
(b) Deterrent Theory of Punishment
(c) Reformative Theory of Punishment
(d) All of the above theories

35. The term 'White-Collar Crime' was first introduced by

(a) C. Barnes
(b) E. Sutherland
(c) A. Cohen
(d) E. Durkheim

36. Nepotism, favouritism and misuse of power are all examples of
(a) Corruption
(b) Ignorance
(c) Conflict
(d) Social solidarity

37. Sampurnanand Ashram is the first 'Open Prison', established in which State?
(a) Madhya Pradesh
(b) Uttar Pradesh
(c) Bihar
(d) Kerala

38. Prison Vocational Training Programmes were introduced for inmates'
(a) Reformation
(b) Rehabilitation
(c) Reformation and Rehabilitation
(d) None of the above

39. According to whom "Societies characterized by too much or too little regulation or integration will have high suicide rates"?
(a) Parsons
(b) Weber
(c) Durkheim
(d) Merton

40. Who has argued that 'punishment is a social reaction to crime, it serves not simply the functions of retribution for the criminal and general deterrence of crime but also maintaining the objection to criminal activity'?
(a) Merton
(b) Parsons
(c) Durkheim
(d) Coser

41. Match the List I with List II given below:

List I (Theories)
(A) Labelling Theory
(B) Imitation Theory
(C) Delinquent Sub-culture Theory
(D) Theory of Suicide

List II (Thinkers)
(i) Tarde
(ii) Becker
(iii) Durkheim
(iv) Cohen

Mark the correct answer from the codes given below:

Codes:	**A**	**B**	**C**	**D**
(a)	(i)	(ii)	(iii)	(iv)
(b)	(ii)	(i)	(iv)	(iii)
(c)	(iv)	(iii)	(ii)	(i)
(d)	(iii)	(iv)	(ii)	(i)

42. Which is the correct sequence of tribal rebellions which took place during the early days of the British rule in 18th and 19th centuries?
(a) Kacha Nagas Rebellion, Birsa Movement among Mundas, Kol Rebellion, Santhal Rebellion
(b) Santhal Rebellion, Kol Rebellion, Birsa Movement among Mundas, Kacha Nagas Rebellion
(c) Kol Rebellion, Santhal Rebellion, Kacha Nagas Rebellion, Birsa Movement among Mundas
(d) Kol Rebellion, Birsa Movement among Mundas, Kacha Nagas Rebellion, Santhal Rebellion

43. Given below are two statements, one is labelled as Assertion (A) and the other as Reason (R):
Assertion (A): In a plural society minority groups often develop mistrust of the majority.
Reason (R): Minority groups are frequent targets of prejudice and discrimination.
Choose the correct answer from the given codes:

Codes:
(a) Both (A) and (R) are true and (R) is the correct explanation of (A).
(b) Both (A) and (R) are true, but (R) is not the correct explanation of (A).
(c) (A) is true, but (R) is false.
(d) (A) is false, but (R) is true.

44. 'Even change in Indian society can be understood by studying its traditions." Who has argued this?
(a) Radha Kamal Mukherjee
(b) D.P. Mukherjee
(c) M.N. Srinivas
(d) S.C. Dube

45. Match the concepts given in List I with the authors given in List II:
List I (Concepts)
(A) Sanskritisation, Westernisation and Modernisation
(B) Universalisation and Parochialisation
(C) Great Tradition and Little Tradition
(D) Universalism Vs. Particularism
List II (Authors)
(i) Mckim Marriot
(ii) Robert Redfield
(iii) M.N. Srinivas
(iv) T. Parsons
(v) B. Malinowski
Select the correct answer from the codes given below:

Codes:	**A**	**B**	**C**	**D**
(a)	(ii)	(i)	(iii)	(v)
(b)	(v)	(ii)	(i)	(iii)
(c)	(iii)	(ii)	(i)	(v)
(d)	(iv)	(i)	(ii)	(iii)

46. Which of the following processes assumes that no special esoteric supernatural forces operate within the world, and that life can be lived in accordance with human rationality?
(a) Secularization
(b) Modernization
(c) Westernization
(d) Desacralization

47. Who, among the following, are associated with Indianisation of Sociology?
(a) G.S. Ghurye, A.K. Saran, D.P. Mukherjee
(b) G.S. Ghurye, T.K. Oommen, A.K. Saran
(c) G.S. Ghurye, A.R. Desai, D.P. Mukerjee
(d) G.S. Ghurye, T.K. Oommen, A.R. Desai

48. Who has argued that 'an empirical sociology of Indian society is not possible'?
(a) G.S. Ghurye
(b) M.N. Srinivas
(c) A.K. Saran
(d) S.C. Dube

49. Who among the early sociologists of India introduced a down-to-earth empiricism in Indian Sociology and Social Anthropology?
(a) G.S. Ghurye
(b) R.K. Mukherjee
(c) A.K. Saran
(d) None of the above

50. Privatization of Education is a consequence of which one of the following?
(a) Urbanization
(b) Globalization
(c) Development of Science and Technology
(d) Increase in Population

51. Who has used the term 'Faction' in the study of rural society at first?

(a) Oscar Lewis
(b) S.C. Dube
(c) Raymond Firth
(d) None of the above

52. Indian Rural Development Programmes widened the gap between rich and poor which resulted into negative consequences
(a) suicides among farmers
(b) richness of farmers
(c) depeasantisation of farmers
(d) depeasantisation and suicides of farmers

53. Jajmani system can best be explained by
(a) mutual trust and co-operation of the people
(b) conflicting interest of the people
(c) oppression and suppressive measures adopted by the jajmans
(d) conflicting interest and distrust of the people

54. 'Rurbanism' is a term that is related to the study of
(a) Villages
(b) Town and cities
(c) Rural areas
(d) Lifestyles of rural-urban people

55. Match List I with List II.

List I
(A) Village India
(B) Indian Village
(C) A Rajasthan Village
(D) The Remembered Village

List II
(i) S.C. Dube
(ii) M.N. Srinivas
(iii) Mckim Marriott
(iv) B.R. Chauhan

Mark the correct answer from the following codes:

Codes:	**A**	**B**	**C**	**D**
(a)	(iv)	(i)	(ii)	(iii)
(b)	(iii)	(i)	(iv)	(ii)
(c)	(ii)	(iii)	(iv)	(i)
(d)	(i)	(ii)	(iii)	(iv)

56. Match List I with List II.

List I (Authors)
(A) B.R. Virmani
(B) S.R. Parker and R.K. Brown et al.
(C) E.V. Schneider
(D) Paul Blumberg

List II (Books)
(i) *Sociology of Industry*
(ii) *Worker's Participation in Management*
(iii) *Industrial Democracy*
(iv) *Industrial Sociology*

Select the correct answer from the codes given below:

Codes:	**A**	**B**	**C**	**D**
(a)	(iv)	(i)	(ii)	(iii)
(b)	(ii)	(i)	(iv)	(iii)
(c)	(i)	(iii)	(ii)	(iv)
(d)	(ii)	(iii)	(iv)	(i)

57. Which is/are the possible ways to settle the industrial disputes between employers and workers by the outsiders?
I. Conciliation
II. Compromise
III. Adjudication
IV. Arbitration

Codes:
(a) I, III, IV
(b) IV only
(c) III only
(d) II, III, IV

58. **Assertion (A):** Nepotism and corruption are rampant in Indian society.
Reason (R): These are due to democracy and bureaucracy.

Codes:
(a) (A) is true, but (R) is false.
(b) Both (A) and (R) are true.
(c) (A) is false and (R) is true.
(d) Both (A) and (R) are false.

59. What is trade union?
(a) An association
(b) Organized interest group
(c) Federation
(d) All of the above

60. Mark the correct sequence of the processes of social stratification:
(a) Evaluation, differentiation, ranking, rewarding
(b) Differentiation, ranking, evaluation, rewarding
(c) Ranking, evaluation, differentiation, rewarding
(d) Differentiation, evaluation, rewarding, ranking

61. Human Development Index (HDI) used by Prof. Mahbubul Haque in order to measure the level of development amongst various countries include the following set of indicators. Mark the right answer.
(a) Health, Education and Income
(b) Freedom, Equality and Fraternity
(c) Equity, Social justice and Liberty
(d) Openness, Freedom and Equality

62. Arrange the following official international conferences on sustainable development in chronological order. Use the codes given below:
I. The Stockholm Conference
II. World Conservation Strategy
III. World Commission on Environment
IV. 'Global 2000' Commission

Codes:
(a) I, II, III, IV
(b) I, IV, II, III
(c) II, III, I, IV
(d) III, II, IV, I

63. Match List I with List II and mark the correct codes given below:

List I
(A) M.K. Gandhi
(B) J.L. Nehru
(C) Amartya Sen
(D) Vinoba Bhave

List II
(i) *Swadeshi Model of Development*
(ii) *Mixed Model of Development*
(iii) *Social Capability Model of Development*
(iv) *Sarvodaya Model of Development*

Codes:	A	B	C	D
(a)	(i)	(ii)	(iii)	(iv)
(b)	(ii)	(iii)	(iv)	(i)
(c)	(iii)	(ii)	(i)	(iv)
(d)	(iv)	(iii)	(ii)	(i)

64. Match List I with List II and mark the correct codes given below:

List I
(A) Centreperiphery
(B) Open-close societies
(C) Centre-Semiperiphery
(D) Trusteeship

List II
(i) M.K. Gandhi
(ii) Samir Amin
(iii) Gunnar Myrdal
(iv) Andre Gunder Frank
(v) Amrita Sen

Codes:	A	B	C	D
(a)	(v)	(iii)	(ii)	(i)
(b)	(iv)	(iii)	(ii)	(i)
(c)	(i)	(ii)	(iii)	(v)
(d)	(ii)	(i)	(iv)	(iii)

65. Match List I (Scientists) and the List II (Theories of Development) given below:

List I (Scientists)
(A) A.G. Frank
(B) Gunnar Myrdal
(C) Max Weber
(D) Samir Amin

List II (Theories of Development)
(i) Soft State
(ii) Uneven development
(iii) Cultural
(iv) Centreperiphery

Select the correct answer from the codes given below:

Codes:	A	B	C	D
(a)	(i)	(iv)	(iii)	(ii)
(b)	(iv)	(i)	(iii)	(ii)
(c)	(ii)	(i)	(iii)	(iv)
(d)	(i)	(ii)	(iii)	(iv)

66. Warren S. Thompson is known for his
(a) Cyclic Theory
(b) Demographic Transition Model
(c) Optimum Population Theory
(d) Social Capillarity Theory

67. Population pyramid is graphic representation of which aspect of population?
(a) Mortality and life expectancy
(b) Age-sex distribution at a given time.
(c) Fertility and birth control.
(d) Mortality and fertility ratio.

68. The following thinkers have contributed to the study of population. Arrange them in chronological order and choose the correct codes.
I. Thomas Malthus
II. Warren S. Thompson
III. Kingsley Davis
IV. Herbert Spencer

Codes:
(a) I, II, III, IV
(b) I, III, II, IV
(c) II, III, IV, I
(d) I, II, IV, III

69. Match the items in List I with the items in List II and choose the correct answer from the codes given below:

List I (Ideas)
(A) Geometric growth of population and arithmetic growth of food supply
(B) Diet Theory
(C) Optimum Population Theory
(D) Social Capillarity

List II (Author)
(i) Doubleday
(ii) Herbert Spencer
(iii) Dalton
(iv) Dumont
(v) Thomas Malthus

Codes:	A	B	C	D
(a)	(i)	(ii)	(iv)	(iii)
(b)	(ii)	(iii)	(iv)	(i)
(c)	(v)	(i)	(iii)	(iv)
(d)	(iii)	(iv)	(i)	(v)

70. Match the items in List I with the items in List II and choose the correct answer from the codes given below:

List I (Books)
(A) *Demography*
(B) *Social Demography: A Systematic Exposition*
(C) *Population and Society*
(D) *Population of India and Pakistan*

List II (Authors)
(i) M.K. Premi
(ii) David M. Heer
(iii) Peter R. Cox
(iv) Kingsley Davis

Codes:	A	B	C	D
(a)	(iii)	(ii)	(iv)	(i)
(b)	(iv)	(iii)	(i)	(ii)
(c)	(iii)	(i)	(ii)	(iv)
(d)	(i)	(ii)	(iii)	(iv)

71. What was the chapter about women which appeared in the Sixth Five-Year Plan?
(a) Women and Welfare Schemes
(b) Women and Development
(c) Women and Education
(d) Women and Health

72. Given below are two statements, one is labelled as Assertion (A) and other as Reason (R):
Assertion (A): Gender as the basis of social inequality is structured into female and male spheres.
Reason (R): All women are not equally unequal in their families and communities.
Select the correct answer from the codes given below:
Codes:
(a) (A) is true, but (R) is false.
(b) Both (A) and (R) are false.
(c) Both (A) and (R) are true, but (R) is not the correct explanation of (A).
(d) (A) is false and (R) is true.

73. Match the List I with the List II given below:
List I (Acts)
(A) Equal Remuneration Act
(B) Domestic Violence Act
(C) National Commission for Women Act
(D) Indecent Representation of Women (Prohibition) Act

List II (Years)
(i) 1990 (ii) 1976
(iii) 1986 (iv) 2005

Select the correct answer from the codes given below:

Codes:	**A**	**B**	**C**	**D**
(a)	(ii)	(iv)	(i)	(iii)
(b)	(ii)	(i)	(iv)	(iii)
(c)	(i)	(iv)	(ii)	(iii)
(d)	(ii)	(iii)	(i)	(iv)

74. Match the List I with the List II given below:
List I (Theories of Gender relations)
(A) Liberal
(B) Radical
(C) Socialist
(D) Postmodernist

List II (Thinkers)
(i) Cixous, Irigaray
(ii) Clara Zetkin, Juliet Mitchell
(iii) Kate Millet, Mary Daly
(iv) Mary Wollstone Craft, Betty Frieden

Select the correct answer from the codes given below:

Codes:	**A**	**B**	**C**	**D**
(a)	(iv)	(iii)	(i)	(ii)
(b)	(iii)	(iv)	(i)	(ii)
(c)	(iv)	(i)	(iii)	(ii)
(d)	(iv)	(iii)	(ii)	(i)

75. Given below are two statements, one is labelled as Assertion (A) and the other as Reason (R):
Assertion (A): It is not sex but gender has been accepted as a form of social stratification.
Reason (R): Women are biologically not equal to men.
Select the correct answer from the codes given below:
Codes:
(a) (A) is false, but (R) is true.
(b) (A) is true, but (R) is false.
(c) Both (A) and (R) are true, but (R) is not the correct explanation of (A).
(d) Both (A) and (R) are true and (R) is the correct explanation of (A).

ANSWERS

1. (c)	2. (c)	3. (a)	4. (c)	5. (c)
6. (c)	7. (b)	8. (b)	9. (c)	10. (c)
11. (c)	12. (a)	13. (a)	14. (c)	15. (c)
16. (b)	17. (c)	18. (b)	19. (d)	20. (c)
21. (b)	22. (a)	23. (c)	24. (c)	25. (a)
26. (a)	27. (c)	28. (c)	29. (a)	30. (b)
31. (b)	32. (a)	33. (b)	34. (c)	35. (b)
36. (a)	37. (b)	38. (c)	39. (c)	40. (c)
41. (b)	42. (c)	43. (a)	44. (b)	45. (c)
46. (d)	47. (a)	48. (c)	49. (a)	50. (b)
51. (c)	52. (d)	53. (a)	54. (d)	55. (b)
56. (b)	57. (a)	58. (a)	59. (b)	60. (b)
61. (a)	62. (b)	63. (a)	64. (b)	65. (b)
66. (b)	67. (b)	68. (d)	69. (c)	70. (c)
71. (b)	72. (c)	73. (a)	74. (d)	75. (c)

DECEMBER–2011

Note: This paper contains Sixty (60) multiple-choice questions, each question carrying two (2) marks. Candidate is expected to answer any Fifty (50) questions. In case more than Fifty (50) questions are attempted, only the first Fifty (50) questions will be evaluated.

PAPER–I

1. Photo bleeding means
   (a) Photo cropping
   (b) Photo placement
   (c) Photo cutting
   (d) Photo colour adjustment

2. While designing communication strategy feed-forward studies are conducted by
   (a) Audience (b) Communicator
   (c) Satellite (d) Media

3. In which language the newspapers have highest circulation?
   (a) English (b) Hindi
   (c) Bengali (d) Tamil

4. Aspect ratio of TV Screen is
   (a) 4 : 3 (b) 3 : 4
   (c) 2 : 3 (d) 2 : 4

5. Communication with oneself is known as
   (a) Organisational Communication
   (b) Grapevine Communication
   (c) Interpersonal Communication
   (d) Intrapersonal Communication

6. The term 'SITE' stands for
   (a) Satellite Indian Television Experiment
   (b) Satellite International Television Experiment
   (c) Satellite Instructional Television Experiment
   (d) Satellite Instructional Teachers Education

7. What is the number that comes next in the sequence?
   2, 5, 9, 19, 37, ___
   (a) 76 (b) 74
   (c) 75 (d) 50

8. Find the next letter for the series MPSV.....
   (a) X (b) Y
   (c) Z (d) A

9. If '367' means 'I am happy'; '748' means 'you are sad' and '469' means 'happy and sad' in a given code, then which of the following represents 'and' in that code?
   (a) 3 (b) 6
   (c) 9 (d) 4

10. The basis of the following classification is 'animal', 'man', 'house', 'book', and 'student':
    (a) Definite descriptions
    (b) Proper names
    (c) Descriptive phrases
    (d) Common names

11. **Assertion (A):** The coin when flipped next time will come up tails.

    Reason (R): Because the coin was flipped five times in a row, and each time it came up heads.

    Choose the correct answer from below:
    (a) Both (A) and (R) are true and (R) is the correct explanation of (A).

(b) Both (A) and (R) are false, and (R) is the correct explanation of (A).
(c) (A) is doubtful, (R) is true, and (R) is not the correct explanation of (A).
(d) (A) is doubtful, (R) is false, and (R) is the correct explanation of (A).

12. The relation 'is a sister of' is
(a) non-symmetrical
(b) symmetrical
(c) asymmetrical
(d) transitive

13. If the proposition "Vegetarians are not meat eaters" is false, then which of the following inferences is correct? Choose from the codes given below:
1. "Some vegetarians are meat eaters" is true.
2. "All vegetarians are meat eaters" is doubtful.
3. "Some vegetarians are not meat eaters" is true.
4. "Some vegetarians are not meat eaters" is doubtful.

Codes:
(a) 1, 2 and 3 (b) 2, 3 and 4
(c) 1, 3 and 4 (d) 1, 2 and 4

14. Determine the nature of the following definition:
'Poor' means having an annual income of ₹ 10,000.
(a) Persuasive (b) Precising
(c) Lexical (d) Stipulative

15. Which one of the following is not an argument?
(a) If today is Tuesday, tomorrow will be Wednesday.
(b) Since today is Tuesday, tomorrow will be Wednesday.
(c) Ram insulted me so I punched him in the nose.
(d) Ram is not at home, so he must have gone to town.

16. Venn diagram is a kind of diagram to
(a) represent and assess the truth of elementary inferences with the help of Boolean Algebra of classes.
(b) represent and assess the validity of elementary inferences with the help of Boolean Algebra of classes.
(c) represent but not assess the validity of elementary inferences with the help of Boolean Algebra of classes.
(d) assess but not represent the validity of elementary inferences with the help of Boolean Algebra of classes.

17. Inductive logic studies the way in which a premise may
(a) support and entail a conclusion
(b) not support but entail a conclusion
(c) neither support nor entail a conclusion
(d) support a conclusion without entailing it

18. Which of the following statements are true?
1. Some arguments, while not completely valid, are almost valid.
2. A sound argument may be invalid.
3. A cogent argument may have a probably false conclusion.
4. A statement may be true or false.

Choose from the codes given below.

Codes:
(a) 1 and 2 (b) 1, 3 and 4
(c) 4 only (d) 3 and 4

19. If the side of the square increases by 40%, then the area of the square increases by
(a) 60% (b) 40%
(c) 196% (d) 96%

20. There are 10 lamps in a hall. Each one of them can be switched on independently. The number of ways in which hall can be illuminated is
(a) 10^2 (b) 1023
(c) 2^{10} (d) 10!

21. How many numbers between 100 and 300 begin or end with 2?
(a) 100 (b) 110
(c) 120 (d) 180

22. In a college having 300 students, every student reads 5 newspapers and every newspaper is read by 60 students. The number of newspapers required is
(a) at least 30 (b) at most 20
(c) exactly 25 (d) exactly 5

The total CO_2 emissions from various sectors are 5 mmt. In the Pie Chart given below, the percentage contribution to CO_2 emissions from various sectors is indicated.

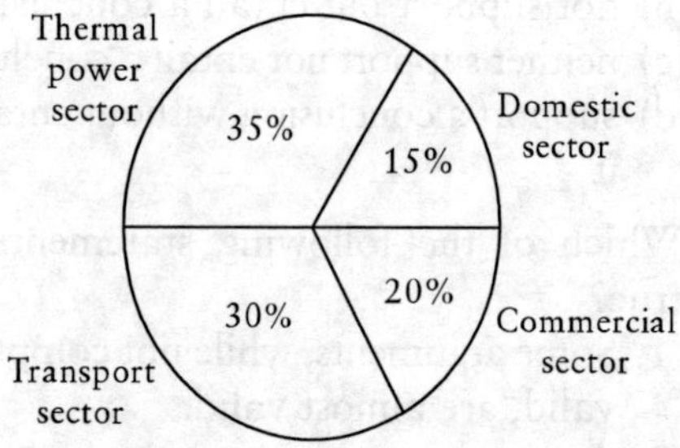

23. What is the absolute CO_2 emission from domestic sector?
(a) 1.5 mmt (b) 2.5 mmt
(c) 1.75 mmt (d) 0.75 mmt

24. What is the absolute CO_2 emission for combined thermal power and transport sectors?
(a) 3.25 mmt (b) 1.5 mmt
(c) 2.5 mmt (d) 4 mmt

25. Which of the following operating system is used on mobile phones?
(a) Windows Vista
(b) Android
(c) Windows XP
(d) All of the above

26. If $(y)_x$ represents a number y in base x, then which of the following numbers is smallest of all?
(a) $(1111)_2$ (b) $(1111)_8$
(c) $(1111)_{10}$ (d) $(1111)_{16}$

27. High level programming language can be converted to machine language using which of the following?
(a) Oracle (b) Compiler
(c) Mat lab (d) Assembler

28. HTML is used to create
(a) machine language program
(b) high level program
(c) web page
(d) web server

29. The term DNS stands for
(a) Domain Name System
(b) Defense Nuclear System
(c) Downloadable New Software
(d) Dependent Name Server

30. IPv4 and IPv6 are addresses used to identify computers on the internet. Find the correct statement out of the following:
(a) Number of bits required for IPv4 address is more than number of bits required for IPv6 address.
(b) Number of bits required for IPv4 address is same as number of bits required for IPv6 address.
(c) Number of bits required for IPv4 address is less than number of bits required for IPv6 address.
(d) Number of bits required for IPv4 address is 64.

31. Which of the following pollutants affects the respiratory tract in humans?
(a) Carbon monoxide
(b) Nitric oxide
(c) Sulphur dioxide
(d) Aerosols

32. Which of the following pollutants is not emitted from the transport sector?
    (a) Oxides of nitrogen
    (b) Chlorofluorocarbons
    (c) Carbon monoxide
    (d) Poly aromatic hydrocarbons

33. Which of the following sources of energy has the maximum potential in India?
    (a) Solar energy
    (b) Wind energy
    (c) Ocean thermal energy
    (d) Tidal energy

34. Which of the following is not a source of pollution in soil?
    (a) Transport sector
    (b) Agriculture sector
    (c) Thermal power plants
    (d) Hydro power plants

35. Which of the following is not a natural hazard?
    (a) Earthquake (b) Tsunami
    (c) Flash floods (d) Nuclear accident

36. Ecological footprint represents
    (a) area of productive land and water to meet the resources requirement
    (b) energy consumption
    (c) CO_2 emissions per person
    (d) forest cover

37. The aim of value education to inculcate in students is
    (a) the moral values
    (b) the social values
    (c) the political values
    (d) the economic values

38. Indicate the number of Regional Offices of University Grants Commission of India.
    (a) 10 (b) 07
    (c) 08 (d) 09

39. One-rupee currency note in India bears the signature of
    (a) The President of India
    (b) Finance Minister of India
    (c) Governor, Reserve Bank of India
    (d) Finance Secretary of Government of India

40. Match the List I with the List II and select the correct answer from the codes given below:

    List I (Commissions and Committees)
    A. First Administrative Reforms Commission
    B. Paul H. Appleby Committee I
    C. K. Santhanam Committee
    D. Second Administrative Reforms Commission

    List II (Year)
    1. 2005 2. 1962
    3. 1966 4. 1953

Codes:	A	B	C	D
(a)	1	3	2	4
(b)	3	4	2	1
(c)	4	2	3	1
(d)	2	1	4	3

41. Constitutionally the registration and recognition of political parties is the function performed by
    (a) The State Election Commission of respective States
    (b) The Law Ministry of Government of India
    (c) The Election Commission of India
    (d) Election Department of the State Governments

42. The members of Gram Sabha are
    (a) Sarpanch, Upsarpanch and all elected Panchas
    (b) Sarpanch, Upsarpanch and Village level worker
    (c) Sarpanch, Gram Sevak and elected Panchas
    (d) Registered voters of Village Panchayat

43. By which of the following methods the true evaluation of the students is possible?
   (a) Evaluation at the end of the course
   (b) Evaluation twice in a year
   (c) Continuous evaluation
   (d) Formative evaluation

44. Suppose a student wants to share his problems with his teacher and he visits the teacher's house for the purpose, the teacher should
   (a) contact the student's parents and solve his problem
   (b) suggest him that he should never visit his house
   (c) suggest him to meet the principal and solve the problem
   (d) extend reasonable help and boost his morale

45. When some students are deliberately attempting to disturb the discipline of the class by making mischief, what will be your role as a teacher?
   (a) Expelling those students
   (b) Isolate those students
   (c) Reform the group with your authority
   (d) Giving them an opportunity for introspection and improve their behaviour

46. Which of the following belongs to a projected aid?
   (a) Blackboard (b) Diorama
   (c) Epidiascope (d) Globe

47. A teacher is said to be fluent in asking questions, if he can ask
   (a) meaningful questions
   (b) as many questions as possible
   (c) maximum number of questions in a fixed time
   (d) many meaningful questions in a fixed time

48. Which of the following qualities is most essential for a teacher?
   (a) He should be a learned person
   (b) He should be a well-dressed person
   (c) He should have patience
   (d) He should be an expert in his subject

49. A hypothesis is a
   (a) Law (b) Canon
   (c) Postulate (d) Supposition

50. Suppose you want to investigate the working efficiency of nationalised bank in India, which one of the following would you follow?
   (a) Area Sampling
   (b) Multi-stage Sampling
   (c) Sequential Sampling
   (d) Quota Sampling

51. Controlled group condition is applied in
   (a) Survey Research
   (b) Historical Research
   (c) Experimental Research
   (d) Descriptive Research

52. Workshops are meant for
   (a) giving lectures
   (b) multiple target groups
   (c) showcase new theories
   (d) hands on training/experience

53. Which one of the following is a research tool?
   (a) Graph (b) Illustration
   (c) Questionnaire (d) Diagram

54. Research is not considered ethical if it
   (a) tries to prove a particular point.
   (b) does not ensure privacy and anonymity of the respondent.
   (c) does not investigate the data scientifically.
   (d) is not of a very high standard.

Read the following passage carefully and answer the questions (55 to 60):

The catalytic fact of the twentieth century is uncontrollable development, consumerist society, political materialism, and spiritual devaluation. This inordinate development has led to the transcendental 'second reality' of sacred perception that biologically transcendence is a part of human life. As the century closes, it dawns with imperative vigour that the 'first reality' of enlightened rationalism and the 'second reality' of the Beyond have to be harmonised in a worthy state of man. The *de facto* values describe what we are, they portray the 'is' of our ethic, they are *est* values (Latin *est* means is). The ideal values tell us what we ought to be, they are *esto* values (Latin *esto* 'ought to be'). Both have to be in the ebb and flow of consciousness. The ever new science and technology and the ever-perennial faith are two modes of one certainty, that is the wholeness of man, his courage to be, his share in being.

The materialistic foundations of science have crumbled down. Science itself has proved that matter is energy, processes are as valid as facts, and affirmed the non-materiality of the universe. The encounter of the 'two cultures', the scientific and the humane, will restore the normal vision, and will be the bedrock of a 'science of understanding' in the new century. It will give new meaning to the ancient perception that quantity (measure) and quality (value) coexist at the root of nature. Human endeavours cannot afford to be humanistically irresponsible.

55. The problem raised in the passage reflects overall on
 (a) Consumerism
 (b) Materialism
 (c) Spiritual devaluation
 (d) Inordinate development

56. The *de facto* values in the passage means
 (a) What is
 (b) What ought to be
 (c) What can be
 (d) Where it is

57. According to the passage, the 'first reality' constitutes
 (a) Economic prosperity
 (b) Political development
 (c) Sacred perception of life
 (d) Enlightened rationalism

58. Encounter of the 'two cultures', the scientific and the human implies
 (a) Restoration of normal vision
 (b) Universe is both material and non-material
 (c) Man is superior to nature
 (d) Co-existence of quantity and quality in nature

59. The contents of the passage are
 (a) Descriptive (b) Prescriptive
 (c) Axiomatic (d) Optional

60. The passage indicates that science has proved that
 (a) universe is material
 (b) matter is energy
 (c) nature has abundance
 (d) humans are irresponsible

ANSWERS

1. (a)	2. (b)	3. (b)	4. (a)	5. (d)
6. (c)	7. (c)	8. (b)	9. (c)	10. (d)
11. (c)	12. (d)	13. (a)	14. (b)	15. (a)
16. (b)	17. (d)	18. (d)	19. (d)	20. (b)
21. (b)	22. (c)	23. (d)	24. (a)	25. (b)
26. (a)	27. (b)	28. (c)	29. (a)	30. (c)
31. (a)	32. (b)	33. (b)	34. (d)	35. (d)
36. (a)	37. (a)	38. (b)	39. (d)	40. (b)
41. (c)	42. (d)	43. (d)	44. (d)	45. (d)
46. (c)	47. (d)	48. (c)	49. (d)	50. (b)
51. (c)	52. (d)	53. (c)	54. (b)	55. (c)
56. (a)	57. (d)	58. (a)	59. (a)	60. (b)

PAPER–II

Note: This paper contains Fifty (50) objective type questions, each question carrying two (2) marks. Attempt all the questions.

1. Who said that society is a super organic aggregate?
   (a) Herbert Spencer
   (b) Charles Darwin
   (c) Emile Durkheim
   (d) Bronislaw Malinowski

2. Who said this, "Social organization is a general social agreement"?
   (a) Herbert Spencer
   (b) A. Comte
   (c) E. Durkheim
   (d) Max Weber

3. In his 'Protestant Ethic and the Spirit of Capitalism' Weber considered religion to be ______ for the development of modern capitalism.
   (a) the only cause of
   (b) of no consequence in
   (c) one of the important causes
   (d) not a cause of

4. The early functionalists often drew an analogy between society and an organism such as the human body. This is called
   (a) organic analogy
   (b) organic similarity
   (c) organic analysis
   (d) organism

5. Many of the founding fathers of Sociology believed that it would be possible to create a science of society based on the same principles and procedures as the natural sciences. This approach is known as
   (a) positivism
   (b) evolutionism
   (c) functionalism
   (d) phenomenology

6. Ideal types are ______.
   (a) tools to be used in the analysis of empirical reality
   (b) tools to be used to trace the evolutionary scheme of societies
   (c) tools to be applied to the study of past societies
   (d) not tools but are examples of actually existing societies

7. **Assertion (A):** Many sub-human species have an orderly system of social life.
   Reason (R): Sub-human social life is based on instinct, and not on social learning.
   (a) Both (A) and (R) are individually true and (R) is the correct explanation of (A).
   (b) Both (A) and (R) are individually true, but (R) is not the correct explanation of (A).
   (c) (A) is true, but (R) is false.
   (d) (A) is false, but (R) is true.

8. **Assertion (A):** A culture is a system of behaviour shared by the members of a society.
   Reason (R): A society is a group of people who share a common culture.
   (a) Both (A) and (R) are individually true and (R) is the correct explanation of (A).
   (b) Both (A) and (R) are individually true, but (R) is not the correct explanation of (A).
   (c) (A) is true, but (R) is false.
   (d) (A) is false, but (R) is true.

9. A Sociologist is primarily interested in
   (a) the ways in which human beings influence each other
   (b) anything which is related in a causal way to the behaviour of man
   (c) the individual, because he is convinced that it is the individual who make the society
   (d) the similarities between human behaviour and the behaviour of other animals
10. According to Durkheim,
   (a) Anomie is a chronic state of disturbance of social affairs in the modern socio-economic system.
   (b) Anomie occurs in modern socio-economic system at the time of economic upheavals.
   (c) Anomie occurs in modern socio-economic system at the lime of political upheavals.
   (d) Anomie does not occur in modern socio-economic system.
11. Under certain conditions the religious beliefs can be a major influence on economic behaviour. Who made use of the above idea in his study on development of capitalism?
   (a) Durkheim
   (b) Marx
   (c) Malinowski
   (d) Weber
12. Merton wrote on how political ideology such as communism can provide a ______ to religion in communist society.
   (a) dysfunction
   (b) functional alternative
   (c) functional unity
   (d) functional pre-requisite
13. Which is the crucial feature of a good sample?
   (a) Small size
   (b) Representativeness
   (c) Easily approachable
   (d) Easy to study
14. Whose view is this "without likeness and the sense of likeness there could be no mutual recognition of belonging together and therefore no society"?
   (a) MacIver
   (b) Durkheim
   (c) Weber
   (d) Ogburn
15. The most essential step in making interview a successful method of data collection is
   (a) use of an interview schedule
   (b) establishing rapport
   (c) obtaining secondary information before the interview
   (d) having a research design
16. Identify the correct sequence of disciplines according to hierarchy of sciences.
   I. Sociology, Biology, Astronomy, Physics
   II. Biology, Physics, Sociology, Astronomy
   III. Physics, Biology, Astronomy, Sociology
   IV. Astronomy, Physics, Biology, Sociology

   Codes:
   (a) I and II are correct.
   (b) III and IV are correct.
   (c) Qnly IV is correct.
   (d) Only II is correct.
17. Population pyramid is a graphic representation of a population's ______.
   (a) fertility and fecundity
   (b) age-sex distribution at a given time
   (c) mortality and morbidity
   (d) fertility and mortality ratio

18. The following social thinkers have contributed to the development of Sociology. Arrange them in the chronological order and choose the correct code.
    I. Karl Marx
    II. Auguste Comte
    III. Talcot Parsons
    IV. George Simmel
    Codes:
    (a) I, II, III, IV
    (b) II, I, III, IV
    (c) III, II, I, IV
    (d) II, I, IV, III
19. In the development of Functional School of Sociology, place the following in sequence of their contribution and choose the correct code:
    I. Auguste Comte
    II. Herbert Spencer
    III. Bronislaw Malinowski
    IV. Radcliffe Brown
    Codes:
    (a) I, III, II, IV
    (b) I, II, IV, III
    (c) I, II, III, IV
    (d) I, IV, III, II
20. **Assertion (A):** According to Durkheim, suicide rate is higher in highly industrialised society.
    Reason (R): There is high division of labour and organic solidarity in industrialised societies.
    In the context of the above two statements, which one of the following is correct?
    Codes:
    (a) (A) is correct, but (R) is wrong.
    (b) Both (A) and (R) are correct.
    (c) (A) is wrong, but (R) is correct.
    (d) Both (A) and (R) are wrong.
21. "Social organisation is a general social agreement" is a statement made by
    (a) Herbert Spencer
    (b) Auguste Comte
    (c) Emile Durkheim
    (d) Max Weber
22. Match the items in List I with the items in List II and choose the correct codes given below:
    List I (Definitions)
    A. A unit about which information is collected and that provides the basis of analysis.
    B. An aggregation of elements from which the sample is actually selected.
    C. An element as set of elements considered for selection in some stage of sampling.
    D. The actual list of sampling units from which the sample is selected.

    List II (Concepts)
    i. Population
    ii Study population
    iii. Element
    iv. Sampling unit
    v. Sampling frame

Codes:	**A**	**B**	**C**	**D**
(a)	iv	iii	ii	i
(b)	iii	ii	iv	v
(c)	i	iii	ii	iv
(d)	iii	v	iv	i

23. Match the items in List I with the items in List II and choose the correct codes given below:
    List I (Explanation)
    A. Patterns of interaction between individuals or groups.
    B. Any form of social encounter between individuals.
    C. Collection of individuals who interact in systematic ways with one another.
    D. The existence of structured inequalities between groups in society.

List II (Concept)
i. Social group
ii. Social structure
iii. Social interaction
iv. Social exclusion
v. Social stratification

Codes:	A	B	C	D
(a)	ii	v	iv	iii
(b)	i	iv	iii	ii
(c)	ii	iii	i	v
(d)	i	iv	iii	v

24. Match the items in List I with the items in List II and choose the correct codes given below:

List I (Residence Rules)
A. A newly married couple settles down with the husband's father's household.
B. A newly married couple settles down with the wife's mother's household.
C. A newly married couple live with either the husband's or wife's family of origin.
D. A newly married couple may choose to live anywhere even far away from their families of origin.

List II (Concept)
i. Avanculocal
ii. Matrilocal
iii. Patrilocal
iv. Bilocal
v. Neolocal

Codes:	A	B	C	D
(a)	iii	ii	iv	v
(b)	iii	i	v	iv
(c)	ii	iii	i	iv
(d)	i	v	iv	ii

23. Match the items in List I with the items in List II and choose the correct codes given below:

List I (Religious Features)
A. Patterns of behaviour that are related to the sacred.
B. The belief in animate, personalised spirits or ghosts of ancestors that have taken an interest in and actively work to influence, human affairs.
C. A belief in divine beings Gods and Goddesses—who shape and mould human affairs.
D. The hierarchy of deities in a religious belief system.

List II (Concepts)
i. Supernaturalism
ii. Pantheon
iii. Animism
iv. Theism
v. Rituals

Codes:	A	B	C	D
(a)	v	iii	iv	ii
(b)	v	iii	i	ii
(c)	i	iv	v	iii
(d)	iv	i	iii	ii

26. Match the items in List I with the items in List II and choose the correct codes given below:

List I (Features of Capitalist Organisation)
A. Domination of industries and markets by a handful of monolithic corporations.
B. A. corporation that controls many other firms in greatly diversified fields.
C. A corporation that does business in more than one country.
D. A formally structured business organisation with an explicit hierarchy definite procedural rules and a well-maintained division of labour.

List II (Concepts)
i. Oligopoly
ii. Multi-National Corporation
iii. Conglomerate
iv. Labour Union
v. Corporate bureaucracy

Codes:	A	B	C	D
(a)	iv	iii	i	ii
(b)	i	v	iv	ii
(c)	i	iii	ii	v
(d)	iii	ii	iv	v

27. Match the items in List I with the items in List II and choose the correct codes given below:

List I (Forms of Government)

A. Social institutions that claim monopoly of the legitimate use of physical force within a society.
B. A political system characterised by representative Government, accountability to an electorate, civilian rule and civil liberties.
C. A political system in which the ultimate authority lies with a single person.
D. The rule by a select few; a form of oligarchy.

List II (Concepts)

i. Democracy
ii. Autocracy
iii. State
iv. Aristocracy
v. Government

Codes:	A	B	C	D
(a)	iii	i	ii	v
(b)	iv	iii	i	ii
(c)	ii	i	iii	v
(d)	iii	i	ii	iv

28. Match the items in List I with the items in List II and choose the correct codes given below:

List I (Explanation)

A. Rules that establishes the legal right of every qualified citizen to run for and hold an office of government.
B. Social liberties that enable people to assemble to express their views and seek to persuade others to engage in organising political activity to vote for whomso-ever they wish.
C. An economic system under which the government owns and controls the major means of production and distribution.
D. A government in which all the power rests ultimately in one person who generally leads the only recognized political party.

List II (Terms)

i. Dictatorship
ii. Public Liberty
iii. Civilian Rule
iv. Socialism
v. Fascism

Codes:	A	B	C	D
(a)	v	iii	ii	i
(b)	ii	iv	iii	v
(c)	iii	v	i	iv
(d)	iii	ii	iv	i

29. Match the items in List I with the items in List II and choose the correct codes given below:

List I (Population Processes)

A. The actual number of births in the population.
B. The annual number of births per 1000 population.
C. The annual number of birth per 1000 women of child bearing age in a population.
D. The frequency of actual deaths in total population.

List II (Concepts)

i. Fertility
ii. Crude death rate
iii. Crude birth rate
iv. Fertility rate
v. Mortality

Codes:	**A**	**B**	**C**	**D**
(a)	i	ii	iv	v
(b)	ii	iii	i	iv
(c)	i	iii	iv	v
(d)	v	ii	i	iii

Direction: Observe the table below and answer the questions 30 to 33 below the table: Expectation of life by age and sex for selected countries

Average future lifetime in years at stated age

	Males						Females					
Country	0	1	10	20	40	60	0	1	10	20	40	60
Burma	40.8	49.8	45.5	36.8	21.1	10.6	43.8	51.6	47.0	38.3	23.7	12.4
Canada	69.3	69.8	61.2	51.7	33.2	17.0	76.4	76.6	67.9	58.2	39.0	21.4
Guatemala	48.3	52.5	51.3	43.2	28.1	14.8	49.7	53.4	52.8	44.6	29.2	14.7
India	41.9	48.4	45.2	36.9	22.1	11.8	40.6	46.0	43.8	35.6	22.4	12.9
Israel	70.3	71.1	62.5	53.1	34.5	17.4	73.9	74.5	65.9	56.1	36.9	19.2
Kenya	46.9	52.6	51.0	43.0	28.3	14.5	51.2	56.6	54.1	45.7	30.3	15.7
Poland	66.8	68.0	59.4	49.8	31.6	15.5	73.8	74.6	66.0	56.2	37.0	19.3
Sweden	72.1	71.9	63.2	53.5	34.7	17.7	77.7	77.3	68.5	58.7	39.4	21.3
Syria	54.5	60.7	56.4	47.4	30.5	15.2	58.7	64.1	59.5	50.5	33.3	17.3
United States	68.7	68.9	60.3	50.8	32.6	16.8	76.5	76.6	67.9	58.1	39.0	21.8

Source: Adapted from United Nations Demographic Yearbook (1978).

30. What is the lowest life expectancy for females at 10 years of age?
(a) 45.2 years (b) 48.4 years
(c) 43.8 years (d) 46.0 years

31. Which country has the lowest life expectancy at birth for males?
(a) India
(b) Burma
(c) Canada
(d) Guatemala

32. What is the life expectancy at birth for females for India?
(a) 41.9 years (b) 48.4 years
(c) 40.6 years (d) 46.0 years

33. Which country has the highest life expectancy at birth for males?
(a) United States
(b) Sweden
(c) Israel
(d) Canada

34. Given below are two statements, one is labelled as Assertion (A) and the other is labelled as Reason (R):
Assertion (A): Inter-religious tensions are endemic in some Indian towns and cities.
Reason (R): The secularization of outlook has not been sufficiently widespread to eradicate communal and sectarian biases.
In the context of the above two statements, choose the correct codes below:
Codes:
(a) Both (A) and (R) are true and (R) is the explanation of (A).
(b) Both (A) and (R) are true, but (R) is not the explanation of (A).
(c) (A) is true, but (R) is false.
(d) (A) is false, but (R) is true.

35. A diagrammatic representation of frequency distribution is known as

(a) Histogram
(b) Monogram
(c) Hologram
(d) Scalogram

36. Match the items in the List I with the items in the List II and choose the correct codes for your answer:

List I (Description)

A. The attempt to develop an initial, rough understanding of some phenomena.
B. The precise measurement and reporting of the characteristics of some population or phenomena under study.
C. A statement of specific expectations about the nature of things, derived from a theory.
D. The discovery and reporting of relationships among different aspects of the phenomena under study.

List II (Terms)

i. Description ii. Exlanation
iii. Exploration iv. Hypothesis
v. Unit of Analysis

Codes:	**A**	**B**	**C**	**D**
(a)	ii	v	iii	iv
(b)	iv	iii	ii	v
(c)	iii	i	iv	ii
(d)	i	iv	ii	iii

37. Arrange the following books in order in which they appeared:

I. The Division of Labour
II. Economics and Society
III. Principles of Sociology
IV. Studies on Positive Philosophy Choose the correct codes for your answer:

Codes:

(a) IV, II, III and I (b) III, IV, I and II
(c) II, III, IV and I (d) IV, III, I and II

38. We have four classical theorists who influenced sociology very much. Identify the correct order in which they appeared in sociology.

(a) Karl Marx, Max Weber, Emile Durkheim, Auguste Comte
(b) August Comte, Max Weber, Karl Marx, Emile Durkheim
(c) August Comte, Karl Marx, Emile Durkheim, Max Weber
(d) Max Weber, Emile Durkheim, Auguste Comte, Karl Marx

39. Given below arc two statements, one labelled as Assertion (A) and the other labelled as Reason (R):

Assertion (A): Marx lived during a period when the overwhelming majority of people in industrial societies were poor.

Reason (R): The rural poor were lured into cities where employment was available in the factories and workshops of the new industrial economies.

In the context of the above statements, which one of the following is correct?

Codes:

(a) (A) is correct, but (R) is wrong.
(b) Both (A) and (R) are correct.
(c) (A) is wrong, but (R) is correct.
(d) Both (A) and (R) are wrong.

40. Given below are two statements, one labelled as Assertion (A) and the other labelled as Reason (R):

Assertion (A): Between 1830 and 1842 Comte wrote his major work, *Cours de Philosophie Positive* in which he coined the term Sociology.

Reason (R): Immediately after the February Revolution of 1848 Comte founded his *Societe Positive* which became the centre for his teaching and attracted his disciples to learn intensely the sociological issues of the time.

In the context of the above statements, which one of the following is correct?

Codes:
(a) Both (A) and (R) are true and (R) is the correct explanation of (A).
(b) Both (A) and (R) are true, but (R) is not the correct explanation of (A).
(c) (A) is true, but (R) is false.
(d) (A) is false, but (R) is true.

41. Given below are two statements, one labelled as Assertion (A) and the other labelled as Reason (R):
Assertion (A): Durkheim believed that individuals are exclusively the product of their social environment.
Reason (R): Durkheim studied suicide as a social phenomenon of deviance and showed that it was surely patterned by social factors rather than exclusively by individual mental disturbances.
In the context of the above two statements which one of the following is correct?
Codes:
(a) (A) is correct, but (R) is wrong.
(b) Both (A) and (R) are correct.
(c) (A) is wrong, but (R) is correct.
(d) Both (A) and (R) are wrong.

42. Given below are two statements, one labelled as Assertion (A) and the other labelled as Reason (R):
Assertion (A): Religion exists in all known societies, although religious beliefs and practices vary from culture to culture.
Reason (R): All religions involve a set of symbols linked to rituals practiced by a community of believers.
In the context of the above two statements, which one of the following is correct?
Codes:
(a) (A) is correct, but (R) is wrong.
(b) Both (A) and (R) are correct.
(c) (A) is wrong, but (R) is correct.
(d) Both (A) and (R) are wrong.

43. Which one of the following pairs is correctly matched? Choose the correct codes:
Codes:
(a) A sociological theory that is concerned with interactionthe meanings people place' in their own and thier's behaviour. – Symbolic
(b) A social process that contributes to the ongoing operation or maintenance of society. – Paradigm
(c) A tested statement about the relationship between two or more empirical variables. – Hypothesis
(d) The tendency for researchers to select data that support their hypothesis and ignore data that appear to contradict it. – Objectivity

44. The term social evolution is used to explain the evolution of
(a) Organism
(b) Animal Society
(c) Animal and human
(d) Human Society

45. ______ said that societies pass through theological, metaphysical and positive stages.
(a) Durkheim
(b) Saint Simon
(c) MacIver
(d) Comte

46. Karl Marx is associated with which theory "of social change"?
(a) Cyclic theory
(b) Functional theory
(c) Conflict theory
(d) Evolutionary theory

47. Who said that conflict is a permanent feature of society not a temporary event?
   (a) Karl Marx
   (b) Herbert Spencer
   (c) George Simmel
   (d) C. Wright Mills

48. According to E. Durkheim, the sociological role of religious beliefs is that
   (a) they enable individuals to face internal and external dangers.
   (b) they provide opportunities to individuals for celebrating rituals and ceremonies.
   (c) they enable individuals to experience the supernatural.
   (d) they provide a stabilizing factor in the social life of individuals.

49. Under certain conditions the religious beliefs can be a major influence on economic behaviour. Who made use of the above belief in his study of development of capitalism?
   (a) E. Durkheim
   (b) Karl Marx
   (c) B. Malinowski
   (d) Max Weber

50. According to Durkheim, the most primitive type of religion is
   (a) Animism (b) Magic
   (c) Totemism (d) Naturism

ANSWERS

1. (a)	2. (b)	3. (c)	4. (a)	5. (a)
6. (b)	7. (b)	8. (c)	9. (c)	10. (a)
11. (d)	12. (b)	13. (b)	14. (a)	15. (b)
16. (c)	17. (b)	18. (d)	19. (c)	20. (b)
21. (b)	22. (b)	23. (d)	24. (a)	25. (a)
26. (c)	27. (d)	28. (d)	29. (c)	30. (c)
31. (b)	32. (c)	33. (b)	34. (b)	35. (a)
36. (c)	37. (d)	38. (c)	39. (b)	40. (b)
41. (b)	42. (b)	43. (d)	44. (d)	45. (a)
46. (c)	47. (a)	48. (a)	49. (a)	50. (c)

JUNE–2011

Note: This paper contains Sixty (60) multiple-choice questions, each question carrying two (2) marks. Candidate is expected to answer any Fifty (50) questions. In case more than Fifty (50) questions are attempted, only the first Fifty (50) questions will be evaluated.

PAPER–I

1. A research paper is a brief report of research work based on
   (a) Primary Data only
   (b) Secondary Data only
   (c) Both Primary and Secondary Data
   (d) None of the above

2. Newton gave three basic laws of motion. This research is categorised as
   (a) Descriptive Research
   (b) Sample Survey
   (c) Fundamental Research
   (d) Applied Research

3. A group of experts in a specific area of knowledge assembled at a place and prepared a syllabus for a new course. The process may be termed as
   (a) Seminar
   (b) Workshop
   (c) Conference
   (d) Symposium

4. In the process of conducting research "Formulation of Hypothesis" is followed by
   (a) Statement of Objectives
   (b) Analysis of Data
   (c) Selection of Research Tools
   (d) Collection of Data

Read the following passage carefully and answer the questions from 5 to 10:

All historians are interpreters of text if they be private letters, government records or parish birthlists or whatever. For most kinds of historians, these are only the necessary means to understanding something other than the texts themselves, such as a political action or a historical trend, whereas for the intellectual historian, a full understanding of his chosen texts is itself the aim of his enquiries. Of course, the intellectual history is particularly prone to draw on the focus of other disciplines that are habitually interpreting texts for purposes of their own, probing the reasoning that ostensibly connects premises and conclusions. Furthermore, the boundaries with adjacent subdisciplines are shifting and indistinct: the history of art and the history of science both claim a certain autonomy, partly just because they require specialised technical skills, but both can also be seen as part of a wider intellectual history, as is evident when one considers, for example, the common stock of knowledge about cosmological beliefs or moral ideals of a period.

Like all historians, the intellectual historian is a consumer rather than a producer of 'methods'. His distinctiveness lies in which aspect of the past he is trying to illuminate, not in having exclusive possession of either a corpus of evidence or a body of techniques. That being said, it does seem that the label 'intellectual history' attracts a disproportionate share of misunderstanding.

It is alleged that intellectual history is the history of something that never really mattered. The long dominance of the historical profession by political historians bred a kind of philistinism, an unspoken belief that power and its exercise was 'what mattered'. The prejudice was reinforced by the assertion that political action was never really the outcome of principles or ideas that were 'more flapdoodle'. The legacy of this precept is still discernible in the tendency to require ideas to have 'licensed' the political class before they can be deemed worthy of intellectual attention, as if there were some reasons why the history of art or science, of philosophy or literature, were somehow of interest and significance than the history of Parties or Parliaments. Perhaps in recent years the mirror-image of this philistinism has been more common in the claim that ideas of any one is of systematic expression or sophistication do not matter, as if they were only held by a minority.

5. An intellectual historian aims to fully understand
   (a) the chosen texts of his own
   (b) political actions
   (c) historical trends
   (d) his enquiries
6. Intellectual historians do not claim exclusive possession of
   (a) conclusions
   (b) any corpus of evidence
   (c) distinctiveness
   (d) habitual interpretation
7. The misconceptions about intellectual history stem from
   (a) a body of techniques
   (b) the common stock of knowledge
   (c) the dominance of political historians
   (d) cosmological beliefs
8. What is philistinism?
   (a) Reinforcement of prejudice
   (b) Fabrication of reasons
   (c) The hold of land-owning classes
   (d) Belief that power and its exercise matter
9. Knowledge of cosmological beliefs or moral ideas of a period can be drawn as part of
   (a) literary criticism
   (b) history of science
   (c) history of philosophy
   (d) intellectual history
10. The claim that ideas of any one is of systematic expression do not matter, as if they were held by a minority, is
    (a) to have a licensed political class
    (b) a political action
    (c) a philosophy of literature
    (d) the mirror-image of philistinism
11. Public communication tends to occur within a more
    (a) complex structure
    (b) political structure
    (c) convenient structure
    (d) formal structure
12. Transforming thoughts, ideas and messages into verbal and non-verbal signs is referred to as
    (a) channelisation
    (b) mediation
    (c) encoding
    (d) decoding
13. Effective communication needs a supportive
    (a) economic environment
    (b) political environment
    (c) social environment
    (d) multi-cultural environment
14. A major barrier in the transmission of cognitive data in the process of communication is an individual's
    (a) personality
    (b) expectation

(c) social status
(d) coding ability

15. When communicated, institutionalised stereotypes become
(a) myths (b) reasons
(c) experiences (d) convictions

16. In mass communication, selective perception is dependent on the receiver's
(a) competence
(b) pre-disposition
(c) receptivity
(d) ethnicity

17. Determine the relationship between the pair of words NUMERATOR : DENOMINATOR and then select the pair of words from the following which have a similar relationship:
(a) fraction : decimal
(b) divisor : quotient
(c) top : bottom
(d) dividend : divisor

18. Find the wrong number in the sequence: 125, 127, 130, 135, 142, 153, 165
(a) 130 (b) 142
(c) 153 (d) 165

19. If HOBBY is coded as IOBY and LOBBY is coded as MOBY; then BOBBY is coded as
(a) BOBY (b) COBY
(c) DOBY (d) OOBY

20. The letters in the first set have certain relationship. On the basis of this relationship, make the right choice for the second set
K/T : 11/20 :: J/R : ?
(a) 10/8 (b) 10/18
(c) 11/19 (d) 10/19

21. If A = 5, B = 6, C = 7, D = 8 and so on, what do the following numbers stand for?
17, 19, 20, 9, 8
(a) Plane (b) Moped
(c) Motor (d) Tonga

22. The price of oil is increased by 25%. If the expenditure is not allowed to increase, the ratio between the reduction in consumption and the original consumption is
(a) 1:3 (b) 1:4
(c) 1:5 (d) 1:6

23. How many 8's are there in the following sequence which are preceded by 5 but not immediately followed by 3?
5 8 3 7 5 8 6 3 8 5 4 5 8 4 7 6 5 5 8 3 5 8 7 5 8 2 8 5
(a) 4 (b) 5
(c) 7 (d) 3

24. If a rectangle were called a circle, a circle a point, a point a triangle and a triangle a square, the shape of a wheel is
(a) Rectangle (b) Circle
(c) Point (d) Triangle

25. Which one of the following methods is best suited for mapping the distribution of different crops as provided in the standard classification of crops in India?
(a) Pie diagram
(b) Chorochromatic technique
(c) Isopleth technique
(d) Dot method

26. Which one of the following does not come under the methods of data classification?
(a) Qualitative
(b) Normative
(c) Spatial
(d) Quantitative

27. Which one of the following is not a source of data?
(a) Administrative records
(b) Population census

(c) GIS
(d) Sample survey

28. If the statement 'some men are cruel' is false, which of the following statements/ statement are/is true?
(i) All men are cruel.
(ii) No men are cruel.
(iii) Some men are not cruel.
Codes:
(a) (i) and (iii) (b) (i) and (ii)
(c) (ii) and (iii) (d) Only (iii)

29. The octal number system consists of the following symbols
(a) 0 – 7
(b) 0 – 9
(c) 0 – 9, A – F
(d) None of the above

30. The binary equivalent of $(-19)_{10}$ in signed magnitude system is
(a) 11101100 (b) 11101101
(c) 10010011 (d) None of these

31. DNS in internet technology stands for
(a) Dynamic Name System
(b) Domain Name System
(c) Distributed Name System
(d) None of these

32. HTML stands for
(a) Hyper Text Markup Language
(b) Hyper Text Manipulation Language
(c) Hyper Text Managing Links
(d) Hyper Text Manipulating Links

33. Which of the following is type of LAN?
(a) Ethernet (b) Token Ring
(c) FDDI (d) All of the above

34. Which of the following statements is true?
(a) Smart cards do not require an operating system.
(b) Smart cards and PCs use some operating system.
(c) COS is smart card operating system.
(d) The communication between reader and card is in full duplex mode.

35. The Ganga Action Plan was initiated during the year
(a) 1986 (b) 1988
(c) 1990 (d) 1992

36. Identify the correct sequence of energy sources in order of their share in the power sector in India.
(a) Thermal > nuclear > hydro > wind
(b) Thermal > hydro > nuclear > wind
(c) Hydro > nuclear > thermal > wind
(d) Nuclear > hydro > wind > thermal

37. Chromium as a contaminant in drinking water in excess of permissible levels, causes
(a) Skeletal damage
(b) Gastrointestinal problem
(c) Dermal and nervous problems
(d) Liver/Kidney problems

38. The main precursors of winter smog are
(a) N_2O and hydrocarbons
(b) NO_x and hydrocarbons
(c) SO_2 and hydrocarbons
(d) SO_2 and ozone

39. Flash floods are caused when
(a) the atmosphere is convectively unstable and there is considerable vertical wind shear
(b) the atmosphere is stable
(c) the atmosphere is convectively unstable with no vertical windshear
(d) winds are catabatic

40. In mega cities of India, the dominant source of air pollution is
(a) transport sector
(b) thermal power
(c) municipal waste
(d) commercial sector

41. The first Open University in India was set up in the State of
 (a) Andhra Pradesh
 (b) Delhi
 (c) Himachal Pradesh
 (d) Tamil Nadu

42. Most of the Universities in India are funded by
 (a) the Central Government
 (b) the State Governments
 (c) the University Grants Commission
 (d) Private bodies and Individuals

43. Which of the following organisations looks after the quality of Technical and Management education in India?
 (a) NCTE (b) MCI
 (c) AICTE (d) CSIR

44. Consider the following statements: Identify the statement which implies natural justice.
 (a) The principle of natural justice is followed by the Courts.
 (b) Justice delayed is justice denied.
 (c) Natural justice is an inalienable right of a citizen.
 (d) A reasonable opportunity of being heard must be given.

45. The President of India is
 (a) the Head of State
 (b) the Head of Government
 (c) both Head of the State and the Head of the Government
 (d) None of the above

46. Who among the following holds office during the pleasure of the President of India?
 (a) Chief Election Commissioner
 (b) Comptroller and Auditor General of India
 (c) Chairman of the Union Public Service Commission
 (d) Governor of a State

Questions 47 to 49 are based upon the following diagram in which there are three interlocking circles A, P and S where A stands for Artists, circle P for Professors and circle S for Sportspersons. Different regions in the figure are lettered from a to g:

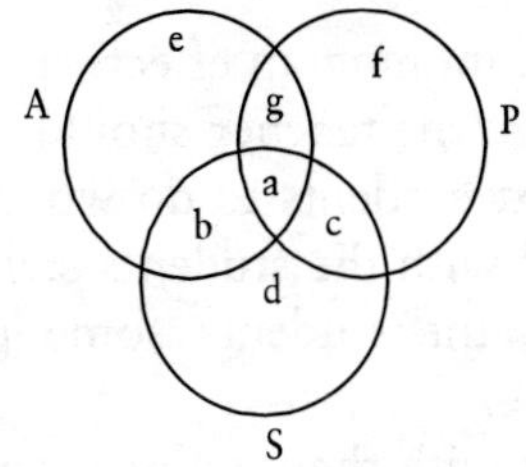

47. The region which represents artists who are neither sportsmen nor professors.
 (a) d (b) e
 (c) b (d) g

48. The region which represents professors, who are both artists and sportspersons.
 (a) a (b) c
 (c) d (d) g

49. The region which represents professors, who are also sportspersons, but not artists.
 (a) e (b) f
 (c) c (d) g

Questions 50 to 52 are based on the following data:

Measurements of some variable X were made at an interval of 1 minute from 10 A.M. to 10:20 A.M. The data, thus, obtained is as follows:

X: 60, 62, 65, 64, 63, 61, 66, 65, 70, 68
63, 62, 64, 69, 65, 64, 66, 67, 66, 64

50. The value of X, which is exceeded 10% of the time in the duration of measurement is
 (a) 69 (b) 68
 (c) 67 (d) 66

51. The value of X, which is exceeded 90% of the time in the duration of measurement is

(a) 63 (b) 62
(c) 61 (d) 60

52. The value of X, which is exceeded 50% of the time in the duration of measurement is
(a) 66 (b) 65
(c) 64 (d) 63

53. For maintaining an effective discipline in the class, the teacher should
(a) allow students to do what they like.
(b) deal with the students strictly.
(c) give the students some problem to solve.
(d) deal with them politely and firmly.

54. An effective teaching aid is one which
(a) is colourful and good looking
(b) activates all faculties
(c) is visible to all students
(d) easy to prepare and use

55. Those teachers are popular among students who
(a) develop intimacy with them
(b) help them solve their problems
(c) award good grades
(d) take classes on extra tuition fee

56. The essence of an effective classroom environment is
(a) a variety of teaching aids
(b) lively student-teacher interaction
(c) pin-drop silence
(d) strict discipline

57. On the first day of his class, if a teacher is asked by the students to introduce himself, he should
(a) ask them to meet after the class
(b) tell them about himself in brief
(c) ignore the demand and start teaching
(d) scold the student for this unwanted demand

58. Moral values can be effectively inculcated among the students when the teacher
(a) frequently talks about values
(b) himself practices them
(c) tells stories of great persons
(d) talks of Gods and Goddesses

59. The essential qualities of a researcher are
(a) spirit of free enquiry
(b) reliance on observation and evidence
(c) systematisation or theorising of knowledge
(d) All of the above

60. Research is conducted to
1. Generate new knowledge
2. Not to develop a theory
3. Obtain research degree
4. Reinterpret existing knowledge

Which of the above are correct?
(a) 1, 3 and 2
(b) 3, 2 and 4
(c) 2, 1 and 3
(d) 1, 3 and 4

ANSWERS

1. (c)	2. (c)	3. (b)	4. (c)	5. (a)
6. (b)	7. (c)	8. (d)	9. (d)	10. (d)
11. (d)	12. (c)	13. (d)	14. (c)	15. (d)
16. (b)	17. (d)	18. (d)	19. (b)	20. (b)
21. (b)	22. (c)	23. (a)	24. (c)	25. (a)
26. (b)	27. (a)	28. (b)	29. (a)	30. (d)
31. (b)	32. (a)	33. (d)	34. (c)	35. (a)
36. (b)	37. (d)	38. (c)	39. (a)	40. (a)
41. (a)	42. (c)	43. (c)	44. (d)	45. (b)
46. (d)	47. (b)	48. (a)	49. (c)	50. (c)
51. (b)	52. (d)	53. (d)	54. (b)	55. (b)
56. (b)	57. (b)	58. (b)	59. (d)	60. (d)

DECEMBER–2010

Note: This paper contains Sixty (60) multiple-choice questions, each question carrying two (2) marks. Candidate is expected to answer any Fifty (50) questions. In case more than Fifty (50) questions are attempted, only the first Fifty (50) questions will be evaluated.

PAPER–I

1. Which of the following variables cannot be expressed in quantitative terms?
   (a) Socio-economic Status
   (b) Marital Status
   (c) Numerical Aptitude
   (d) Professional Attitude

2. A doctor studies the relative effectiveness of two drugs of dengue fever. His research would be classified as
   (a) Descriptive Survey
   (b) Experimental Research
   (c) Case Study
   (d) Ethnography

3. The term 'phenomenology' is associated with the process of
   (a) Qualitative Research
   (b) Analysis of Variance
   (c) Correlational Study
   (d) Probability Sampling

4. The 'Sociogram' technique is used to study
   (a) Vocational Interest
   (b) Professional Competence
   (c) Human Relations
   (d) Achievement Motivation

Read the following passage carefully and answer the questions from 5 to 10.

It should be remembered that the nationalist movement in India, like all nationalist movements, was essentially a bourgeois movement. It represented the natural historical stage of development, and to consider it or to criticise it as a working-class movement is wrong. Gandhi represented that movement and the Indian masses in relation to that movement to a supreme degree, and he became the voice of Indian people to that extent. The main contribution of Gandhi to India and the Indian masses has been through the powerful movements which he launched through the National Congress. Through nation-wide action he sought to mould the millions, and largely succeeded in doing so, and changing them from a demoralised, timid and hopeless mass, bullied and crushed by every dominant interest, and incapable of resistance, into a people with self-respect and self-reliance, resisting tyranny, and capable of united action and sacrifice for a larger cause.

Gandhi made people think of political and economic issues and every village and every bazaar hummed with argument and debate on the new ideas and hopes that filled the people. That was an amazing psychological change. The time was ripe for it, of course, and circumstances and world conditions worked for this change. But a great leader is necessary to take advantage of circumstances and conditions. Gandhi was that leader, and he released many of the bonds that imprisoned and disabled our minds, and none of us who experienced it can ever forget that great feeling of release and exhilaration that came over the Indian people.

Gandhi has played a revolutionary role in India of the greatest importance because he knew how to make the most of the objective conditions and could reach the heart of the masses, while groups with a more advanced ideology functioned largely in the air because they did not fit in with those conditions and could therefore not evoke any substantial response from the masses.

It is perfectly true that Gandhi, functioning in the nationalist plane, does not think in terms of the conflict of classes, and tries to compose their differences. But the action he has indulged and taught the people has inevitably raised mass consciousness tremendously and made social issues vital. Gandhi and the Congress must be judged by the policies they pursue and the action they indulge in. But behind this, personality counts and colours those policies and activities. In the case of very exceptional person like Gandhi the question of personality becomes especially important in order to understand and appraise him. To us he has represented the spirit and honour of India, the yearning of her sorrowing millions to be rid of their innumerable burdens, and an insult to him by the British Government or others has been an insult to India and her people.

5. Which one of the following is true of the given passage?
   (a) The passage is a critique of Gandhi's role in Indian movement for independence
   (b) The passage hails the role of Gandhi in India's freedom movement
   (c) The author is neutral on Gandhi's role in India's freedom movement
   (d) It is an account of Indian National Congress's support to the working-class movement

6. The change that the Gandhian movement brought among the Indian masses was
   (a) Physical (b) Cultural
   (c) Technological (d) Psychological

7. To consider the nationalist movement or to criticise it as a working-class movement was wrong because it was a
   (a) historical movement
   (b) voice of the Indian people
   (c) bourgeois movement
   (d) movement represented by Gandhi

8. Gandhi played a revolutionary role in India because he could
   (a) preach morality
   (b) reach the heart of Indians
   (c) see the conflict of classes
   (d) lead the Indian National Congress

9. Groups with advanced ideology functioned in the air as they did not fit in with
   (a) objective conditions of masses
   (b) the Gandhian ideology
   (c) the class consciousness of the people
   (d) the differences among masses

10. The author concludes the passage by
   (a) criticising the Indian masses
   (b) the Gandhian movement
   (c) pointing out the importance of the personality of Gandhi
   (d) identifying the sorrows of millions of Indians

11. Media that exist in an interconnected series of communication—points are referred to as
   (a) Networked media
   (b) Connective media
   (c) Nodal media
   (d) Multimedia

12. The information function of mass communication is described as

(a) diffusion (b) publicity
(c) surveillance (d) diversion

13. An example of asynchronous medium is
(a) Radio
(b) Television
(c) Film
(d) Newspaper

14. In communication, connotative words are
(a) explicit
(c) abstract
(b) simple
(d) cultural

15. A message beneath a message is labelled as
(a) embedded text
(b) internal text
(c) inter-text
(d) sub-text

16. In analogue mass communication, stories are
(a) static
(b) dynamic
(c) interactive
(d) exploratory

17. Determine the relationship between the pair of words ALWAYS : NEVER and then select from the following pair of words which have a similar relationship
(a) often : rarely
(b) frequently : occasionally
(c) constantly : frequently
(d) intermittently : casually

18. Find the wrong number in the sequence 52, 51, 48, 43, 34, 27, 16
(a) 27 (b) 34
(c) 43 (d) 48

19. In a certain code, PAN is written as 31 and PAR as 35, then PAT is written in the same code as
(a) 30 (b) 37
(c) 39 (d) 41

20. The letters in the first set have certain relationship. On the basis of this relationship, make the right choice for the second set:
AF : IK : : LQ : ?
(a) MO (b) NP
(c) OR (d) TV

21. If 5472 = 9, 6342 = 6, 7584 = 6, what is 9236?
(a) 2 (b) 3
(c) 4 (d) 5

22. In an examination, 35% of the total students failed in Hindi, 45% failed in English and 20% in both. The percentage of those who passed in both subjects is
(a) 10 (b) 20
(c) 30 (d) 40

23. Two statements I and II given below are followed by two conclusions (a) and (b). Supposing the statements are true, which of the following conclusions can logically follow?

Statements:
I. Some flowers are red.
II. Some flowers are blue.

Conclusions:
(i) Some flowers are neither red nor blue.
(ii) Some flowers are both red and blue.

Codes:
(a) Only (i) follows
(b) Only (ii) follows
(c) Both (i) and (ii) follows
(d) Neither (i) nor (ii) follows

24. If the statement 'all students are intelligent' is true, which of the following statements are false?
(i) No students are intelligent.
(ii) Some students are intelligent.
(iii) Some students are not intelligent.

(a) (i) and (ii) (b) (i) and (iii)
(c) (ii) and (iii) (d) Only (i)

25. A reasoning where we start with certain particular statements and conclude with a universal statement is called
(a) Deductive Reasoning
(b) Inductive Reasoning
(c) Abnormal Reasoning
(d) Transcendental Reasoning

26. What is the smallest number of ducks that could swim in this formation—two ducks in front of a duck, two ducks behind a duck and a duck between two ducks?
(a) 5 (b) 7
(c) 4 (d) 3

27. Mr. A, Miss B, Mr. C and Miss D are sitting around a table and discussing their trades.
(i) Mr. A sits opposite to the cook.
(ii) Miss B sits right to the barber.
(iii) The washerman sits right to the barber.
(iv) Miss D sits opposite to Mr. C.
What are the trades of A and B?
(a) Tailor and barber
(b) Barber and cook
(c) Tailor and cook
(d) Tailor and washerman

28. Which one of the following methods serve to measure correlation between two variables?
(a) Scatter Diagram
(b) Frequency Distribution
(c) Two-way table
(d) Coefficient of Rank Correlation

29. Which one of the following is not an Internet Service Provider (ISP)?
(a) MTNL
(b) BSNL
(c) ERNET India
(d) Infotech India Ltd.

30. The hexadecimal number system consists of the symbols
(a) 0 - 7 (b) 0 - 9, A - F
(c) 0 - 7, A - F (d) None of these

31. The binary equivalent of $(-15)_{10}$ is (2's complement system is used)
(a) 11110001 (b) 11110000
(c) 10001111 (d) None of these

32. 1 GB is equal to
(a) 2^{30} bits (b) 2^{30} bytes
(c) 2^{20} bits (d) 2^{20} bytes

33. The set of computer programs that manage the hardware/software of a computer is called
(a) Compiler system
(b) Operation system
(c) Operating system
(d) None of these

34. SMIME in Internet technology stands for
(a) Secure Multipurpose Internet Mail Extension
(b) Secure Multimedia Internet Mail Extension
(c) Simple Multipurpose Internet Mail Extension
(d) Simple Multimedia Internet Mail Extension

35. Which of the following is not covered in 8 missions under the Climate Action Plan of Government of India?
(a) Solar power
(b) Waste to energy conversion
(c) Afforestation
(d) Nuclear energy

36. The concentration of Total Dissolved Solids (TDS) in drinking water should not exceed
(a) 500 mg/L
(b) 400 mg/L
(c) 300 mg/L
(d) 200 mg/L

37. Chipko movement was first started by
   (a) Arundhati Roy
   (b) Medha Patkar
   (c) Ila Bhatt
   (d) Sunderlal Bahuguna

38. The constituents of photochemical smog responsible for eye irritation are
   (a) SO_2 and O_3
   (b) SO_2 and NO_2
   (c) HCHO and PAN
   (d) SO_2 and SPM

39. **Assertion (A):** Some carbonaceous aerosols may be carcinogenic.
   Reason (R): They may contain polycyclic aromatic hydrocarbons (PAHs).
   (a) Both (A) and (R) are correct and (R) is the correct explanation of (A).
   (b) Both (A) and (R) are correct, but (R) is not the correct explanation of (A).
   (c) (A) is correct, but (R) is false.
   (d) (A) is false, but (R) is correct.

40. Volcanic eruptions affect
   (a) atmosphere and hydrosphere
   (b) hydrosphere and biosphere
   (c) lithosphere, biosphere and atmosphere
   (d) lithosphere, hydrosphere and atmosphere

41. India's first Defence University is in the State of
   (a) Haryana
   (b) Andhra Pradesh
   (c) Uttar Pradesh
   (d) Punjab

42. Most of the Universities in India
   (a) conduct teaching and research only
   (b) affiliate colleges and conduct examinations
   (c) conduct teaching/research and examinations
   (d) promote research only

43. Which one of the following is not a Constitutional Body?
   (a) Election Commission
   (b) Finance Commission
   (c) Union Public Service Commission
   (d) Planning Commission

44. Which one of the following statements is not correct?
   (a) Indian Parliament is supreme.
   (b) The Supreme Court of India has the power of judicial review.
   (c) There is a division of powers between the Centre and the States.
   (d) There is a Council of Ministers to aid and advise the President.

45. Which one of the following statements reflects the republic character of Indian democracy?
   (a) Written constitution
   (b) No State religion
   (c) Devolution of power to local government institutions
   (d) Elected President and directly or indirectly elected Parliament

46. Who among the following appointed by the Governor can be removed by only the President of India?
   (a) Chief Minister of a State
   (b) A member of the State Public Service Commission
   (c) Advocate-General
   (d) Vice Chancellor of a State University

47. If two small circles represent the class of the 'men' and the class of the 'plants' and the big circle represents 'mortality', which one of the following figures represent the proposition 'All men are mortal.'?

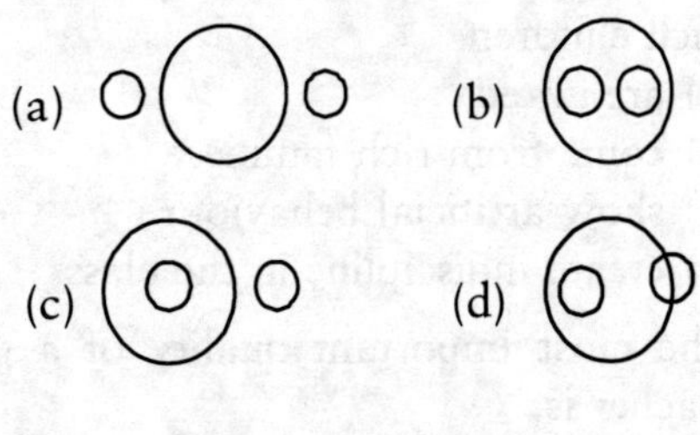

The following table presents the production of electronic items (TVs and LCDs) in a factory during the period from 2006 to 2010. Study the table carefully and answer the questions from 48 to 52:

Year	2006	2007	2008	2009	2010
TVs	6000	9000	13000	11000	8000
LCDs	7000	9400	9000	10000	12000

48. In which year, the total production of electronic items is maximum?
(a) 2006 (b) 2007
(c) 2008 (d) 2010

49. What is the difference between averages of production of LCDs and TVs from 2006 to 2008?
(a) 3000 (b) 2867
(c) 3015 (d) None of these

50. What is the year in which production of TVs is half the production of LCDs in the year 2010?
(a) 2007 (b) 2006
(c) 2009 (d) 2008

51. What is the ratio of production of LCDs in the years 2008 and 2010?
(a) 4:3 (b) 3:4
(c) 1:3 (d) 2:3

52. What is the ratio of production of TVs in the years 2006 and 2007?
(a) 6:7 (b) 7:6
(c) 2:3 (d) 3:2

53. Some students in a class exhibit great curiosity for learning. It may be because such children
(a) are gifted
(b) come from rich families
(c) show artificial behaviour
(d) create indiscipline in the class

54. The most important quality of a good teacher is
(a) Sound knowledge of subject matter
(b) Good communication skills
(c) Concern for students' welfare
(d) Effective leadership qualities

55. Which one of the following is appropriate in respect of teacher-student relationship?
(a) Very informal and intimate
(b) Limited to classroom only
(c) Cordial and respectful
(d) Indifferent

56. The academic performance of students can be improved if parents are encouraged to
(a) supervise the work of their wards
(b) arrange for extra tuition
(c) remain unconcerned about it
(d) interact with teachers frequently

57. In a lively classroom situation, there is likely to be
(a) occasional roars of laughter
(b) complete silence
(c) frequent teacher-student dialogue
(d) loud discussion among students

58. If a parent approaches the teacher to do some favour to his/her ward in the examination, the teacher should
(a) try to help him
(b) ask him not to talk in those terms
(c) refuse politely and firmly
(d) ask him rudely to go away

59. Which of the following phrases is not relevant to describe the meaning of research as a process?
(a) Systematic Activity
(b) Objective Observation
(c) Trial and Error
(d) Problem Solving

60. Which of the following is not an example of a continuous variable?
(a) Family size
(b) Intelligence
(c) Height
(d) Attitude

ANSWERS

1. (d)	2. (b)	3. (a)	4. (c)	5. (b)
6. (d)	7. (c)	8. (b)	9. (a)	10. (c)
11. (a)	12. (c)	13. (d)	14. (d)	15. (d)
16. (a)	17. (a)	18. (b)	19. (b)	20. (d)
21. (a)	22. (b)	23. (c)	24. (d)	25. (b)
26. (a)	27. (c)	28. (d)	29. (d)	30. (b)
31. (d)	32. (b)	33. (c)	34. (a)	35. (d)
36. (a)	37. (d)	38. (b)	39. (a)	40. (d)
41. (a)	42. (c)	43. (d)	44. (b)	45. (d)
46. (b)	47. (c)	48. (c)	49. (d)	50. (b)
51. (b)	52. (c)	53. (a)	54. (b)	55. (c)
56. (d)	57. (c)	58. (c)	59. (c)	60. (c)

PAPER–II

Note: This paper contains Fifty (50) objective type questions, each question carrying two (2) marks. All questions are compulsory.

1. "We belong to associations, not to institutions." Who among the following said so?
   (a) Ogburn
   (b) Sutherland
   (c) Giddens
   (d) MacIver

2. Which of the following statements are correct? Answer by using the correct codes given below:
   (i) A class system of social stratification may be regarded as a 'closed' system.
   (ii) It may be regarded as an 'open' system.
   (iii) In the class system, a person cannot move up or down in the social hierarchy.
   (iv) The class system is usually distinguished by social mobility.

   Codes:
   (a) (ii) and (iii) (b) (ii) and (iv)
   (c) (i) and (iv) (d) (i) and (iii)

3. An example of an ex-criminal's conformity to social norms may be called
   (a) Socialisation
   (b) Re-socialisation
   (c) De-socialisation
   (d) Non-socialisation

4. Match the following methods of investigation of social phenomena (List I) with the names (List II) of authors associated with them:

List I	List II
A. Logico-experimental	i. Durkheim
B. Dialectical	ii. Pareto
C. Ideal typical	iii. Marx
D. Functional	iv. Weber

Codes:	A	B	C	D
(a)	iii	ii	i	iv
(b)	ii	iii	iv	i
(c)	iv	iii	ii	i
(d)	i	iii	iv	ii

5. Which one of the following is not an example of a community?
   (a) The Red Indians
   (b) The Muria
   (c) The Andman Icelanders
   (d) The Rashtriya Swayamsewak Sangh

6. Match List I with List II and select the correct answer from the codes given below the lists:

   List I
   A. Sub-culture
   B. Contra-culture
   C. Vehicle of culture
   D. Culture clash

   List II
   i. Hippie
   ii. Language
   iii. Army
   iv. Ayodhya Temple Movement

Codes:	A	B	C	D
(a)	iv	ii	iii	i
(b)	i	ii	iii	iv
(c)	iii	i	ii	iv
(d)	i	iv	ii	iii

7. Who among the following used sociometry for the first time?
(a) Lundberg (b) Moreno
(c) Bogardus (d) Burgess

8. One of the following does not form part of social action typology presented by Weber. Identify.
(a) Democratic
(b) Traditional
(c) Evaluative
(d) Rational

9. Identify which one of the following does not constitute an element of culture:
(a) Family
(b) Values
(c) Dress
(d) Ways of behaviour

10. In his sociological explanation of religion, Durkheim made certain observations. Select the correct ones from the codes given below:
(i) Religion is mental illness.
(ii) God is only society personified.
(iii) Religion brings salvation for the suffering humanity.
(iv) The kingdom of heaven is a glorified society.

Codes:
(a) (i) and (ii) (b) (ii) and (iii)
(c) (i) and (iii) (d) (ii) and (iv)

11. Which of the following is not an example of primary group?
(a) Neighbourhood
(b) School
(c) Friends Circle
(d) The State Bank of India

12. The State is an example of which of the following?
(a) Primary group
(b) Community
(c) Association
(d) Government

13. Classification of groups into ingroup and outgroup categories was presented by who among the following?
(a) Tonnies (b) Cooley
(c) Homans (d) Sumner

14. Who has divided functions of family into following six categories?
(i) Affectional (ii) Economic
(iii) Recreational (iv) Protective
(v) Religious (vi) Educational
(a) MacIver
(b) Ogburn and Nimkoff
(c) G.H. Sprott
(d) Arnold Green

15. Who has defined the Hindu Joint Family as "a group constituted of known ancestors and adopted sons and relatives related to these sons through marriage"?
(a) Henry Maine
(b) Kingsley Davis
(c) R.M. MacIver
(d) H.M. Johnson

16. The first significant contribution to the study of kinship was made by
(a) Tylor
(b) Morgan
(c) Malinowski
(d) Redcliffe-Brown

17. Match List I with List II and select the correct answer from the codes given below the list:

List I
A. Family and kinship among Pandits of Kashmir
B. Kinship and Marriage

C. Elementary structures of kinship
D. Family and kin, in Indo-European culture

List II
i. Robin Fox
ii. G.S. Ghurye
iii. Radhakamal Mukherjee
iv. T.N. Madan
v. C. Levi-Strauss

Codes:	A	B	C	D
(a)	iii	i	v	ii
(b)	iv	i	v	ii
(c)	iv	ii	iii	v
(d)	ii	i	iv	iii

18. Given below are two statements, one labelled as Assertion (A) and the other labelled as Reason (R).
Assertion (A): Caste as a social group cannot be called a community.
Reason (R): Caste does have social coherence but it lacks the community's territorial basis.
In the context of the above two statements, which one of the following is correct?
Codes:
(a) Both (A) and (R) are true and (R) is the correct explanation of (A).
(b) Both (A) and (R) are true, but (R) is not the correct explanation of (A).
(c) (A) is true, but (R) is false.
(d) (A) is false, but (R) is true.

19. Which of the following pairs are correctly matched?

(1) Sanskritization	M.N. Srinivas
(2) Little and Great Tradition	McKim Marriott
(3) Brahminisation	Aiyappan
(4) Parochialization	F.G. Bailey

Select the correct answer using the codes given below:
Codes:
(a) 2, 3 and 4 (b) 1, 3 and 4
(c) 1, 2 and 4 (d) 1, 2 and 3

20. Match List I with List II and select the correct answer using the codes given below the lists:
List I
A. Caste is a closed system
B. Caste is a closed organic stratification
C. Caste is an extreme form of equality
D. Caste is an expression of hierarchy rather than stratification

List II
i. Louis Dumont
ii. Gunar Myrdal
iii. Fredrick Bailey
iv. Max Weber

Codes:	A	B	C	D
(a)	i	ii	iii	iv
(b)	iv	iii	ii	i
(c)	i	iii	ii	iv
(d)	iv	ii	iii	i

21. Match List I with List II and select the correct answer using the codes given below the lists:
List I
A. Opposition of purity-pollution.
B. Tribe-caste-Peasant continuum
C. Attributional and International analysis

List II
i. S. Sinha
ii. L. Dumont
iii. McKim Marriott
iv. M.N. Srinivas

Codes:	A	B	C
(a)	i	iv	ii
(b)	i	iii	iv
(c)	ii	i	iii
(d)	ii	iii	i

22. Choose the right arrangement of the following stages of socialization in a sequence from the codes given below:
(a) Anticipatory
(b) Child
(c) Infant
(d) Adult
(e) Adolescent
Codes:
(a) a c b e d
(b) e c b d a
(c) c b e d a
(d) b c d e a

23. Which one of the following is an example of 'generalized others'?
(a) Community
(b) Friends
(c) Peer group
(d) Parents

24. Who among the following has analysed the stages of social evolution as simple, compound, double compound and trebly compound?
(a) L.H. Morgan
(b) E.B. Tylor
(c) E. Durkheim
(d) H. Spencer

25. Some social change occurs without being noticed by most members of a society is known as
(a) Manifest change
(b) Latent change
(c) Relative change
(d) Absolute change

26. Who among the following does not belong to cyclical theory of social change?
(a) Spencer
(b) Toynbee
(c) Lipset
(d) Hobhouse

27. Match List I with List II and select the correct answer from the codes given below:

List I	List II
A. Cyclical	i. Vico
B. Linear	ii. Sorokin
C. Fluctuation	iii. Spengler
D. Spiral	iv. Spencer

Codes:	A	B	C	D
(a)	iii	iv	ii	i
(b)	iii	ii	i	iv
(c)	ii	iii	i	iv
(d)	ii	i	iv	iii

28. According to Radcliffe-Brown, a society with a condition of functional disunity rarely dies, instead, it
(i) Struggles towards the new state of eunomia.
(ii) Might change its structural pattern.
(iii) Throws itself into disarray.
(iv) Changes its identity.
Select the correct answer from the codes given below:
Codes:
(a) (i) and (ii) are correct
(b) (ii) and (iii) are correct
(c) (i) and (iii) are correct
(d) (iii) and (iv) are correct

29. Which one of the following is not associated with Malinowski's three levels of system in hierarchic order?
(a) Symbolic system
(b) Social structural system
(c) Personality system
(d) Biological system

30. Who laid down the distinction between historical and functional types of inquiry?
(a) Radcliffe-Brown
(b) Durkheim
(c) Parsons
(d) Merton

31. Match the List I with List II and choose the correct answer from the codes given below the lists.

List I

A. Affectivity-affective neutrality
B. Diffuseness-specificity
C. Universalism-particularism
D. Achievement-ascriptive

List II

i. Whether actors be assessed in terms of same standards
ii. Whether actors be assessed in terms of achievement or ascription
iii. Appropriate emotional expression in an interaction
iv. Appropriate obligations in a relationship

Codes:	A	B	C	D
(a)	iv	i	iii	ii
(b)	iii	iv	i	ii
(c)	ii	i	iii	iv
(d)	i	ii	iv	iii

32. Which of the following functional imperatives of Talcott Parsons is associated with 'Pattern maintenance and tension management'?
(a) Adaptation
(b) Goal attainment
(c) Integration
(d) Latency

33. Robert K. Merton stated that a cultural item can have diverse and varied consequences for individuals, groups, society and culture. To which of his functional postulates this statement is related?
(a) Functional unity
(b) Universal functionalism
(c) Functional indispensability
(d) None of the above

34. 'An action is determined by a conscious belief in the value for its own sake.' This statement is applicable to which of the following types of action propounded by Max Weber?
(a) Action based on Means-end rationality
(b) Action based on value rationality
(c) Affectual action
(d) Traditional action

35. Which one of the following is associated with Pareto's concept of non-logical action?
(a) Non-scientific belief systems are the determinants of action
(b) Non-scientific belief systems are not the determinants of action.
(c) Non-scientific belief systems are the expressions of deep seated sentiments.
(d) None of the above.

36. Which of the following statements distinguishes 'I' from 'Me'?
(a) 'I' is given importance in modern society and 'Me' is given importance in primitive society.
(b) Important values are located in 'I' but not in 'Me'.
(c) 'I' is immediate response to others while 'Me' is the organised set of attitudes of others.
(d) None of the above.

37. Which of the following is not related to functional theory of Durkheim?
(a) Society can be reduced to parts.
(b) Society can be decomposed into its constituent parts.
(c) System parts fufill basic needs of the whole.
(d) System can be normal only when equilibrium is maintained.

38. Who paid attention to positive dimensions of conflict?
(a) Coser (b) Dahrendorf
(c) Collins (d) Simmel

39. Two statements are given here, one is labelled as Assertion (A) and other as Reason (R).
Assertion (A): Symbolic interactionist tend to accord causal significance to social interaction.
Reason (R): Meaning stems from not from solitary mental process but from interaction.
Select the correct answer from the codes given below:
Codes:
(a) Both (A) and (R) are true and (R) is the correct explanation of (A).
(b) Both (A) and (R) are true, but (R) is not the correct explanation of (A).
(c) (A) is true, but (R) is false.
(d) (A) is false, but (R) is true.

40. Who has used historical comparative method in the study of West European societies?
(a) Emile Durkheim
(b) Max Weber
(c) L.H. Morgan
(d) T. Veblen

41. Who among the classical sociologists has used quantitative method in comparative analysis?
(a) Karl Marx
(b) Max Weber
(c) Emile Durkheim
(d) Auguste Comte

42. Who among the following propounded the idea of sociology as 'a natural science of society'?
(a) B. Malinowski
(b) Talcott Parsons
(c) Claude Levi-Strauss
(d) A.R. Radcliffe-Brown

43. Who argued that 'structure is a method not a reality'?
(a) Claude Levi-Strauss
(b) A.R. Radcliffe-Brown
(c) S.F. Nadel
(d) Talcott Parsons

44. Who is known to have used 'participant observation' method in the study of American society?
(a) B. Malinowski
(b) W.F. Whyte
(c) W.J. Goode
(d) P.F. Hatt

45. In which research design hypothesis is not necessarily required?
(a) Descriptive
(b) Experimental
(c) Diagnostic
(d) Exploratory

46. Case-study involves
(a) Quantitative analysis
(b) Quantitative and Qualitative analysis
(c) Qualitative analysis
(d) All of the above

47. Which of the following takes into account quantity of a position in the array?
(a) Mean (b) Mode
(c) Median (d) All of the above

48. Who is said to be the founding father of survey research?
(a) Charles Booth
(b) R.F. Lazarsfeld
(c) R.K. Merton
(d) W.J. Goode

49. Match List I with List II and select the correct answer from the codes given below the lists:
List I (Term)
A. Qualitative variables
B. Quantitative variables
C. Frequency distribution
D. Probability

List II (Statistic)
i. Tabulation ii. Sampling
iii. Attributes iv. Variates
v. Deviation

Codes:	A	B	C	D
(a)	i	ii	iii	iv
(b)	ii	iii	iv	v
(c)	iii	iv	i	ii
(d)	iv	i	ii	iii

50. Match List I with List II and select the correct answer from the codes given below the lists:

List I (Concepts)
A. Participant observation
B. Content Analysis
C. Conjuctural history
D. Research Design

List II (Authors)
i. Jahoda
ii. Charles Booth
iii. Malinowski
iv. Radcliffe-Brown
v. Merton

Codes:	A	B	C	D
(a)	v	iv	iii	ii
(b)	iii	v	iv	i
(c)	iv	iii	ii	i
(d)	ii	iv	iii	v

ANSWERS

1. (b)	2. (c)	3. (c)	4. (b)	5. (b)
6. (a)	7. (a)	8. (d)	9. (d)	10. (a)
11. (d)	12. (b)	13. (c)	14. (a)	15. (d)
16. (d)	17. (a)	18. (b)	19. (b)	20. (c)
21. (b)	22. (a)	23. (b)	24. (c)	25. (b)
26. (a)	27. (a)	28. (b)	29. (c)	30. (d)
31. (c)	32. (c)	33. (c)	34. (a)	35. (a)
36. (a)	37. (b)	38. (a)	39. (a)	40. (c)
41. (c)	42. (c)	43. (d)	44. (d)	45. (d)
46. (b)	47. (a)	48. (b)	49. (c)	50. (b)

JUNE–2010

Note: This paper contains Sixty (60) multiple-choice questions, each question carrying two (2) marks. Candidate is expected to answer any Fifty (50) questions. In case more than Fifty (50) questions are attempted, only the first Fifty (50) questions will be evaluated.

PAPER–I

1. Which one of the following is the most important quality of a good teacher?
   (a) Punctuality and sincerity
   (b) Content mastery
   (c) Content mastery and reactive
   (d) Content mastery and sociable

2. The primary responsibility for the teacher's adjustment lies with
   (a) The children
   (b) The principal
   (c) The teacher himself
   (d) The community

3. As per the NCTE norms, what should be the staff strength for a unit of 100 students at B.Ed. level?
   (a) 1 + 7 (b) 1 + 9
   (c) 1 + 10 (d) 1 + 5

4. Research has shown that the most frequent symptom of nervous instability among teachers is
   (a) Digestive upsets
   (b) Explosive behaviour
   (c) Fatigue
   (d) Worry

5. Which one of the following statements is correct?
   (a) Syllabus is an annexure to the curriculum.
   (b) Curriculum is the same in all educational institutions.
   (c) Curriculum includes both formal and informal education.
   (d) Curriculum does not include methods of evaluation.

6. A successful teacher is one who is
   (a) Compassionate and disciplinarian
   (b) Quite and reactive
   (c) Tolerant and dominating
   (d) Passive and active

Read the following passage carefully and answer the questions from 7 to 12:

The phrase "What is it like?" stands for a fundamental thought process. How does one go about observing and reporting on things and events that occupy segments of earth space? Of all the infinite variety of phenomena on the face of the earth, how does one decide what phenomena to observe? There is no such thing as a complete description of the earth or any part of it, for every microscopic point on the earth's surface differs from every other such point. Experience shows that the things observed are already familiar, because they are like phenomena that occur at home or because they resemble the abstract images and models developed in the human mind.

How are abstract images formed? Humans alone among the animals possess language; their words symbolise not only specific things but also mental images of classes of things. People can remember what they have seen or experienced because they attach a word symbol to them.

During the long record of our efforts to gain more and more knowledge about the face of the earth as the human habitat, there has been a continuing interplay between things and events. The direct observation through the senses is described as a percept; the mental image is described as a concept. Percepts are what some people describe as reality, in contrast to mental images, which are theoretical, implying that they are not real.

The relation of Percept to Concept is not as simple as the definition implies. It is now quite clear that people of different cultures or even individuals in the same culture develop different mental images of reality and what they perceive is a reflection of these preconceptions. The direct observation of things and events on the face of the earth is so clearly a function of the mental images of the mind of the observer that the whole idea of reality must be reconsidered.

Concepts determine what the observer perceives, yet concepts are derived from the generalizations of previous percepts. What happens is that the educated observer is taught to accept a set of concepts and then sharpens or changes these concepts during a professional career. In any one field of scholarship, professional opinion at one time determines what concepts and procedures are acceptable, and these form a kind of model of scholarly behaviour.

7. The problem raised in the passage reflects on
   (a) thought process
   (b) human behaviour
   (c) cultural perceptions
   (d) professional opinion

8. According to the passage, human beings have mostly in mind
   (a) Observation of things
   (b) Preparation of mental images
   (c) Expression through language
   (d) To gain knowledge

9. Concept means
   (a) a mental image
   (b) a reality
   (c) an idea expressed in language form
   (d) All of the above

10. The relation of Percept to Concept is
    (a) Positive
    (b) Negative
    (c) Reflective
    (d) Absolute

11. In the passage, the earth is taken as
    (a) The Globe
    (b) The Human Habitat
    (c) A Celestial Body
    (d) A Planet

12. Percept means
    (a) Direct observation through the senses
    (b) A conceived idea
    (c) Ends of a spectrum
    (d) An abstract image

13. Action research means
    (a) A longitudinal research
    (b) An applied research
    (c) A research initiated to solve an immediate problem
    (d) A research with socio-economic objective

14. Research is
    (a) searching again and again
    (b) finding solution to any problem
    (c) working in a scientific way to search for truth of any problem
    (d) None of the above

15. A common test in research demands much priority on
    (a) Reliability
    (b) Usability
    (c) Objectivity
    (d) All of the above
16. Which of the following is the first step in starting the research process?
    (a) Searching sources of information to locate problem
    (b) Survey of related literature
    (c) Identification of problem
    (d) Searching for solutions to the problem
17. If a researcher conducts a research on finding out which administrative style contributes more to institutional effectiveness? This will be an example of
    (a) Basic Research
    (b) Action Research
    (c) Applied Research
    (d) None of the above
18. Normal Probability Curve should be
    (a) Positively skewed
    (b) Negatively skewed
    (c) Leptokurtic skewed
    (d) Zero skewed
19. In communication, a major barrier to reception of messages is
    (a) audience attitude
    (b) audience knowledge
    (c) audience education
    (d) audience income
20. Post-modernism is associated with
    (a) Newspapers
    (b) Magazines
    (c) Radio
    (d) Television
21. Didactic communication is
    (a) intra-personal
    (b) inter-personal
    (c) organisational
    (d) relational
22. In communication, the language is
    (a) the non-verbal code
    (b) the verbal code
    (c) the symbolic code
    (d) the iconic code
23. Identify the correct sequence of the following:
    (a) Source, channel, message, receiver
    (b) Source, receiver, channel, message
    (c) Source, message, receiver, channel
    (d) Source, message, channel, receiver
24. **Assertion (A):** Mass media promote a culture of violence in the society.

    Reason (R): Because violence sells in the market as people themselves are violent in character.
    (a) Both (A) and (R) are true and (R) is the correct explanation of (A).
    (b) Both (A) and (R) are true, but (R) is not the correct explanation of (A).
    (c) (A) is true, but (R) is false.
    (d) Both (A) and (R) are false.
25. When an error of 1% is made in the length of a square, the percentage error in the area of a square will be
    (a) 0 (b) 1/2
    (c) 1 (d) 2
26. On January 12, 1980, it was a Saturday. The day of the week on January 12, 1979 was
    (a) Thursday
    (b) Friday
    (c) Saturday
    (d) Sunday
27. If water is called food, food is called tree, tree is called earth, earth is called world, which of the following grows a fruit?

(a) Water (b) Tree
(c) World (d) Earth

28. E is the son of A, D is the son of B, E is married to C, C is the daughter of B. How is D related to E?
(a) Brother
(b) Uncle
(c) Father-in-law
(d) Brother-in-law

29. If INSURANCE is coded as ECNARUSNI, how HINDRANCE will be coded?
(a) CADNIHWCE
(b) HANODEINR
(c) AENIRHDCN
(d) ECNARDNIH

30. Find the next number in the following series: 2, 5, 10, 17, 26, 37, 50, ?
(a) 63 (b) 65
(c) 67 (d) 69

31. Which of the following is an example of circular argument?
(a) God created man in his image and man created God in his own image.
(b) God is the source of a scripture and the scripture is the source of our knowledge of God.
(c) Some of the Indians are great because India is great.
(d) Rama is great because he is Rama.

32. Lakshmana is a morally good person because
(a) he is religious
(b) he is educated
(c) he is rich
(d) he is rational

33. Two statements I and II given below are followed by two conclusions (i) and (ii). Supposing the statements are true, which of the following conclusions can logically follow?

Statements:
I. Some religious people are morally good.
II. Some religious people are rational.

Conclusions:
(i) Rationally religious people are good morally.
(ii) Non-rational religious persons are not morally good.
(a) Only (i) follows
(b) Only (ii) follows
(c) Both (i) and (ii) follow
(d) Neither (i) nor (ii) follows

34. Certainty is
(a) an objective fact
(b) emotionally satisfying
(c) logical
(d) ontological

Questions from 35 to 36 are based on the following diagram in which there are three intersecting circles I, S and P where circle I stands for Indians, circle S stands for Scientists and circle P for Politicians. Different regions of the figure are lettered from a to g.

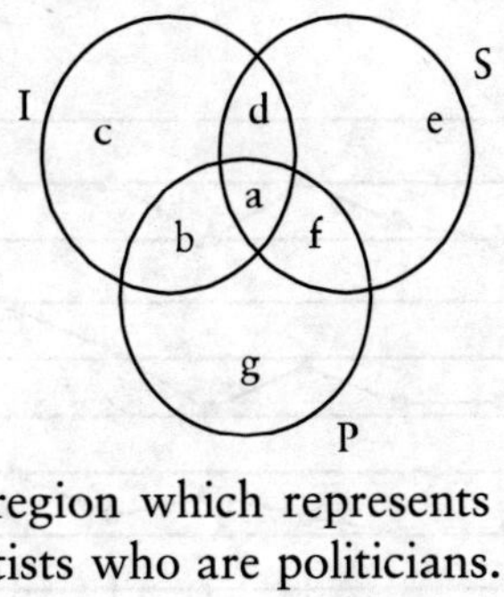

35. The region which represents non-Indian scientists who are politicians.
(a) f (b) d
(c) a (d) c

36. The region which represents politicians who are Indians as well as scientists.

(a) b (b) c
(c) a (d) d

37. The population of a city is plotted as a function of time (years) in graphic form below:

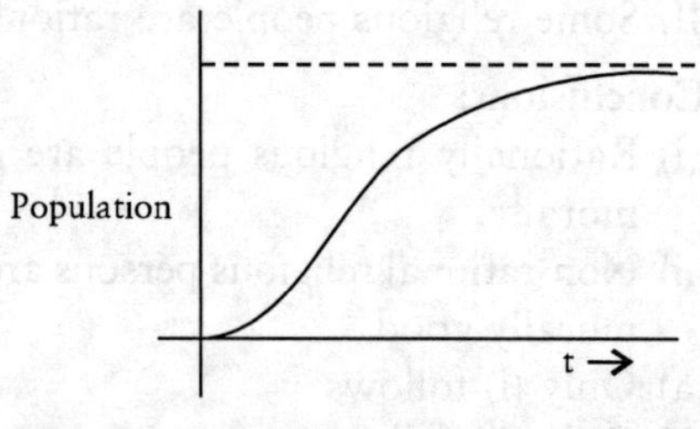

Which of the following inference can be drawn from above plot?
(a) The population increases exponentially.
(b) The population increases in parabolic fashion.
(c) The population initially increases in a linear fashion and then stabilises.
(d) The population initially increases exponentially and then stabilises.

In the following chart, the price of logs is shown in per cubic metre and that of Plywood and Saw Timber in per tonnes. Study the chart and answer the following questions 38, 39 and 40.

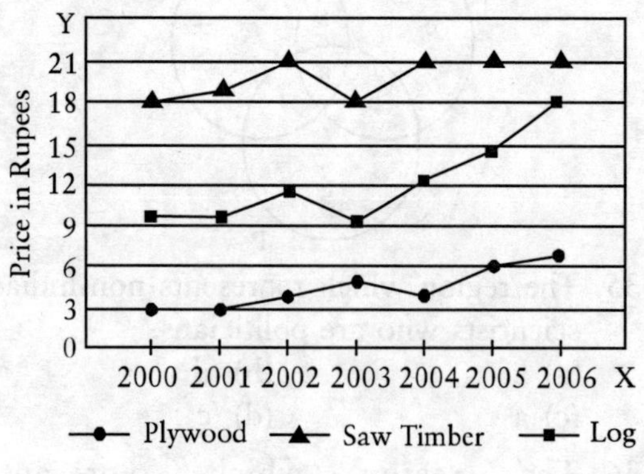

38. Which product shows the maximum percentage increase in price over the period?
(a) Saw timber
(b) Plywood
(c) Log
(d) None of the above

39. What is the maximum percentage increase in price per cubic metre of log?
(a) 6 (b) 12
(c) 18 (d) None of these

40. In which year the prices of two products increased and that of the third increased?
(a) 2000 (b) 2002
(c) 2003 (d) 2006

41. Which one of the following is the oldest Archival source of data in India?
(a) National Sample Surveys
(b) Agricultural Statistics
(c) Census
(d) Vital Statistics

42. In a large random data set following normal distribution, the ratio (%) of number of data points which are in the range of (mean ± standard deviation) to the total number of data points is
(a) ~ 50% (b) ~ 67%
(c) ~ 97% (d) ~ 47%

43. Which number system is usually followed in a typical 32-bit computer?
(a) 2 (b) 8
(c) 10 (d) 16

44. Which one of the following is an example of Operating System?
(a) Microsoft Word
(b) Microsoft Excel
(c) Microsoft Access
(d) Microsoft Windows

45. Which one of the following represent the binary equivalent of the decimal number 23?
(a) 01011 (b) 10111
(c) 10011 (d) None of these

46. Which one of the following is different from other members?
(a) Google
(b) Windows
(c) Linux
(d) Mac

47. Where does a computer add and compare its data?
(a) CPU
(b) Memory
(c) Hard disk
(d) Floppy disk

48. Computers on an internet are identified by
(a) e-mail address
(b) street address
(c) IP address
(d) None of the above

49. The Right to Information Act, 2005 makes the provision of
(a) Dissemination of all types of information by all Public authorities to any person
(b) Establishment of Central, State and District Level Information Commissions as an appellate body
(c) Transparency and accountability in Public authorities
(d) All of the above

50. Which type of natural hazards cause maximum damage to property and lives?
(a) Hydrological
(b) Hydro-meteorological
(c) Geological
(d) Geo-chemical

51. Dioxins are produced from
(a) Wastelands
(b) Power plants
(c) Sugar factories
(d) Combustion of plastics

52. The slogan "A tree for each child" was coined for
(a) Social forestry program
(b) Clean Air program
(c) Soil conservation program
(d) Environmental protection program

53. The main constituents of biogas are
(a) Methane and Carbon dioxide
(b) Methane and Nitric oxide
(c) Methane, Hydrogen and Nitric oxide
(d) Methane and Sulphur dioxide

54. **Assertion (A):** In the world as a whole, the environment has degraded during past several decades.

Reason (R): The population of the world has been growing significantly.
(a) (A) is correct, (R) is correct and (R) is the correct explanation of (A).
(b) (A) is correct, (R) is correct and (R) is not the correct explanation of (A).
(c) (A) is correct, but (R) is false.
(d) (A) is false, but (R) is correct.

55. Climate change has implications for
1. soil moisture
2. forest fires
3. biodiversity
4. groundwater

Identify the correct combination according to the code:

Codes:
(a) 1 and 3 (b) 1, 2 and 3
(c) 1, 3 and 4 (d) 1, 2, 3 and 4

56. The accreditation process by National Assessment and Accreditation Council

(NAAC) differs from that of National Board of Accreditation (NBA) in terms of

(a) Disciplines covered by both being the same, there is duplication of efforts.
(b) One has institutional grading approach and the other has program grading approach.
(c) Once get accredited by NBA or NAAC, the institution is free from renewal of grading, which is not a progressive decision.
(d) This accreditation amounts to approval of minimum standards in the quality of education in the institution concerned.

57. Which option is not correct?
(a) Most of the educational institutions of National repute in scientific and technical sphere fall under 64th entry of Union list.
(b) Education, in general, is the subject of concurrent list since 42nd Constitutional Amendment Act 1976.
(c) Central Advisory Board on Education (CABE) was first established in 1920.
(d) India had implemented the right to Free and Compulsory Primary Education in 2002 through 86th Constitutional Amendment.

58. Which statement is not correct about the "National Education Day" of India?
(a) It is celebrated on 5th September every year.
(b) It is celebrated on 11th November every year.
(c) It is celebrated in the memory of India's first Union Minister of Education, Dr. Abul Kalam Azad.
(d) It is being celebrated since 2008.

59. Match List I with List II and select the correct answer from the codes given below:

List I (Articles of the Constitution)
A. Article 280
B. Article 324
C. Article 323
D. Article 315

List II (Institutions)
1. Administrative Tribunals
2. Election Commission of India
3. Finance Commission at Union level
4. Union Public Service Commission

Codes:	A	B	C	D
(a)	1	2	3	4
(b)	3	2	1	4
(c)	2	3	4	1
(d)	2	4	3	1

60. Deemed Universities declared by UGC under Section 3 of the UGC Act 1956, are not permitted to
(a) offer programs in higher education and issue degrees
(b) give affiliation to any institute of higher education
(c) open off-campus and off-shore campus anywhere in the country and overseas respectively without the permission of the UGC
(d) offer distance education programs without the approval of the Distance Education Council

ANSWERS

1. (b)	2. (c)	3. (c)	4. (b)	5. (c)	31. (b)	32. (a)	33. (d)	34. (c)	35. (a)
6. (a)	7. (c)	8. (a)	9. (a)	10. (c)	36. (c)	37. (d)	38. (c)	39. (d)	40. (b)
11. (b)	12. (a)	13. (c)	14. (c)	15. (d)	41. (c)	42. (b)	43. (a)	44. (d)	45. (b)
16. (c)	17. (c)	18. (d)	19. (c)	20. (d)	46. (b)	47. (a)	48. (c)	49. (d)	50. (c)
21. (b)	22. (b)	23. (d)	24. (d)	25. (d)	51. (d)	52. (d)	53. (a)	54. (b)	55. (d)
26. (b)	27. (c)	28. (d)	29. (d)	30. (b)	56. (c)	57. (a)	58. (a)	59. (b)	60. (b)

DECEMBER–2009

Note: This paper contains Sixty (60) multiple-choice questions, each question carrying two (2) marks. Candidate is expected to answer any Fifty (50) questions. In case more than Fifty (50) questions are attempted, only the first Fifty (50) questions will be evaluated.

PAPER–I

1. The University which telecasts interaction educational programs through its own channel is
   (a) Osmania University
   (b) University of Pune
   (c) Annamalai University
   (d) Indira Gandhi National Open University (IGNOU)

2. Which of the following skills are needed for present day teacher to adjust effectively with the classroom teaching?
   1. Knowledge of technology
   2. Use of technology in teaching learning
   3. Knowledge of students' needs
   4. Content mastery

   (a) 1 and 3 (b) 2 and 3
   (c) 2, 3 and 4 (d) 2 and 4

3. Who has signed as MoU for Accreditation of Teacher Education Institutions in India?
   (a) NAAC and UGC
   (b) NCTE and NAAC
   (c) UGC and NCTE
   (d) NCTE and IGNOU

4. The primary duty of the teacher is to
   (a) raise the intellectual standard of the students
   (b) improve the physical standard of the students
   (c) help all-round development of the students
   (d) imbibe value system in the students

5. Micro teaching is more effective
   (a) during the preparation for teaching-practice
   (b) during the teaching-practice
   (c) after the teaching-practice
   (d) always

6. What quality the students like the most in a teacher?
   (a) Idealist philosophy
   (b) Compassion
   (c) Discipline
   (d) Entertaining

7. A null hypothesis is
   (a) when there is no difference between the variables
   (b) the same as research hypothesis
   (c) subjective in nature
   (d) when there is difference between the variables

8. The research which is exploring new facts through the study of the past is called
   (a) Philosophical research
   (b) Historical research
   (c) Mythological research
   (d) Content analysis

9. Action research is
   (a) An applied research
   (b) A research carried out to solve immediate problems
   (c) A longitudinal research
   (d) Simulative research

10. The process not needed in Experimental Researches is
    (a) Observation
    (b) Manipulation
    (c) Controlling
    (d) Content Analysis
11. Manipulation is always a part of
    (a) Historical research
    (b) Fundamental research
    (c) Descriptive research
    (d) Experimental research
12. Which correlation co-efficient best explains the relationship between creativity and intelligence?
    (a) 1.00 (b) 0.6
    (c) 0.5 (d) 0.3

Read the following passage and answer the questions from 13 to 18:

The decisive shift in British Policy really came about under mass pressure in the autumn and winter of 1945 to 46—the months which Penderel Moon while editing Wavell's Journal has perceptively described as 'The Edge of a Volcano'. Very foolishly, the British initially decided to hold public trials of several hundreds of the 20,000 I.N.A. prisoners (as well as dismissing from service and detaining without trial no less than 7,000). They compounded the folly by holding the first trial in the Red Fort, Delhi in November 1945, and putting on the dock together a Hindu, a Muslim and a Sikh (P.K. Sehgal, Shah Nawaz, Gurbaksh Singh Dhillon). Bhulabhai Desai, Tejbahadur Sapru and Nehru appeared for the defence (the latter putting on his barrister's gown after 25 years), and the Muslim League also joined the countrywide protest. On 20 November, an Intelligence Bureau note admitted that "there has seldom been a matter which has attracted so much Indian public interest and, it is safe to say, sympathy...this particular brand of sympathy cuts across communal barriers". A journalist (B. Shiva Rao) visiting the Red Fort prisoners on the same day reported that 'There is not the slightest feeling among them of Hindu and Muslim.... A majority of the men now awaiting trial in the Red Fort is Muslim. Some of these men are bitter that Mr. Jinnah is keeping alive a controversy about Pakistan.' The British became extremely nervous about the I.N.A. spirit spreading to the Indian Army, and in January the Punjab Governor reported that a Lahore reception for released I.N.A. prisoners had been attended by Indian soldiers in uniform.

13. Which heading is more appropriate to assign to the above passage?
    (a) Wavell's Journal
    (b) Role of Muslim League
    (c) I.N.A. Trials
    (d) Red Fort Prisoners
14. The trial of P.K. Sehgal, Shah Nawaz and Gurbaksh Singh Dhillon symbolises
    (a) communal harmony
    (b) threat to all religious persons
    (c) threat to persons fighting for the freedom
    (d) British reaction against the natives
15. I.N.A. stands for
    (a) Indian National Assembly
    (b) Indian National Association
    (c) Inter-national Association
    (d) Indian National Army
16. 'There has seldom been a matter which has attracted so much Indian Public Interest and, it is safe to say, sympathy... this particular brand of sympathy cuts across communal barriers.' Who sympathises to whom and against whom?

(a) Muslims sympathised with Shah Nawaz against the British
(b) Hindus sympathised with P.K. Sehgal against the British
(c) Sikhs sympathised with Gurbaksh Singh Dhillon against the British
(d) Indians sympathised with the persons who were to be trialled

17. The majority of people waiting for trial outside the Red Fort and criticising Jinnah were the
(a) Hindus
(b) Muslims
(c) Sikhs
(d) Hindus and Muslims both

18. The sympathy of Indian soldiers in uniform with the released I.N.A. prisoners at Lahore indicates
(a) Feeling of Nationalism and Fraternity
(b) Rebellious nature of Indian soldiers
(c) Simply to participate in the reception party
(d) None of the above

19. The country which has the distinction of having the two largest circulated newspapers in the world is
(a) Great Britain
(b) The United States
(c) Japan
(d) China

20. The chronological order of non-verbal communication is
(a) Signs, symbols, codes, colours
(b) Symbols, codes, signs, colours
(c) Colours, signs, codes, symbols
(d) Codes, colours, symbols, signs

21. Which of the following statements is not connected with communication?
(a) Medium is the message.
(b) The world is an electronic cocoon.
(c) Information is power.
(d) Telepathy is technological.

22. Communication becomes circular when
(a) the decoder becomes an encoder
(b) the feedback is absent
(c) the source is credible
(d) the channel is clear

23. The site that played a major role during the terrorist attack on Mumbai (26/11) in 2008 was
(a) Orkut
(b) Facebook
(c) Amazon.com
(d) Twitter

24. **Assertion (A):** For an effective classroom communication at times it is desirable to use the projection technology.
Reason (R): Using the projection technology facilitates extensive coverage of course contents.
(a) Both (A) and (R) are true and (R) is the correct explanation.
(b) Both (A) and (R) are true, but (R) is not the correct explanation.
(c) (A) is true, but (R) is false.
(d) (A) is false, but (R) is true.

25. January 1, 1995 was a Sunday. What day of the week lies on January 1, 1996?
(a) Sunday
(b) Monday
(c) Wednesday
(d) Saturday

26. When an error of 1% is made in the length and breadth of a rectangle, the percentage error (%) in the area of a rectangle will be
(a) 0 (b) 1
(c) 2 (d) 4

27. The next number in the series 2, 5, 9, 19, 37, ? will be

(a) 74 (b) 75
(c) 76 (d) None of these

28. There are 10 true-false questions in an examination. Then these questions can be answered in
(a) 20 ways
(b) 100 ways
(c) 240 ways
(d) 1024 ways

29. What will be the next term in the following?
DCXW, FEVU, HGTS, ?
(a) AKPO (b) ABYZ
(c) JIRQ (d) LMRS

30. Three individuals X, Y, Z hired a car on a sharing basis and paid ₹ 1,040. They used it for 7, 8, 11 hours, respectively. What are the charges paid by Y?
(a) ₹ 290 (b) ₹ 320
(c) ₹ 360 (d) ₹ 440

31. Deductive argument involves
(a) sufficient evidence
(b) critical thinking
(c) seeing logical relations
(d) repeated observation

32. Inductive reasoning is based on or presupposes
(a) uniformity of nature
(b) God created the world
(c) unity of nature
(d) laws of nature

33. To be critical, thinking must be
(a) practical
(b) socially relevant
(c) individually satisfying
(d) analytical

34. Which of the following is an analogous statement?
(a) Man is like God
(b) God is great
(c) Gandhiji is the Father of the Nation
(d) Man is a rational being

Questions from 35 to 36 are based on the following diagram in which there are three intersecting circles. H representing *The Hindu*, I representing *Indian Express* and T representing *The Times of India*. A total of 50 persons were surveyed and the number in the Venn diagram indicates the number of persons reading the newspapers.

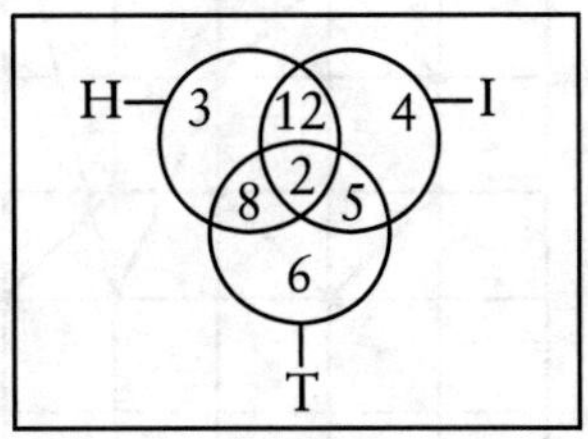

35. How many persons would be reading at least two newspapers?
(a) 23 (b) 25
(c) 27 (d) 29

36. How many persons would be reading almost two newspapers?
(a) 23 (b) 25
(c) 27 (d) 48

37. Which of the following graphs does not represent regular (periodic) behaviour of the variable f(t)?

1. 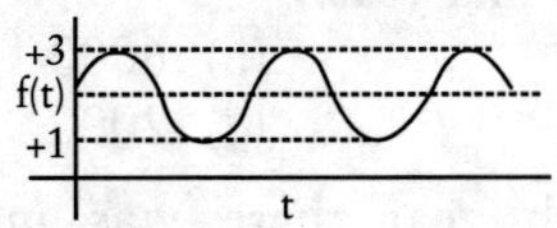

2. 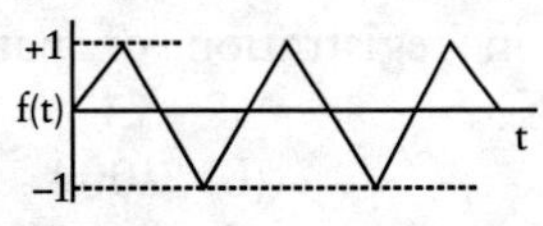

3. 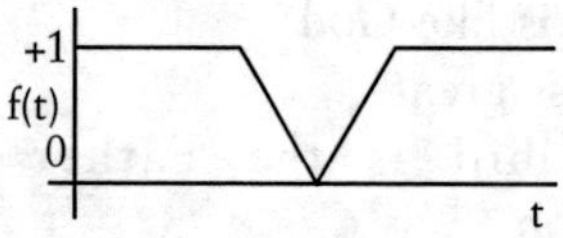

4. 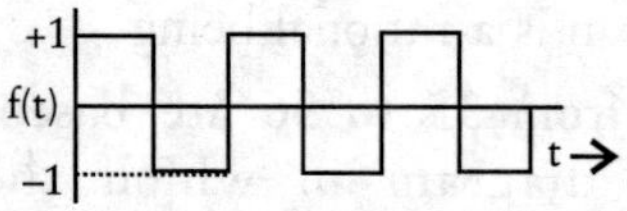

(a) 1 (b) 2
(c) 3 (d) 4

Study the following graph and answer the questions from 38 to 40:

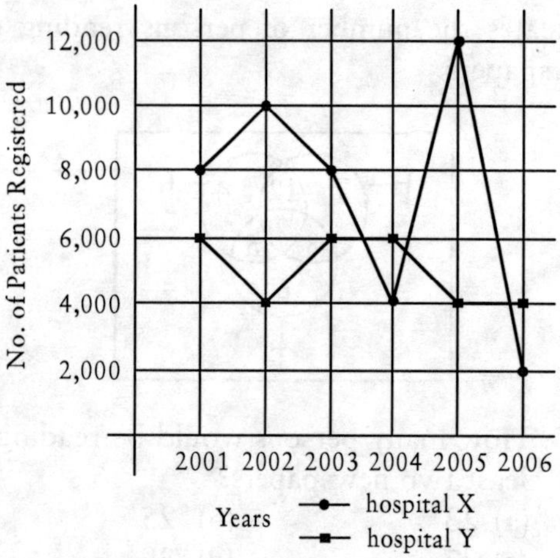

38. In which year total number of patients registered in hospital X and hospital Y was the maximum?
(a) 2003 (b) 2004
(c) 2005 (d) 2006

39. What is the maximum dispersion in the registration of patients in the two hospitals in a year?
(a) 8000 (b) 6000
(c) 4000 (d) 2000

40. In which year there was maximum decrease in registration of patients in hospital X?
(a) 2003 (b) 2004
(c) 2005 (d) 2006

41. Which of the following sources of data is not based on primary data collection?
(a) Census of India
(b) National Sample Survey
(c) Statistical Abstracts of India
(d) National Family Health Survey

42. Which of the four data sets have more dispersion?
(a) 88 91 90 92 89 91
(b) 0 1 1 0 –1 –2
(c) 3 5 2 4 1 5
(d) 0 5 8 10 –2 –8

43. Which of the following is not related to information security on the Internet?
(a) Data Encryption
(b) Water Marking
(c) Data Hiding
(d) Information Retrieval

44. Which is the largest unit of storage among the following?
(a) Terabyte (b) Megabyte
(c) Kilobyte (d) Gigabyte

45. bit stands for
(a) binary information term
(b) binary digit
(c) binary tree
(d) Bivariate Theory

46. Which one of the following is not a linear data structure?
(a) Array
(b) Binary Tree
(c) Queue
(d) Stack

47. Which one of the following is not a network device?
(a) Router (b) Switch
(c) Hub (d) CPU

48. A compiler is used to convert the following to object code which can be executed

(a) High-level language
(b) Low-level language
(c) Assembly language
(d) Natural language

49. The great Indian Bustard bird is found in
(a) Thar Desert of Rajasthan
(b) Malabar Coast
(c) Coastal regions of India
(d) Delta regions

50. The Sagarmanthan National Park has been established to preserve the eco-system of which mountain peak?
(a) Kanchenjunga
(b) Mount Everest
(c) Annapurna
(d) Dhaulavira

51. Maximum soot is released from
(a) Petrol vehicles
(b) CNG vehicles
(c) Diesel vehicles
(d) Thermal Power Plants

52. Surface Ozone is produced from
(a) Transport sector
(b) Cement plants
(c) Textile industry
(d) Chemical industry

53. Which one of the following non-conventional energy sources can be exploited most economically?
(a) Solar
(b) Wind
(c) Geothermal
(d) Ocean Thermal Energy Conversion (OTEC)

54. The most recurring natural hazard in India is
(a) Earthquakes
(b) Floods
(c) Landslides
(d) Volcanoes

55. The recommendation of National Knowledge Commission for the establishment of 1500 Universities is to
(a) create more teaching jobs
(b) ensure increase in student enrolment in higher education
(c) replace or substitute the privately managed higher education institutions by public institutions
(d) enable increased movement of students from rural areas to urban areas

56. According to Article 120 of the Constitution of India, the business in Parliament shall be transacted in
(a) Only English
(b) Only Hindi
(c) Both English and Hindi
(d) All the languages included in Eighth Schedule of the Constitution

57. Which of the following is more interactive and student centric?
(a) Seminar
(b) Workshop
(c) Lecture
(d) Group Discussion

58. The Parliament in India is composed of
(a) Lok Sabha and Rajya Sabha
(b) Lok Sabha, Rajya Sabha and Vice-President
(c) Lok Sabha, Rajya Sabha and President
(d) Lok Sabha, Rajya Sabha with their Secretariats

59. The enrolment in higher education in India is contributed both by Formal System of Education and by System of Distance Education. Distance education contributes
(a) 50% of formal system
(b) 25% of formal system

(c) 10% of the formal system
(d) Distance education system's contribution is not taken into account while considering the figures of enrolment in higher education

60. **Assertion (A):** The UGC Academic Staff Colleges came into existence to improve the quality of teachers.
Reason (R): University and college teachers have to undergo both orientation and refresher courses.
(a) Both (A) and (R) are true and (R) is the correct explanation of (A).
(b) Both (A) and (R) are correct but (R) is not the correct explanation of (A).
(c) (A) is correct and (R) is false.
(d) (A) is false and (R) is correct.

ANSWERS

1. (d)	2. (c)	3. (b)	4. (c)	5. (b)
6. (c)	7. (a)	8. (b)	9. (b)	10. (b)
11. (c)	12. (b)	13. (c)	14. (a)	15. (d)
16. (d)	17. (b)	18. (a)	19. (c)	20. (a)
21. (d)	22. (a)	23. (a)	24. (a)	25. (b)
26. (c)	27. (b)	28. (d)	29. (c)	30. (b)
31. (c)	32. (a)	33. (b)	34. (a)	35. (c)
36. (d)	37. (c)	38. (c)	39. (a)	40. (d)
41. (c)	42. (d)	43. (d)	44. (a)	45. (b)
46. (b)	47. (d)	48. (a)	49. (a)	50. (b)
51. (d)	52. (a)	53. (a)	54. (b)	55. (b)
56. (c)	57. (d)	58. (c)	59. (b)	60. (a)

JUNE–2009

Note: This paper contains Fifty (50) objective type questions, each question carrying two (2) marks. Attempt all the questions.

PAPER–I

1. Good evaluation of written material should not be based on
   (a) Linguistic expression
   (b) Logical presentation
   (c) Ability to reproduce whatever is read
   (d) Comprehension of subject

2. Why do teachers use teaching aid?
   (a) To make teaching fun-filled
   (b) To teach within understanding level of students
   (c) For students' attention
   (d) To make students attentive

3. Attitudes, concepts, skills and knowledge are products of
   (a) Learning
   (b) Research
   (c) Heredity
   (d) Explanation

4. Which among the following gives more freedom to the learner to interact?
   (a) Use of film
   (b) Small group discussion
   (c) Lectures by experts
   (d) Viewing country-wide classroom program on TV

5. Which of the following is not a product of learning?
   (a) Attitudes
   (b) Concepts
   (c) Knowledge
   (d) Maturation

6. How can the objectivity of the research be enhanced?
   (a) Through its impartiality
   (b) Through its reliability
   (c) Through its validity
   (d) All of the above

7. Action-research is
   (a) An applied research
   (b) A research carried out to solve immediate problems
   (c) A longitudinal research
   (d) All of the above

8. The basis on which assumptions are formulated
   (a) Cultural background of the country
   (b) Universities
   (c) Specific characteristics of the castes
   (d) All of the above

9. Which of the following is classified in the category of the developmental research?
   (a) Philosophical research
   (b) Action research
   (c) Descriptive research
   (d) All of the above

10. We use Factorial Analysis
    (a) To know the relationship between two variables
    (b) To test the Hypothesis
    (c) To know the difference between two variables
    (d) To know the difference among the many variables

Read the following passage and answer the questions from 11 to 15:

While the British rule in India was detrimental to the economic development of the country, it did help in starting of the process of modernising Indian society and formed several progressive institutions during that process. One of the most beneficial institutions, which were initiated by the British, was democracy. Nobody can dispute that despite its many shortcomings, democracy was and is far better alternative to the arbitrary rule of the rajas and nawabs, which prevailed in India in the pre-British days.

However, one of the harmful traditions of British democracy inherited by India was that of conflict instead of cooperation between elected members. This was its essential feature. The party, which got the support of the majority of elected members, formed the government while the others constituted a standing opposition. The existence of the opposition to those in power was and is regarded as a hallmark of democracy.

In principle, democracy consists of rule by the people; but where direct rule is not possible, it's rule by persons elected by the people. It is natural that there would be some differences of opinion among the elected members as in the rest of the society.

Normally, members of any organisations have differences of opinion between themselves on different issues but they manage to work on the basis of a consensus and they do not normally form a division between some who are in majority and are placed in power, while treating the others as in opposition.

The members of an organisation usually work on consensus. Consensus simply means that after an adequate discussion, members agree that the majority opinion may prevail for the time being. Thus, persons who form a majority on one issue and whose opinion is allowed to prevail may not be on the same side if there is a difference on some other issue.

It was largely by accident that instead of this normal procedure, a two-party system came to prevail in Britain and that is now being generally taken as the best method of democratic rule.

Many democratically inclined persons in India regret that such a two-party system was not brought about in the country. It appears that to have two parties in India—of more or less equal strength—is a virtual impossibility. Those who regret the absence of a two-party system should take the reasons into consideration.

When the two-party system got established in Britain, there were two groups among the rules (consisting of a limited electorate) who had the same economic interests among themselves and who therefore formed two groups within the selected members of Parliament.

There were members of the British aristocracy (which landed interests and consisting of lord, barons, etc.) and members of the new commercial class consisting of merchants and artisans. These groups were more or less of equal strength and they were able to establish their separate rule at different times.

Answer the following questions:

11. In pre-British period, when India was ruled by the independent rulers
    (a) Peace and prosperity prevailed in the society
    (b) People were isolated from political affairs
    (c) Public opinion was inevitable for policy making
    (d) Law was equal for one and all

12. What is the distinguishing feature of the democracy practised in Britain?
(a) End to the rule of might is right.
(b) Rule of the people, by the people and for the people.
(c) It has stood the test of time.
(d) Cooperation between elected members.

13. Democracy is practised where
(a) elected members form a uniform opinion regarding policy matter.
(b) opposition is more powerful than the ruling combine.
(c) representatives of masses.
(d) None of these.

14. Which of the following is true about the British rule in India?
(a) It was behind the modernisation of the Indian society.
(b) India gained economically during that period.
(c) Various establishments were formed for the purpose of progress.
(d) None of these.

15. Who became the members of the new commercial class during that time?
(a) British Aristocrats
(b) Lord and Barons
(c) Political Persons
(d) Merchants and Artisans

16. Which one of the following Telephonic Conferencing with a radio link is very popular throughout the world?
(a) TPS
(b) Telepresence
(c) Video conference
(d) Video teletext

17. Which is not 24 hours news channel?
(a) NDTV 24×7
(b) ZEE News
(c) Aajtak
(d) Lok Sabha Channel

18. The main objective of FM station in radio is
(a) Information, Entertainment and Tourism
(b) Entertainment, Information and Interaction
(c) Tourism, Interaction and Entertainment
(d) Entertainment only

19. In communication chatting on internet is
(a) Verbal communication
(b) Non-verbal communication
(c) Parallel communication
(d) Grapevine communication

20. Match List I with List II and select the correct answer using the codes given below:

List I (Artists)
A. Pandit Jasraj
B. Kishan Maharaj
C. Ravi Shankar
D. Udai Shankar

List II (Art)
1. Hindustani vocalist
2. Sitar
3. Tabla
4. Dance

Codes:	A	B	C	D
(a)	1	2	3	4
(b)	1	3	4	2
(c)	1	3	2	4
(d)	3	2	1	4

21. Insert the missing number in the following.
3, 8, 18, 23, 33, ?, 48
(a) 37 (b) 40
(c) 38 (d) 45

22. In a certain code, CLOCK is written as KCOLC. How would STEPS be written in that code?
(a) SPEST (b) SPSET
(c) SPETS (d) SEPTS

23. The letters in the first set have a certain relationship. On the basis of this relationship mark the right choice for the second set
BDFH : OMKI :: GHIK : ?
(a) FHJL (b) RPNL
(c) LNPR (d) LJHF

24. What was the day of the week on 1st January 2001?
(a) Friday
(b) Monday
(c) Sunday
(d) Wednesday

25. Find out the wrong number in the sequence.
52, 51, 48, 43, 34, 27, 16
(a) 27 (b) 34
(c) 43 (d) 48

26. In a deductive argument conclusion is
(a) Summing up of the premises
(b) Not necessarily based on premises
(c) Entailed by the premises
(d) Additional to the premises

27. 'No man are mortal' is contradictory of
(a) Some man are mortal
(b) Some man are not mortal
(c) All men are mortal
(d) No mortal is man

28. A deductive argument is valid if
(a) premises are false and conclusion is true
(b) premises are false and conclusion is also false
(c) premises are true and conclusion is false
(d) premises are true and conclusion is true

29. Structure of logical argument is based on
(a) Formal validity
(b) Material truth
(c) Linguistic expression
(d) Aptness of examples

30. Two ladies and two men are playing bridge and seated at North, East, South and West of a table. No lady is facing East. Persons sitting opposite to each other are not of the same sex. One man is facing South. Which direction are the ladies facing to?
(a) East and West
(b) North and West
(c) South and East
(d) None of these

Questions 31 and 32 are based on the following venn diagram in which there are three intersecting circles representing Hindi knowing persons, English knowing persons and persons who are working as teachers. Different regions so obtained in the figure are marked as a, b, c, d, e, f and g.

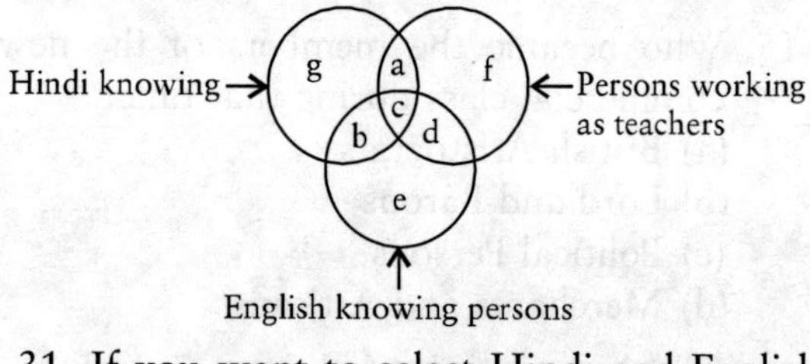

31. If you want to select Hindi and English knowing teachers, which of the following is to be selected?
(a) g (b) b
(c) c (d) e

32. If you want to select persons, who do not know English and are not teachers, which of the region is to be selected?
(a) e (b) g
(c) b (d) a

Study the following graph carefully and answer the questions form 33 to 35.

Export of Engineering Goods

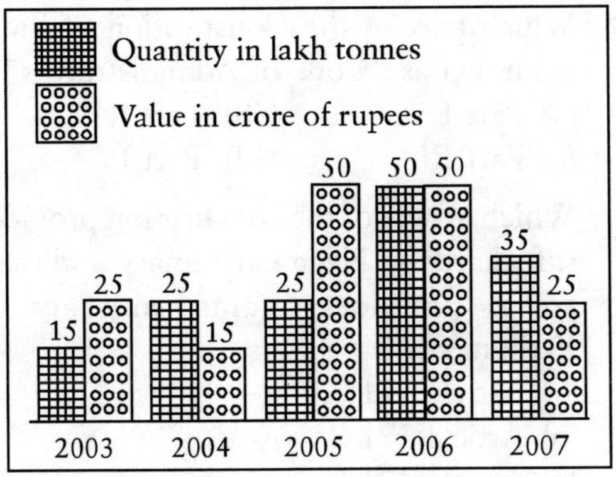

33. In which year the quantity of engineering goods' exports was maximum?
(a) 2005 (b) 2006
(c) 2004 (d) 2007

34. In which year the value of engineering goods decreased by 50 per cent compared to the previous year?
(a) 2004 (b) 2007
(c) 2005 (d) 2006

35. In which year the quantity of exports was 100 per cent higher than the quantity of previous year?
(a) 2004 (b) 2005
(c) 2006 (d) 2007

36. What do you need to put your web pages on the www?
(a) a connection to internet
(b) a web browser
(c) a web server
(d) All of the above

37. Which was the first company to launch mobile phone services in India?
(a) Essar
(b) BPL
(c) Hutchison
(d) Airtel

38. Chandrayan I was launched on 22nd October, 2008 in India from
(a) Bangalore
(b) Sri Harikota
(c) Chennai
(d) Ahmedabad

39. What is blog?
(a) Online music
(b) Intranet
(c) A personal or corporate website in the form of an online journal
(d) A personal or corporate Google search

40. Which is not online Indian Matrimonial website?
(a) www.jeevansathi.com
(b) www.bharatmatrimony.com
(c) www.shaadi.com
(d) www.u.k.singlemuslim.com

41. Environmental impact assessment is an objective analysis of the probable changes in
(a) physical characteristics of the environment
(b) biophysical characteristics of the environment
(c) socio-economic characteristics of the environment
(d) All of the above

42. Bog is a wetland that receives water from
(a) nearby water bodies
(b) melting
(c) Only rainfall
(d) Only sea

43. Which of the following region is in the very high risk zone of earthquakes?
(a) Central Indian Highland
(b) Coastal region

(c) Himalayan region
(d) Indian desert

44. Match List I with List II and select the correct answer using the codes given below:

List I (Institutes)
A. Central Arid Zone Institute
B. Space Application Centre
C. Indian Institute of Public Administration
D. Headquarters of Indian Science Congress

List II (Cities)
1. Kolkata
2. New Delhi
3. Ahmedabad
4. Jodhpur

Codes:	A	B	C	D
(a)	4	3	2	1
(b)	4	2	1	3
(c)	3	1	2	4
(d)	1	2	4	3

45. Indian coastal areas experienced Tsunami disaster in the year
(a) 2005 (b) 2004
(c) 2006 (d) 2007

46. The Kothari Commission's report was entitled on
(a) Education and National Development
(b) Learning to be adventure
(c) Diversification of Education
(d) Education and socialisation in democracy

47. Which of the following is not a Dualmode University?
(a) Delhi University
(b) Bangalore University
(c) Madras University
(d) Indira Gandhi National Open University

48. Which part of the Constitution of India is known as "Code of Administrators"?
(a) Part I (b) Part II
(c) Part III (d) Part IV

49. Which article of the constitution provides safeguards to Naga Customary and their social practices against any act of Parliament?
(a) Article 371 A
(b) Article 371 B
(c) Article 371 C
(d) Article 263

50. Which one of the following is not the tool of good governance?
(a) Right to Information
(b) Citizens' Charter
(c) Social Auditing
(d) Judicial Activism

ANSWERS

1. (a)	2. (a)	3. (a)	4. (b)	5. (d)
6. (d)	7. (b)	8. (a)	9. (d)	10. (d)
11. (b)	12. (d)	13. (a)	14. (c)	15. (a)
16. (b)	17. (d)	18. (b)	19. (b)	20. (c)
21. (c)	22. (c)	23. (b)	24. (b)	25. (b)
26. (c)	27. (c)	28. (d)	29. (b)	30. (b)
31. (c)	32. (b)	33. (b)	34. (b)	35. (c)
36. (d)	37. (d)	38. (b)	39. (c)	40. (d)
41. (d)	42. (a)	43. (b)	44. (a)	45. (b)
46. (a)	47. (d)	48. (d)	49. (a)	50. (d)

PAPER–II

Note: This paper contains Fifty (50) multiple-choice questions, each question carrying two (2) marks. Attempt all of them.

1. The concept of 'Sanskritisation' is closely related to the concept of
   (a) reference group
   (b) primary group
   (c) interest group
   (d) tertiary group
2. Which one of the following states in India has the highest percentage of reservation for the Scheduled Castes?
   (a) Maharashtra
   (b) Uttar Pradesh
   (c) Punjab
   (d) Tamil Nadu
3. Which one of the following statements is correct?
   (a) Article 341 of the Constitution defines the term Scheduled Caste
   (b) The Constitution empowers the Parliament to define the term Scheduled Caste
   (c) The Constitution does not contain a definition of the term Scheduled Caste
   (d) The term Scheduled Caste is defined in the Government of India Act. 1918
4. Which one of the following is the basic concern of Article 17 of the Indian Constitution?
   (a) Representation of backward classes
   (b) The abolition of untouchability
   (c) Reservation of posts in services for the Scheduled Castes
   (d) Political representation to Scheduled Castes
5. Who was the first Chairman of the 'Backward classes Commission' in India?
   (a) B.P. Mandal
   (b) B.R. Ambedkar
   (c) Kaka Kalelkar
   (d) M.K. Gandhi
6. Who first used the term 'Rites de passage'?
   (a) Marx
   (b) Weber
   (c) A. Van Gennep
   (d) Cooley
7. Under ______, each group within a village is expected to give certain standardised services to the other castes.
   (a) commensality
   (b) jajmani system
   (c) prescriptions
   (d) mutuality
8. According to Weber ______ within each of the main classes would forestall any move in the direction of internal unity and coherence
   (a) pressure groups
   (b) power blocs
   (c) status groups
   (d) parties
9. Which ofthe following terms has been identified as a dimension of accorded status by most sociologists?
   (a) Status
   (b) Social class
   (c) Class
   (d) Caste
10. Who said this? 'The differential distribution of authority leads to class formation and class conflict'.
    (a) Karl Papper
    (b) Ralph Dahrendorf
    (c) Karl Mark
    (d) Wright Mills
11. The social classes are large groups of people who differ from each other by their relation to the means of social production. Whose view is this?

(a) Marx
(b) Ralph Dahrendorf
(c) Weber
(d) Lenin

12. Marx differentiated various classes in ______.
(a) objective terms
(b) subjective terms
(c) both subjective and objective terms
(d) absolute terms

13. From Marxian perspective, political power derives from ______.
(a) economic power
(b) social prestige
(c) landed property
(d) religious sanction

14. The person who gives service to the Jajman is called
(a) Parjan
(b) Kamin
(c) Karmin
(d) Purohit

15. According to Marx, a class which has come into being but which is not yet conscious of its fundamental interests is a ______.
(a) class in itself
(b) class for itself
(c) bourgeoisie
(d) None of the above

16. Gopal's father who was a big business man lost all his money in gambling. Which of the following connects best the above statement to the concept of class?
(a) A man is responsible for the class to which he belongs
(b) Gambling is a bad habit and is accountable for downward mobility
(c) Class membership can change in an individual's life time
(d) None of the above

17. Subjective class concept locates individuals in the stratification hierarchy according to judgments of
(a) analyst
(b) society
(c) individual himself
(d) community

18. According to Weber, the status order tends to be
(a) universalistic and achievement oriented
(b) particularistic and ascriptive
(c) particularistic and achievement oriented
(d) universalistic and ascriptive

19. According to Weber, as the division of labour becomes more complex, class ______.
(a) becomes more advanced
(b) becomes more heterogeneous
(c) remain essentially the same
(d) None of the above

20. ______ constitutes the primary model of the estate system
(a) Medieval European feudal society
(b) Spanish society
(c) Ancient Greek society
(d) Medieval Indian society

21. The Caste system is ______ in nature.
(a) hierarchical
(b) symmetrical
(c) contradictory
(d) None of the above

22. Due to financial problems at home, a land less labourer from a village moved to city to work as a factory labourer. This is an example of
(a) horizontal mobility
(b) vertical downward mobility
(c) vertical mobility
(d) social mobility

23. If a person becomes a minister from an ordinary shopkeeper, the mobility is called
    (a) upward mobility
    (b) downward mobility
    (c) horizontal mobility
    (d) None of the above

24. The functionalists are primarily concerned with the ______ of social stratification, with is contribution to the maintenance and well being of society
    (a) function (b) aims
    (c) value (d) nature

25. According to Weber, communal division is an example of ______.
    (a) status groups
    (b) class
    (c) party
    (d) caste

Directions: The following question consist of two statements, one labelled as 'Assertion (A)' and the other labelled as 'Reason (R)'. You are to examine these two statements carefully and decide if the Assertion (A) and the Reason (R) are individually true and if so, whether the Reason is a correct explanation of the Assertion.

Select your answers to these items using the codes given below and mark your answer sheet accordingly.
(a) Both A and R are true and R is the correct explanation of A
(b) Both A and R are true, but R is not the correct explanation of A
(c) A is true, but R is false
(d) A is false, but R is true

26. **Assertion (A):** There is a considerable ethno-linguistic diversity in India.
    Reason (R): This prohibits equal opportunity.

27. Which one of the following pairs is not correctly matched?
    (a) Schumpeter : Enterpreneur
    (b) China : Cultural revolution
    (c) Russia : Industrial revolution
    (d) Max Weber : Bureaucracy

28. Which one of the following statements is true about 'Mana'?
    (a) The respect the father commands from his sons whose belief in 'life after death' tends to deity the father.
    (b) The sacred animal which is a symbol of deep group based sentiments and feelings.
    (c) A benign supernatural force that has no shape of its own but inhabits living or inaminate things.
    (d) A ritual that is arranged to felicitate a women on her first pregnancy in a tribal society in North-East India.

29. Which one of the following pairs is correctly matched?
    (a) Hindus — parallel cousin marriage
    (b) Santhals — Assam
    (c) Endogamy — Totemism
    (d) Indian kinship system — Avoidance

30. Match List I with List II and select the correct answer:

List I (Concepts)
A. Evolutionary Universals
B. Spectrum of Reciprocity
C. Theory of Surplus Value
D. Creative Destruction

List II (Thinkers)
i. Schumpeter
ii. Parsons
iii. Sahlins
iv. Marx

Codes:	A	B	C	D
(a)	iii	ii	iv	i
(b)	ii	iii	i	iv
(c)	ii	iii	iv	i
(d)	iii	ii	i	iv

31. Which of the following pairs are correctly matched?
    1. Marx : Mode of Production
    2. Weber : Class, Caste and Power
    3. Centers : Subjective characteristics
    4. Warner : Self-identification

    Select the correct answer using the codes given below:

    Codes:
    (a) 1, 2, 3 and 4 (b) 1, 3 and 4
    (c) 2 and 4 (d) 1, 2 and 3

32. Match List I with List II and select the correct answer:

    List I
    A. Dialetics
    B. Social dynamics
    C. Unilinear evolution
    D. Super-organic evolution

    List II
    i. Morgan ii. Comte
    iii. Herbert Spencer iv. Hegel

Codes:	A	B	C	D
(a)	ii	iv	iii	i
(b)	ii	iv	i	iii
(c)	iv	ii	i	iii
(d)	iv	ii	iii	i

33. Match List I (Sociologists) with List II (Their contribution) and select the correct answer:

    List I
    A. Louis Wirth B. Elton Mayo
    C. Robert Redfield D. Fredrick Taylor

    List II
    i. Folk-urban continuum
    ii. Scientific management
    iii. Urbanism as a way of life
    iv. Human Relations

Codes:	A	B	C	D
(a)	iii	iv	ii	i
(b)	iii	iv	i	ii
(c)	iv	iii	i	ii
(d)	iv	iii	ii	i

34. **Assertion (A):** Altruistic suicides occur more in over-integrated societies.

    Reason (R): Suicide is the desperate act of an individual.

    (a) Both A and R are true and R is the correct explanation of A
    (b) Both A and R are true, but R is not the correct explanation of A
    (c) A is true, but R is false
    (d) A is false, but R is true

35. **Assertion (A):** It is witnessed that even the rational persons put some food and the burial pit of dead persons.

    Reason (R): Modes of action persist more than the modes of thinking.

    (a) Both A and R are true and R is the correct explanation of A
    (b) Both A and R are true, but R is not the correct explanation of A
    (c) A is true, but R is false
    (d) A is false, but R is true

36. Match List I (Concept) with List II (Scholar) and select the correct answer using the codes given below the lists:

    List I
    A. Rational goal-oriented action
    B. Gesellschaft
    C. Theory of Collective Behaviour
    D. Historical materialism

    List II
    i. Ferdinand Tonnies
    ii. Friedrich Engels
    iii. Max Weber
    iv. N.J. Smelser

Codes:	A	B	C	D
(a)	iv	i	iii	ii
(b)	iii	ii	iv	i
(c)	iv	ii	iii	i
(d)	iii	i	iv	ii

37. Will is primarily responsible for the emergence of

(a) Reference group
(b) Gesellschaft
(c) Gemeinschaft
(d) Secondary group

38. Caste is an ______ group.
(a) exogamous
(b) utilitarian
(c) endogamous
(d) indispensable

39. Weber defines ______ as groups which are specifically concerned with influencing policies and making decisions in the interests of their membership.
(a) Status groups (b) Classes
(c) Parties (d) Castes

40. According to Weber ______.
(a) status and class are always co-related
(b) status and class are co-related but there are many cases in which they are not
(c) class determines status
(d) status determines class

41. In which of the following the first literary traces of caste system are found?
(a) Rig veda (b) Atharva veda
(c) Yajur veda (d) Sama veda

42. Weber posits the views that ______ reach their most developed form in the caste system of traditional Hindu Society.
(a) status groups
(b) castes
(c) jajmani system
(d) None of the above

43. Consider the following types of society:
1. Bourgeois society
2. Primitive Communism
3. Feudal society
4. Ancient society

Which of the following is the correct chronological sequence of these societies as conceived by Karl Marx?
(a) 3-1-2-4 (b) 2-4-3-1
(c) 3-4-2-1 (d) 2-1-3-1

44. Which one of the following is asserted by the organic theory of society?
(a) The society is like a living/biological organism
(b) The society is unlike a human organism
(c) The units of society are fixed
(d) Each unit of a society performs definite universal function

45. Which one of the following facts, according to Lewis H. Morgan, distinguishes civilization from the preceding stages in the evolution of human society?
(a) Technological inventions
(b) Scientific inventions
(c) Smelting of iron ores
(d) Invention of alphabets, phonetics and writing

46. Who among the following introduced the distinction of cultures into ideational and sensate categories?
(a) P.A. Sorokin
(b) Sigmund Freud
(c) A.L. Koreber
(d) O. Spengler

47. Consider the following statements:
1. Crude death rate is very strongly affected by the age composition of the population.
2. The life expectancy at birth is a good measure of mortality conditions in a country because it adjusts for age composition by using prevailing birth rates at each age to estimate the average number of years a person may expect to live.

Which of the statements given above is/are correct?

(a) 1 only
(b) 2 only
(c) Both 1 and 2
(d) Neither 1 nor 2

48. What is the spread of cultural traits from one society to another commonly called?
(a) Acculturation (b) Diffusion
(c) Enculturation (d) Discrimination

49. What happens: "When changes in material culture precede changes in adaptive culture, adjustments cannot start before change requiring them has taken place. But old customs persist and bring about quite harmful consequences"?
(a) Cultural deprivation
(b) Cultural lag
(c) Cultural diffusion
(d) Cultural determinism

50. What does cultural relativism mean?
(a) There are no universal cultural norms that we follow
(b) One's view of social institutions is coloured by one's cultural perspective
(c) Functions and meanings of cultural traits are according to their social settings
(d) The belief that one's own culture is superior to others

ANSWERS

1. (a)	2. (d)	3. (c)	4. (b)	5. (c)
6. (c)	7. (b)	8. (c)	9. (b)	10. (b)
11. (a)	12. (a)	13. (a)	14. (a)	15. (a)
16. (c)	17. (c)	18. (b)	19. (b)	20. (a)
21. (a)	22. (a)	23. (a)	24. (a)	25. (a)
26. (c)	27. (c)	28. (c)	29. (d)	30. (c)
31. (b)	32. (c)	33. (b)	34. (c)	35. (a)
36. (b)	37. (c)	38. (c)	39. (c)	40. (b)
41. (a)	42. (a)	43. (b)	44. (a)	45. (d)
46. (a)	47. (d)	48. (b)	49. (b)	50. (b)

DECEMBER–2008

Note: This paper contains Fifty (50) objective type questions, each question carrying two (2) marks. Attempt all the questions.

PAPER–I

1. According to Swami Vivekananda, teacher's success depends on
   (a) His renunciation of personal gain and service to others
   (b) His professional training and creativity
   (c) His concentration on his work and duties with a spirit of obedience to God
   (d) His mastery on the subject and capacity in controlling the students
2. Which of the following teacher will be liked most?
   (a) A teacher of high idealistic attitude
   (b) A loving teacher
   (c) A teacher who is disciplined
   (d) A teacher who often amuses his students
3. A teacher's most important challenge is
   (a) to make students do their home work
   (b) to make teaching-learning process enjoyable
   (c) to maintain discipline in the class-room
   (d) to prepare the question paper
4. Value-education stands for
   (a) making a student healthy
   (b) making a student to get a job
   (c) inculcation of virtues
   (d) all-round development of personality
5. When a normal student behaves in an erratic manner in the class, you would
   (a) pull up the student then and there
   (b) talk to the student after the class
   (c) ask the student to leave the class
   (d) ignore the student
6. The research is always
   (a) verifying the old knowledge
   (b) exploring new knowledge
   (c) filling the gap between knowledge
   (d) All of these
7. The research that applies the laws at the time of field study to draw more and more clear ideas about the problem is
   (a) Applied research
   (b) Action research
   (c) Experimental research
   (d) None of these
8. When a research problem is related to heterogeneous population, the most suitable sampling method is
   (a) Cluster Sampling
   (b) Stratified Sampling
   (c) Convenient Sampling
   (d) Lottery Method
9. The process not needed in experimental research is
   (a) Observation
   (b) Manipulation and replication
   (c) Controlling
   (d) Reference collection

10. A research problem is not feasible only when
    (a) it is researchable
    (b) it is new and adds something to knowledge
    (c) it consists of independent and dependent variables
    (d) it has utility and relevance

Read the following passage carefully and answer the questions from 11 to 15:

Radically changing monsoon patterns, reduction in the winter rice harvest and a quantum increase in respiratory diseases all part of the environmental doomsday scenario which is reportedly playing out in South Asia. According to a United Nations Environment Program report, a deadly three-kilometer deep blanket of pollution comprising a fearsome, cocktail of ash, acids, aerosols and other particles has enveloped in this region. For India, already struggling to cope with a drought, the implication of this are devastating and further crop failure will amount to a life and death question for many Indians. The increase in premature deaths will have adverse social and economic consequences and a rise in morbidities will place an unbearable burden on our crumbling health system. And there is no one to blame but ourselves. Both official and corporate India has always been allergic to any mention of clean technology. Most mechanical two wheelers roll of the assembly line without proper pollution control system. Little effort is made for R&D on simple technologies, which could make a vital difference to people's lives and the environment.

However, while there is no denying that South Asia must clean up its act, skeptics might question the timing of the haze report. The Kyoto meet on climate change is just two weeks away and the stage is set for the usual battle between the developing world and the West, particularly the United States of America. President Mr. Bush has adamantly refused to sign any protocol, which would mean a change in American consumption level. U.N. environment report will likely find a place in the U.S. arsenal as it plants an accusing finger towards controls like India and China. Yet the U.S.A. can hardly deny its own dubious role in the matter of erasing trading quotas.

Richer countries can simply buy up excess credits from poorer countries and continue to pollute. Rather than try to get the better of developing countries, who undoubtedly have taken up environmental shortcuts in their bid to catch up with the West, the USA should take a look at the environmental profigacy, which is going on within. From opening up virgin territories for oil exploration to relaxing the standards for drinking water, Mr. Bush's policies are not exactly beneficial, not even to America's interests. We realise that we are all in this together and that pollution anywhere should be a global concern otherwise there will only be more tunnels at the end of the tunnel.

11. Both official and corporate India is allergic to
    (a) Failure of Monsoon
    (b) Poverty and Inequality
    (c) Slowdown in Industrial Production
    (d) Mention of Clean Technology

12. If the rate of premature death increases it will
    (a) Exert added burden on the crumbling economy
    (b) Have adverse social and economic consequences
    (c) Make positive effect on our effort to control population
    (d) Have less job aspirants in the society

13. According to the passage, the two wheeler industry is not adequately concerned about
    (a) Passenger safety on the roads
    (b) Life cover insurance of the vehicle owner
    (c) Pollution control system in the vehicle
    (d) Rising cost of the two wheelers

14. What could be the reason behind timing of the haze report just before the Kyoto meet?
    (a) United Nations is working hand-in-glove with U.S.A.
    (b) Organisers of the forthcoming meet to teach a lesson to the U.S.A.
    (c) Drawing attention of the world towards devastating effects of environment degradation.
    (d) U.S.A. wants to use it as a handle against the developing countries in the forthcoming meet.

15. Which of the following is the indication of environmental degradation in South Asia?
    (a) Social and economic inequality
    (b) Crumbling health care system
    (c) Inadequate pollution control system
    (d) Radically changing monsoon pattern

16. Community Radio is a type of radio service that caters to the interest of
    (a) Local audience
    (b) Education
    (c) Entertainment
    (d) News

17. Orcut is a part of
    (a) Intra personal Communication
    (b) Mass Communication
    (c) Group Communication
    (d) Inter personal Communication

18. Match List I with List II and select the correct answer using the codes given below:

List I (Artists)
(A) Amrita Shergill
(B) T. Swaminathan Pillai
(C) Bhimsen Joshi
(D) Padma Subramaniyam

List II (Art)
i. Flute ii. Classical Song
iii. Painting iv. Bharat Natyam

Codes:	A	B	C	D
(a)	iii	i	ii	iv
(b)	ii	iii	i	iv
(c)	iv	ii	iii	i
(d)	i	iv	ii	iii

19. Which is not correct in latest communication award?
    (a) Salman Rushdie – Booker's Prize—July 20, 2008
    (b) Dilip Sanghavi – Business Standard CEO Award, July 22, 2008
    (c) Tapan Sinha – Dada Saheb Falke Award, July 21, 2008
    (d) Gautam Ghosh – Osians Lifetime Achievement Award, July 11, 2008

20. Firewalls are used to protect a communication network system against
    (a) Unauthorised attacks
    (b) Virus attacks
    (c) Data-driven attacks
    (d) Fire attacks

21. Insert the missing number in the following:
    $\frac{2}{3}, \frac{4}{7}, ?, \frac{11}{21}, \frac{16}{31},$
    (a) $\frac{10}{8}$ (b) $\frac{6}{10}$
    (c) $\frac{5}{10}$ (d) $\frac{7}{13}$

22. In a certain code, GAMESMAN is written as AGMEMSAN. How would DISCLOSE be written in that code?
(a) IDSCOLSE (b) IDCSOLES
(c) IDSCOLES (d) IDSCLOSE

23. The letters in the first set have a certain relationship. On the basis of this relationship mark the right choice for the second set : AST : BRU :: NQV: ?
(a) ORW (b) MPU
(c) MRW (d) OPW

24. On what dates of April, 1994 did Sunday fall?
(a) 2, 9, 16, 23, 30
(b) 3, 10, 17, 24
(c) 4, 11, 18, 25
(d) 1, 8, 15, 22, 29

25. Find out the wrong number in the sequence:
125, 127, 130, 135, 142, 153, 165
(a) 130 (b) 142
(c) 153 (d) 165

26. There are five books A, B, C, D and E. The book C lies above D, the book E is below A and B is below E. Which is at the bottom?
(a) E (b) B
(c) A (d) C

27. Logical reasoning is based on
(a) Truth of involved propositions
(b) Valid relation among the involved propositions
(c) Employment of symbolic language
(d) Employment of ordinary language

28. Two propositions with the same subject and predicate terms but different in quality are
(a) Contradictory
(b) Contrary
(c) Subaltern
(d) Identical

29. The premises of a valid deductive argument
(a) Provide some evidence for its conclusion
(b) Provide no evidence for its conclusion
(c) Are irrelevant for its conclusion
(d) Provide conclusive evidence for its conclusion

30. Syllogistic reasoning is
(a) Deductive
(b) Inductive
(c) Experimental
(d) Hypothetical

Study the following Venn diagram and answer the questions from 31 to 33:

Three circles representing Graduates, Clerks and Government employeer are intersecting. The intersections are marked A, B, C, e, f, g and h. Which part best represents the statements in questions 31 to 33?

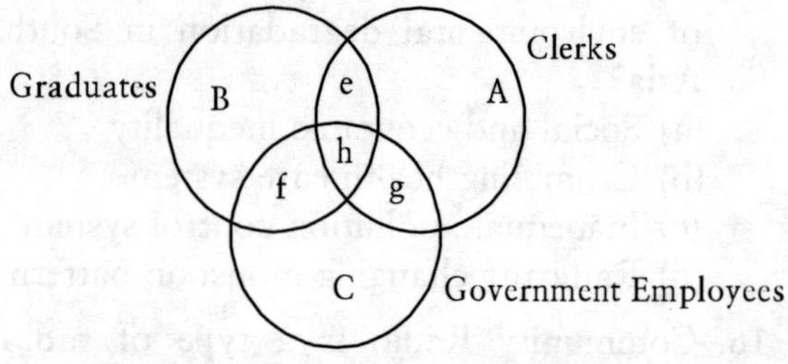

31. Some graduates are government employees but not as clerks.
(a) h (b) g
(c) f (d) e

32. Clerks who are graduates as well as government employees.
(a) e (b) f
(c) g (d) h

33. Some graduates are clerks but not government employees.
(a) f (b) g
(c) h (d) e

Study the following graph and answer the questions from 34 to 35:

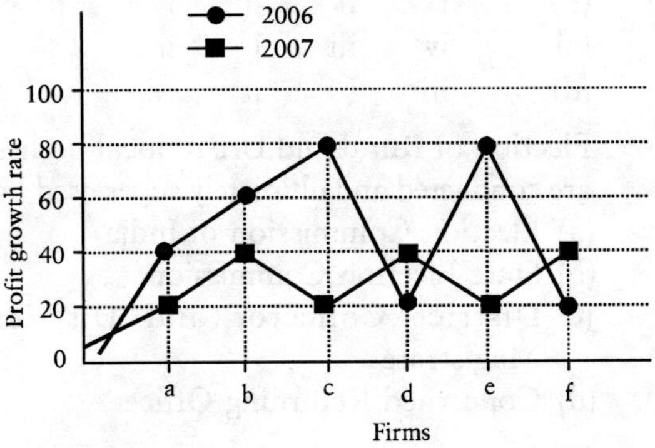

34. Which of the firms got maximum profit growth rate in the year 2006?
(a) ab (b) ce
(c) cd (d) ef

35. Which of the firms got maximum profit growth rate in the year 2007?
(a) bdf (b) acf
(c) bed (d) ace

36. The accounting software 'Tally' was developed by
(a) HCL (b) TCS
(c) Infosys (d) Wipro

37. Errors in computer programs are called
(a) Follies (b) Mistakes
(c) Bugs (d) Spam

38. HTML is basically used to design
(a) Webpage
(b) Website
(c) Graphics
(d) Tables and Frames

39. 'Micro Processing' is made for
(a) Computer
(b) Digital System
(c) Calculator
(d) Electronic Goods

40. Information, a combination of graphics, text, sound, video and animation is called
(a) Multiprogram
(b) Multifacet
(c) Multimedia
(d) Multiprocess

41. Which of the following pairs regarding typical composition of hospital wastes is incorrect?
(a) Plastic - 9-12%
(b) Metals - 1-2%
(c) Ceramic - 8-10%
(d) Biodegradable - 35-40%

42. Fresh water achieves its greatest density at
(a) –4°C (b) 0°C
(c) 4°C (d) –2.5°C

43. Which one of the following is not associated with earthquakes?
(a) Focus
(b) Epicenter
(c) Seismograph
(d) Swells

44. The tallest trees in the world are found in the region
(a) Equatorial region
(b) Temperate region
(c) Monsoon region
(d) Mediterranean region

45. Match List I with List II and select the correct answer from the codes given below:

List I (National Parks)
(A) Periyar
(B) Nandan Kanan
(C) Corbett National Park
(D) Sariska Tiger Reserve

List II (States)
1. Orissa
2. Kerala
3. Rajasthan
4. Uttarakhand

Codes:	A	B	C	D
(a)	2	1	4	3
(b)	1	2	4	3
(c)	3	2	1	4
(d)	1	2	3	4

46. According to Radhakrishnan Commission, the aim of Higher Education is
(a) To develop the democratic values, peace and harmony
(b) To develop great personalities who can give their contributions in politics, administration, industry and commerce
(c) Both (a) and (b)
(d) None of these

47. The National Museum at New Delhi is attached to
(a) Delhi University
(b) a Deemed University
(c) a Subordinate Office of the JNU
(d) Part of Ministry of Tourism and Culture

48. Match List I with List II and select the correct answer from the codes given below:

List I (Institutions)
(A) National Law Institute
(B) Indian Institute of Advanced Studies
(C) National Judicial Academy
(D) National Savings Institute

List II (Locations)
i. Shimla
ii. Bhopal
iii. Hyderabad
iv. Nagpur

Codes:	A	B	C	D
(a)	iii	ii	iv	i
(b)	i	ii	iii	iv
(c)	iv	iii	i	ii
(d)	iii	i	ii	iv

49. Election of Rural and Urban local bodies are conducted and ultimately supervised by
(a) Election Commission of India
(b) State Election Commission
(c) District Collector and District Magistrate
(d) Concerned Returning Officer

50. Which opinion is not correct?
(a) Education is a subject of concurrent list of VII schedule of Constitution of India
(b) University Grants Commission is a statutory body
(c) Patent, inventions, design, copyright and trade marks are the subject of concurrent list
(d) Indian Council of Social Science Research is a statutory body related to research in social sciences.

ANSWERS

1. (d)	2. (c)	3. (b)	4. (c)	5. (b)
6. (d)	7. (a)	8. (b)	9. (d)	10. (b)
11. (d)	12. (b)	13. (c)	14. (c)	15. (d)
16. (a)	17. (d)	18. (a)	19. (b)	20. (a)
21. (d)	22. (a)	23. (d)	24. (b)	25. (d)
26. (b)	27. (b)	28. (a)	29. (d)	30. (a)
31. (c)	32. (d)	33. (d)	34. (b)	35. (a)
36. (b)	37. (c)	38. (a)	39. (a)	40. (c)
41. (d)	42. (c)	43. (d)	44. (b)	45. (a)
46. (c)	47. (d)	48. (d)	49. (b)	50. (c)

PAPER–II

Note: This paper contains Fifty (50) objective type questions, each question carrying two (2) marks. Attempt all the questions.

1. The sun will tan your skin if we exposed ourselves to it. This is a case of
   (a) Biological adaptation
   (b) Physical adaptation
   (c) Social adaptation
   (d) None of the above
2. Fishes adapting to a marine environment is a case of
   (a) Physical adaptation
   (b) Social adaptation
   (c) Biological adaptation
   (d) All of the above
3. Consider the following statements:
   1. Social adaptation always involves some standard of values
   2. Social adaptation is conditional adaptation
   3. When we speak of Maladaptation or maladjament, we do not mean that universal principles of physical adaptation is defeated

   Codes:
   (a) 1 and 2 are correct
   (b) 2 and 3 are incorrect
   (c) 1 and 3 are correct
   (d) All the above are correct
4. Consider the following statements:
   1. The inner environment of man includes social heritage.
   2. The outer environment of man includes non-material culture
   3. The inner and outer environment of man are always interactive
   4. Man is adjusted to inner environment through conscious response and habitation

   Codes:
   (a) 1, 2, 3 are correct
   (b) 2, 3, 4 are incorrect
   (c) 1, 3, 4 are correct
   (d) All of the above are correct
5. 'Professional skill of surgeon' is
   (a) Habit
   (b) Custom
   (c) Neither habit nor custom
   (d) Norm
6. Nadel's conception of structure is based on which of the following?
   1. Repetitiveness
   2. Durability
   3. Uniqueness
   4. Equilibrium

   Codes:
   (a) 1, 2, 3 (b) 2, 3, 4
   (c) 1, 2, 4 (d) All of the above
7. Consider the following statements.
   1. Nadel contends that a particular social structure as described at a moment is accurate only for a particular period of time.
   2. According to Nadel, structure and variance are not inherently contradictory: rather the former is defined or built up through taking account of the latter.

   Codes:
   (a) Both 1 and 2 are correct
   (b) Both 1 and 2 are incorrect
   (c) Only 1 is correct
   (d) Only 2 is correct
8. Who among the following defined social structure in terms of institution, orders and spheres?
   (a) Levi-Strauss
   (b) Gerth and Mills
   (c) Evans
   (d) Meyer Fortes

9. Consider the following statements:
   1. Institutions are the basic building blocks of social structure
   2. Social structure is more than mere inter-relations of institutions

   Codes:
   (a) Both 1 and 2 are correct
   (b) Both 1 and 2 are incorrect
   (c) Only 1 is correct
   (d) Only 2 is correct

10. The term 'schedule Caste' was coined in the year
   (a) 1927 (b) 1930
   (c) 1935 (d) 1948

11. A man who has accumulated a lot of black money, constructs a hospital for cancer patients and poses himself as a saviour of the downtrodden. This is an example of
   (a) role insulation
   (b) counterfeit role
   (c) false role
   (d) role-set

12. Who among the following is not a contributor to the studies on acculturation?
   (a) Linton
   (b) Redfield
   (c) Herskovits
   (d) Ogburn

13. Routinisation of charisma refers to
   (a) the process by which the personal qualities of a charismatic leader are incorporated in the characteristics of an organisation
   (b) the wide acceptance of the leadership quality of the charismatic leader by his followers
   (c) the high normative standard of the actions of charismatic leader
   (d) the ultimate goal which the charismatic leader has attained

14. Consider the following characteristics:
   1. A network of social relationships
   2. Totality of population
   3. Provision for membership by birth
   4. Comprehensive culture

   The major characteristics of society would include
   (a) 1, 2 and 3
   (b) 2, 3 and 4
   (c) 1, 2 and 4
   (d) 1, 3 and 4

15. Who held the view that the primary groups are "the breeding grounds of our mores and the nurse of our loyalties"?
   (a) Cooley
   (b) Tonnies
   (c) MacIver
   (d) Sumner

Directions: The following 5 (Five) items consist of two statements, one labelled as the 'Assertion (A)' and the other as 'Reason (R)'. You are to examine these two statements carefully and select the answers to these items using the codes given below:

(a) Both (A) and (R) are individually true and (R) is the correct explanation of (A).
(b) Both (A) and (R) are individually true, but (R) is not the correct explanation of (A).
(c) (A) is true, but (R) is false.
(d) (A) is false, but (R) is true.

16. **Assertion (A):** It is not merely equality under law that determines the status of women in Society.
   Reason (R): Traditions and customs are involved in everyday social interactions.

17. **Assertion (A):** forces of urbanisation induce family disorganisation.
   Reason (R): Urban values are hostile to abiding relationships.

18. **Assertion (A):** The behaviour between maternal uncle and niece, and between mother-in-law and son-in-law falls under the same pattern.
Reason (R): Both behaviours are classified as joking-relationship.

19. **Assertion (A):** Ascribed social status acquired from one's family of orientation does not automatically persist throughout one's life.
Reason (R): Social training acquired in the family of orientation fosters a continuity of status when a family of procreation is established.

20. **Assertion (A):** The role of maternal uncle in a matrilineal family is crucial to the extent of safeguarding his sister and her daughters.
Reason (R): He is not a custodian of his sister's wealth and property.

21. Caste is an ______ group.
(a) exogamous
(b) utilitarian
(c) endogamous
(d) indispensable

22. Weber defines ______ as groups which are specifically concerned with influencing policies and making decisions in the inferests of their membership.
(a) status groups
(b) classes
(c) parties
(d) castes

23. According to Weber ______.
(a) status and class are always co-related
(b) status and class are co-related but there are many cases in which they are not
(c) class determines status
(d) status determines class

24. In which of the following the first literary traces of caste system are found?
(a) *Rig veda* (b) *Atharva veda*
(c) *Yajur veda* (d) *Sama veda*

25. Weber posits the views that ______ reach their most developed form in the caste system of traditional Hindu Society.
(a) status groups
(b) castes
(c) jajmani system
(d) None of the above

26. In which of the following States did the Naxalite movement emerge in 1960s?
(a) Bihar
(b) West Bengal
(c) Orissa
(d) Madhya Pradesh

27. Who among the following has referred to integrative orientation and alienating orientation as two types of social movements?
(a) Rajni Kothari
(b) Andre Beteille
(c) Katheleen Gough
(d) Yogendra Singh

28. Which of the following is not an essential feature of social movement?
(a) Collective mobilization
(b) Revolution
(c) Ideology
(d) Orientation towards change

29. Which one of the following tribes initiated the Jharkhand movement?
(a) Bhil (b) Bodo
(c) Santhal (d) Birhor

30. Which one of the following was a peasant movement?
(a) Khilafat Movement
(b) Women Liberation Movement
(c) Telengana Movement
(d) Jharkhand Movement

31. Who among the following has proposed a model to explain the differentiation of social system, based on an analysis of the

way in which a particular system responds to forces for change?
(a) N.J. Smelser
(b) Talcott Parsons
(c) Daniel Bell
(d) Ulrich Beck

32. Which of the following group(s) of factors was/were used by Koreber to classify kinship terminology?
1. Descen, Gender, Polarity, Bifurcation and Lineage
2. Kinderd, Class, Affinity, Gender and Polarity
3. Generation, Gender, Afinity, Bifurcation and Polarity

Select the correct answer using the codes given below:

Codes:
(a) 1 only (b) 3 only
(c) 2 and 3 (d) 1 and 3

33. A special role, similar to that of a maternal uncle, for one's father's sister is designated as
(a) Amitate (b) Couvade
(c) Avunculate (d) Teknonymy

34. Consider the following statements:
1. Extended family consists of two mates of opposite sex and their offspring.
2. Conjugal family consists of two mates of opposite sex and their offspring.
3. Consanguineous family consists of two mats of opposite sex and their offspring.

Which of the statements given above is correct?
(a) 1 only (b) 2 only
(c) 3 only (d) None

35. When two or more sibs exist in a community, they may be called
(a) Moieties
(b) Phrateries
(c) Exogamous clans
(d) Endogamous clans

36. Marx believed that western society had developed through the following main epochs. They are
(a) primitive communism, ancient society, feudal society and capitalist society
(b) savagery, feudalism and capitalism
(c) slavery, barbarism and feudalism
(d) feudalism, capitalism and socialism

37. Who first introduced the concept of alienation into sociological theory?
(a) Hegel
(b) August Comte
(c) Marx
(d) Herbert Spencer

38. Changes in social positions with regard to variations in occupations, prestige, income, wealth, power and social class are referred to as ______.
(a) social change
(b) international mobility
(c) social mobility
(d) migration

39. Vertical mobility involves
(a) change in role
(b) change in occupation
(c) change in group
(d) change in social class position

40. ______ refers to the division of a population into strata one on top of another, on the basis of the possession of certain characteristics which the society regards as desirable or less desirable
(a) Social inequality
(b) Social stratification
(c) Caste
(d) Hierarchy

41. Match List I with List II and select the correct answer using the codes given below the lists:

List I
A. Opposition of purity and pollution
B. Dominant caste

C. Tribe-caste-peasant continuum
D. Attributional and interactional analysis of caste

List II

i. Surajit Sinha
ii. L. Dumont
iii. McKim Marriott
iv. M.N. Srinivas

Codes:	A	B	C	D
(a)	i	iv	ii	iii
(b)	ii	iii	i	iv
(c)	i	iii	ii	iv
(d)	ii	iv	i	iii

42. Match List I (Interpretation of Caste) with List II (Scholar) and select the correct answer using the codes given below the lists:

List I

A. Caste is a closed system
B. Closed organic stratification
C. Caste is an extreme form
D. Caste is an expression of hierarchy rather than stratification

List II

i. Louis Dumont
ii. Gunnar Myrdal
iii. Fredrick Bailey
iv. Max Weber

Codes:	A	B	C	D
(a)	i	ii	iii	iv
(b)	iv	iii	ii	i
(c)	i	iii	ii	iv
(d)	iv	ii	iii	i

43. According to Karl Marx, where does the capitalist class derive profit from?
(a) Absolute control over property
(b) The surplus values created by the workers
(c) Greater investment of capital to production
(d) Increase of means of production

44. Who looks into social stratification as 'the unequal division of material rewards and social prestige'?
(a) Max Weber
(b) Kingsley Davis and Wilbert Moore
(c) Karl Marx
(d) Melvin Tumin

45. Match List I with List II and select the correct answer using the codes given below the lists:

List I

A. Social position of men into groups based on their consumption pattern
B. Besides capitalists and workers, there are also other classes and strata in capitalist society
C. Status attainment through achievement motivation
D. Exploitation through appropriation of surplus value

List II

i. Kingsley Davis and Wilbert Moore
ii. Max Weber
iii. Karl Marx
iv. Wesoloski

Codes:	A	B	C	D
(a)	ii	iv	i	iii
(b)	iii	i	iv	ii
(c)	ii	i	iv	iii
(d)	iii	iv	i	ii

46. Only when ______ attitudes develop does the class struggle really emerge
(a) fur sich
(b) an sick
(c) nationalistic
(d) capitalistic

47. _____ refers to the rules and prescriptions about intercaste relations, particularly to eating and drinking of water.
(a) Prohibition
(b) Commensality
(c) Regulations
(d) Prescriptions

48. Alienation for Marx is a/an ______.
(a) objective condition
(b) subjective condition
(c) individual condition
(d) class condition

49. Status groups, according to Weber are identified by
(a) education
(b) occupation
(c) styles of life
(d) family background

50. According to Marx, when a class becomes aware of its interests and organizes itself, it becomes a
(a) class in itself
(b) revolutionary class
(c) class for itself
(d) bourgeoisie

ANSWERS

1. (b)	2. (c)	3. (d)	4. (c)	5. (a)
6. (c)	7. (a)	8. (b)	9. (a)	10. (c)
11. (b)	12. (b)	13. (a)	14. (c)	15. (c)
16. (a)	17. (b)	18. (c)	19. (a)	20. (d)
21. (c)	22. (c)	23. (b)	24. (a)	25. (a)
26. (b)	27. (d)	28. (b)	29. (c)	30. (c)
31. (b)	32. (b)	33. (a)	34. (b)	35. (b)
36. (a)	37. (c)	38. (c)	39. (d)	40. (b)
41. (d)	42. (b)	43. (b)	44. (b)	45. (a)
46. (a)	47. (a)	48. (a)	49. (c)	50. (c)

JUNE–2008

Note: This paper contains Fifty (50) objective type questions, each question carrying two (2) marks. Attempt all the questions.

PAPER–I

1. The teacher has been glorified by the phrase "Friend, philosopher and guide" because
   (a) He has to play all vital roles in the context of society
   (b) He transmits the high value of humanity to students
   (c) He is the great reformer of the society
   (d) He is a great patriot

2. The most important cause of failure for teacher lies in the area of
   (a) inter personal relationship
   (b) lack of command over the knowledge of the subject
   (c) verbal ability
   (d) strict handling of the students

3. A teacher can establish rapport with his students by
   (a) becoming a figure of authority
   (b) impressing students with knowledge and skill
   (c) playing the role of a guide
   (d) becoming a friend to the students

4. Education is a powerful instrument of
   (a) Social transformation
   (b) Personal transformation
   (c) Cultural transformation
   (d) All of the above

5. A teacher's major contribution towards the maximum self-realisation of the student is affected through
   (a) Constant fulfilment of the students' needs
   (b) Strict control of classroom activities
   (c) Sensitivity to students' needs, goals and purposes
   (d) Strict reinforcement of academic standards

6. Research problem is selected from the stand point of
   (a) Researcher's interest
   (b) Financial support
   (c) Social relevance
   (d) Availability of relevant literature

7. Which one is called non-probability sampling?
   (a) Cluster sampling
   (b) Quota sampling
   (c) Systematic sampling
   (d) Stratified random sampling

8. Formulation of hypothesis may not be required in
   (a) Survey method
   (b) Historical studies
   (c) Experimental studies
   (d) Normative studies

9. Fieldwork based research is classified as
   (a) Empirical
   (b) Historical
   (c) Experimental
   (d) Biographical

10. Which of the following sampling method is appropriate to study the prevalence of

AIDS amongst male and female in India in 1976, 1986, 1996 and 2006?
(a) Cluster sampling
(b) Systematic sampling
(c) Quota sampling
(d) Stratified random sampling

Read the following passage and answer the questions from 11 to 15:

The fundamental principle is that Article 14 forbids class legislation but permits reasonable classification for the purpose of legislation which classification must satisfy the twin tests of classification being founded on an intelligible differentia which distinguishes persons or things that are grouped together from those that are left out of the group and that differentia must have a rational nexus to the object sought to be achieved by the Statute in question. The thrust of Article 14 is that the citizen is entitled to equality before law and equal protection of laws. In the very nature of things the society being composed of unequals a welfare State will have to strive by both executive and legislative action to help the less fortunate in society to ameliorate their condition so that the social and economic inequality in the society may be bridged. This would necessitate a legislative application to a group of citizens otherwise unequal and amelioration of whose lot is the object of state affirmative action. In the absence of the doctrine of classification such legislation is likely to flounder on the bedrock of equality enshrined in Article 14. The Court realistically appraising the social and economic inequality and keeping in view the guidelines on which the State action must move as constitutionally laid down in Part IV of the Constitution evolved the doctrine of classification. The doctrine was evolved to sustain a legislation or State action designed to help weaker sections of the society or some such segments of the society in need of succour. Legislative and executive action may accordingly be sustained if it satisfies the twin tests of reasonable classification and the rational principle correlated to the object sought to be achieved.

The concept of equality before the law does not involve the idea of absolute equality among human beings which is a physical impossibility. All that Article 14 guarantees is a similarity of treatment contra-distinguished from identical treatment. Equality before law means that among equals the law should be equal and should be equally administered and that the likes should be treated alike. Equality before the law does not mean that things which are different shall be as though they are the same. It of course means denial of any special privilege by reason of birth, creed or the like. The legislation as well as the executive government, while dealing with diverse problems arising out of an infinite variety of human relations must of necessity have the power of making special laws, to attain any particular object and to achieve that object it must have the power of selection or classification of persons and things upon which such laws are to operate.

11. Right to equality, one of the fundamental rights, is enunciated in the constitution under Part III, Article
(a) 12 (b) 13
(c) 14 (d) 15

12. The main thrust of Right to equality is that it permits
(a) class legislation
(b) equality before law and equal protection under the law
(c) absolute equality
(d) special privilege by reason of birth

13. The social and economic inequality in the society can be bridged by

(a) executive and legislative action
(b) universal suffrage
(c) identical treatment
(d) None of the above

14. The doctrine of classification is evolved to
(a) Help weaker sections of the society
(b) Provide absolute equality
(c) Provide identical treatment
(d) None of the above

15. While dealing with diverse problems arising out of an infinite variety of human relations, the government
(a) must have the power of making special laws
(b) must not have any power to make special laws
(c) must have power to withdraw equal rights
(d) None of the above

16. Communication with oneself is known as
(a) Group communication
(b) Grapevine communication
(c) Interpersonal communication
(d) Intrapersonal communication

17. Which broadcasting system for TV is followed in India?
(a) NTSE (b) PAL
(c) SECAM (d) NTCS

18. All India Radio before 1936 was known as
(a) Indian Radio Broadcasting
(b) Broadcasting Service of India
(c) Indian State Broadcasting Service
(d) All India Broadcasting Service

19. The biggest news agency of India is
(a) PTI
(b) UNI
(c) NANAP
(d) Samachar Bharati

20. Prasar Bharati was launched in the year
(a) 1995 (b) 1997
(c) 1999 (d) 2001

21. A statistical measure based upon the entire population is called parameter while measure based upon a sample is known as
(a) Sample parameter
(b) Inference
(c) Statistics
(d) None of these

22. The importance of the correlation co-efficient lies in the fact that
(a) There is a linear relationship between the correlated variables
(b) It is one of the most valid measure of statistics
(c) It allows one to determine the degree or strength of the association between two variables
(d) It is a non-parametric method of statistical analysis

23. The F-test
(a) is essentially a two tailed test
(b) is essentially a one tailed test
(c) can be one tailed as well as two tailed depending on the hypothesis
(d) can never be a one tailed test

24. What will be the next letter in the following series
DCXW, FEVU, HGTS, ______
(a) AKPO (b) JBYZ
(c) JIRQ (d) LMRS

25. The following question is based on the diagram given below. If the two small circles represent formal classroom education and distance education and the big circle stands for university system of education, which figure represents the university systems.

(a)  (b) 

(c) 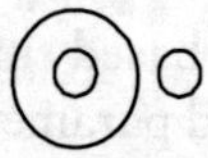 (d) 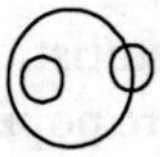

26. The statement, *To be non-violent is good* is a
    (a) Moral judgement
    (b) Factual judgement
    (c) Religious judgement
    (d) Value judgement
27. **Assertion (A):** Man is a rational being.
    Reason (R): Man is a social being.
    (a) Both (A) and (R) are true and (R) is the correct explanation of (A)
    (b) Both (A) and (R) are true, but (R) is not the correct explanation of (A)
    (c) (A) is true, but (R) is false
    (d) (A) is false, but (R) is true
28. Value Judgements are
    (a) Factual Judgements
    (b) Ordinary Judgements
    (c) Normative Judgements
    (d) Expression of public opinion
29. Deductive reasoning proceeds from
    (a) general to particular
    (b) particular to general
    (c) one general conclusion to another general conclusion
    (d) one particular conclusion to another particular conclusion
30. AGARTALA is written in code as 14168171, the code for AGRA is
    (a) 1641 (b) 1416
    (c) 1441 (d) 1461
31. Which one of the following is the most comprehensive source of population data?
    (a) National Family Health Surveys
    (b) National Sample Surveys
    (c) Census
    (d) Demographic Health Surveys
32. Which one of the following principles is not applicable to sampling?
    (a) Sample units must be clearly defined
    (b) Sample units must be dependent on each other
    (c) Same units of sample should be used throughout the study
    (d) Sample units must be chosen in a systematic and objective manner
33. If January 1st, 2007 is Monday, what was the day on 1st January 1995?
    (a) Sunday
    (b) Monday
    (c) Friday
    (d) Saturday
34. Insert the missing number in the following series:
    4 16 8 64 ? 256
    (a) 16 (b) 24
    (c) 32 (d) 20
35. If an article is sold for ₹ 178 at a loss of 11%; what would be its selling price in order to earn a profit of 11%?
    (a) ₹ 222.50 (b) ₹ 267
    (c) ₹ 222 (d) ₹ 220
36. WYSIWYG—describes the display of a document on screen as it will actually print
    (a) What you state is what you get
    (b) What you see is what you get
    (c) What you save is what you get
    (d) What you suggest is what you get
37. Which of the following is not a Computer language?
    (a) PASCAL
    (b) UNIX
    (c) FORTRAN
    (d) COBOL

38. A keyboard has at least
(a) 91 keys (b) 101 keys
(c) 111 keys (d) 121 keys

39. An E-mail address is composed of
(a) two parts (b) three parts
(c) four parts (d) five parts

40. Corel Draw is a popular
(a) Illustration programme
(b) Programming language
(c) Text programme
(d) None of the above

41. Human ear is most sensitive to noise in which of the following ranges
(a) 1-2 KHz
(b) 100-500 Hz
(c) 10-12 KHz
(d) 13-16 KHz

42. Which one of the following units is used to measure intensity of noise?
(a) decible (b) Hz
(c) Phon (d) Watts/m^2

43. If the population growth follows a logistic curve, the maximum sustainable yield
(a) is equal to half the carrying capacity
(b) is equal to the carrying capacity
(c) depends on growth rates
(d) depends on the initial population

44. Chemical weathering of rocks is largely dependent upon
(a) high temperature
(b) strong wind action
(c) heavy rainfall
(d) glaciation

45. Structure of earth's system consists of the following:
Match List I with List II and give the correct answer:

List I (Zone)
A. Atmosphere
B. Biosphere
C. Hydrosphere
D. Lithosphere

List II (Chemical Character)
1. Inert gases
2. Salt, freshwater, snow and ice
3. Organic substances, skeleton matter
4. Light silicates

Codes:	A	B	C	D
(a)	2	3	1	4
(b)	1	3	2	4
(c)	2	1	3	4
(d)	3	1	2	4

46. NAAC is an autonomous institution under the aegis of
(a) ICSSR (b) CSIR
(c) AICTE (d) UGC

47. National Council for Women's Education was established in
(a) 1958 (b) 1976
(c) 1989 (d) 2000

48. Which one of the following is not situated in New Delhi?
(a) Indian Council of Cultural Relations
(b) Indian Council of Scientific Research
(c) National Council of Educational Research and Training
(d) Indian Institute of Advanced Studies

49. Autonomy in higher education implies freedom in
(a) Administration
(b) Policy-making
(c) Finance
(d) Curriculum development

50. Match List I with List II and select the correct answer from the codes given below:

List I (Institutions)
A. Dr. Hari Singh Gour University
B. S.N.D.T. University

C. M.S. University
D. J.N. Vyas University

List II (Locations)
1. Mumbai
2. Baroda
3. Jodhpur
4. Sagar

Codes:	A	B	C	D
(a)	4	1	2	3
(b)	1	2	3	4
(c)	3	1	2	4
(d)	2	4	1	3

ANSWERS

1. (b)	2. (b)	3. (b)	4. (d)	5. (c)
6. (c)	7. (b)	8. (b)	9. (a)	10. (d)
11. (c)	12. (b)	13. (a)	14. (a)	15. (a)
16. (d)	17. (b)	18. (c)	19. (a)	20. (b)
21. (a)	22. (c)	23. (c)	24. (c)	25. (b)
26. (a)	27. (b)	28. (c)	29. (a)	30. (d)
31. (c)	32. (b)	33. (d)	34. (a)	35. (c)
36. (b)	37. (b)	38. (b)	39. (a)	40. (a)
41. (b)	42. (a)	43. (a)	44. (c)	45. (b)
46. (d)	47. (a)	48. (d)	49. (c)	50. (a)

PAPER–II

Note: This paper contains Fifty (50) objective type questions, each question carrying two (2) marks. Attempt all the questions.

1. Among the following implements, which on led to "silent revolution" from nomadic to agricultural society?
(a) Flint stone
(b) Catapult
(c) Mandate
(d) Hoe

2. Match List I (Author) with List II (Contribution) and select the correct answer using the codes given below the lists:

List I
A. Max Weber
B. R. Dahrendorf
C. Emile Durkheim
D. T. Veblen

List II
i. Division of Labour
ii. The Leisure Class
iii. Economy and Society
iv. Class and Class Conflict in Industrial Society

Codes:	A	B	C	D
(a)	i	iv	iii	ii
(b)	iv	iii	i	iv
(c)	i	ii	iii	iv
(d)	iii	iv	i	ii

3. Who among the following has divided religious organisations into denominations and cults?
(a) Max Weber
(b) Ernst Troeltsch
(c) Howard Becker
(d) Robert K. Merton

4. Match List I with List II and select the correct answer using the codes given below the lists:

List I (Concept)
A. Rationalization
B. Military society and industrial society
C. Mechanical solidarity and organic solidarity
D. Primary, secondary and tertiary sectors

List II (Thinker)
i. Saint Simon
ii. Collin Clark
iii. Max Weber
iv. Emile Durkheim

Codes:	A	B	C	D
(a)	iii	ii	iv	i
(b)	iv	ii	iii	ii
(c)	iii	i	iv	ii
(d)	iv	ii	iii	i

5. Which among the following are the two orientations with regard to the two types of social movements as given by Yogender Singh?
   1. Integrative
   2. Alternative
   3. Alienating
   4. Reformative

   Select the correct answer using the codes given below:

   Codes:
   (a) 1 and 2 (b) 1 and 3
   (c) 3 and 4 (d) 1 and 4

6. What does the term 'Patrician' stand for?
   (a) Landowner
   (b) Landless labourer
   (c) Slave
   (d) Salve master

7. With whom among the following are the concepts universalisation and parochrialisation associated?
   (a) Robert R. Marret
   (b) McKim Marriott
   (c) R. Redfield
   (d) Meyer Fortes

8. Who among the following has suggested a three-fold division of the agricultural population into Malik, Kisan and Mazdoor?
   (a) Daniel Thorner
   (b) D.N. Dhanagre
   (c) K. Gough
   (d) A. Amitai Etzioni

9. Consider the following statements:
   1. Tribal Economy often has a market place but not a market system.
   2. Reciprocity and redistribution create the integrative patterns prevalent in tribal economy.
   3. Tribal production is contractual and voluntary.
   4. A distinguishing feature of primitive life is fusion of social and economic institutions.

   Which of the statements given above are correct?
   (a) 1 and 4 (b) 2 and 4
   (c) 1, 2 and 4 (d) 1, 2 and 3

10. Which among the following tribes has started the Tana Bhagat Movement?
    (a) Santal (b) Khasi
    (c) Oraon (d) Kuki

11. Match List I (Typology) with List II (Tribal Movement) and select the correct answer, using the codes given below the lists:

    List I
    A. Ethni B. Reform
    C. Secessionist D. Subnational

    List II
    i. Naga Movement
    ii. Jharkhand Movement
    iii. Birsa Movement
    iv. Bhagat Movement

Codes:	A	B	C	D
(a)	iii	ii	i	iv
(b)	i	iv	iii	ii
(c)	iii	iv	i	ii
(d)	i	ii	iii	iv

12. Match List I (Dormitory) with List II (Tribe) and select the correct answer using the codes given below the lists:

List I	List II
A. Rangbang	i. Munda
B. Ghotul	ii. Ao Naga
C. Yo	iii. Bhotia
D. Ggitora	iv. Muria

Codes:	A	B	C	D
(a)	ii	i	iii	iv
(b)	iii	iv	ii	i
(c)	ii	iv	iii	i
(d)	iii	i	ii	iv

13. Consider the following statements: R.K. Merton refers to the Hopi rain dance in connection with
    1. laten function
    2. relative deprivation
    3. reference group
    4. manifest function

    Which of the statements given above is/are correct?
    (a) 1 only (b) 2 and 3
    (c) 1 and 4 (d) 4 only

14. Consider the following statements
    1. Power has become independent of class than what it was in the past.
    2. Ownership of land is no longer the decisive factor in acquiring power.
    3. Mobility in the caste system has always been an extremely slow and, gradual process.

    Which of the statements given above are correct according to Andre Beteille with regard to power?
    (a) 1 and 3 (b) 2 and 3
    (c) 1 and 2 (d) 1, 2 and 3

15. Match List I with List II and select the correct answer using the codes given below the lists:

    List I
    A. Urbanism
    B. Folk urban continuum
    C. Little tradition and great tradition
    D. Culture of poverty

    List II
    i. Oscar Lewis
    ii. L. Wirth
    iii. R. Redfield
    iv. Milton Singer

Codes:	A	B	C	D
(a)	iv	i	ii	iii
(b)	ii	iii	iv	i
(c)	iv	iii	ii	i
(d)	ii	i	iii	iv

16. Lewis Mumford used the term "container" to characterise the city of
    (a) Neolithic period
    (b) Paleolithic period
    (c) Mesolithic period
    (d) Feudal period

17. The scientific stage of society began in the 19th century and it corresponded to the industrial society. Who among the following used the term "industrial society" in this content?
    (a) Auguste Comte
    (b) Emile Durkheim
    (c) Karl Marx
    (d) Max Weber

18. People in the cybernetic age are categorised into 'Alpha' and 'Beta'. Which one of the following belongs to 'Alpha category'?
    (a) Illiterate tribal
    (b) Cultivator
    (c) Village shopkeeper
    (d) Trained scientist and professional

19. Who expressed the view that demographic density is a major determinant of societal evolution?
    (a) Talcott Parsons
    (b) Emile Durkheim
    (c) George Simmel
    (d) L. Cosere

20. What does population pyramid deal with?
    (a) Age and marriage structure
    (b) Age and sex structure
    (c) Age and labour force structure
    (d) Age and literacy structure

21. Who introduced the term 'stateless society'?

(a) Paul Bohannan
(b) E.E. Evans-Pritchard
(c) A. Powell
(d) A. Giddens

22. Which one of the following principles in not relater to P.A. Sorokin's cultural theory of change?
(a) The principle of cyclical change
(b) The principle of immanent change
(c) The principle of limit
(d) The principle of social equilibrium

23. Match List I (Article) with List II (Provision) and select the correct answer using the codes given below the lists:

List I

A. Article 15 B. Article 330
C. Article 46 D. Article 17

List II

i. Abolition of untouchability
ii. Promotion of education and economic interests of SC/ST and other weaker sections
iii. Prohibition of discrimination on the basis of religion, race, caste, sex or place of birth
iv. Reservation of seats for SC and ST in the Lok Sabha

Codes:	A	B	C	D
(a)	ii	iv	iii	i
(b)	iii	i	ii	iv
(c)	ii	i	iii	iv
(d)	iii	iv	ii	i

24. When was the Kaka Kalelkar Commission constituted by the then President of India?
(a) 1952 (b) 1953
(c) 1954 (d) 1951

25. Which of the concepts given below are concerned with analysis of cyclical change?
(a) Social statics and social dynamics
(b) Morphostatics and morphogenesis
(c) Social telesis and social genesis
(d) Residues and derivations

26. Who among the following is regarded as technological determinist of social change?
(a) E. Durkheim
(b) W.F. Ogburn
(c) Pitrim A. Sorokin
(d) Thorstein Veblen

27. Who among the following offered a cyclic theory of social change which views the societies oscillating between three different types of mentalities?
(a) V. Pareto (b) P.A. Sorokin
(c) T. Veblen (d) K. Marx

28. According to Hindu view of life there are four ages. Which one of the following is the correct sequence?
(a) Satyayuga – Dwapara – Treta – Kaliyuga
(b) Kaliyuga – Dwapara – Satyayuga – Treta
(c) Satyayuga – Treta – Dwapara – Kaliyuga
(d) Treta – Dwapara – Satyayuga – Kaliyuga

29. Who among the following has said that all cultures go through a regular succession of stages corresponding to spring, summer, autumn and winter?
(a) A. Toynbee
(b) Oswald Spengler
(c) F.S. Chapin
(d) A.L. Koreber

30. Who among the following developed notions of stratification that included both the institutional gains of stratification and the conflict inherent in societal inequalities?
(a) Ralph Dahrendrof
(b) Talcott Parsons

(c) Max Weber
(d) Herbert Spencer

31. Which one of the following statements is correct?
The concept of social role, according to E. Goffman has originated in a
(a) theatrical setting
(b) social life
(c) system of social stratification
(d) the process of role adaptation

32. Which one of the following pairs is not correctly matched?
(a) A.R. Radcliffe Brown : Four functional prerequisites
(b) R.K. Merton : Reference groups
(c) Emile Durkheim : Social facts
(d) E.H. Cooley : Primary and secondary groups

33. Who regards deviance as functional for society?
(a) A. Cohen (b) E. Durkheim
(c) R.K. Merton (d) L.K. White

34. What does law in a society mean?
1. To transform informal social norms into formal ones.
2. To elevate vague obligations and privileges into rights and duties.
3. A realm of formal obligation.
4. A fear imposed on people to avoid certain actions.
Select the correct answer using the codes given below:
(a) 1, 2 and 4 (b) 1, 3 and 4
(c) 1, 2 and 3 (d) 2, 3 and 4

35. Consider the following factors about socialization, as conceived by Sigmund Freud:
1. 'Super-ego' develops in an individual when the latter assimilates his/her parent's ideas of right and wrong.
2. The rational part of the individual's 'id' takes the form of ago.
3. The individual's organism contacts the external world.
4. Innate tendencies, stored in the 'id' seek satisfaction in the external world.
Which one of the following is the correct sequence of the factors given above?
(a) 2-1-4-3 (b) 4-3-2-1
(c) 2-3-4-1 (d) 4-1-2-3

36. What is the process, under which one culture merges itself with the dominant culture, called?
(a) Adaptation
(b) Accommodation
(c) Assimilation
(d) Acculturation

37. What is the most important and basic factor for social integration according to the functionalists?
(a) Value consensus
(b) Maintenance of relative stability
(c) Structural interdependence
(d) Condition of anomie

38. Which one of the following is not covered under the "element of Social Structure"?
(a) Deviation (b) Observance
(c) Sanction (d) Group action

39. What are social norms?
(a) Rules whose observance is expected in a society
(b) Laws whose violation invariably leads to punishment
(c) Principles accepted as normal by sociology
(d) Codes which are prescribed in sacred texts

40. Which one of the following theories is considered as a cause of social protests?
(a) Absolute deprivation
(b) Political mobilisation of the oppressed
(c) Relative deprivation
(d) Absolute poverty

41. Who among the following authors developed the social distance scale?
(a) L. Guttman
(b) Paulin Young
(c) W.J. Goode and P.K. Hatt
(d) E.S. Bogardus

42. Who among the following originally used the term 'Relative Deprivation'?
(a) Samuel A. Stouffer
(b) R.K. Merton
(c) W.G. Summer
(d) A. Henderson

43. What is the marriage of a widow to her deceased husband's brother termed as?
(a) Widow marriage
(b) Sororate
(c) Polyandry
(d) Levirate

44. In which one of the following concepts has M.N. Srinivas explained caste mobility as a process of social and cultural change?
(a) Sanskritization
(b) Secularization
(c) Westernization
(d) Modernization

45. Which of the following social groups practiced the custom of visiting husbands as a form of marriage?
(a) Bhils (b) Santhals
(c) Nairs (d) Nagas

46. What is a marriage between social strata, where the woman is a member of the upper stratum; designated as?
(a) Hypogamy
(b) Hypergamy
(c) Exogamy
(d) Endogamy

47. Which one of the following situations does sororal polygyny refer to?
(a) Several sisters marry the same man
(b) A woman's marriage with her husband's brother after the husband's death
(c) A man's marriage with his sister's daughter
(d) A man's marriage with the sister of his sister's husband

48. In which one of the following terminological system, each term designates only one type of relative?
(a) Classificatory kinship terminology
(b) Kinship terminology
(c) Colloquial terminology
(d) Descriptive kinship terminology

49. What is the most important feature of the social system of the Manus tribal of Admiralty Islands which Margaret mead called "Gentes"?
(a) Patrilineal clan
(b) Matrilineal clan
(c) Teknonymy
(d) Adelphic Polyandry

50. Match List I (Concept) with List II (Propounded By) and select the correct answer using the codes given below the lists:

List I
A. Third World
B. Bureaucracy
C. Iron Law of Oligarchy
D. Law of Mystical participation

List II
i. Lucian Levy-Bruhl
ii. Monsieur de Gournay
iii. Robert Michels
iv. Alfred Sauvy

Codes:	A	B	C	D
(a)	iv	i	iii	ii
(b)	iii	ii	iv	i
(c)	iv	ii	iii	i
(d)	iii	i	iv	ii

ANSWERS

1. (d)	2. (d)	3. (d)	4. (c)	5. (d)
6. (d)	7. (b)	8. (a)	9. (b)	10. (c)
11. (c)	12. (d)	13. (c)	14. (d)	15. (b)
16. (d)	17. (a)	18. (d)	19. (b)	20. (b)
21. (b)	22. (d)	23. (d)	24. (b)	25. (b)
26. (b)	27. (b)	28. (c)	29. (b)	30. (a)
31. (b)	32. (a)	33. (b)	34. (c)	35. (b)
36. (c)	37. (a)	38. (a)	39. (a)	40. (c)
41. (b)	42. (a)	43. (d)	44. (a)	45. (c)
46. (a)	47. (a)	48. (d)	49. (d)	50. (c)

DECEMBER–2007

Note: This paper contains Fifty (50) objective type questions, each question carrying two (2) marks. Attempt all the questions.

PAPER–I

1. Verbal guidance is least effective in the learning of
   (a) Aptitudes (b) Skills
   (c) Attitudes (d) Relationship
2. Which is the most important aspect of the teacher's rule in learning?
   (a) The development of insight into what constitutes an adequate performance
   (b) The development of insight into what constitutes the pitfalls and dangers to be avoided
   (c) The provision of encouragement and moral support
   (d) The provision of continuous diagnostic and remedial help
3. The most appropriate purpose of learning is
   (a) personal adjustment
   (b) modification of behaviour
   (c) social and political awarness
   (d) preparing oneself for employment
4. The students who keep on asking questions in the class should be
   (a) encouraged to find answer independently
   (b) advised to meet the teacher after the class
   (c) encouraged to continue questioning
   (d) advised not to disturb during the lecture
5. Maximum participation of students is possible in teaching through
   (a) discussion method
   (b) lecture method
   (c) audio-visual aids
   (d) textbook method
6. Generalised conclusion on the basis of a sample is technically known as
   (a) Data analysis and interpretation
   (b) Parameter inference
   (c) Statistical inference
   (d) All of the above
7. The experimental study is based on
   (a) The manipulation of variables
   (b) Conceptual parameters
   (c) Replication of research
   (d) Survey of literature
8. The main characteristic of scientific research is
   (a) empirical (b) theoretical
   (c) experimental (d) All of the above
9. Authenticity of a research finding is its
   (a) Originality (b) Validity
   (c) Objectivity (d) All of the above
10. Which technique is generally followed when the population is finite?
    (a) Area Sampling Technique
    (b) Purposive Sampling Technique
    (c) Systematic Sampling Technique
    (d) None of the above

Read the following passage and answer the questions from 11 to 15:

Gandhi's overall social and environmental philosophy is based on what human beings need rather than what they want. His early introduction to the teachings of Jains, Theosophists, Christian sermons, Ruskin and Tolstoy, and most significantly the *Bhagavad Gita*, were to have profound impact on the development of Gandhi's holistic thinking on humanity, nature and their ecological interrelation. His deep concern for the disadvantaged, the poor and rural population created an ambience for an alternative social thinking that was at once far-sighted, local and immediate. For Gandhi was acutely aware that the demands generated by the need to feed and sustain human life, compounded by the growing industrialisation of India, far outstripped the finite resources of nature. This might nowadays appear naive or commonplace, but such pronouncements were as rare as they were heretical a century ago. Gandhi was also concerned about the destruction, under colonial and modernist designs, of the existing infrastructures which had more potential for keeping a community flourishing within ecologically-sensitive traditional patterns of subsistence, especially in the rural areas, than did the incoming Western alternatives based on nature-blind technology and the enslavement of human spirit and energies.

Perhaps the moral principle for which Gandhi is best known is that of active non-violence, derived from the traditional moral restraint of not injuring another being. The most refined expression of this value is in the great epic of the *Mahabharata*, (c. 100 BCE to 200 CE), where moral development proceeds through placing constraints on the liberties, desires and acquisitiveness endemic to human life. One's action is judged in terms of consequences and the impact it is likely to have on another. Jainas had generalised this principle to include all sentient creatures and biocommunities alike. Advanced Jaina monks and nuns will sweep their path to avoid harming insects and even bacteria. Non-injury is a non-negotiable universal prescription.

11. Which one of the following have a profound impact on the development of Gandhi's holistic thinking on humanity, nature and their ecological interrelations?
    (a) Jain teachings
    (b) Christian sermons
    (c) *Bhagavad Gita*
    (d) Ruskin and Tolstoy
12. Gandhi's overall social and environmental philosophy is based on human beings'
    (a) need (b) desire
    (c) wealth (d) welfare
13. Gandhiji's deep concern for the disadvantaged, the poor and rural population created an ambience for an alternative
    (a) rural policy
    (b) social thinking
    (c) urban policy
    (d) economic thinking
14. Colonial policy and modernisation led to the destruction of
    (a) major industrial infrastructure
    (b) irrigation infrastructure
    (c) urban infrastructure
    (d) rural infrastructure
15. Gandhi's active non-violence is derived from
    (a) Moral restraint of not injuring another being
    (b) Having liberties, desires and acquisitiveness
    (c) Freedom of action
    (d) Nature-blind technology and enslavement of human spirit and energies
16. DTH service was started in the year
    (a) 2000 (b) 2002
    (c) 2004 (d) 2006

17. National Press day is celebrated on
(a) 16th November (b) 19th November
(c) 21st November (d) 30th November

18. The total number of members in the Press Council of India are
(a) 28 (b) 14
(c) 17 (d) 20

19. The right to impart and receive information is guaranteed in the Constitution of India by Article
(a) 19(2)(a) (b) 19(16)
(c) 19(2) (d) 19(1)(a)

20. Use of radio for higher education is based on the presumption of
(a) Enriching curriculum based instruction
(b) Replacing teacher in the long run
(c) Everybody having access to a radio set
(d) Other means of instruction getting outdated

21. Find out the number which should come at the place of question mark which will complete the following series.
5, 4, 9, 17, 35, ? = 139
(a) 149 (b) 79
(c) 49 (d) 69

Questions 22 to 24 are based on the following diagram in which there are three interlocking circles I, S and P, where circle I stands for Indians, circle S for Scientists and circle P for Politicians. Different regions in the figure are lettered from a to g.

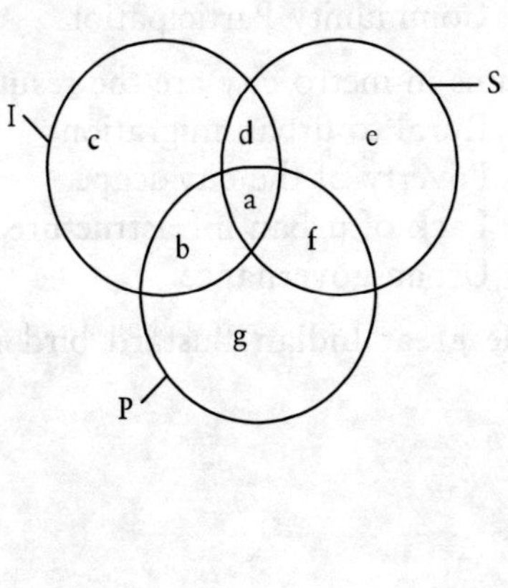

22. The region which represents Non-Indian Scientists who are Politicians.
(a) f (b) d
(c) a (d) c

23. The region which represents Indians who are neither Scientists nor Politicians.
(a) g (b) c
(c) f (d) a

24. The region which represents Politicians who are Indians as well as Scientists.
(a) b (b) c
(c) a (d) d

25. Which number is missing in the following series:
2, 5, 10, 17, 26, 37, 50, ?
(a) 63 (b) 65
(c) 67 (d) 69

26. The function of measurement includes.
(a) Prognosis (b) Diagnosis
(c) Prediction (d) All of the above

27. Logical arguments are based on
(a) Scientific reasoning
(b) Customary reasoning
(c) Mathematical reasoning
(d) Syllogistic reasoning

28. Insert the missing number 4 : 17 : : 7 : ?
(a) 48 (b) 49
(c) 50 (d) 51

29. Choose the odd word.
(a) Nun (b) Knight
(c) Monk (d) Priest

30. Choose the number which is different from others in the group.
(a) 49 (b) 63
(c) 77 (d) 81

31. Probability sampling implies.
(a) Stratified Random Sampling
(b) Systematic Random Sampling
(c) Simple Random Sampling
(d) All of the above

32. Insert the missing number.

$\frac{36}{62}, \frac{39}{63}, \frac{43}{61}, \frac{48}{64}, ?$

(a) $\frac{51}{65}$ (b) $\frac{56}{60}$

(c) $\frac{54}{65}$ (d) $\frac{33}{60}$

33. At what time between 3 and 4 o'clock will the hands of a watch point in opposite directions?
(a) 40 minutes past three
(b) 45 minutes past three
(c) 50 minutes past three
(d) 55 minutes past three

34. Mary has three children. What is the probability that none of the three children is a boy?

(a) $\frac{1}{2}$ (b) $\frac{1}{3}$

(c) $\frac{3}{4}$ (d) 1

35. If the radius of a circle is increased by 50 per cent. Its area is increased by
(a) 125 per cent (b) 100 per cent
(c) 75 per cent (d) 50 per cent

36. CD ROM stands for
(a) Computer Disk Read Only Memory
(b) Compact Disk Read Over Memory
(c) Compact Disk Read Only Memory
(d) Computer Disk Read Over Memory

37. The 'brain' of a computer which keeps peripherals under its control is called
(a) Common Power Unit
(b) Common Processing Unit
(c) Central Power Unit
(d) Central Processing Unit

38. Data can be saved on backing storage medium known as
(a) Compact Disk Recordable
(b) Computer Disk Rewritable
(c) Compact Disk Rewritable
(d) Computer Data Rewritable

39. RAM means
(a) Random Access Memory
(b) Rigid Access Memory
(c) Rapid Access Memory
(d) Revolving Access Memory

40. www represents
(a) who what and where
(b) weird wide web
(c) word wide web
(d) world wide web

41. Deforestation during the recent decades has led to
(a) Soil erosion
(b) Landslides
(c) Loss of bio-diversity
(d) All of the above

42. Which one of the following natural hazards is responsible for causing highest human disaster?
(a) Earthquakes
(b) Volcanic eruptions
(c) Snowstorms
(d) Tsunami

43. Which one of the following is appropriate for natural hazard mitigation?
(a) International AID
(b) Timely Warning System
(c) Rehabilitation
(d) Community Participation

44. Slums in metro city are the result of
(a) Rural to urban migration
(b) Poverty of the city-scape
(c) Lack of urban infrastructure
(d) Urban-governance

45. The great Indian Bustard bird is found in

(a) Thar Desert of India
(b) Coastal regions of India
(c) Temperate Forests in the Himalaya
(d) Tarai zones of the Himalayan Foot

46. The first Indian Satellite for serving the educational sector is known as
(a) SATEDU (b) INSAT-B
(c) EDUSAT (d) INSAT-C

47. Exclusive educational channel of IGNOU is known as
(a) Gyan Darshan (b) Gyan Vani
(c) Door Darshan (d) Prasar Bharati

48. The headquarter of Mahatma Gandhi Antarrashtriya Hindi Vishwavidyalaya is situated in
(a) Sevagram (b) New Delhi
(c) Wardha (d) Ahmedabad

49. Match List I with List II and select the correct answer using the codes given below:

List I (Institutes)
A. Central Institute of English and Foreign Languages
B. Gramodaya Vishwavidyalaya
C. Central Institute of Higher Tibetan Studies
D. IGNOU

List II (Locations)
1. Chitrakoot
2. Hyderabad
3. New Delhi
4. Dharmasala

Codes:	A	B	C	D
(a)	2	1	4	3
(b)	4	3	2	1
(c)	3	4	1	2
(d)	1	2	4	3

50. The aim of vocationalisation of education is
(a) preparing students for a vocation along with knowledge
(b) converting liberal education into vocational education
(c) giving more importance to vocational than general education
(d) making liberal education job-oriented

ANSWERS

1. (b)	2. (a)	3. (b)	4. (a)	5. (a)
6. (c)	7. (c)	8. (c)	9. (d)	10. (c)
11. (c)	12. (a)	13. (b)	14. (c)	15. (a)
16. (d)	17. (a)	18. (a)	19. (d)	20. (b)
21. (d)	22. (a)	23. (b)	24. (c)	25. (b)
26. (d)	27. (d)	28. (c)	29. (b)	30. (c)
31. (d)	32. (c)	33. (c)	34. (d)	35. (a)
36. (c)	37. (d)	38. (c)	39. (a)	40. (d)
41. (d)	42. (a)	43. (b)	44. (a)	45. (a)
46. (c)	47. (a)	48. (c)	49. (a)	50. (d)

PAPER–II

Note: This paper contains Fifty (50) objective type questions, each question carrying two (2) marks. All questions are compulsory.

1. Who of the following has differentiated between 'Character structure' and 'social structure'?
(a) Levi-Strauss
(b) Merion
(c) Gerth and Mills
(d) Meyer Frotes

2. Character structure and social structure is united by
(a) Status (b) Role
(c) Norm (d) Institution

3. According to Merton, causes of anomie lie in
(a) Individual's nature
(b) Social structure
(c) Deregulated institutions
(d) All of the above

4. Merton's concept of deviance states that deviance is a product of incompatibility between
(a) Societal goals and cultural means
(b) Institutionalized goals and cultural means
(c) Cultural goals and institutionalized means
(d) Institutionalised goals and societal means

5. Match List I with List II and choose the correct answers from the codes given below the lists:

List I
A. Innovation B. Ritualism
C. Retreatism D. Rebellion

List II
i. Organised political action
ii. Vagabonds
iii. Overtly cautious bureaucrat
iv. Embeezzlement

Codes:	A	B	C	D
(a)	iii	iv	ii	i
(b)	iii	iv	i	ii
(c)	iv	iii	i	ii
(d)	iv	iii	ii	i

6. When the prevailing institutionalized arrangements are perceived to be unjust to the realization of legitimized goals, the stage is set for
(a) Innovation (b) Ritualism
(c) Retreatism (d) Rebellion

7. Who of the following constitute the true aliens, according to Merton?
(a) Innovalist (b) Ritualism
(b) Retreatism (d) Rebellion

8. Which of the following is a privatized rather than a collective mode of adaptation of the socially disinherited according to Merton?
(a) Innovation (b) Ritualism
(c) Retreatism (d) Rebellion

9. Consider the following statements:
1. Howard Odum is a regionalist.
2. Regionalists seek out the potential as well as the actual interaction between man's physical environment and man's social life.

Codes:
(a) Both 1 and 2 are correct
(b) Both 1 and 2 are incorrect
(c) Only 1 is correct
(d) Only 2 is correct

10. Consider the following statements:
1. Purely physical adjustment is always on going, is never 'maladjustments'.
2. We speak of 'maladaptation' in case of biological adaptation.

Codes:
(a) Both 1 and 2 are correct
(b) Both 1 and 2 are incorrect
(c) Only 1 is correct
(d) Only 2 is correct

11. The sun will tan your skin if we exposed ourselves to it. This is a case of
(a) Biological adaptation
(b) Physical adaptation
(c) Social adaptation
(d) None of the above

12. Fishes adapting to a marine environment is a case of
(a) Physical adaptation
(b) Social adaptation
(c) Biological adaptation
(d) All of the above

13. Consider the following statements:
    1. Social adaptation always involves some standard of values
    2. Social adaptation is conditional adaptation
    3. When we speak of Maladaptation or maladjament, we do not mean that universal principles of physical adaptation is defeated

    Codes:
    (a) 1 and 2 are correct
    (b) 2 and 3 are incorrect
    (c) 1 and 3 are correct
    (d) All of the above are correct
14. Consider the following statements:
    1. The inner environment of man includes social heritage.
    2. The outer environment of man includes non-material culture
    3. The inner and outer environment of man are always interactive
    4. Man is adjusted to inner environment through conscious response and habitation

    Codes:
    (a) 1, 2, 3 are correct
    (b) 2, 3, 4 are incorrect
    (c) 1, 3, 4 are correct
    (d) All of the above are correct
15. 'Professional skill of surgeon' is
    (a) Habit
    (b) Custom
    (c) Neither Habit nor custom
    (d) Norm
16. The people of certain age can be classified as
    (a) Group
    (b) Quasi group
    (c) Statistical aggregate
    (d) Community
17. Which of the following are true for 'Social Class'?
    1. Like attitude of groups members
    2. Most inclusive range of interests
    3. Indefinite social organization
    4. Interest conscious unities

    Codes:
    (a) 1, 2, 3 (b) 2, 3, 4
    (c) 1, 3, 4 (d) All of the above
18. Interest conscious unities with definite organization are known as
    (a) Institutions (b) Association
    (c) Community (d) Nation
19. Which of the following are primary groups?
    (a) Play group
    (b) The gang
    (c) The tribal council
    (d) Church

    Codes:
    (a) 1 and 2 (b) 1 and 3
    (c) 1, 2, 3 (d) 1, 2, 4
20. Common interest groups is one in which
    (a) Momentary curiosity becomes common
    (b) Common curiosity becomes momentary
    (c) Curiosity becomes of long duration
    (d) Curiosity and interest clash
21. Which of the following traits of metropells is explained by its being called a radical and cultural melting pot?
    (a) Complexity of lifestyle
    (b) Density
    (c) Mobility
    (d) Heterogeneity
22. When cultural traits spread from one society to another, the process is known as
    (a) Assimilation
    (b) Marginalisation
    (c) Diffusion
    (d) Parallelism

23. Which of the following necessitates the establishment of international order?
    (a) Only under international order can the common and the complementary interest of peoples be safeguarded and advanced.
    (b) Every state, and particularly every great state, is treat to the security of all others.

Codes:
(a) Both 1 and 2 are correct
(b) Both 1 and 2 are incorrect
(c) Only 1 is correct
(d) Only 2 is correct

24. Who of the following has written the book *The Acquisitive Society*?
    (a) Peter Blau (b) R.H. Tawnye
    (c) M. Foucault (d) K. Pearson

25. Consider the following statements and state which are correct?
    1. In the economics association, men seek wealth in conjunction, but ultimately in order to gain individual control or possession.
    2. The political method socializes or communizes wealth.
    3. Socialised or communized goods are removed from the sphere of exchange and of the regulating economic forces of supply and demand.
    4. Communised goods may also be unequally distributed.

Codes:
(a) 1, 2 (b) 1, 2, 3
(c) 2, 3 (d) All of the above

26. Which of the following are the results of 'incorporation' of associations?
    1. It gives to an association a specific legal personality.
    2. It defines and limits the functions of an association.
    3. It defines and limits the liabilities of its members.
    4. It turns association into an agency, acting through appointed officials resulting in separation of ownership from management.

Codes:
(a) 2, 4 (b) 1, 2, 4
(c) 1, 3, 4 (d) All of the above

27. Who among the following links the education system with the system of social stratification?
    (a) Herbert Gintis
    (b) Goode
    (c) Davis and Moore
    (d) M. Foucault

28. Consider the following statements about human biogrammar state which is correct?
    1. Biogrammar is genetically based programme which predisposes mankind to behave in certain ways.
    2. Predispositions of man according to biogrammar are same as instinct.

Codes:
(a) Both 1 and 2 are correct
(b) Both 1 and 2 are incorrect
(c) Only 1 is correct
(d) Only 2 is correct

29. Lionel Tiger and Robin Fox see dominance as
    (a) Sex linked characteristics
    (b) Cultural linked characteristics
    (c) Both Sex and Culture linked characteristics
    (d) None of the above

30. According to Lionel Tiger and Robin Fox, the basic family unit is
    (a) Father and child
    (b) Husband and wife
    (c) Mother and child
    (d) Father, mother and their children

31. According to Lionel Tiger and Robin Fox, male and female biogrammars are adapted to
(a) Sexual division of labour in hunting society
(b) Sexual division of labour in feudal society
(c) Sexual division of labour in industrial society
(d) Sexual division of labour in agricultural society

32. According to Lionel Tiger and Ribon Fox, who among the following is most essential for the well being of a child?
(a) Father
(b) Mother
(c) Brothers and sisters
(d) Whole family

33. Consider the following statements and state which are correct?
(a) G.P. Murdock sees biological differences between men and women as the basis of the sexual division of labour in society.
(b) G.P. Murdock sees sexual division of labour in society as the basis of biological differences.
(c) According to G.P. Murdock, given the biological differences between men and women, a sexual division of labour is most different way of organizing.

Codes:
(a) 1, 2 (b) 1, 3
(c) 2, 3 (d) All of the above

34. The concept of 'principle of polarization' was put forward by
(a) Ogburn
(b) Sorokin
(c) K. Mannluim
(d) Arnold Toymbee

35. Consider the following statements:
1. Marx made a distinction between "class in itself and class for itself" to reflect the movement from a class' self awareness to actual self awareness.
2. According to Marx, super structure determines infrastructure in society.

Codes:
(a) Both 1 and 2 are correct
(b) Both 1 and 2 are incorrect
(c) Only 1 is correct
(d) Only 2 is correct

36. Marx referred to small capitalists as
1. Petil bourgeoisie
2. Lumpenproletariat

Codes:
(a) Both 1 and 2 are correct
(b) Both 1 and 2 are incorrect
(c) Only 1 is correct
(d) Only 2 is correct

37. According to Marx, the value of any commodity is determined by
(a) Value of ingredients
(b) Value of amount of labour
(c) Capitalists
(d) Market forces

38. Who among the following claim that underdevelopment of the third-world countries is initiated and aggravated by the capitalist system of developed countries which have sterilized and exploited developing countries?
(a) Marx
(b) Andre Guilder Frank
(c) Herbert Marcuse
(d) Habermas

39. Consider the following statements about Herbert Spencer and state which are correct?

1. He was born on 27th April 1820
2. He was British
3. He was an engineer

Codes:

(a) 1, 2 (b) 2, 3
(c) 1, 3 (d) All of the above

40. Who among the following has defined social organization as "the systematic ordering of social relations by acts of choices and decisions"?
(a) M. Ginsberg (b) R. Firth
(c) K. Davis (d) S.F. Nadel

41. Match List I with List II and choose correct answers from the codes given below the lists:

List I

A. Gemeinshaft and geselschaft
B. Mechinical solidarity and organic solidarity
C. Status and ontract
D. Militant and industrial societies

List II

i. Henry Mine ii. Spencer
iii. Tonnies iv. Durkhiem

Codes:	A	B	C	D
(a)	iv	iii	ii	i
(b)	iii	iv	ii	i
(c)	iv	iii	i	ii
(d)	iii	iv	i	ii

42. Who among the following has provided a distinction between 'tribal' and 'open' societies into
(a) K. Davis
(b) K.R. Popper
(c) B.B. Mishra
(d) Robert Redfield

43. Who among the following has classified societies into
1. Simple societies
2. Simple poly segmentary societies
3. Simple compounded poly segmentary societies
4. Double sompounded poly segmentary societies

Codes:

(a) Durkhiem (b) Spencer
(c) Cooley (d) H.M. Johnson

44. Match List I with List II and choose the correct answers from the codes given below the lists:

List I

A. From Tribe to empire
B. Morals in Evolution
C. Contribution to the Critique of political economy
D. The political systems of Empire

List II

i. Hobbhouse
ii. A Moret and G. Davy
iii. S.N. Eisenstadt
iv. Marx

Codes:	A	B	C	D
(a)	iii	i	iv	ii
(b)	ii	i	iv	iii
(c)	iii	iv	i	ii
(d)	ii	iv	i	iii

45. Who among the following has put forward the concept of "Hydraulic society"?
(a) Karl Marx
(b) Karl Mannhiem
(c) K. Wittfogel
(d) H. Pirenne

46. Nadel's conception of structure is based on which of the following?
1. Repetitiveness 2. Durability
3. Uniqueness 4. Equilibrium

Codes:

(a) 1, 2, 3 (b) 2, 3, 4
(c) 1, 2, 4 (d) All of the above

47. Consider the following statements.
1. Nadel contends that a particular social structure as described at a moment is

accurate only for a particular period of time.

2. According to Nadel, structure and variance are not inherently contradictory: rather the former is defined or built up through taking account of the latter.

Codes:

(a) Both 1 and 2 are correct
(b) Both 1 and 2 are incorrect
(c) Only 1 is correct
(d) Only 2 is correct

48. Who among the following defined social structure in terms of institution, orders and spheres?
(a) Levi-Strauss
(b) Gerth and Mills
(c) Evans
(d) Meyer Fortes

49. Consider the following statements:
1. Institutions are the basic building blocks of social structure.
2. Social structure is more than mere inter-relations of institutions.

Codes:

(a) Both 1 and 2 are correct
(b) Both 1 and 2 are incorrect
(c) Only 1 is correct
(d) Only 2 is correct

50. The term 'schedule Caste' was coined in the year
(a) 1927 (b) 1930
(c) 1935 (d) 1948

ANSWERS

1. (c)	2. (b)	3. (b)	4. (c)	5. (d)
6. (d)	7. (c)	8. (c)	9. (a)	10. (a)
11. (b)	12. (c)	13. (d)	14. (c)	15. (a)
16. (c)	17. (c)	18. (b)	19. (c)	20. (a)
21. (d)	22. (c)	23. (a)	24. (b)	25. (d)
26. (d)	27. (c)	28. (c)	29. (a)	30. (c)
31. (a)	32. (b)	33. (b)	34. (b)	35. (c)
36. (a)	37. (b)	38. (b)	39. (d)	40. (b)
41. (d)	42. (b)	43. (a)	44. (b)	45. (c)
46. (c)	47. (a)	48. (b)	49. (a)	50. (c)

JUNE–2007

Note: This paper contains Fifty (50) objective type questions, each question carrying two (2) marks. Attempt all the questions.

PAPER–I

1. Teacher uses visual-aids to make learning
   (a) simple
   (b) more knowledgeable
   (c) quicker
   (d) interesting
2. The teacher's role at the higher educational level is to
   (a) provide information to students
   (b) promote self-learning in students
   (c) encourage healthy competition among students
   (d) help students to solve their personal problems
3. Which one of the following teachers would you like the most?
   (a) Punctual
   (b) Having research aptitude
   (c) Loving and having high idealistic philosophy
   (d) Who often amuses his students
4. Micro teaching is most effective for the student-teacher
   (a) during the practice-teaching
   (b) after the practice-teaching
   (c) before the practice-teaching
   (d) None of the above
5. Which is the least important factor in teaching?
   (a) Punishing the students
   (b) Maintaining discipline in the class
   (c) Lecturing in impressive way
   (d) Drawing sketches and diagrams on the blackboard
6. To test null hypothesis, a researcher uses
   (a) t test   (b) ANOVA
   (c) x^2 (d) factorial analysis
7. A research problem is feasible only when
   (a) it has utility and relevance
   (b) it is researchable
   (c) it is new and adds something to knowledge
   (d) All of the above
8. Bibliography given in a research report
   (a) shows vast knowledge of the researcher
   (b) helps those interested in further research
   (c) has no relevance to research
   (d) All of the above
9. Fundamental research reflects the ability to
   (a) Synthesize new ideals
   (b) Expound new principles
   (c) Evaluate the existing material concerning research
   (d) Study the existing literature regarding various topics
10. The study in which the investigators attempt to trace an effect is known as
    (a) Survey Research
    (b) *Ex-post Facto* Research

(c) Historical Research
(d) Summative Research

Read the following passage and answer the questions from 11 to 15:

All political systems need to mediate the relationship between private wealth and public power. Those that fail risk a dysfunctional government captured by wealthy interests. Corruption is one symptom of such failure with private willingness-to-pay trumping public goals. Private individuals and business firms pay to get routine services and to get to the head of the bureaucratic queue. They pay to limit their taxes, avoid costly regulations, obtain contracts at inflated prices and get concessions and privatised firms at low prices. If corruption is endemic, public officials—both bureaucrats and elected officials—may redesign programs and propose public projects with few public benefits and many opportunities for private profit. Of course, corruption, in the sense of bribes, pay-offs and kickbacks, is only one type of government failure. Efforts to promote "good governance" must be broader than anti-corruption campaigns. Governments may be honest but inefficient because no one has an incentive to work productively, and narrow elites may capture the state and exert excess influence on policy. Bribery may induce the lazy to work hard and permit those not in the inner circle of cronies to obtain benefits. However, even in such cases, corruption cannot be confined to 'functional' areas. It will be a temptation whenever private benefits are positive. It may be a reasonable response to a harsh reality but, over time, it can facilitate a spiral into an even worse situation.

11. The governments which fail to focus on the relationship between private wealth and public power are likely to become
(a) Functional
(b) Dysfunctional
(c) Normal functioning
(d) Good governance

12. One important symptom of bad governance is
(a) Corruption
(b) High taxes
(c) Complicated rules and regulations
(d) High prices

13. When corruption is rampant, public officials always aim at many opportunities for
(a) Public benefits (b) Public profit
(c) Private profit (d) Corporate gains

14. Productivity linked incentives to public/private officials is one of the indicatives for
(a) Efficient government
(b) Bad governance
(c) Inefficient government
(d) Corruption

15. The spiralling corruption can only be contained by promoting
(a) Private profit
(b) Anti-corruption campaign
(c) Good governance
(d) Pay-offs and kickbacks

16. Press Council of India is located at
(a) Chennai (b) Mumbai
(c) Kolkata (d) Delhi

17. Adjusting the photo for publication by cutting is technically known as
(a) Photo cutting
(b) Photo bleeding
(c) Photo cropping
(d) Photo adjustment

18. Feedback of a message comes from
(a) Satellite (b) Media
(c) Audience (d) Communicator

19. Collection of information in advance before designing communication strategy is known as

(a) Feedback (b) Feed-forward
(c) Research study (d) Opinion poll

20. The aspect ratio of TV screen is
(a) 4:3 (b) 4:2
(c) 3:5 (d) 2:3

21. Which is the number that comes next in the sequence?
9, 8, 8, 8, 7, 8, 6, __
(a) 5 (b) 6
(c) 8 (d) 4

22. If in a certain language PUNCTUAL is coded as 16598623, how would ACTUPULN be coded?
(a) 834536 (b) 29861635
(c) 834530 (d) 834539

23. The question to be answered by factorial analysis of the quantitative data does not explain one of the following
(a) Is 'X' related to 'Y'?
(b) How is 'X' related to 'Y'?
(c) How does 'X' affect the dependent variable 'Y' at different levels of another independent variable 'K' or 'M'?
(d) How is 'X' by 'K' related to 'M'?

24. January 12, 1980 was Saturday, what day was January 12, 1979?
(a) Saturday (b) Friday
(c) Sunday (d) Thursday

25. How many Mondays are there in a particular month of a particular year, if the month ends on Wednesday?
(a) 5 (b) 4
(c) 3 (d) None of these

26. From the given four statements, select the two which cannot be true but yet both can be false. Choose the right pair.
1. All men are mortal
2. Some men are mortal
3. No man is mortal
4. Some men are not mortal
(a) 1 and 2 (b) 3 and 4
(c) 1 and 3 (d) 2 and 4

27. A Syllogism must have
(a) Three terms (b) Four terms
(c) Six terms (d) Five terms

28. Copula is that part of proposition which denotes the relationship between
(a) Subject and predicate
(b) Known and unknown
(c) Major premise and minor premise
(d) Subject and object

29. "E" denotes
(a) Universal Negative Proposition
(b) Particular Affirmative Proposition
(c) Universal Affirmative Proposition
(d) Particular Negative Proposition

30. 'A' is the father of 'C' and 'D' is the son of 'B'. 'E' is the brother of 'A'. If 'C' is the sister of 'D' how is 'B' related to 'E'?
(a) Daughter (b) Husband
(c) Sister-in-law (d) Brother-in-law

31. Which of the following methods will you choose to prepare choropleth map of India showing urban density of population?
(a) Quartiles (b) Quintiles
(c) Mean and SD (d) Break-point

32. Which of the following methods is best suited to show on a map the types of crops being grown in a region?
(a) Choropleth
(b) Chorochromatic
(c) Choroschematic
(d) Isopleth

33. A ratio represents the relation between
(a) Part and Part
(b) Part and Whole
(c) Whole and Whole
(d) All of the above

34. Out of four numbers, the average of the first three numbers is thrice the fourth

number. If the average of the four numbers is 5, the fourth number is
(a) 4.5 (b) 5
(c) 2 (d) 4

35. Circle graphs are used to show
(a) How various sections share in the whole
(b) How various parts are related to the whole
(c) How one whole is related to other wholes
(d) How one part is related to other parts

36. On the keyboard of computer each character has an "ASCII" value which stands for
(a) American Stock Code for Information Interchange
(b) American Standard Code for Information Interchange
(c) African Standard Code for Information Interchange
(d) Adaptable Standard Code for Information Change

37. Which part of the Central Processing Unit (CPU) performs calculation and makes decisions
(a) Arithmetic Logic Unit
(b) Alternating Logic Unit
(c) Alternate Local Unit
(d) American Logic Unit

38. "Dpi" stands for
(a) Dots per inch
(b) Digits per unit
(c) Dots pixel inch
(d) Diagrams per inch

39. The process of laying out a document with text, graphics, headlines and photographs is involved in
(a) Deck Top Publishing
(b) Desk Top Printing
(c) Desk Top Publishing
(d) Deck Top Printing

40. Transfer of data from one application to another line is known as
(a) Dynamic Disk Exchange
(b) Dodgy Data Exchange
(c) Dogmatic Data Exchange
(d) Dynamic Data Exchange

41. Tsunami occurs due to
(a) Mild earthquakes and landslides in the oceans
(b) Strong earthquakes and landslides in the oceans
(c) Strong earthquakes and landslides in mountains
(d) Strong earthquakes and landslides in deserts

42. Which of the natural hazards have big effect on Indian people each year?
(a) Cyclones (b) Floods
(c) Earthquakes (d) Landslides

43. Comparative Environment Impact Assessment study is to be conducted for
(a) the whole year
(b) three seasons excluding monsoon
(c) any three seasons
(d) the worst season

44. Sea level rise results primarily due to
(a) Heavy rainfall
(b) Melting of glaciers
(c) Submarine volcanism
(d) Seafloor spreading

45. The plume rise in a coal based power plant depends on
1. Buoyancy
2. Atmospheric stability
3. Momentum of exhaust gases identify

Codes:
(a) (1) and (2)
(b) (2) and (3)
(c) (1) and (3)
(d) (1), (2) and (3)

46. Value education makes a student
   (a) Good citizen
   (b) Successful businessman
   (c) Popular teacher
   (d) Efficient manager
47. Networking of libraries through electronic media is known as
   (a) Inflibnet (b) Libinfnet
   (c) Internet (d) HTML
48. The University which telecasts interactive educational programs through its own channel is
   (a) B.R. Ambedkar Open University, Hyderabad
   (b) I.G.N.O.U.
   (c) University of Pune
   (d) Annamalai University
49. The Government established the University Grants Commission by an Act of Parliament in the year
   (a) 1980 (b) 1948
   (c) 1950 (d) 1956
50. Universities having central campus for imparting education are called
   (a) Central Universities
   (b) Deemed Universities
   (c) Residential Universities
   (d) Open Universities

ANSWERS

1. (d)	2. (a)	3. (a)	4. (b)	5. (a)
6. (c)	7. (d)	8. (b)	9. (b)	10. (b)
11. (b)	12. (a)	13. (c)	14. (a)	15. (c)
16. (d)	17. (c)	18. (c)	19. (d)	20. (a)
21. (c)	22. (b)	23. (c)	24. (b)	25. (d)
26. (b)	27. (a)	28. (b)	29. (a)	30. (d)
31. (b)	32. (c)	33. (b)	34. (c)	35. (a)
36. (a)	37. (a)	38. (a)	39. (c)	40. (d)
41. (b)	42. (b)	43. (a)	44. (b)	45. (d)
46. (a)	47. (a)	48. (b)	49. (d)	50. (b)

PAPER–II

Note: This paper contains Fifty (50) objective type questions, each question carrying two (2) marks. Attempt all the questions.

1. When a person believes that his culture is superior to other cultures, it is called
   (a) ethnicity
   (b) ethnocentrism
   (c) cultural snobbery
   (d) cultural relativism
2. Role conflict arise when
   (a) an individual has to perform a number of roles simultaneously
   (b) an individual has to perform a role which is socially not approved
   (c) an individual has to perform two roles in compatible with one another
   (d) The performance of a role pushes the individual into conflict with other individuals
3. Who among the following used the distinction between the repressive and the restitutive law as the basis for classifying societies?
   (a) Max Weber
   (b) Henry Maine
   (c) Montesquieu
   (d) Emile Durkheim
4. Which of the following characteristics are used for defining a law?
   1. A rule
   2. Justice
   3. Political authority
   4. State power

Select the correct answer using the codes given below:

Codes:

(a) 1, 2, and 3 (b) 2 and 4
(c) 1, 3, and 4 (d) 2, 3 and 4

5. Consider the following groups:
   1. A political party of one's choice
   2. One's religion
   3. One's enemy
   4. One's favourite teacher

   Among these groups reference group(s) would include
   (a) 1, 2, 3 and 4 (b) 1, 3 and 4
   (c) 2 and 4 (d) 2 only

6. The concept of recruitment roles was used by
   (a) Ralph Linton (b) Talcott Parsons
   (c) S.F. Nadel (d) E. Goffman

7. Which of the following characteristics is/are related to Associations?
   1. Definite ends
   2. Specific interests
   3. Close interaction
   4. Fixed criteria for membership

   Select the correct answer using the codes given below:

   Codes:
   (a) 1, 2 and 3 (b) 1 and 4
   (c) 2 and 3 (d) 1, 2, 3 and 4

8. Who among the following maintains that social structure has nothing to do with empirical reality?
   (a) C. Levi-Strauss
   (b) Marion J. Levy
   (c) Raymond Firth
   (d) Evans Pritchard

9. Which one of the following statements about "deviance" is not correct?
   (a) Failure to conform to the customary norms of society
   (b) A tendency on the part of an individual to behave in such a way as to disturb the equilibrium of interactive process
   (c) The concept of deviance is relative and not absolute
   (d) Deviant behaviour is never socially useful

10. The process of accommodation is adopted in society to avoid
    (a) competition between people
    (b) competition between ideologies
    (c) conflict between equals and non-equals
    (d) integration between the formal and the informal

11. Which one of the following statements corresponds to the essence of the concept of "looking glass-self"?
    (a) What ego thinks ego is
    (b) What alter thinks ego is
    (c) What ego and alter thinks ego is
    (d) What ego thinks alter is

12. Which of the following are the characteristics of society?
    1. Territory
    2. State
    3. Individuals
    4. System of interrelationships
    5. Common culture

    Select the correct answer using the codes given below:

    Codes:
    (a) 1, 2, and 3 (b) 3, 4 and 5
    (c) 2, 3, 4 and 5 (d) 1, 4 and 5

13. Which of the following are the characteristics of a modern urban society?
    1. Organic solidarity
    2. Mechanical solidarity
    3. Strong collective consciousness
    4. Weak collective consciousness

Select the correct answer using the codes given below:

Codes:

(a) 2 and 3 (b) 2 and 4
(c) 1 and 3 (d) 1 and 4

14. The statement that "Indian culture is superior to Western culture" an example of
(a) cultural relativity
(b) ethnocentrism
(c) fundamentalism
(d) xenophobia

15. Who among the following developed the concept of "primordial primary group"?
(a) Edward Shills
(b) C.H. Cooley
(c) Erich Fromm
(d) George Homans

16. The term "relative deprivation" was used originally by
(a) Samuel A. Stouffer
(b) R.K. Merton
(c) Herbert Hyman
(d) K. Davis

17. Promised rewards for compliance and threatened penalties for non-compliance with group expectations, is called
(a) norms (b) values
(c) sanctions (d) mores

18. Who among the following identified four major types of co-operation, that is, spontaneous traditional, directed and contractual?
(a) L. Coser
(b) George Simmel
(c) Robert Nisbet
(d) George C. Homans

19. Dudhlautawa as a form of cross-cousin marriage, is prevalent among the
(a) Gonds of Madhya Pradesh
(b) Santhals of Orissa
(c) Mundas of Chhotanagpur
(d) Bhils of Rajasthan.

20. Marriage between single pairs, without involving the rights of exclusive cohabitation with each other is referred to as
(a) syndyasmian family
(b) conjugal family
(c) patriarchal family
(d) promiscuous family

21. A person belonging to a *dalit* caste gives up eating non-vegetarian food and adopts ritualistic worship. Which one of the following best describes this behaviour?
(a) Sanskritisation
(b) Acculturation
(c) Enculturation
(d) Socialisation

22. Which one of the following was believed to represent the vertical unit of castes?
(a) Varna system
(b) Jajmani system
(c) Sanskritisation
(d) Endogamy

23. Consider the following statements: According to the Imperial Gazetteer of India, a tribe is a
   1. collection of families with a common name.
   2. community using ancient means of production.
   3. community speaking a common dialect.
   4. community which is usually exogamous.
   5. community occupying a common territory.

Which of the above statements are correct?

(a) 1, 2, 3 and 4 (b) 2, 3 and 4
(c) 1, 2 and 5 (d) 1, 3 and 5

24. With whose name would one associate the study of the economy of Trobriand Islanders?
(a) J.P.S. Uberoi
(b) E. Evans Pritchard
(c) B. Malinowski
(d) R. Firth

25. Which one of the following States has the lowest density of population as per 2001 Census?
(a) Arunachal Pradesh
(b) Mizoram
(c) Sikkim
(d) Manipur

26. The first synchronic all India Census was organised in the year
(a) 1871 (b) 1872
(c) 1901 (d) 1951

27. Consider the following States:
1. Kerala 2. Uttar Pradesh
3. Madhya Pradesh 4. Punjab
The correct sequence of these states in descending order in terms of sex ratios (females per thousand males as per 1991 Census) of their population is:
(a) 3, 1, 2 and 4 (b) 3, 1, 4 and 2
(c) 1, 3, 2 and 4 (d) 1, 3, 4 and 2

28. Spencer viewed all evolution in terms of two types of society, the
(a) agrarian and industrial
(b) military and industrial
(c) pastoral and industrial
(d) tribal und industrial

29. According to T. Parsons, there are three modes of motivational orientation. Which one of the following is not included in these modes?
(a) Cognitive orientation
(b) Cathetic orientation
(c) Appreciative orientation
(d) Evaluative orientation

30. Clark Wissler demonstrated that in each restricted area of a culture, a central point of dispersal could be identified. People living on the borders of two culture areas share the features of both, such areas are called
(a) areas of cultural parallels
(b) areas of cultural similarities
(c) areas of cultural amalgamation
(d) marginal areas

31. A man who has accumulated a lot of black money, constructs a hospital for cancer patients and poses himself as a saviour of the downtrodden. This is an example of
(a) role insulation
(b) counterfeit role
(c) false role
(d) role-set

32. Who among the following is not a contributor to the studies on acculturation?
(a) Linton (b) Redfield
(c) Herskovits (d) Ogburn

33. Routinisation of charisma refers to
(a) the process by which the personal qualities of a charismatic leader are incorporated in the characteristics of an organisation
(b) the wide acceptance of the leadership quality of the charismatic leader by his followers
(c) the high normative standard of the actions of charismatic leader
(d) the ultimate goal which the charismatic leader has attained

34. Consider the following characteristics:
1. A network of social relationships
2. Totality of population
3. Provision for membership by birth
4. Comprehensive culture

The major characteristics of society would include

(a) 1, 2 and 3 (b) 2, 3 and 4
(c) 1, 2 and 4 (d) 1, 3 and 4

35. Who held the view that the primary groups are "the breeding grounds of our mores and the nurse of our loyalties"?
(a) Cooley (b) Tonnies
(c) MacIver (d) Sumner

36. Which one of the following pairs is correctly matched?

(a) Kinship usage	:	Agnates
(b) Classificatory kinshipterm	:	Class relationship
(c) Descriptive kinshipterm	:	Specific relationship
(d) Avunculate	:	Paternal uncle

37. Irawati Karve speaks of four-clan rule, practised in North India in mate selection restrictions. Which one of the following is not included in the four-clan rule?
A man must not marry a woman from his
(a) father's gotra
(b) mother's gotra
(c) father's mother's gotra
(d) mother's father's gotra

38. P. Kolenda has given some compositional categories of nuclear family in India. Which one of the following is not one of the categories presented by Kolenda?
(a) Supplemented nuclear
(b) Sub-nuclear
(c) Single person household
(d) Supplemented lineal

39. Consider the following characteristics:
1. Segmental division of society
2. Unrestricted division of occupations
3. Civil and religious disabilities and privileges
Which of these are the characteristics of the caste system?
(a) 1, 2 and 3 (b) 1 and 2
(c) 2 and 3 (d) 1 and 3

40. Robert Park and Burgess arranged modern cities in a series of the following concentric zones:
1. Commuter's zone
2. Zone in transition
3. Central business district
4. Zone of the working population
5. Residential zone
According to Park and Burgess, the correct sequence of the above mentioned live concentric zones starting from the centre and going outward is
(a) 3, 4, 2, 5 and 1
(b) 3, 2, 4, 5 and 1
(c) 3, 5, 1, 4 and 2
(d) 4, 5, 2, 3 and 1

41. Family and kinship ties were adversely affected by
(a) industry
(b) technology
(c) new work ethics
(d) All of these

42. For development of modern capitalism, it is necessary to have
(a) formal and value rationalities
(b) formal and instrumental rationalities
(c) instrumental and value rationalities
(d) instrumental rationality

43. When urban population grows and the proportion of urban population to the total population remains constant, it is known as
(a) urbanisation
(b) over-urbanisation
(c) urban growth
(d) population stability

44. Which one of the following is based on the belief in the sanctity of habit and obedience to a person who occupies customary position of authority?

(a) Feudal authority
(b) Traditional authority
(c) Charismatic authority
(d) Legal authority

45. An untouchable getting converted to Christianity, is an example of
(a) horizontal mobility
(b) vertical mobility
(c) social mobility
(d) None of the above

46. The first person or set of persons to have used the term "Political Socialisation" was
(a) Herbert Hyman
(b) Herbert Spencer
(c) Almond Powell
(d) Easton and Dennis

47. The status of organisations like the FICCI und CII the political system is that of a/an
(a) economic institution
(b) trade association
(c) pressure group
(d) interest group

48. Which one of the following group of thinkers belong to the linear view of social change?
(a) Comte, Pareto and Marx
(b) Pareto, Sorokin and Ogburn
(c) Comte, Ogburn and Marx
(d) Comte, Spencer and Pareto

Directions: For Q. 49-50. For each question, there is an Assertion (A) and a Reason (R). There can be four possibilities:
(a) Both (A) and (R) are right and (R) is right explanation of (A).
(b) Both (A) and (R) are right, but (R) is not right explanation of (A).
(c) (A) is right, but (R) is wrong.
(d) (R) is right, but (A) is wrong.

49. **Assertion (A):** According to Mallet, automation will revitalize trade union movement.
Reason (R): Automation integrates the working class into the structure of capitalist society.

50. **Assertion (A):** In order to survive, an authoritarian state resorts to repression, permanent mobilisation and manipulation.
Reason (R): In a authoritarian state, the bureaucratic apparatus becomes responsive to the needs of the masses.

ANSWERS

1. (b)	2. (c)	3. (d)	4. (b)	5. (d)
6. (a)	7. (a)	8. (d)	9. (c)	10. (b)
11. (b)	12. (d)	13. (b)	14. (b)	15. (a)
16. (c)	17. (b)	18. (a)	19. (a)	20. (a)
21. (a)	22. (d)	23. (c)	24. (a)	25. (b)
26. (d)	27. (b)	28. (c)	29. (c)	30. (d)
31. (b)	32. (b)	33. (a)	34. (c)	35. (c)
36. (a)	37. (d)	38. (c)	39. (d)	40. (b)
41. (d)	42. (b)	43. (a)	44. (b)	45. (a)
46. (a)	47. (c)	48. (c)	49. (a)	50. (b)

DECEMBER–2006

Note: This paper contains Fifty (50) objective type questions, each question carrying two (2) marks. Attempt all the questions.

PAPER–I

1. Which of the following is not instructional material?
   (a) Over Head Projector
   (b) Audio Cassette
   (c) Printed Material
   (d) Transparency

2. Which of the following statement is not correct?
   (a) Lecture Method can develop reasoning
   (b) Lecture Method can develop knowledge
   (c) Lecture Method is one way process
   (d) During Lecture Method students are passive

3. The main objective of teaching at Higher Education Level is
   (a) To prepare students to pass examination
   (b) To develop the capacity to take decisions
   (c) To give new information
   (d) To motivate students to ask questions during lecture

4. Which of the following statement is correct?
   (a) Reliability ensures validity
   (b) Validity ensures reliability
   (c) Reliability and validity are independent of each other
   (d) Reliability does not depend on objectivity

5. Which of the following indicates evaluation?
   (a) Ram got 45 marks out of 200
   (b) Mohan got 38 percent marks in English
   (c) Shyam got First Division in final examination
   (d) All of the above

6. Research can be conducted by a person who?
   (a) has studied research methodology
   (b) holds a postgraduate degree
   (c) possesses thinking and reasoning ability
   (d) is a hard worker

7. Which of the following statements is correct?
   (a) Objectives of research are stated in first chapter of the thesis
   (b) Researcher must possess analytical ability
   (c) Variability is the source of problem
   (d) All of the above

8. Which of the following is not the Method of Research?
   (a) Observation (b) Historical
   (c) Survey (d) Philosophical

9. Research can be classified as
   (a) Basic, Applied and Action Research
   (b) Quantitative and Qualitative Research
   (c) Philosophical, Historical, Survey and Experimental Research
   (d) All of the above

10. The first step of research is
    (a) Selecting a problem
    (b) Searching a problem
    (c) Finding a problem
    (d) Identifying a problem

Read the following passage and answer the questions from 11 to 15:

After almost three decades of contemplating Swarovski-encrusted navels on increasing flat abs, the Mumbai film industry is on a discovery of India and itself. With budgets of over 30 crore each, four soon to be released movies by premier directors are exploring the idea of who we are and redefining who the other is. It is a fundamental question which the bling-bling, glam-sham and disham-disham tends to avoid. It is also a question which binds an audience when the lights go dim and the projector rolls : as a nation, who are we? As a people, where are we going?

The Germans coined a word for it, Zeitgeist, which perhaps Yash Chopra would not care to pronounce. But at 72, he remains the person who can best capture it. After being the first to project the diasporic Indian on screen in Lamhe in 1991, he has returned to his roots in a new movie. Veer-Zaara, set in 1986, where Pakistan, the traditional other, the part that got away, is the lover and the saviour. In Subhash Ghai's Kisna, set in 1947, the other is the English woman. She is not a memsahib, but a mehbooba. In Ketan Mehta's The Rising, the East India Englishman is not the evil oppressor of countless cardboard characterisations, which span the spectrum from Jewel in the Crown to Kranti, but an honourable friend.

This is Manoj Kumar's Desh Ki Dharti with a difference: there is culture, not contentious politics; balle balle, not bombs: no dooriyan (distance), only nazdeekiyan (closeness).

All four films are heralding a new hero and heroine. The new hero is fallible and vulnerable, committed to his dharma, but also not afraid of failure-less of a boy and more of a man. He even has a grown up name: Veer Pratap Singh in Veer-Zaara and Mohan Bhargav in Swades. The new heroine is not a babe, but often a bebe, dressed in traditional Punjabi clothes, often with the stereotypical body type as well, as in Bride and Prejudice of Gurinder Chadha.

11. Which word Yash Chopra would not be able to pronounce?
    (a) Bling-bling (b) Zeitgeist
    (c) Montaz (d) Dooriyan

12. Who made Lamhe in 1991?
    (a) Subhash Ghai (b) Yash Chopra
    (c) Aditya Chopra (d) Sakti Samanta

13. Which movie is associated with Manoj Kumar?
    (a) Jewel in the Crown
    (b) Kisna
    (c) Zaara
    (d) Desh Ki Dharti

14. Which is the latest film by Yash Chopra?
    (a) Deewar
    (b) Kabhi Kabhi
    (c) Dilwale Dulhaniya Le Jayenge
    (d) Veer-Zaara

15. Which is the dress of the heroine in Veer-Zaara?
    (a) Traditional Gujarati Clothes
    (b) Traditional Bengali Clothes
    (c) Traditional Punjabi Clothes
    (d) Traditional Madrasi Clothes

16. Which one of the following can be termed as verbal communication?
    (a) Prof. Sharma delivered the lecture in the classroom.
    (b) Signal at the cross-road changed from green to orange.
    (c) The child was crying to attract the attention of the mother.
    (d) Dipak wrote a letter for leave application.

17. Which is the 24 hours English Business news channel in India?
(a) *Zee News* (b) *NDTV 24×7*
(c) *CNBC* (d) *India News*

18. Consider the following statements in communication:
(i) Hema Malini is the Chairperson of the Children's Film Society, India.
(ii) Yash Chopra is the Chairman of the Central Board of Film Certification of India.
(iii) Sharmila Tagore is the Chairperson of National Film Development Corporation.
(iv) Dilip Kumar, Raj Kapoor and Preeti Zinta have all been recipients of Dada Saheb Phalke Award.

Which of the statements given above is/are correct?
(a) (i) and (iii) (b) (ii) and (iii)
(c) (iv) only (d) (iii) only

19. Which of the following pair is not correctly matched?
(a) N. Ram : *The Hindu*
(b) Barkha Dutt : *Zee News*
(c) Pranay Roy : *NDTV 24×7*
(d) Prabhu Chawla : *Aaj taak*

20. "Because you deserve to know" is the punchline used by
(a) *The Times of India*
(b) *The Hindu*
(c) *Indian Express*
(d) *Hindustan Times*

21. In the sequence of numbers 8, 24, 12, X, 18, 54 the missing number X is
(a) 26 (b) 24
(c) 36 (d) 32

22. If A stands for 5, B for 6, C for 7, D for 8 and so on, then the following numbers stand for 17, 19, 20, 9 and 8
(a) PLANE (b) MOPED
(c) MOTOR (d) TONGA

23. The letters in the first set have certain relationship. On the basis of this relationship what is the right choice for the second set?

AST : BRU : : NQV : ?
(a) ORW (b) MPU
(c) MRW (d) OPW

24. In a certain code, PAN is written as 31 and PAR as 35. In this code PAT is written as
(a) 30 (b) 37
(c) 38 (d) 39

25. The sides of a triangle are in the ratio of $\frac{1}{2}:\frac{1}{3}:\frac{1}{4}$. If its perimeter is 52 cm, the length of the smallest side is
(a) 9 cm (b) 10 cm
(c) 11 cm (d) 12 cm

26. Which one of the following statements is completely non-sensical?
(a) He was a bachelor, but he married recently.
(b) He is a bachelor, but he married recently.
(c) When he married, he was not a bachelor.
(d) When he was a bachelor, he was not married.

27. Which of the following statements are mutually contradictory?
(i) All flowers are not fragrant.
(ii) Most flowers are not fragrant.
(iii) None of the flowers is fragrant.
(iv) Most flowers are fragrant.

Choose the correct answer from the codes given below:

Codes:
(a) (i) and (ii) (b) (i) and (iii)
(c) (ii) and (iii) (d) (iii) and (iv)

28. Which of the following statements say the same thing?

(i) "I am a teacher" (said by Arvind)
(ii) "I am a teacher" (said by Binod)
(iii) "My son is a teacher" (said by Binod's father)
(iv) "My brother is a teacher" (said by Binod's sister)
(v) "My brother is a teacher" (said by Binod's only sister)
(vi) "My sole enemy is a teacher" (said by Binod's only enemy)

Choose the correct answer from the codes given below:

Codes:
(a) (i) and (ii)
(b) (ii), (iii), (iv) and (v)
(c) (ii) and (vi)
(d) (v) and (vi)

29. Which of the following are correct ways of arguing?
(i) There can be no second husband without a second wife.
(ii) Anil is a friend of Bob, Bob is a friend of Raj, hence Anil is a friend of Raj.
(iii) A is equal to B, B is equal to C, hence A is equal to C.
(iv) If everyone is a liar, then we cannot prove it.

Choose the correct answer from the codes given below:

Codes:
(a) (iii) and (iv)
(b) (i), (iii) and (iv)
(c) (ii), (iii) and (iv)
(d) (i), (ii), (iii) and (iv)

30. Which of the following statement/s is are always false?
(i) The sun will not rise in the East some day.
(ii) A wooden table is not a table.
(iii) Delhi city will be drowned under water.
(iv) Cars run on water as fuel.

Choose the correct answer from the codes given below:

Codes:
(a) (i), (iii) and (iv) (b) (iii) only
(c) (i), (ii) and (iii) (d) (ii) only

Study the following graph and answer question numbers 31 to 33:

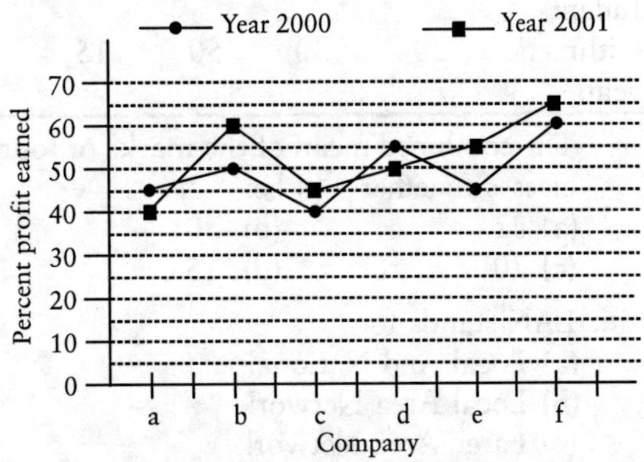

31. In the year 2000, which of the following Companies earned maximum percent profit?
(a) a (b) b
(c) d (d) f

32. In the year 2001, which of the following Companies earned minimum percent profit?
(a) a (b) c
(c) d (d) e

33. In the years 2000 and 2001, which of the following Companies earned maximum average percent profit?
(a) f (b) e
(c) d (d) b

34. Human Development Report for 'each' of the year at global level has been published by
(a) UNDP (b) WTO
(c) IMF (d) World Bank

35. The number of students in four classes A, B, C, D and their respective mean marks obtained by each of the class are given below:

	Class A	Class B	Class C	Class D
Number of students	10	40	30	20
Arithmetic mean	20	30	50	15

The combined mean of the marks of four classes together will be:
(a) 32 (b) 50
(c) 20 (d) 15

36. LAN stands for
(a) Local And National
(b) Local Area Network
(c) Large Area Network
(d) Live Area Network

37. Which of the following statement is correct?
(a) Modem is a software
(b) Modem helps in stabilizing the voltage
(c) Modem is the operating system
(d) Modem converts the analog signal into digital signal and vice versa

38. Which of the following is the appropriate definition of a computer?
(a) Computer is a machine that can process information.
(b) Computer is an electronic device that can store, retrieve and process both qualitative and quantitative data quickly and accurately.
(c) Computer is an electronic device that can store, retrieve and quickly process only quantitative data.
(d) Computer is a machine that can store, retrieve and process quickly and accurately only qualitative information

39. Information and Communication Technology includes
(a) On line learning
(b) Learning through the use of EDUSAT
(c) Web Based Learning
(d) All of the above

40. Which of the following is the appropriate format of URL of e-mail?
(a) www_mail.com
(b) www@mail.com
(c) WWW@mail.com
(d) www.mail.com

41. The most significant impact of volcanic erruption has been felt in the form of
(a) change in weather
(b) sinking of islands
(c) loss of vegetation
(d) extinction of animals

42. With absorption and decomposition of CO_2 in ocean water beyond desired level, there will be
(a) decrease in temperature
(b) increase in salinity
(c) growth of phyto plankton
(d) rise in sea level

43. Arrange column II in proper sequence so as to match it with column I and choose the correct answer from the codes given below:

Column I (Water Quality)	Column II (pH Value)
(A) Neutral	(i) 5
(B) Moderately acidic	(ii) 7
(C) Alkaline	(iii) 4
(D) Injurious	(iv) 8

Codes:	(A)	(B)	(C)	(D)
(a)	(ii)	(iii)	(i)	(iv)
(b)	(i)	(iii)	(ii)	(iv)
(c)	(ii)	(i)	(iv)	(iii)
(d)	(iv)	(ii)	(iii)	(i)

44. The maximum emission of pollutants from fuel sources in India is caused by
(a) Coal
(b) Firewood
(c) Refuse burning
(d) Vegetable waste product

45. The urbanisation process accounts for the wind in the urban centres during nights to remain
(a) faster than that in rural areas
(b) slower than that in rural areas
(c) the same as that in rural areas
(d) cooler than that in rural areas

46. The University Grants Commission was constituted on the recommendation of
(a) Dr. Sarvapalli Radhakrishnan Commission
(b) Mudaliar Commission
(c) Sargent Commission
(d) Kothari Commission

47. Which one of the following Articles of the Constitution of India safeguards the rights of Minorities to establish and run educational institutions of their own liking?
(a) Article 19 (b) Article 29
(c) Article 30 (d) Article 31

48. Match List I (Institutions) with List II (Functions) and select the correct answer by using the codes given below:

List I (Institutions)
(A) Parliament
(B) C & A.G.
(C) Ministry of Finance
(D) Executing Departments

List II (Functions)
(i) Formulation of Budget
(ii) Enactment of Budget
(iii) Implementation of Budget
(iv) Legality of expenditure
(v) Justification of Income

Codes:	(A)	(B)	(C)	(D)
(a)	(iii)	(iv)	(ii)	(i)
(b)	(ii)	(iv)	(i)	(iii)
(c)	(v)	(iii)	(iv)	(ii)
(d)	(iv)	(ii)	(iii)	(v)

49. Foundation training to the newly recruited IAS (Probationers) is imparted by
(a) Indian Institute of Public Administration
(b) Administrative Staff College of India
(c) L.B.S. National Academy of Administration
(d) Centre for Advanced Studies

50. Electoral disputes arising out of Presidential and Vice-Presidential Elections are settled by
(a) Election Commission of India
(b) Joint Committee of Parliament
(c) Supreme Court of India
(d) Central Election Tribunal

ANSWERS

1. (d)	2. (a)	3. (b)	4. (b)	5. (d)
6. (c)	7. (d)	8. (b)	9. (d)	10. (d)
11. (b)	12. (b)	13. (d)	14. (d)	15. (c)
16. (c)	17. (c)	18. (d)	19. (b)	20. (d)
21. (c)	22. (b)	23. (d)	24. (b)	25. (d)
26. (b)	27. (b)	28. (b)	29. (a)	30. (d)
31. (b)	32. (a)	33. (a)	34. (a)	35. (a)
36. (b)	37. (d)	38. (b)	39. (d)	40. (b)
41. (a)	42. (c)	43. (c)	44. (c)	45. (b)
46. (a)	47. (c)	48. (b)	49. (c)	50. (c)

PAPER–II

1. Which one of the following statements is correct?
   Industrial society refers to
   (a) Durkheim's concept of mechanical solidarity
   (b) Tonnie's model of Gesellschaft
   (c) Parson's model of collective orientation
   (d) Redfield's type of archaic society
2. Match List I (Concept) with List II (Thinker) and select the correct answer using the codes given below the lists:
   List I
   A. Post Capitalist Society
   B. Post Modern Era
   C. Post Bourgeois Order
   D. Post Economic Society
   List II
   i. Kahn and Wiener
   ii. Ralf Dahrendorf
   iii. Amitai Etzioni
   iv. George Lichtheim

Codes:	**A**	**B**	**C**	**D**
(a)	ii	iii	iv	i
(b)	iv	i	ii	iii
(c)	ii	i	iv	iii
(d)	iv	iii	ii	i

3. Consider the following statements:
   The significant characteristics of industrial society are
   1. profit orientation
   2. bureaucratic organization
   3. reliance on animate energy
   4. class segregation
   Which of the statements given above are correct?
   (a) 1, 2 and 3 (b) 1, 2 and 4
   (c) 1, 3 and 4 (d) 2, 3 and 4

Directions: The following 8 (Eight) items consist of two statements, one labelled as the 'Assertion (A)' and the other as 'Reason (R)'. You are to examine these two statements carefully and select the answers to these items using the codes given below:
(a) Both (A) and (R) are individually true and (R) is the correct explanation of (A).
(b) Both (A) and (R) are individually true, but (R) is not the correct explanation of (A).
(c) (A) is true, but (R) is false.
(d) (A) is false, but (R) is true.

4. **Assertion (A):** It is not merely equality under law that determines the status of women in Society.
   Reason (R): Traditions and customs are involved in everyday social interactions.
5. **Assertion (A):** Forces of urbanisation induce family disorganisation.
   Reason (R): Urban values are hostile to abiding relationships.
6. **Assertion (A):** The behaviour between maternal uncle and niece, and between mother-in-law and son-in-law falls under the same pattern.
   Reason (R): Both behaviours are classified as joking-relationship.
7. **Assertion (A):** Ascribed social status acquired from one's family of orientation does not automatically persist throughout one's life.
   Reason (R): Social training acquired in the family of orientation fosters a continuity of status when a family of procreation is established.
8. **Assertion (A):** The role of maternal uncle in a matrilineal family is crucial to the extent of safeguarding his sister and her daughters.
   Reason (R): He is not a custodian of his sister's wealth and property.
9. **Assertion (A):** Ascetic Protestantism contained the seeds of its own destruction.

Reason (R): Once its teachings were incorporated into a rational capitalist system, religious direction and validation were rapidly eroded.

10. **Assertion (A):** In a democracy participation is the most important indicator of political stratification.
    Reason (R): Access to opportunities to participate and the actual sue of these opportunities is not the basis of stratification in a society.

11. **Assertion (A):** According to P.A. Sorokin, change occurs from within the society aided by the external factors.
    Reason (R): Change is a latent process.

12. Match List I (Concept) with List II (Scholar) and select the correct answer using the codes given below the lists:
    List I
    A. Rational goal-oriented action
    B. Gesellschaft
    C. Theory of Collective Behaviour
    D. Historical materialism

    List II
    i. Ferdinand Tonnies
    ii. Friedrich Engels
    iii. Max Weber
    iv. N.J. Smelser

Codes:	**A**	**B**	**C**	**D**
(a)	iv	i	iii	ii
(b)	iii	ii	iv	i
(c)	iv	ii	iii	i
(d)	iii	i	iv	ii

13. Will is primarily responsible for the emergence of
    (a) Reference group
    (b) Gesellschaft
    (c) Gemeinschaft
    (d) Secondary group

14. Consider the following types of society:
    1. Bourgeois society
    2. Primitive Communism
    3. Feudal society
    4. Ancient society

    Which of the following is the correct chronological sequence of these societies as conceived by Karl Marx?
    (a) 3-1-2-4 (b) 2-4-3-1
    (c) 3-4-2-1 (d) 2-1-3-4

15. Which one of the following is asserted by the organic theory of society?
    (a) The society is like a living/biological organism
    (b) The society is unlike a human organism
    (c) The units of society are fixed
    (d) Each unit of a society performs definite universal function

16. Which one of the following facts, according to Lewis H. Morgan, distinguishes civilization from the preceding stages in the evolution of human society?
    (a) Technological inventions
    (b) Scientific inventions
    (c) Smelting of iron ores
    (d) Invention of alphabets, phonetics and writing

17. Who among the following introduced the distinction of cultures into ideational and sensate categories?
    (a) P.A. Sorokin
    (b) Sigmund Freud
    (c) A.L. Koreber
    (d) O. Spengler

18. Consider the following statements:
    1. Crude death rate is very strongly affected by the age composition of the population.

2. The life expectancy at birth is a good measure of mortality conditions in a country because it adjusts for age composition by using prevailing birth rates at each age to estimate the average number of years a person may expect to live.

Which of the statements given above is/are correct?
(a) 1 only
(b) 2 only
(c) Both 1 and 2
(d) Neither 1 nor 2

19. What is the spread of cultural traits from one society to another commonly called?
(a) Acculturation
(b) Diffusion
(c) Enculturation
(d) Discrimination

20. What happens: "When changes in material culture precede changes in adaptive culture, adjustments cannot start before change requiring them has taken place. But old customs persist and bring about quite harmful consequences"?
(a) Cultural deprivation
(b) Cultural lag
(c) Cultural diffusion
(d) Cultural determinism

21. What does cultural relativism mean?
(a) There are no universal cultural norms that we follow
(b) One's view of social institutions is coloured by one's cultural perspective
(c) Functions and meanings of cultural traits are according to their social settings
(d) The belief that one's own culture is superior to others

22. What is a situation in which people regard their own cultural values to be universally valid and superior to all other cultures, called?
(a) Cultural absorption
(b) Accommodation
(c) Ethnocentrism
(d) Cultural ambivalence

23. Consider the following statements: According to the functionalist perspective of Talcott Parsons, all societies must solve the functional problems of
1. pattern maintenance
2. goal attainment
3. adaptation
4. integration

Which of the statements given is/are correct?
(a) 1 only (b) 1 and 2
(c) 2 and 3 (d) 1, 2, 3, and 4

24. A family falls in the category of primary group. What are the other terms sociologists use to indicate family as a primary group?
(a) Genetic, involuntary, in-group, blood relations
(b) Genetic, voluntary, in-group, associations
(c) Genetic, involuntary, out-group, institution
(d) Involuntary, institutional, blood relations, associations

25. Which one of the following pairs is not correctly matched?
(a) C.H. Cooley : Primary group
(b) Talcott Parsons : Positivism
(c) R.K. Merton : Reverence groups
(d) W.G. Summer : In-group, out-group

26. To which of the following patterns of social change, can the process of Sankritisation in India be compared?
(a) Anomie
(b) Horizontal mobility

(c) Evolutionary process
(d) Reference-group model

27. Which one of the following statements in respect of status is not correct?
(a) Status is the rank-order position
(b) Status is a position in the general institutional system
(c) Status is the worth of a person as estimated by a group
(d) Status is a cultural attribute of an individual

28. Consider the following statements:
1. Auguste Comte proposed a theory of evolutionary social change dividing it into three stages of thought; the religious stage, the metaphysical stage and the scientific stage.
2. According to Herbert Spencer's evolutionary theory, human societies evolve from "barbarian" to "civilized".

Which of the statements given above is/are correct?
(a) 1 only
(b) 2 only
(c) Both 1 and 2
(d) Neither 1 nor 2

29. Who among the following has/have used the concept of "unitary coded substance" that explains the process of pollution among Hindus?
(a) Pauline Kolenda
(b) McKim Marriott and R.B. Inden
(c) M.N. Srinivas
(d) T.N. Madan

30. Which of the following is not a criterion of caste?
(a) Hereditary occupation
(b) Endogamy
(c) Exogamy
(d) Hierarchy

31. Match List I with List II and select the correct answer using the codes given below the lists:

List I
A. Opposition of purity and pollution
B. Dominant caste
C. Tribe-caste-peasant continuum
D. Attributional and interactional analysis of caste

List II
i. Surajit Sinha
ii. L. Dumont
iii. McKim Marriott
iv. M.N. Srinivas

Codes:	A	B	C	D
(a)	i	iv	ii	iii
(b)	ii	iii	i	iv
(c)	i	iii	ii	iv
(d)	ii	iv	i	iii

32. Match List I (Interpretation of Caste) with List II (Scholar) and select the correct answer using the codes given below the lists:

List I
A. Caste is a closed system
B. Closed organic stratification
C. Caste is an extreme form
D. Caste is an expression of hierarchy rather than stratification

List II
i. Louis Dumont
ii. Gunnar Myrdal
iii. Fredrick Bailey
iv. Max Weber

Codes:	A	B	C	D
(a)	i	ii	iii	iv
(b)	iv	iii	ii	i
(c)	i	iii	ii	iv
(d)	iv	ii	iii	i

33. According to Karl Marx, where does the capitalist class derive profit from?

(a) Absolute control over property
(b) The surplus values created by the workers
(c) Greater investment of capital to production
(d) Increase of means of production

34. Who looks into social stratification as 'the unequal division of material rewards and social prestige'?
(a) Max Weber
(b) Kingsley Davis and Wilbert Moore
(c) Karl Marx
(d) Melvin Tumin

35. Match List I with List II and select the correct answer using the codes given below the lists:

List I
A. Social position of men into groups based on their consumption pattern
B. Besides capitalists and workers, there are also other classes and strata in capitalist society
C. Status attainment through achievement motivation
D. Exploitation through appropriation of surplus value

List II
i. Kingsley Davis and Wilbert Moore
ii. Max Weber
iii. Karl Marx
iv. Wesoloski

Codes:	A	B	C	D
(a)	ii	iv	i	iii
(b)	iii	i	iv	ii
(c)	ii	i	iv	iii
(d)	iii	iv	i	ii

36. Which one of the following statements is correct?
In "marumakkatthayam" practice inheritance is through
(a) the father
(b) the mother
(c) the paternal uncle
(d) the maternal uncle

37. Which one of the following pairs is not correctly matched?
(a) Patrilolity : Patrilineal
(b) Avunculocality : Matrilineal
(c) Matrilocality : Sororal Polygyny
(d) Bilocality : Double descent

38. Match List I (Theory Regarding Origin of Religion) with List II (Propounder) and select the correct answer using the codes given below the lists:

List I	**List II**
A. Animism	i. Malinowski
B. Naturism	ii. Max Muller
C. Functional	iii. Tylor
	iv. Marett

Codes:	A	B	C
(a)	ii	i	iii
(b)	iii	ii	i
(c)	ii	iv	iii
(d)	iii	i	iv

39. Consider the following statements
Under matrilocal residence
1. Wife has to life in husband's father's house
2. Mother has to live son-in-law's house
3. Husband has to live in wife's mother's house
4. Father has to live in daughter-in-law's house

Which of the above statements is/are correct?
(a) 1 and 3
(b) 2 only
(c) 3 only
(d) 2 and 3

40. Match List I with List II and select the correct answer using the codes given below the lists:

List I
A. Cognate
B. Modern family
C. Socialisation
D. Avunculate

List II

i. Family function
ii. Maternal uncle
iii. Common ancestor
iv. Narrow range kinship
v. Classificatory Kin

Codes:	A	B	C	D
(a)	ii	iv	i	iii
(b)	iii	i	iv	ii
(c)	ii	i	iv	iii
(d)	iii	iv	i	ii

41. Which of the following is an example of matrilineal Kin group?
(a) Irula (b) Kadar
(c) Khasi (d) Toda

42. Match List I (Concept) with List II (Residence Rule) and select the correct answer using the codes given below the lists:

List I

A. Neolocal B. Bilocal
C. Matrilocal D. Patrilocal

List II

i. Married couple lives in wife's mother's household
ii. Married couple is allowed to live with either husband's or wife's family of origin
iii. Married couple lives anywhere on their own outside their respective families
iv. Married couple lives in husband's father's household

Codes:	A	B	C	D
(a)	i	iv	iii	ii
(b)	iii	ii	i	iv
(c)	i	ii	iii	iv
(d)	iii	iv	i	ii

43. What is the term given to the relationship which is governed by formal rules to restrict interaction between designated categories of relatives?
(a) Avoidance relationships
(b) Joking relationships
(c) Conflicting relationship
(d) Intimate relationship

44. Who divided the science of Sociology into two major parts—Social statics and Social dynamics?
(a) Max Weber
(b) Karl Marx
(c) Satin Simon
(d) Auguste Comte

45. Which one of the following statements correctly describes Wergild?
(a) An ordeal performed by the culprit to prove himself not guilty
(b) A kind of bride price arranged by a groom among the tribals
(c) A fine by which homicide and other heinous crimes against the person were expiated among the Teutonic people
(d) A kind of sacrificial and sacramental meals among the tribes

46. A particular social status involves not a single associated role, but an array of as sociated roles. What was this termed as by R.K. Merton?
(a) Status set
(b) Multiple statuses
(c) Multiple roles
(d) Role set

47. What did the 'Satyashodhak Samaj' established in 1873 aim at?
(a) To bring all castes together
(b) To create a non-idol-worshipping, reason-based faith anchored to truth.
(c) To fight against British rule
(d) To fight for women's rights

48. Consider the following statements:
1. The functionalist theory of social stratification has not focused on explaining social stratification as a system of rewards resulting in differences ins social prestige.

2. Generally, functionalist theories of social stratification have been assumed, as far as public policy is concerned, because they mirror and support the status quo.

Which of the statements given above is/are correct?

(a) 1 only (b) 2 only
(c) Both 1 and 2 (d) Neither 1 nor 2

49. Which of the following concepts are applied to analyse the process of civilization change?
(a) Gemeinschaft and Gesellschaft
(b) Zweckrationaitat and Wertrationalitat
(c) Mechanical and organic solidarity
(d) Sensate and ideational culture

50. Who was the Maharaja under whose patronage the Dalit movement flourished in Maharashtra?
(a) The Maharaja of Kolhapur
(b) The Maharaja of Raigarh
(c) The Maharaja of Nagpur
(d) The Maharaja of Amaravati

ANSWERS

1. (b)	2. (a)	3. (b)	4. (a)	5. (b)
6. (c)	7. (a)	8. (d)	9. (a)	10. (d)
11. (c)	12. (b)	13. (c)	14. (b)	15. (a)
16. (d)	17. (a)	18. (d)	19. (b)	20. (b)
21. (b)	22. (c)	23. (d)	24. (a)	25. (b)
26. (d)	27. (d)	28. (a)	29. (b)	30. (c)
31. (d)	32. (b)	33. (b)	34. (b)	35. (a)
36. (b)	37. (c)	38. (d)	39. (c)	40. (d)
41. (c)	42. (b)	43. (a)	44. (d)	45. (c)
46. (d)	47. (b)	48. (b)	49. (d)	50. (a)

JUNE–2006

Note: This paper contains Fifty (50) objective type questions, each question carrying two (2) marks. Attempt all the questions.

PAPER–I

1. Which of the following comprise teaching skill?
   (a) Blackboard writing
   (b) Questioning
   (c) Explaining
   (d) All of the above
2. Which of the following statements is most appropriate?
   (a) Teachers can teach.
   (b) Teachers help can create in a student a desire to learn.
   (c) Lecture method can be used for developing thinking.
   (d) Teachers are born.
3. The first Indian chronicler of Indian history was
   (a) Megasthenes (b) Fa-Hien
   (c) Hiuen-Tsang (d) Kalhan
4. Which of the following statements is correct?
   (a) Syllabus is a part of curriculum.
   (b) Syllabus is an annexure to curriculum.
   (c) Curriculum is the same in all educational institutions affiliated to a particular university.
   (d) Syllabus is not the same in all educational institutions affiliated to a particular university.
5. Which of the two given options is of the level of understanding?
   (I) Define noun.
   (II) Define noun in your own words.
   (a) Only I (b) Only II
   (c) Both I and II (d) Neither I nor II
6. Which of the following options are the main tasks of research in modern society?
   (I) to keep pace with the advancement in knowledge.
   (II) to discover new things.
   (III) to write a critique on the earlier writings.
   (IV) to systematically examine and critically analyse the investigations/sources with objectivity.
   (a) IV, II and I (b) I, II and III
   (c) I and III (d) II, III and IV
7. Match List I (Interviews) with List II (Meaning) and select the correct answer from the codes given below:

   List I (Interviews)
   (A) Structured interviews
   (B) Unstructured interviews
   (C) Focussed interviews
   (D) Clinical interviews

   List II (Meaning)
   (i) greater flexibility approach
   (ii) attention on the questions to be answered
   (iii) individual life experience
   (iv) pre-determined question
   (v) non-directive

Codes:	A	B	C	D
(a)	(iv)	(i)	(ii)	(iii)
(b)	(ii)	(iv)	(i)	(iii)
(c)	(v)	(ii)	(iv)	(i)
(d)	(i)	(iii)	(v)	(iv)

8. What do you consider as the main aim of interdisciplinary research?
   (a) To bring out holistic approach to research.
   (b) To reduce the emphasis of single subject in research domain.
   (c) To over simplify the problem of research.
   (d) To create a new trend in research methodology.
9. One of the aims of the scientific method in research is to
   (a) improve data interpretation
   (b) eliminate spurious relations
   (c) confirm triangulation
   (d) introduce new variables
10. The depth of any research can be judged by
   (a) title of the research.
   (b) objectives of the research.
   (c) total expenditure on the research.
   (d) duration of the research.

Read the following passage and answer the questions from 11 to 15:

The superintendence, direction and control of preparation of electoral rolls for, and the conduct of, elections to Parliament and State Legislatures and elections to the offices of the President and the Vice-President of India are vested in the Election Commission of India. It is an independent constitutional authority.

Independence of the Election Commission and its insulation from executive interference is ensured by a specific provision under Article 324 (5) of the constitution that the Chief Election Commissioner shall not be removed from his office except in like manner and on like grounds as a Judge of the Supreme Court and conditions of his service shall not be varied to his disadvantage after his appointment.

In C.W.P. No. 4912 of 1998 (Kushra Bharat Vs. Union of India and others), the Delhi High Court directed that information relating to Government dues owed by the candidates to the departments dealing with Government accommodation, electricity, water, telephone and transport, etc. and any other dues should be furnished by the candidates and this information should be published by the election authorities under the commission.

11. The text of the passage reflects or raises certain questions
   (a) The authority of the commission cannot be challenged.
   (b) This would help in stopping the criminalization of Indian politics.
   (c) This would reduce substantially the number of contesting candidates.
   (d) This would ensure fair and free elections.
12. According to the passage, the Election Commission is an independent constitutional authority. This is under Article
   (a) 324 (b) 356
   (c) 246 (d) 161
13. Independence of the Commission means
   (a) have a constitutional status.
   (b) have legislative powers.
   (c) have judicial powers.
   (d) have political powers.
14. Fair and free election means
   (a) transparency
   (b) to maintain law and order
   (c) regional considerations
   (d) role for pressure groups
15. The Chief Election Commissioner can be removed from his office under Article
   (a) 125 (b) 352
   (c) 226 (d) 324
16. The function of mass communication of supplying information regarding the processes, issues, events and societal developments is known as

(a) content supply (b) surveillance
(c) gratification (d) correlation

17. The science of the study of feedback systems in humans, animals and machines is known as
(a) cybernetics
(b) reverse communication
(c) selectivity study
(d) response analysis

18. Networked media exist in inter-connected
(a) social environments
(b) economic environments
(c) political environments
(d) technological environments

19. The combination of computing, telecommunications and media in a digital atmosphere is referred to as
(a) online communication
(b) integrated media
(c) digital combine
(d) convergence

20. A dialogue between a human-being and a computer programme that occurs simultaneously in various forms is described as
(a) man-machine speak
(b) binary chat
(c) digital talk
(d) interactivity

21. Insert the missing number:

$\frac{16}{32}, \frac{15}{33}, \frac{17}{31}, \frac{14}{34}, ?$

(a) $\frac{19}{35}$ (b) $\frac{19}{30}$
(c) $\frac{18}{35}$ (d) $\frac{18}{30}$

22. Monday falls on 20th March 1995. What was the day on 3rd November 1994?
(a) Thursday (b) Sunday
(c) Tuesday (d) Saturday

23. The average of four consecutive even numbers is 27. The largest of these numbers is
(a) 36 (b) 32
(c) 30 (d) 28

24. In a certain code, FHQK means GIRL. How will WOMEN be written in the same code?
(a) VNLDM (b) FHQKN
(c) XPNFO (d) VLNDM

25. At what time between 4 and 5 o'clock will the hands of a watch point in opposite directions?
(a) 45 min. past 4
(b) $40\frac{4}{11}$ min. past 4
(c) 50 min. past 4
(d) $54\frac{6}{11}$ min. past 4

26. Which of the following conclusions is logically valid based on statement given below?
Statement: Most teachers are hard working.
Conclusions: (I) Some teachers are hard working.
(II) Some teachers are not hard working.
(a) Only (I) is implied
(b) Only (II) is implied
(c) Both (I) and (II) are implied
(d) Neither (I) nor (II) is implied

27. Who among the following can be asked to make a statement in Indian Parliament?
(a) Any MLA
(b) Chief of Army Staff
(c) Solicitor General of India
(d) Mayor of Delhi

28. Which of the following conclusions is logically valid based on statement given below?

Statement: Most of the Indian states existed before independence.

Conclusions: (I) Some Indian States existed before independence.

(II) All Indian States did not exist before independence.

(a) Only (I) is implied
(b) Only (II) is implied
(c) Both (I) and (II) are implied
(d) Neither (I) nor (II) is implied

29. Water is always involved with landslides. This is because it
(a) reduces the shear strength of rocks
(b) increases the weight of the overburden
(c) enhances chemical weathering
(d) is a universal solvent

30. Direction for this question:
Given below are two Statements (a) and (b) followed by two Conclusions (i) and (ii).
Considering the statements to be true, indicate which of the following conclusions logically follow from the given statements by selecting one of the four response alternatives given below the conclusion:

Statements: (a) All businessmen are wealthy.

(b) All wealthy people are hard working.

Conclusions: (i) All businessmen are hard working.

(ii) All hardly working people are not wealthy.

(a) Only (i) follows
(b) Only (ii) follows
(c) Both (i) and (ii) follows
(d) Neither (i) nor (ii) follows

31. Using websites to pour out one's grievances is called
(a) cyberventing (b) cyber ranting
(c) web hate (d) web plea

32. In web search, finding a large number of documents with very little relevant information is termed
(a) poor recall
(b) web crawl
(c) poor precision rate
(d) poor web response

33. The concept of connect intelligence is derived from
(a) virtual reality
(b) fuzzy logic
(c) bluetooth technology
(d) value added networks

34. Use of an ordinary telephone as an Internet applicance is called
(a) voicenet (b) voice telephone
(c) voice line (d) voice portal

35. Video transmission over the Internet that looks like delayed live casting is called
(a) virtual video
(b) direct broadcast
(c) video shift
(d) real-time video

36. Which is the smallest North-east State in India?
(a) Tripura (b) Meghalaya
(c) Mizoram (d) Manipur

37. Tamil Nadu coastal belt has drinking water shortage due to
(a) high evaporation
(b) sea water flooding due to tsunami
(c) over exploitation of ground water by tubewells
(d) seepage of sea water

38. While all rivers of Peninsular India flow into the Bay of Bengal, Narmada and Tapti flow into the Arabian Sea because these two rivers
   (a) Follow the slope of these rift valleys
   (b) The general slope of the Indian peninsula is from east to west
   (c) The Indian peninsula north of the Satpura ranges, is tilted towards the west
   (d) The Indian peninsula south of the satpura ranges is tilted towards east

39. Soils in the Mahanadi delta are less fertile than those in the Godavari delta because of
   (a) erosion of top soils by annual floods
   (b) inundation of land by sea water
   (c) traditional agriculture practices
   (d) the derivation of alluvial soil from red-soil hinterland

40. Which of the following institutions in the field of education is set up by the MHRD Government of India?
   (a) Indian council of World Affair, New Delhi
   (b) Mythic Society, Bangalore
   (c) National Bal Bhawan, New Delhi
   (d) India International Centre, New Delhi

41. **Assertion (A):** Aerosols have potential for modifying climate
   Reason (R): Aerosols interact with both short waves and radiation.
   (a) Both (A) and (R) are true, and (R) is the correct explanation of (A)
   (b) Both (A) and (R) are true, but (R) is not the correct explanation of (A)
   (c) (A) is true, but (R) is false
   (d) (A) is false, but (R) is true

42. 'SITE' stands for
   (a) System for International technology and Engineering
   (b) Satellite Instructional Television Experiment
   (c) South Indian Trade Estate
   (d) State Institute of Technology and Engineering

43. What is the name of the Research station established by the Indian Government for 'Conducting Research at Antarctic?
   (a) Dakshin Gangotri
   (b) Yamunotri
   (c) Uttari Gangotri
   (d) None of the above

44. Ministry of Human Resource Development (HRD) includes
   (a) Department of Elementary Education and Literacy
   (b) Department of Secondary Education and Higher Education
   (c) Department of Women and Child Development
   (d) All of the above

45. Parliament can legislate on matters listed in the State list
   (a) With the prior permission of the President.
   (b) Only after the constitution is amended suitably.
   (c) In case of inconsistency among State legislatures.
   (d) At the request of two or more States.

The following pie chart indicates the expenditure of a country on various sports during a particular year. Study the pie chart and answer question number 46 to 50.

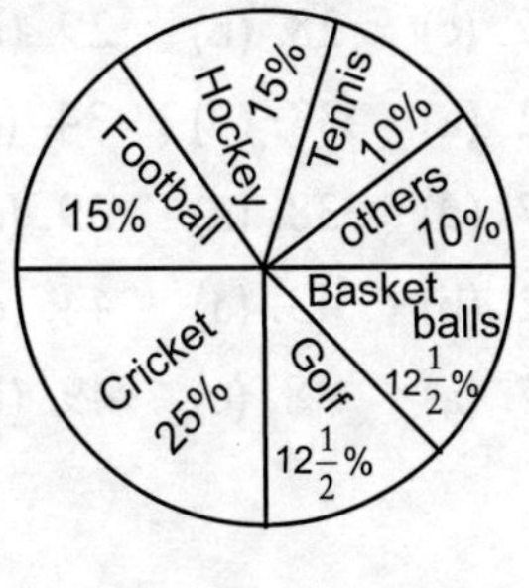

46. The ratio of the total expenditure on football to that of expenditure on hockey is
(a) 1 : 15 (b) 1 : 1
(c) 15 : 1 (d) 3 : 20

47. If the total expenditure on sports during the year was ₹ 1,20,000,00 how much was spent on basket ball?
(a) ₹ 9,50,000 (b) ₹ 10,00,000
(c) ₹ 12,00,000 (d) ₹ 15,00,000

48. The chart shows that the most popular game of the country is
(a) Hockey (b) Football
(c) Cricket (d) Tennis

49. Out of the following country's expenditure is the same on
(a) Hockey and Tennis
(b) Golf and Basket ball
(c) Cricket and Football
(d) Hockey and Golf

50. If the total expenditure on sport during the year was ₹ 1,50,00,000 the expenditure on cricket and hockey together was
(a) ₹ 60,00,000 (b) ₹ 50,00,000
(c) ₹ 37,50,000 (d) ₹ 25,00,000

ANSWERS

1. (d)	2. (b)	3. (d)	4. (a)	5. (b)
6. (a)	7. (a)	8. (a)	9. (b)	10. (b)
11. (d)	12. (a)	13. (a)	14. (b)	15. (d)
16. (a)	17. (a)	18. (d)	19. (d)	20. (d)
21. (d)	22. (a)	23. (c)	24. (c)	25. (d)
26. (c)	27. (c)	28. (b)	29. (b)	30. (a)
31. (a)	32. (a)	33. (d)	34. (c)	35. (d)
36. (c)	37. (d)	38. (a)	39. (a)	40. (c)
41. (a)	42. (b)	43. (a)	44. (d)	45. (d)
46. (b)	47. (a)	48. (c)	49. (b)	50. (a)

PAPER–II

1. Which one of the following statements is correct?
Feminism in the western societies
(a) is a militant movement of women's rights supporters
(b) is a homogenous ideology built like Marxism, theoretically, over the years
(c) has emerged as a generic term encompassing various ideological positions vis-a-vis society's treatment of women
(d) is a metaphysical notion that nobody wishes to question or challenge

2. In which of the following States did the Naxalite movement emerge in 1960s?
(a) Bihar
(b) West Bengal
(c) Orissa
(d) Madhya Pradesh

3. Who among the following has referred to integrative orientation and alienating orientation as two types of social movements?
(a) Rajni Kothari
(b) Andre Beteille
(c) Katheleen Gough
(d) Yogendra Singh

4. Which of the following is not an essential feature of social movement?
(a) Collective mobilization
(b) Revolution
(c) Ideology
(d) Orientation towards change

5. Which one of the following tribes initiated the Jharkhand movement?
(a) Bhil (b) Bodo
(c) Santhal (d) Birhor

6. Which one of the following was a peasant movement?

(a) Khilafat Movement
(b) Women Liberation Movement
(c) Telengana Movement
(d) Jharkhand Movement

7. Who among the following has proposed a model to explain the differentiation of social system, based on an analysis of the way in which a particular system responds to forces for change?
(a) N.J. Smelser
(b) Talcott Parsons
(c) Daniel Bell
(d) Ulrich Beck

8. Which of the following group(s) of factors was/were used by Koreber to classify kinship terminology?
1. Descen, Gender, Polarity, Bifurcation and Lineage
2. Kinderd, Class, Affinity, Gender and Polarity
3. Generation, Gender, Afinity, Bifurcation and Polarity

Select the correct answer using the codes given below:
Codes:
(a) 1 only (b) 3 only
(c) 2 and 3 (d) 1 and 3

9. A special role, similar to that of a maternal uncle, for one's father's sister is designated as
(a) Amitate (b) Couvade
(c) Avunculate (d) Teknonymy

10. Consider the following statements:
1. Extended family consists of two mates of opposite sex and their offspring
2. Conjugal family consists of two mates of opposite sex and their offspring
3. Consanguineous family consists of two mats of opposite sex and their offspring.

Which of the statements given above is correct?
(a) 1 only (b) 2 only
(c) 3 only (d) None

11. When two or more sibs exist in a community, they may be called
(a) Moieties
(b) Phrateries
(c) Exogamous clans
(d) Endogamous clans

12. Match List I with List II and select the correct answer using the codes given below the lists:

List I
A. Joking relationships
B. Taboo
C. Classificatory terminology
D. Tolemism

List II
i. L.H. Morgan
ii. F.J. Pedlar
iii. E. Durkheim
iv. Sir James Frazer

Codes:	A	B	C	D
(a)	i	iv	ii	iii
(b)	ii	iii	i	iv
(c)	i	iii	ii	iv
(d)	ii	iv	i	iii

13. Consider the following statements about family:
1. Family regulates sexual behaviour through incest taboo.
2. Family provides ethnics identity.
3. Family serves as an occupational guild.
4. Family provides predictable social contexts within which its children are to be socialised.

Which of the above statements are correct?
(a) 1, 2 and 3 (b) 1, 2 and 4
(c) 1 and 3 (d) 2 and 4

14. What is the smallest unit of Tharwawad called?
(a) Tavazhi (b) Nambudiri
(c) Cheri (d) Koli

15. Match List I (Book) with List II (Author) and select the correct answer using the codes given below the lists:

List I
A. *Family, Kinship and Marriage in India*
B. *Kinship Organisation in India*
C. *Family and Kinship: A Study of Pandits of Rural Kashmir*
D. *Marriage and Family in India*

List II
i. Irawati Karve
ii. T.N. Madan
iii. Patricia Uberoi
iv. K.M. Kapadia

Codes:	**A**	**B**	**C**	**D**
(a)	iv	ii	i	iii
(b)	iii	i	ii	iv
(c)	iv	i	ii	iii
(d)	iii	ii	i	iv

16. Among the Muslims, a wife can obtain release from her marriage by giving consideration to husband whose consent is essential. What is this type of divorce called?
(a) Mehar (b) Tafweez
(c) Khula (d) Talaq

17. What is a Hindu marriage in which the daughter is gifted to a priest, called?
(a) Brahma marriage
(b) Daiva marriage
(c) Sacred marriage
(d) Arsha marriage

18. In traditional Hindu society which of the following forms of mate selection were undesirable?
(a) Asura, Rakshasa and Paisacha
(b) Brahma, Asura, Arsha and Gandharva
(c) Rakshasa, Daiva, Prajapatya and Paisacha
(d) Brahma, Arsha and Rakshasa

19. What is according to Hindu traditional law, marriage by abduction, called?
(a) Gandharva (b) Paisacha
(c) Arsha (d) Rakshasa

20. What is a cross-cousin marriage as practiced by Gonds of Madhya Pradesh called?
(a) Sahahadlautwa
(b) Gheelautwa
(c) Paanilautwa
(d) Daudhlautwa

21. One of the important elements of the ethos of science is
(a) emotional value
(b) organised scepticism
(c) organised scholasticism
(d) commitment to human values

Directions: The following question consist of two statements, one labelled as 'Assertion (A)' and the other labelled as 'Reason (R)'. You are to examine these two statements carefully and decide if the Assertion (A) and the Reason (R) are individually true and if so, whether the Reason is a correct explanation of the Assertion.

Select your answers to these items using the codes given below and mark your answer sheet accordingly.
(a) Both (A) and (R) are true and (R) is the correct explanation of (A)
(b) Both (A) and (R) are true, but (R) is not the correct explanation of (A)
(c) (A) is true, but (R) is false
(d) (A) is false, but (R) is true

22. **Assertion (A):** There is a considerable ethnolinguistic diversity in India.
Reason (R): This prohibits equal opportunity.

23. Which one of the following pairs is not correctly matched?
(a) Schumpeter : Enterpreneur
(b) China : Cultural revolution
(c) Russia : Industrial revolution
(d) Max Weber : Bureaucracy

24. Which one of the following statements is true about 'Mana'?
(a) The respect the father commands from his sons whose belief in 'life after death' tends to deity the father.
(b) The sacred animal which is a symbol of deep group based sentiments and feelings.
(c) A benign supernatural force that has no shape of its own but inhabits living or inanimate things.
(d) A ritual that is arranged to felicitate a women on her first pregnancy in a tribal society in North-East India.

25. Which one of the following pairs is correctly matched?
(a) Hindus – Parallel cousin marriage
(b) Santhals – Assam
(c) Endogamy – Totemism
(d) Indian kinship system – Avoidance

26. Match List I with List II and select the correct answer:
List I (Concepts)
A. Evolutionary Universals
B. Spectrum of Reciprocity
C. Theory of Surplus Value
D. Creative Destruction

List II (Thinkers)
i. Schumpeter ii. Parsons
iii. Sahlins iv. Marx

Codes:	A	B	C	D
(a)	iii	ii	iv	i
(b)	ii	iii	i	iv
(c)	ii	iii	iv	i
(d)	iii	ii	i	iv

27. Which of the following pairs are correctly matched?
1. Marx : Mode of Production
2. Weber : Class, Caste and Power
3. Centers : Subjective characteristics
4. Warner : Self-identification

Select the correct answer using the codes given below:
(a) 1, 2, 3 and 4 (b) 1, 3 and 4
(c) 2 and 4 (d) 1, 2 and 3

28. Match List I with List II and select the correct answer:
List I
A. Dialectics
B. Social dynamics
C. Unilinear evolution
D. Super-organic evolution

List II
i. Morgan
ii. Comte
iii. Herbert Spencer
iv. Hegel

Codes:	A	B	C	D
(a)	ii	iv	iii	i
(b)	ii	iv	i	iii
(c)	iv	ii	i	iii
(d)	iv	ii	iii	i

29. Match List I (Sociologists) with List II (Their contribution) and select the correct answer:
List I
A. Louis Wirth
B. Elton Mayo
C. Robert Redfield
D. Fredrick Taylor

List II
i. Folk-urban continuum
ii. Scientific management
iii. Urbanism as a way of life
iv. Human Relations

Codes:	**A**	**B**	**C**	**D**
(a)	iii	iv	ii	i
(b)	iii	iv	i	ii
(c)	iv	iii	i	ii
(d)	iv	iii	ii	i

30. **Assertion (A):** Altruistic suicides occur more in over-integrated societies.
Reason (R): Suicide is the desperate act of an individual.

31. **Assertion (A):** It is witnessed that even the rational persons put some food and eatables on the burial pit of dead persons.
Reason (R): Modes of action persist more obstinately than the modes of thinking.

32. **Assertion (A):** In a given society, the rate of suicide, is significantly higher in cities than in villages.
Reason (R): Autonomy of individual increases with increasing social division of labour.

33. **Assertion (A):** There is a proliferation of voluntary associations in cities.
Reason (R): The hold of collective consciousness declines with an increase in organic solidarity.

34. Consider the following pairs:
   1. Marriage : Group
   2. Family : Institution
   3. Clan : Kindered
   4. Tribe : Community

   Select the correct answer using the codes given below:
   Codes:
   (a) 2, 3 and 4 (b) 1 and 4
   (c) 2 and 3 (d) 1, 2, 3 and 4

35. Who among the following said that the approach to human development encompasses Jamma, Karma and Bhakti?
(a) Mahatma Gandhi
(b) Swami Vivekananda
(c) Amartya Sen
(d) Morari Bapu

36. The women of Bishnoi community hugged the trees to prevent the woodcutters from cutting the trees to build a palace in
(a) Gujarat (b) Haryana
(c) Rajasthan (d) Uttar Pradesh

37. Who among the following treated magic as a Pseudoscience?
(a) Tylor (b) Frazer
(c) Morgan (d) Malinowski

38. **Assertion (A):** Commercial revolution was the main reason for the development of medieval cities.
Reason (R): Colonization and conquests opened up the East to the Western market.

39. Which one of the following practices of child-rearing is better suited for democratisation of social life?
(a) Children may be seen but not heard
(b) Criticising the child
(c) "I say you do"
(d) Showing proper ways of doing things

40. Which one of the following pairs is not correctly matched?
(a) Dialectical Materialism : Karl Marx
(b) Power Elite : C. Wright Mill
(c) Collective Consciousness : Durkheim
(d) Ideal Type : Sumner

41. The concept of 'Sanskritisation' is closely related to the concept of
(a) reference group
(b) primary group
(c) interest group
(d) tertiary group

42. Which one of the following states in India has the highest percentage of reservation for the Scheduled Castes?

(a) Maharashtra (b) Uttar Pradesh
(c) Punjab (d) Tamil Nadu

43. Which one of the following statements is correct?
(a) Article 341 of the Constitution defines the term Scheduled Caste
(b) The Constitution empowers the Parliament to define the term Scheduled Caste
(c) The Constitution does not contain a definition of the term Scheduled Caste
(d) The term Scheduled Caste is defined in the Government of India Act. 1918

44. Which one of the following is the basic concern of Article 17 of the Indian Constitution?
(a) Representation of backward classes
(b) The abolition of untouchability
(c) Reservation of posts in services for the Scheduled Castes
(d) Political representation to Scheduled Castes

45. Who was the first Chairman of the 'Backward classes Commission' in India?
(a) B.P. Mandal
(b) B.R. Ambedkar
(c) Kaka Kalelkar
(d) M.K. Gandhi

46. "Women have acquired all the follies and vices of civilization, and miss the useful Fruit." Who made the above statement?
(a) Beatric Webb
(b) Mary Wollstonecraft
(c) Nancy Chodorow
(d) Margaret Mead

47. Which of the following Articles of the Constitution protects Schedules Tribes representation in Lok Sabha and Vidhan Sabha in proportion to their population?
(a) 330 and 332 (b) 275
(c) 365 (d) 340 and 342

48. The term 'Backward Class' is used in which Article of the Constitution of India?
(a) 15 (4) (b) 16 (4)
(c) 17 (4) (d) 23 (4)

49. Which three stages of the following socio-cultural evolution are propounded by L. H. Morgan?
(a) Ancient, Feudal and Industrial
(b) Savagery, Barbarism and Civilisation
(c) Lower, Intermediate and Modern
(d) Primitive, Traditional and Technological

50. In India, a special Ministry for Women and Social Welfare was formed at the Centre in the year
(a) 1983 (b) 1986
(c) 1976 (d) 1991

ANSWERS

1. (c)	2. (b)	3. (d)	4. (b)	5. (c)
6. (c)	7. (b)	8. (b)	9. (a)	10. (b)
11. (b)	12. (d)	13. (d)	14. (a)	15. (b)
16. (c)	17. (b)	18. (a)	19. (d)	20. (d)
21. (d)	22. (c)	23. (c)	24. (c)	25. (d)
26. (c)	27. (b)	28. (c)	29. (b)	30. (c)
31. (a)	32. (d)	33. (d)	34. (b)	35. (b)
36. (c)	37. (b)	38. (b)	39. (d)	40. (d)
41. (a)	42. (d)	43. (c)	44. (b)	45. (c)
46. (b)	47. (a)	48. (b)	49. (b)	50. (c)

DECEMBER–2005

Note: This paper contains Fifty (50) objective type questions, each question carrying two (2) marks. Attempt all the questions.

PAPER–I

1. Team teaching has the potential to develop
   (a) Competitive spirit
   (b) Cooperation
   (c) The habit of supplementing the teaching of each other
   (d) Highlighting the gaps in each other's teaching
2. Which of the following is the most important characteristic of Open Book Examination system?
   (a) Students become serious.
   (b) It improves attendance in the classroom.
   (c) It reduces examination anxiety amongst students.
   (d) It compels students to think.
3. Which of the following methods of teaching encourages the use of maximum senses?
   (a) Problem-solving method
   (b) Laboratory method
   (c) Self-study method
   (d) Team-teaching method
4. Which of the following statement is correct?
   (a) Communicator should have fine senses
   (b) Communicator should have tolerance power
   (c) Communicator should be soft spoken
   (d) Communicator should have good personality
5. An effective teacher is one who can
   (a) control the class
   (b) give more information in less time
   (c) motivate students to learn
   (d) correct the assignments carefully
6. One of the following is not a quality of researcher
   (a) Unison with that of which he is in search
   (b) He must be of alert mind
   (c) Keenness in enquiry
   (d) His assertion to outstrip the evidence
7. A satisfactory statistical quantitative method should not possess one of the following qualities
   (a) Appropriateness (b) Measurability
   (c) Comparability (d) Flexibility
8. Books and records are the primary sources of data in
   (a) historical research
   (b) participatory research
   (c) clinical research
   (d) laboratory research
9. Which of the following statement is correct?
   (a) Objectives should be pinpointed
   (b) Objectives can be written in statement or question form
   (c) Another word for problem is variable
   (d) All of the above
10. The important pre-requisites of a researcher in sciences, social sciences and humanities are

(a) laboratory skills, records, supervisor, topic
(b) Supervisor, topic, critical analysis, patience
(c) archives, supervisor, topic, flexibility in thinking
(d) topic, supervisor, good temperament, pre-conceived notions

Read the following passage and answer the questions from 11 to 15:

Knowledge creation in many cases requires creativity and idea generation. This is especially important in generating alternative decision support solutions. Some people believe that an individual's creative ability stems primarily from personality traits such as inventiveness, independence, individuality, enthusiasm, and flexibility. However, several studies have found that creativity is not so much a function of individual traits as was once believed, and that individual creativity can be learned and improved. This understanding has led innovative companies to recognise that the key to fostering creativity may be the development of an idea-nurturing work environment. Idea-generation methods and techniques, to be used by individuals or in groups, are consequently being developed. Manual methods for supporting idea generation, such as brainstorming in a group, can be very successful in certain situations. However, in other situations, such an approach is either not economically feasible or not possible. For example, manual methods in group creativity sessions will not work or will not be effective when: (1) there is no time to conduct a proper idea-generation session; (2) there is a poor facilitator (or no facilitator at all); (3) it is too expensive to conduct an idea-generation session; (4) the subject matter is too sensitive for a face-to-face session; or (5) there are not enough participants, the mix of participants is not optimal, or there is no climate for idea generation. In such cases, computerised idea-generation methods have been tried, with frequent success.

Idea-generation software is designed to help stimulate a single user or a group to produce new ideas, options and choices. The user does all the work, but the software encourages and pushes, something like a personal trainer. Although idea-generation software is still relatively new, there are several packages on the market. Various approaches are used by idea-generating software to increase the flow of ideas to the user. Idea Fisher, for example, has an associate lexicon of the English language that cross-references words and phrases. These associative links, based on analogies and metaphors, make it easy for the user to be fed words related to a given theme. Some software packages use questions to prompt the user towards new, unexplored patterns of thought. This helps users to break out of cyclical thinking patterns, conquer mental blocks, or deal with bouts of procrastination.

11. The author in this passage has focussed on
(a) knowledge creation
(b) idea-generation
(c) creativity
(d) individual traits

12. Fostering creativity needs an environment of
(a) decision support systems
(b) idea-nurturing
(c) decision support solutions
(d) alternative individual factors

13. Manual methods for the support of idea-generation in certain occasions
(a) are alternatively effective
(b) can be less expensive
(c) do not need a facilitator
(d) require a mix of optimal participants

14. Idea-generation software works as if it is a
    (a) stimulant
    (b) knowledge package
    (c) user-friendly trainer
    (d) climate creator
15. Mental blocks, bouts of procrastination and cyclical thinking patterns can be won when
    (a) innovative companies employ electronic thinking methods
    (b) idea-generation software prompts questions
    (c) manual methods are removed
    (d) individuals acquire a neutral attitude towards the software
16. Level C of the effectiveness of communication is defined as
    (a) channel noise
    (b) semantic noise
    (c) psychological noise
    (d) source noise
17. Recording a television programme on a VCR is an example of
    (a) time-shifting
    (b) content reference
    (c) mechanical clarity
    (d) media synchronisation
18. A good communicator is the one who offers to his audience
    (a) plentiful of information
    (b) a good amount of statistics
    (c) concise proof
    (d) repetition of facts
19. The largest number of newspapers in India is published from the state of
    (a) Kerala (b) Maharashtra
    (c) West Bengal (d) Uttar Pradesh
20. Insert the missing number:
    8 24 12 ? 18 54
    (a) 26 (b) 24
    (c) 36 (d) 32
21. January 1, 1995 was Sunday. What day of the week lies on January 1, 1996?
    (a) Sunday (b) Monday
    (c) Saturday (d) None of these
22. The sum of a positive number and its reciprocal is twice the difference of the number and its reciprocal. The number is
    (a) $\sqrt{2}$ (b) $\frac{1}{\sqrt{2}}$
    (c) $\sqrt{3}$ (d) $\frac{1}{\sqrt{3}}$
23. In a certain code, ROUNDS is written as RONUDS. How will PLEASE will be written in the same code?
    (a) LPAESE (b) PLAESE
    (c) LPAEES (d) PLASEE
24. At what time between 5.30 and 6.00 will the hands of an clock be at right angles?
    (a) $43\frac{5}{11}$ min. past 5
    (b) $43\frac{7}{11}$ min. past 5
    (c) 40 min. past 5
    (d) 45 min. past 5
25. **Statements:** I. All students are ambitious.
    II. All ambitious persons are hard working.
    Conclusions: (i) All students are hard working.
    (ii) All hardly working people are not ambitious.
    Which of the following is correct?
    (a) Only (i) is correct
    (b) Only (ii) is correct
    (c) Both (i) and (ii) are correct
    (d) Neither (i) nor (ii) is correct
26. **Statement:** Most students are intelligent
    Conclusions: (i) Some students are intelligent
    (ii) All students are not intelligent

Which of the following is implied?
(a) Only (i) is implied
(b) Only (ii) is implied
(c) Both (i) and (ii) are implied
(d) Neither (i) nor (ii) is implied

27. **Statement:** Most labourers are poor.
Conclusions: (i) Some labourers are poor.
(ii) All labourers are not poor.
Which of the following is implied?
(a) Only (i) is implied
(b) Only (ii) is implied
(c) Both (i) and (ii) are implied
(d) Neither (i) nor (ii) is implied

28. Line access and avoidance of collision are the main functions of
(a) the CPU
(b) the monitor
(c) network protocols
(d) wide area networks

29. In the hypermedia database, information bits are stored in the form of
(a) signals (b) cubes
(c) nodes (d) symbols

30. Communications bandwidth that has the highest capacity and is used by microwave, cable and fibre optics lines is known as
(a) hyper-link
(b) broadband
(c) bus width
(d) carrier wave

31. An electronic bill board that has a short text or graphical advertising message is referred to as
(a) bulletin (b) strap
(c) bridge line (d) banner

32. Which of the following is not the characteristic of a computer?
(a) Computer is an electrical machine
(b) Computer cannot think at its own
(c) Computer processes information error free
(d) Computer can hold data for any length of time

33. Bitumen is obtained from
(a) Forests and Plants
(b) Kerosene oil
(c) Crude oil
(d) Underground mines

34. Malaria is caused by
(a) bacterial infection
(b) viral infection
(c) parasitic infection
(d) fungal infection

35. The cloudy nights are warmer compared to clear nights (without clouds) during winter days. This is because
(a) clouds radiate heat towards the earth
(b) clouds prevent cold wave from the sky, descend on earth
(c) clouds prevent escaping of the heat radiation from the earth
(d) clouds being at great heights from earth absorb heat from the sun and send towards the earth

36. Largest soil group of India is
(a) Red soil (b) Black soil
(c) Sandy soil (d) Mountain soil

37. Main pollutant of the Indian coastal water is
(a) oil spill
(b) municipal sewage
(c) industrial effluents
(d) aerosols

38. Human ear is most sensitive to noise in the following frequency ranges
(a) 1-2 KHz (b) 100-500 Hz
(c) 10-12 KHz (d) None of these

39. Which species of chromium is toxic in water?
(a) Cr + 2 (b) Cr + 3
(c) Cr + 6 (d) Cr is non-toxic element

40. Match List I (Dams) with List II (River) in the following:

List I (Dams)	List II (River)
(A) Bhakra	(i) Krishna
(B) Nagarjunasagar	(ii) Damodar
(C) Panchet	(iii) Sutlej
(D) Hirakud	(iv) Bhagirathi
(E) Tehri	(v) Mahanadi

Codes:	A	B	C	D	E
(a)	v	iii	iv	ii	i
(b)	iii	i	ii	v	iv
(c)	i	ii	iv	iii	v
(d)	ii	iii	iv	i	v

41. A negative reaction to a mediated communication is described as
(a) flak
(b) fragmented feedback
(c) passive response
(d) non-conformity

42. The launch of satellite channel by IGNOU on 26th January 2003 for technological education for the growth and development of distance education is
(a) Eklavya channel
(b) Gyandarshan channel
(c) Rajrishi channel
(d) None of these

43. Match List I with List II and select the correct answer from the codes given below:

List I (Institutions)	List II (Locations)
(A) The Indian Council of Historical Reasearch (ICHR)	(i) Shimla
(B) The Indian Institute of Advanced Studies (IIAS)	(ii) New Delhi
(C) The Indian Council of Philosophical Research (ICPR)	(iii) Banglore
(D) The Central Institute of Coastal Engineering for Fisheries	(iv) Lucknow

Codes:	A	B	C	D
(a)	ii	i	iv	iii
(b)	i	ii	iii	iv
(c)	ii	iv	i	iii
(d)	iv	iii	ii	i

44. Which of the following is not a Fundamental Right?
(A) Right to equality
(b) Right against exploitation
(c) Right to freedom of speech and expression
(d) Right of free compulsory education of all children upto the age of 14

45. The Lok Sabha can be dissolved before the expiry of its normal five year term by
(a) The Prime Minister
(b) The Speaker of Lok Sabha
(c) The President on the recommendation of the Prime Minister
(d) None of the above

Study the following graph carefully and answer Q.No. from 46 to 50 given below it:

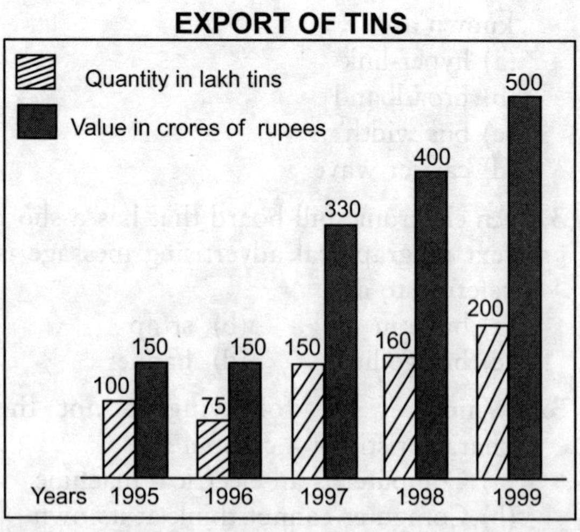

46. In which year the value per tin was minimum?
(a) 1995 (b) 1996
(c) 1998 (d) 1999

47. What was the difference between the tins exported in 1997 and 1998?
(a) 10 (b) 1000
(c) 100000 (d) 1000000

48. What was the approximate percentage increase in export value from 1995 to 1999?
(a) 350 (b) 330.3
(c) 433.3 (d) None of these

49. What was the percentage drop in export quantity from 1995 to 1996?
(a) 75 (b) 50
(c) 25 (d) None of these

50. If in 1998, the tins were exported at the same rate per tin as that in 1997, what would be the value (in crores of rupees) of export in 1998?
(a) 400 (b) 375
(c) 352 (d) 330

ANSWERS

1. (c)	2. (d)	3. (b)	4. (a)	5. (c)
6. (d)	7. (d)	8. (a)	9. (a)	10. (b)
11. (a)	12. (b)	13. (a)	14. (a)	15. (b)
16. (a)	17. (d)	18. (a)	19. (d)	20. (c)
21. (b)	22. (d)	23. (b)	24. (b)	25. (c)
26. (b)	27. (b)	28. (c)	29. (a)	30. (b)
31. (b)	32. (a)	33. (d)	34. (c)	35. (c)
36. (a)	37. (c)	38. (d)	39. (c)	40. (b)
41. (c)	42. (a)	43. (a)	44. (d)	45. (c)
46. (a)	47. (a)	48. (d)	49. (c)	50. (c)

PAPER–II

1. Marx believed that western society had developed through the following main epochs. They are
(a) primitive communism, ancient society, feudal society and capitalist society
(b) savagery, feudalism and capitalism
(c) slavery, barbarism and feudalism
(d) feudalism, capitalism and socialism

2. Who first introduced the concept of alienation into sociological theory?
(a) Hegel
(b) August Comte
(c) Marx
(d) Herbert Spencer

3. Changes in social positions with regard to variations in occupations, prestige, income, wealth, power and social class are referred to as
(a) social change
(b) international mobility
(c) social mobility
(d) migration

4. Vertical mobility involves
(a) change in role
(b) change in occupation
(c) change in group
(d) change in social class position

5. _____ refers to the division of a population into strata one on top of another, on the basis of the possession of certain characteristics which the society regards as desirable or less desirable
(a) Social inequality
(b) Social stratification
(c) Caste
(d) Hierarchy

6. Gopal's father who was a big business man lost all his money in gambling. Which of the following connects best the above statement to the concept of class?
   (a) A man is responsible for the class to which he belongs
   (b) Gambling is a bad habit and is accountable for downward mobility
   (c) Class membership can change in an individual's life time
   (d) None of the above
7. Subjective class concept locates individuals in the stratification hierarchy according to judgments of
   (a) analyst
   (b) society
   (c) individual himself
   (d) community
8. According to Weber, the status order tends to be
   (a) universalistic and achievement oriented
   (b) particularistic and ascriptive
   (c) particularistic and achievement oriented
   (d) universalistic and ascriptive
9. According to Weber, as the division of labour becomes more complex, class
   (a) becomes more advanced
   (b) becomes more heterogeneous
   (c) remain essentially the same
   (d) None of the above
10. ______ constitutes the primary model of the estate system.
   (a) Medieval European feudal society
   (b) Spanish society
   (c) Ancient Greek Society
   (d) Medieval Indian Society
11. The Caste system is ______ in nature.
   (a) hierarchical
   (b) symmetrical
   (c) contradictory
   (d) None of the above
12. Due to financial problems at home, a land less labourer from a village moved to city to work as a factory labourer. This is an example of
   (a) horizontal mobility
   (b) vertical downward mobility
   (c) vertical mobility
   (d) social mobility
13. If a person becomes a minister from an ordinary shopkeeper, the mobility is called
   (a) upward mobility
   (b) downward mobility
   (c) horizontal mobility
   (d) None of the above
14. The functionalists are primarily concerned with the ______ of social stratification, with is contribution to the maintenance and well being of society.
   (a) function (b) aims
   (c) value (d) nature
15. According to Weber, communal division is an example of
   (a) status groups (b) class
   (c) party (d) caste
16. According to ______, a social class is any portion of a community marked off from the rest by the social status,
   (a) MacIver and Page
   (b) Weber
   (c) Marshall
   (d) Sorokin
17. According to ______, castes are the modified forms of guilds.
   (a) occupational theory
   (b) political theory
   (c) evolutionary theory
   (d) None of the above

18. Social stratification is the mechanism which attaches unequal rewards and privileges to the different positions in society. Whom is this statement attributed to?
(a) Parsons
(b) Tumin
(c) Weber
(d) Davis and Moore

19. Interdependence among castes is termed as by Srinivas.
(a) Jajmani system (b) Vertical unity
(c) Horizontal unity (d) Mutuality

20. According to ______, class is determined by a person's market situation.
(a) Marx
(b) Weber
(c) Ralph Dahrendorf
(d) Lenin

21. Which of the following statements is true?
(a) Class is more open than caste
(b) The caste system is believed to have been divinely ordained whereas classes are not founded on religious dogmas
(c) Caste is more open then class
(d) Both (a) and (b) are true

22. While discussing stratification who of the following has/have referred to effective role allocation and performance?
(a) Parsons
(b) Tumin
(c) Davis and Tumin
(d) Davis and Moore

23. "Function and function alone is responsible for the origin of caste structure is India's." Who said this?
(a) Majumdar (b) Ghurye
(c) Nesfield (d) Risley

24. Who has pointed out three sets of characteristics used as a basis of ranking, viz., possessions, qualities and performances?
(a) Max Weber (b) Functionalists
(c) Talcott Parsons (d) R.K. Merton

25. The concept of ______ is fundamental to the caste system and every type of caste relation is governed by it.
(a) rites (b) pollution
(c) power (d) prestige

26. According to ______, class is a historical category.
(a) Weber
(b) Engels
(c) Marx
(d) Ralph Dahrendorf

27. According to Sir Herbert Risley, caste system originated in India due to
(a) an artificial creation by the clever priesthood for permanent division and subjection
(b) racial differences and hypergamy
(c) specialization, of religious duties
(d) hereditary occupations and endogamy

28. Jajmani system is ______.
(a) achieved
(b) hereditary
(c) contractual in nature
(d) None of the above

29. ______ argues that stratification system derive from common values.
(a) Talcott Parsons (b) Weber
(c) Davis and Moore (d) Tumin

30. Pre-revolutionary Russia, as a/an ______ society in which the clergy, the nobility, merchants and peasants were separated into social strata that depended on birth and were controlled by law.
(a) classless (b) caste ridden
(c) estate (d) agricultural

31. Who maintained that those who perform successfully in terms of society's values

will be ranked highly and they will be likely to receive a variety of rewards?
(a) Parsons
(b) Davis
(c) Durkheim
(d) Redcliffe Brown

32. Which of the following is employed to mean the numerous subdivisions of a *varna*?
(a) Jati (b) Caste
(c) Gotra (d) None of the above

33. According to Marx, various forms of exploitative mode of production have been
(a) slavery, feudalism, and capitalism
(b) slavery, barbarism, and capitalism
(c) slavery, bourgeoisie, and capitalism
(d) None of the above

34. According to Marx's classic phrase, the proletariat are a
(a) class in themselves
(b) class for themselves
(c) class by themselves
(d) class through themselves

35. According to Weber, ______ refers to the unequal distribution of economic rewards whereas ______ refers to the unequal distribution of social honour.
(a) class, caste
(b) power, prestige
(c) class, status
(d) caste, class

36. According to ______, social stratification originated on account of religious principles and customs.
(a) Hocart (b) Risley
(c) Ghurye (d) Senart

37. The word 'Caste' owes its origin to ______ word 'Casta'.
(a) Spanish (b) German
(c) Latin (d) Polynesian

38. Who maintained that basically, alienation involves compulsive conformity to norms
(a) Weber (b) Functionalists
(c) Marx (d) Durkheim

39. Membership in the caste is
(a) ascribed
(b) given by the govt.
(c) achieved
(d) God's gift

40. ______ are stratified according to the principles of their consumption of goods as represented by special styles of life.
(a) Classes (b) Status group
(c) Parties (d) Castes

41. According to ______, the Origin of caste system can be found in the nature and quality of social work performed by the various groups of people
(a) guild theory
(b) political theory
(c) occupational theory
(d) racial theory

42. Self-identification is important in determining
(a) objective status
(b) accorded status
(c) subjective status
(d) status

43. According to ______, when a class is somewhat strictly hereditary, we may call it a caste.
(a) MacIver (b) Weber
(c) Sorokin (d) Cooley

44. Objective class concept locates individuals in the stratification hierarchy according to judgments of
(a) analyst
(b) society
(c) community
(d) individual himself

45. According to _____, when status is wholly predetermined, so that men are born to their lot without any hope of changing it, then class takes the extreme form of caste.
   (a) Weber (b) Marx
   (c) MacIver (d) Davis

46. Caste is an _____ group.
   (a) exogamous (b) utilitarian
   (c) endogamous (d) indispensable

47. Weber defines _____ as groups which are specifically concerned with influencing policies and making decisions in the interests of their membership.
   (a) Status groups (b) Classes
   (c) Parties (d) Castes

48. According to Weber
   (a) status and class are always co-related
   (b) status and class are co-related but there are many cases in which they are not
   (c) class determines status
   (d) status determines class

49. In which of the following the first literary traces of caste system are found?
   (a) *Rig veda* (b) *Atharva veda*
   (c) *Yajur veda* (d) *Soma veda*

50. Weber posits the views that _____ reach their most developed form in the caste system of traditional Hindu Society.
   (a) status groups
   (b) castes
   (c) jajmani system
   (d) None of the above

ANSWERS

1. (a)	2. (c)	3. (c)	4. (d)	5. (b)
6. (c)	7. (c)	8. (b)	9. (b)	10. (a)
11. (a)	12. (a)	13. (a)	14. (a)	15. (a)
16. (a)	17. (d)	18. (d)	19. (b)	20. (b)
21. (d)	22. (d)	23. (c)	24. (c)	25. (b)
26. (c)	27. (b)	28. (b)	29. (a)	30. (c)
31. (a)	32. (a)	33. (a)	34. (a)	35. (c)
36. (a)	37. (a)	38. (a)	39. (a)	40. (b)
41. (c)	42. (c)	43. (d)	44. (a)	45. (c)
46. (c)	47. (c)	48. (b)	49. (a)	50. (a)

PRACTICE PAPERS

MOCK TEST–1
PAPER–I

1. A teacher is called the leader of the class because
   (a) he is autocratic emperor of his class
   (b) he masters the art of oratory like a political leader
   (c) he is a maker of the future of his students
   (d) he belongs to a recognised teachers' union

2. The aim of introducing career courses in schools and colleges is to
   (a) increase G.K. in students
   (b) develop the ability to make the intelligent choice of jobs
   (c) provide professional knowledge to students
   (d) All of the above

3. The most effective attribute for a teacher is
   (a) Teaching skills (b) Knowledge
   (c) Feedback (d) Management

4. Those teachers are preferred most by students who
   (a) are themselves disciplined
   (b) give important questions before examination
   (c) dictate notes in the class
   (d) can clear their difficulties regarding subject-matter

5. The qualities of a teacher is/are
   (i) He must not give any false promise
   (ii) He must not have any bad habits
   (iii) He should be mentally and physically fit
   (iv) He must not be superstitious about his class and students
   (a) (iii), (iv) and (ii)
   (b) (iv), (i) and (ii)
   (c) (i), (iii) and (iv)
   (d) All of the above

6. A teacher is more effective who can
   (a) motivate students to learn
   (b) control the class
   (c) correct the assignments carefully
   (d) give more information in less time

7. A teacher ought to know the problems prevalent in the field of education because
   (a) he can tell the government about it
   (b) with this knowledge, he can have information about education
   (c) he can tell about the same to another teacher
   (d) only he can do something about solving them

8. We can judge the quality of a research by the
   (a) experience of researcher
   (b) relevance of research
   (c) depth of the research
   (d) methodology followed in conducting the research

9. The theory or model developed through the fundamental research to the actual solution of the problems is applied in
   (a) educational research
   (b) action research

(c) applied research
(d) basic research

10. A write-up based on studies of the census data of a given area is called
(a) Research paper (b) Article
(c) Research report (d) Thesis

Direction: (11-16) Study the following passage and give answer to the questions based on it.

Knowledge creation in many cases requires creativity and idea generation. This is especially important in generating alternative decision support solutions. Some people believe that an individual's creative ability stems primarily from personality traits such as inventiveness, independence, individuality, enthusiasm, and flexibility. However, several studies have found that creativity is not so much a function of individual traits as was once believed, and that individual creativity can be learned and improved. This understanding has led innovative companies to recognise that the key to fostering creativity may be the development of an idea-nurturing work environment. Idea-generation methods and techniques, to be used by individuals or in groups, are consequently being developed. Manual methods for supporting idea generation, such as brain-storming in a group, can be very successful in certain situations. However, in other situations, such an approach is either not economically feasible or not possible. For example, manual methods in group creativity sessions will not work or will not be effective when: (a) there is no time to conduct a proper idea-generation session; (b) there is a poor facilitator (or no facilitator at all); (c) it is too expensive to conduct an idea-generation session; (d) the subject matter is too sensitive for a face-to-face session; or (e) there are not enough participants, the mix of participants is not optimal, or there is no climate for idea generation. In such cases, computerised idea-generation methods have been tried, with frequent success. Idea-generation software is designed to help stimulate a single user or a group to produce new ideas, options and choices. The user does all the work, but the software encourages and pushes, something like a personal trainer. Although idea-generation software is still relatively new, there are several packages on the market. Various approaches are used by idea-generating software to increase the flow of ideas to the user. Idea Fisher, for example, has an associate lexicon of the English language that cross-references words and phrases. These associative links, based on analogies and metaphors, make it easy for the user to be fed words related to a given theme. Some software packages use questions to prompt the user towards new, unexplored patterns of thought. This helps users to break out of cyclical thinking patterns, conquer mental blocks, or deal with bouts of procrastination.

11. The author, in this passage has focused on
(a) individual traits
(b) knowledge creation
(c) creativity
(d) idea-generation

12. Idea-generation software works as if it is a
(a) user-friendly trainer
(b) stimulant
(c) climate creator
(d) knowledge package

13. Which among the following personality traits is not believed to be a factor contributing to an individual's creative ability?
(a) Flexibility (b) Individuality
(c) Sophistication (d) Enthusiasm

14. In certain occasions, manual methods for the support of idea-generation
(a) can be less expensive
(b) do not need a facilitator

(c) require a mix of optimal participants
(d) are alternatively effective

15. Mental blocks, bouts of procrastination and cyclical thinking patterns can be won when
(a) idea-generation software prompts questions
(b) individuals acquire a neutral attitude towards the software
(c) manual methods are removed
(d) innovative companies employ electronic thinking methods

16. Fostering creativity needs an environment of
(a) decision support systems
(b) alternative individual factors
(c) idea-nurturing
(d) decision support solutions

17. For controlling noise in a classroom, the best method of communication is
(a) remaining calm and just looking at student
(b) saying 'don't talk'
(c) continue teaching without caring for noise
(d) raising one's voice above students voice

18. In India, Education TV was first introduced in the year
(a) 1978 (b) 1959
(c) 1987 (d) 1998

19. The failure of the teacher to communicate his ideas well to students may result into:
I. Classroom indiscipline.
II. Decrease in attendance in class.
III. Loss of student's interest in class.
(a) Only II (b) Only III
(c) Only I (d) All of these

20. Visualisation in the instructional process cannot increase
(a) curiosity and concentration
(b) interest and motivation
(c) stress and boredom
(d) retention and adaptation

21. Communication helps in
(a) entertainment
(b) integration of country
(c) cultural promotion
(d) All of the above

22. "Because you deserve to know" is the punchline used by
(a) *Hindustan Times*
(b) *The Telegraph*
(c) *The Times of India*
(d) *India Today*

23. Find the odd one out from the following groups of letters.
(a) UlmnE (b) AbcdE
(c) ApqrL (d) IfghO

24. The ambitious computerisation program of the Government of India aimed at connecting 60,000 government schools through internet is known as
(a) Vidya Vahini (b) Gyan Vahini
(c) Kalpana project (d) Vidya Vani

25. Find the wrong number in the following sequence.
225, 336, 447, 557, 669, 771
(a) 669 (b) 557
(c) 336 (d) 771

26. In this question two words are given which have certain relationship followed by four paired lettered words. Select the paired words, that has the same relation as original pair.
ROOF : FOUNDATION
(a) Plateau : Valley
(b) Peak : Valley
(c) Mountain : Grassland
(d) Hill : Mountain

27. "Communication is a verbal process by which we understand each other and reduce uncertainty through the use of

symbol." Who is the author of this statement?

(a) David K. Barlo
(b) Dance
(c) P.S.K. Serichavenko
(d) K.J. Newman

28. Find out the missing number:

8 24 12 ? 18 54

(a) 28 (b) 32
(c) 36 (d) 38

29. A D C F
C F E H
O R ? ?

(a) JK (b) RN
(c) SU (d) QT

30. 3, 12, 27, 48, 75, (?), 147.

(a) 111 (b) 108
(c) 117 (d) 122

31. In this question four words have been given, out of which three are alike in some manner and the fourth one is different. Choose the odd one out.

(a) Epigraphy (b) Ecology
(c) Archaeology (d) Palaeontology

32. Which of the following figures will represent the right relationship between, societies, societies who run schools, DPS society.

(a)  (b) 

(c)  (d) 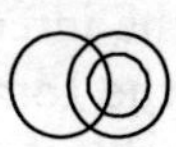

33. **Statements:**

I. All students are ambitious.
II. All ambitious persons are hard working.

Conclusions:

(i) All students are hard working.
(ii) All hardly working people are not ambitious.

Which of the following is correct?

(a) Only (i) is correct
(b) Only (ii) is correct
(c) Both (i) and (ii) are correct
(d) Neither (i) nor (ii) is correct

34. In a certain code language:

'pit dit mit' means: 'Reena went to Delhi'.
'dit ket set' means: 'Delhi is closing'.
'mit set un' means: 'Reena is educated'.
Then what is the code for 'went'?

(a) dit (b) mit
(c) pit (d) None of these

35. EDITOR : MAGAZINE

Choose the pair from the answer choices that best expresses the relationship similar to that expressed by the question pair.

(a) Novel : Writer
(b) Director : Film
(c) Poem : Poet
(d) Chair : Carpenter

36. Should education in India be made free?

Arguments:

I. Yes, this is the only way to improve the level of literacy.
II. No, this would add already heavy burden on the exchequer.

(a) Only argument I is strong
(b) Only argument II is strong
(c) Both the arguments are strong
(d) None of these

Direction: (37-41) Study the table and answer the questions:

Export of Pulses and Import of Onion (in ₹ crores)

Year	Export of Pulses (in ₹ crores)	Import of Onion (in ₹ crores)
1998-99	44	58
1999-00	45	50

2000-01	60	54
2001-02	56	60
2002-03	92	68
2003-04	100	78
2004-05	68	60

37. During which year there was a maximum fall in export?
(a) 2004-05 (b) 2001-02
(c) 2003-04 (d) None of these

38. The percent of increase of imports in 2003-04 over 2002-03 is
(a) 14.9% (b) 14.7%
(c) 18.4% (d) 18.9%

39. In 1999-2000, the ratio of export to the import is
(a) 19:11 (b) 11:9
(c) 13:17 (d) 9:10

40. During which year there was maximum increase in import over its preceding year?
(a) 2003-04 (b) 2000-01
(c) 2001-02 (d) 2002-03

41. During which year there was minimum increase in import over its preceding year?
(a) 2003-04 (b) 2002-03
(c) 2001-02 (d) None of these

42. The sum of a positive number and its reciprocal is twice the difference of the number and its reciprocal. The number is
(a) $\sqrt{3}$ (b) $\sqrt{2}$
(c) $\frac{1}{\sqrt{2}}$ (d) $\frac{1}{\sqrt{3}}$

43. Which one of the following states has the maximum number of Wildlife Sanctuaries (National Park and Sanctuaries)?
(a) Madhya Pradesh
(b) Rajasthan
(c) Uttar Pradesh
(d) West Bengal

Directions: (44-48) Answer the following questions based on the graph given below:

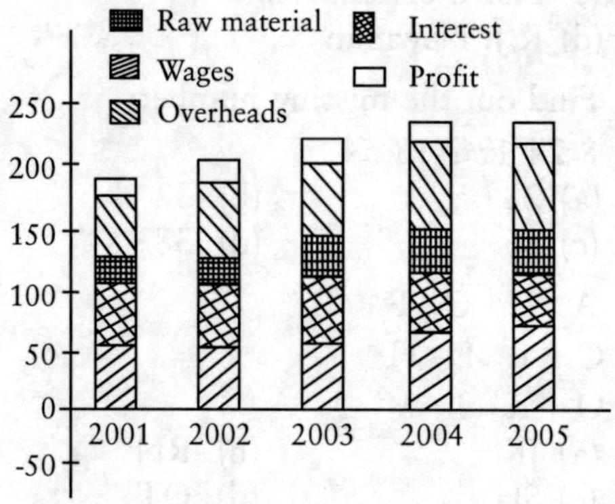

44. Which component of the cost of production has remained almost unchanged over the period 2001-05?
(a) Wages (b) Interest
(c) Raw material (d) Overheads

45. In which year was the increase in raw material maximum?
(a) 2004 (b) 2002
(c) 2003 (d) 2001

46. What percent of costs did the profits from over the period?
(a) 7% (b) 5%
(c) 2% (d) 1%

47. In which period was the change in profit maximum?
(a) 2002-03 (b) 2001-02
(c) 2004-05 (d) 2003-04

48. If the interest component is not included in the total cost calculation, which year would show the maximum profit per unit cost?
(a) 2001 (b) 2002
(c) 2003 (d) 2005

49. How many types of emergencies have been envisaged by the constitution?

(a) One (b) Two
(c) Three (d) Four

50. Photocopying and other electrical equipments produce
(a) methane
(b) ethane
(c) ozone
(d) hydrogen dioxide

PAPER–II

1. Who coined the term 'sociology' and is generally considered to be the 'founder' of sociology?
(a) Auguste Comte
(b) Karl Marx
(c) Emile Durkheim
(d) Max Weber

2. The general fertility rate fell between 1964 and 2000 because of
(a) there being fewer women of childbearing age than there were in the first half of the century.
(b) increases in the age of marriage and the age at which childbearing begins.
(c) the risk of diseases caused by poverty, poor housing and bad sanitation.
(d) errors in the measurement of birth rates and production of statistics.

3. **Assertion (A):** Between the years 1618 to 1648, European population decreased substantiality.
Reason (R): Between the years 1618 to 1648, European countries witnessed revolutionary change in science and technology and were passing through a period of relative peace and tranquility.
Codes:
(a) If both (A) and (R) are true and (R) is the correct explanation of (A).
(b) If both (A) and (R) are true, but (R) is not the correct explanation of (A).
(c) If (A) is true, but (R) is false.
(d) If (A) is false, but (R) is true.

4. Society symbolises the network of
(a) orientations
(b) inter-connections
(c) social relationships
(d) human relationships

5. The Shuddhi movement for bringing back to the Hindu fold people converted to other religions from Hinduism was launched by
(a) Ram-Krishna Mission
(b) Prarthana Sabha
(c) Arya Samaj
(d) Brahmo Samaj

6. Socialisation is
(a) a tendency of social theorists to explain everything in terms of social causes.
(b) the formation of an attachment bond between an infant and his carer.
(c) the historical process by which societies change from traditional to modern.
(d) the process of becoming part of a society by learning its norms and values.

7. Match List I (Concepts) with List II (Meaning) and select the correct answer using the codes given below the lists:
List I (Concepts)
A. Vertical mobility
B. Horizontal mobility
C. Inter-generational mobility
D. Intra-generational mobility

List II (Meaning)
i. Change in role but not in status
ii. Son's occupational status being different from that of the father

iii. A person's second job being lower than the first one
iv. A caste improving its status
v. Movement from a village to a city

Codes:	A	B	C	D
(a)	iv	i	ii	iii
(b)	iii	v	ii	i
(c)	iv	iii	i	ii
(d)	ii	i	iv	iii

8. Peer group is a group whose members share similar
(a) values
(b) study circle and books
(c) playground
(d) circumstances

9. Chodorow (1978) argued that gender socialization occurred through
(a) girls being attached to their mothers but then breaking away.
(b) both boys and girls being closely attached to their mothers, but then boys breaking away.
(c) boys being attached to their fathers and girls to their mothers.
(d) both boys and girls being closely attached to their fathers, but girls breaking away.

10. A social group is a
(a) organisation of people for purpose.
(b) association of people.
(c) system of social interaction.
(d) gathering of people.

11. The concept which Mckim Marriott put forward as the opposite of his concept of 'universalisation' for explaining social change in village India is
(a) Traditionalisation
(b) Parochialisation
(c) Localisation
(d) Globalisation

12. Which tribe practises non-fraternal polyandry?
(a) Toda of Nilgiri
(b) Nayars of Malabar
(c) Kot of Kerala
(d) Khasi tribe

13. In Parsons' view, the function of the sick role was to
(a) provide normative expectations to minimise the disruptive effects of illness on social life.
(b) provide a set of guidelines for medical staff to treat patients in hospital.
(c) create a sense of meaning and order out of the illness experience.
(d) create a scapegoat for people to blame, in the context of family life.

14. Durkheim defined social facts as
(a) the way scientists construct knowledge in a social context.
(b) ways of acting, thinking, and feeling that are collective and social in origin.
(c) ideas and theories that have no basis in the external, physical world.
(d) data collected about social phenomena that are proven to be correct.

15. Ethnographic research produces qualitative data because
(a) it is conducted over a period of several years.
(b) the findings are amenable to statistical analysis.
(c) it compares findings from a number of different cases.
(d) it uncovers rich, detailed accounts from an insider's perspective.

16. 'Pattern variables' are _____ in number
(a) five (b) three
(c) six (d) four

17. It is useful to have a diversity of theories in sociology because

(a) sociologists can choose the theory that best fits the data they have collected.
(b) human behaviour is so complicated that no single theory would be adequate.
(c) innumerable theories have been developed in the many fields of sociology.
(d) it removes the need to assess a theory according to the empirical evidence.

18. To whose name this diagram may be associated?

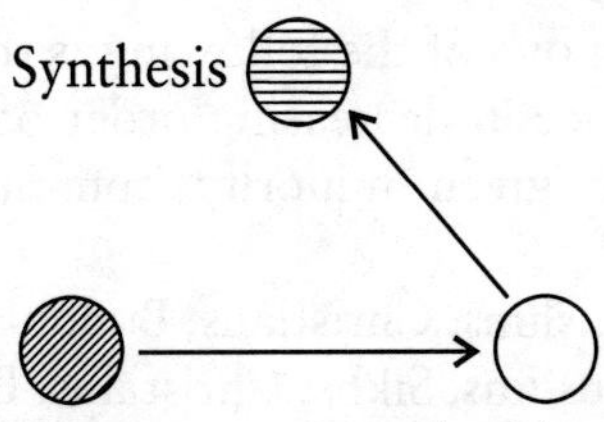

(a) Marx (b) Weber
(c) Pareto (d) Mosca

19. Stratification refers to a division of society into
(a) group
(b) economic activity
(c) individual basis
(d) kinship

20. Which among the following statements is not correct?
(a) No community can be self sufficient these days.
(b) In past communities used to be self sufficient, politically, socially or economically.
(c) The term community denotes almost uniformly and permanently shared lives of people over a definite range.
(d) Every community is self sufficient these days.

21. Social Stratification
(a) causes social disintegration.
(b) gives support to untouchability.
(c) is an unavoidable phenomenon.
(d) weakens existing social structure.

22. Critics of the spread of Western cultural products across the globe argue that a cultural empire has been created. What term do they use to describe this?
(a) Media globalization
(b) Media saturation
(c) Media imperialism
(d) Media penetration

23. Who defined sociology as "a scheme for scientific social development."
(a) Montesque (b) J.B. Mckee
(c) Auguste Comte (d) G.D. Mitchell

24. A social group is a
(a) organisation of people for purpose.
(b) association of people.
(c) system of social interaction.
(d) gathering of people.

25. In the context of Randall Collin's analysis, identify the correct one
(a) Moves from macro-level to Meso-level and to micro-level social processes
(b) Moves from micro-level to Meso-level and to micro-level social processes
(c) Moves from micro-level to macro-level social processes
(d) Moves from macro-level to micro-level processes being closely attached to their fathers, but girls breaking away.

26. Agency refers to
(a) purposeful action.
(b) how far you trust doctors and politicians.
(c) personal qualities and desires.
(d) the power you can exert in a relationship.

27. The view of anti-psychiatrists like Scheff was that mental illness was

(a) a socially negotiated 'insanity role' into which anyone could drift.
(b) shaped by the processes of interaction taking place within the family and community.
(c) a form of deviance, occurring when people challenged taken for granted expectations about interaction.
(d) All of the above.

28. Durkheim defined social facts as
(a) the way scientists construct knowledge in a social context.
(b) ways of acting, thinking, and feeling that are collective and social in origin.
(c) ideas and theories that have no basis in the external, physical world.
(d) data collected about social phenomena that are proven to be correct.

29. Ethnographic research produces qualitative data because
(a) it is conducted over a period of several years.
(b) the findings are amenable to statistical analysis.
(c) it compares findings from a number of different cases.
(d) it uncovers rich, detailed accounts from an insider's perspective.

30. "Ad-hocracy" is the system whereby there will be an administrative system with transient project teams, task forces and ad hoc committees which would give dynamism and replace bureaucracies. This terms was coined by
(a) Alvin Toffler (b) Goldthorpe
(c) Peter Blau (d) A. Etzioni

31. When might unplanned multi-stage research be described as a "salvage operation"?
(a) When the second research strategy is used to explain unexpected or puzzling results.
(b) When the researcher abandons their original strategy and starts all over again.
(c) When it is ethically unsound to use only one research strategy.
(d) When there is a paradigm shift from quantitative to qualitative research.

32. Who is the author of the work *Class and Class Conflict in an Industrial Society*?
(a) Karl Marx
(b) S.M. Lipset
(c) Ralf Dahrendorf
(d) Raymond Aron

33. Which one of the following is the correct sequence in decreasing order of the sizes of the given minority communities in India?
(a) Muslims, Christians, Buddhists, Sikhs.
(b) Muslims, Sikhs, Christians, Buddhists.
(c) Christians, Muslims, Sikhs, Buddhists.
(d) Muslims, Christians, Sikhs, Buddhists.

34. Human and animal societies share all but one of the following characteristics
(a) Shared beliefs and collective destiny.
(b) Population and common territory.
(c) Both sexes and all ages.
(d) None of the above.

35. When studying the subject of aggression and violence, sociologists are most likely to consider?
(a) Why levels of aggression are higher in some societies or groups than in others.
(b) The cognitive processes through which anger can explode in aggressive behaviour.
(c) The aggressive images activated in individuals by different types of weapons.
(d) The affective processes through which anger can explode in aggressive behaviour.

36. According to W.E.B. Dubois, progress for African-Americans in the aftermath of slavery
(a) required them to move to large cities where they would be accepted as equals in government, religion, and education.
(b) depended on the small group of African-Americans receiving the same thorough and extensive education as the most talented White Americans were able to access.
(c) involved their use of skills they already had from farming, domestic work, and labors of rural life rather than being forced to learn new skills in the late 1800s.
(d) required that they be trained and prepared as craftspeople and service employees so they could become immediately self-sufficient.

37. Functionalism in social anthropology arose as a critique of
(a) individualism and positivism
(b) evolutionism and particularism
(c) positivism and organicism
(d) evolutionism and diffusionism

38. A social mechanism for preventing certain kinship bonds from falling into neglect in a matrilineal society is
(a) Kin Cherishing
(b) Kin-contact
(c) Amitate
(d) Control mechanism

39. For understanding why Sanskritisation has gone such a short way in so long line in the festival of Kishan Garhi, the concept of primary or endogenous process of civilisation offers useful guidance. By definition, an endogenous civilisation is one whose great tradition originates by the universalization process. Who was of this opinion?
(a) Mckim Marriott
(b) S.C. Dubey
(c) Milton Senger
(d) Oscar Lewis

40. I once asked an Australian native why he had to avoid his mother-in-law, and his reply was 'because she is my best friend in the world, she has given me my wife, the mutual respect between son-in-law and parents-in-law is a mode of friendship,—to whom does this statement belong?
(a) Slegman
(b) Emile Durkheim
(c) W.H.R. Rivers
(d) Radcliffe Brown

41. The 'demographic transition' is a social trend that involves
(a) a change in the principal causes of death and disease since industrialization.
(b) a reduction in population size, caused by a higher rate of emigration than immigration.
(c) a decline in the birth rate, greater life expectancy, and an ageing population.
(d) increased birth and death rates, resulting in a relatively young population.

42. **Assertion (A):** Rapid change in the occupational structure may raise the question of whether a particular movement is vertical or merely horizontal.
Reason (R): Information we have about social mobility in earlier times is less than exact and is not easy to compare with our knowledge of the amount of mobility in recent times.

Codes:

(a) Both (A) and (R) are true and (R) is the correct explanation for (A).
(b) Both (A) and (R) are true, but (R) is not the correct explanation for (A).
(c) (A) is true, but (R) is false.
(d) (A) is false, but (R) is true.

43. Who among the following started self-respect movement. Advocated the rejection of Brahman priests in rituals of weddings, forcible temple entry, the burning of Manusmriti and finally the rejection of religion and the propagation of atheism?
(a) E.V. Ramaswami Naicker
(b) Sri Narayana Guru
(c) K. Kamraj
(d) B.R. Ambedkar

44. Which of the following statements are true?
1. All social movements strive only for elevation of status.
2. Reform movements aim to change some parts of a society while revolutionary movements went to reconstruct the entire social order.
3. Social movements help an individual in a society to relate himself to a larger group in that society.

Codes:

(a) 2 and 3 (b) 1 and 2
(c) 1, 2 and 3 (d) 3 only

45. Mark out from among the following the racial group, that is said to have come from the North Eastern side.
(a) Mediterranean
(b) Later Mediterranean
(c) Mongoloid
(d) Proto-Australoids

46. Freud's notion of the 'ego' referred to
(a) the unconscious mass of instinctive drives that may be repressed.
(b) the self as a whole: an unstable mix of conscious and unconscious elements.
(c) the conscious part of the mind that regulates emotional drives on a practical, rational level.
(d) the neurotic part of the mind that longs for belonging and may suffer an inferiority complex.

47. In the United States social darwinism enjoyed a great vogue in the late nineteenth century, and profound by influenced sociological theorising. Who was its chief exponent?
(a) W.G. Sumner (b) Robert Redfield
(c) Morgan (d) Albion Small

48. Peer group is a group whose members share similar
(a) values
(b) study circle and books
(c) playground
(d) circumstances

49. Stratification refers to a division of society into
(a) group
(b) economic activity
(c) individual basis
(d) kinship

50. Regional community aims at
(a) cultural exchange
(b) economic co-operation
(c) balanced development
(d) All of the above

PAPER–III

1. "Tribe is an indigenous unit speaking a common language, claiming a common descent, living in a particular geographical area, backward in technology, pre-literate, loyally observing social and political

customs based on kinship." Whose definition is this?
(a) Radcliffe Brown
(b) Indigenous People Conference, Sav Paulo 1937
(c) A conference at Shillong in 1962
(d) Earth Summit at Rio in 1992

2. **Assertion (A):** According to structural functionalism, social life is maintained despite a complete turnover in its membership.
Reason (R): In every generation each society develops structures which are found appropriate for meeting the demands of social life.
Codes:
(a) If both (A) and (R) are true and (R) is the correct explanation of (A).
(b) If both (A) and (R) are true, but (R) is not the correct explanation of (A).
(c) If (A) is true, but (R) is false.
(d) If (A) is false, but (R) is true.

3. Society is defined as a group of individuals
(a) who share common territory.
(b) each of whom interacts with each of the other members somewhat frequently.
(c) who share common culture.
(d) with common blood group.

4. A researcher mailed 1,000 questionnaires to members of a labor union and received 300 back. Most of those who returned the questionnaires indicated that they were dissatisfied with the union. Results based only on the returned questionnaires are most likely contaminated by
(a) statistical regression.
(b) response rate bias.
(c) researcher bias.
(d) confusing correlation and causation.

5. Consider the following statements.
Sri Narayana Dharma Paripalana Movement started in Kerala by Sri Narayana Guru Swamy focussed on
1. Right of admission to schools.
2. Reservation in government jobs.
3. Scheduling of deprived castes.
4. Entry into temple roads.
Codes:
(a) 3 only (b) 1, 2 and 4
(c) 1, 2 and 3 (d) 2, 3 and 4

6. Nearly universal norm for marriage in all societies is
(a) Parallel-cousin marriage
(b) Clan exogamy
(c) Clan endogamy
(d) Lineage endogamy

7. Match List I (Book) with List II (Authors) and select the correct answer using the codes given below the lists.
List I (Books)
A. *Social and Cultural Mobility*
B. *Education in Ancient India*
C. *Caste, Class and Power*
D. *India's Path of Development*

List II (Authors)
i. Pilrim A. Sorokin ii. A.S. Altekar
iii. Andra Beleille iv. P.K. Bose
v. M.N. Srinivas

Codes:	**A**	**B**	**C**	**D**
(a)	v	iv	ii	i
(b)	v	iii	i	ii
(c)	iv	v	iii	ii
(d)	i	ii	iii	iv

8. What constitutes the legal sovereign? Mark out the legal sovereign.
(a) The Prime Minister in Parliament
(b) The President in Parliament
(c) The Speaker of Lok Sabha
(d) The Chairman of Rajya Sabha

9. Polyandry may be classified into two groups. Which among the following is that?
(a) Hypergamy and hypogamy
(b) Cross cousin and parallel cousin

(c) Levirate and sororate
(d) Adelphic and Non-adelphic

10. Anne Sociologique was founded in 1898 by
(a) Thomas Hobbes
(b) Saint Simon
(c) Emile Durkheim
(d) Herbert Spencer

11. Which among the following is correct? The term role-set has been coined to refer
(a) to the total number of occupants of the correlative social positions when a particular occupant of a particular position is taken as a point of reference.
(b) to the total complex of other social positions with which any particular social position is characteristically connected.
(c) Both (a) and (b) are false.
(d) Both (a) and (b) are true.

12. Broadly, there are two main approaches to the study of social stratification. They are
(a) International and conflict
(b) Functional and liberal
(c) Functional and international
(d) Functional and conflict

13. The concept which Mckim Marriott put forward as the opposite of his concept of 'universalisation' for explaining social change in village India is
(a) Traditionalisation
(b) Parochialisation
(c) Localisation
(d) Globalisation

14. In Parsons' view, the function of the sick role was to
(a) provide normative expectations to minimise the disruptive effects of illness on social life.
(b) provide a set of guidelines for medical staff to treat patients in hospital.
(c) create a sense of meaning and order out of the illness experience.
(d) create a scapegoat for people to blame, in the context of family life.

15. According to whom the 'self' develops in a social context and is nurtured by primary groups?
(a) Mead
(b) Freud
(c) Charles H. Cooley
(d) Ruth Benedict

16. One of the ethical problems with covert participant observation is
(a) deceiving the respondents as to the reason for your presence.
(b) not being able to write comprehensive fieldnotes or record conversations.
(c) subjecting the participants to physical harm.
(d) observing people outside of their natural setting.

17. What does the acronym "CAQDAS" stand for?
(a) Complicated Analytical Questions Deserving Answers Soon.
(b) Computer Assisted Qualitative Data Analysis Software.
(c) Content Analysis Quantification: Durkheim and Statistics.
(d) Constant Aggravation Queried Directly and Swiftly.

18. Why is it argued that qualitative research may not really be 'naturalistic'?
(a) Because it is concerned with the social world rather than the natural world.
(b) Because participant observation has to be overt and so causes reactivity effects.
(c) Because methods such as interviews and focus groups constitute artificial social settings.

(d) Because quantitative methods such as structured observation tend to take place in more naturalistic environments.

19. Who was of the opinion that strict adherence to the norms of society itself produces a type of deviance?
(a) Robert M. Williams
(b) Howard Becker
(c) Sutherland
(d) Parsons

20. Orientalists were scholars who studied the cultures of
(a) Egypt and Mesopotamia.
(b) Far-East countries.
(c) India and China.
(d) Greek and Roman.

21. Which of the following is not one of the basic assumptions of C.A.?
(a) Analysis is grounded in data.
(b) Talk is structured.
(c) Talk is forged contextually.
(d) Talk can be measured and predicted.

22. Under which of the following circumstances folkways develop into more?
1. Their fulfilment comes to be regarded as necessary and vital to the groups welfare.
2. Society begins to show more tolerance including their violations.
3. People come, to resort to informal sanctions such as ridicule and mild criticism.
4. The idea of morality, right and wrong comes to be attached to them.

Codes:
(a) 1 and 4 (b) 3 and 2
(c) 1 and 3 (d) 2 and 4

23. Which among the following is not correct regarding the advantages of polyandry?
(a) Members feel security
(b) It leads to sterility
(c) Divorce is not easy
(d) Division of property is not easy.

24. While analysing the development of self who has used the concept 'significant others'?
(a) Mead (b) Giddings
(c) MacIver (d) Cooley

25. Social norms are
(a) the symbolic representation of social groups in the mass media.
(b) creative activities such as gardening, cookery and craftwork.
(c) rules and expectations about interaction that regulate social life.
(d) religious beliefs about how the world ought to be.

26. Earliest reaction to Brahmanic ritualism came from
(a) Upanishadic thinkers
(b) Lord Mahavira
(c) Lord Buddha
(d) Vedas

27. Economic aid has largely failed to promote modernization in the developing countries because
(a) the United Nations has refused to call on rich countries to provide it.
(b) there are no clearly defined projects into which the money can be directed.
(c) debt repayments with interest can be greater than the amount of money received.
(d) debt repayments with interest can be greater than the amount of money received.

28. In Marx's theory, the 'mode of production' means

(a) the average measure of productivity under capitalism.
(b) the way in which products are made in a factory.
(c) an integral part of the superstructure of a society.
(d) the organization of a society's technical and human resources.

29. What does an empiricist believe?
(a) It is the sociologist's aim to understand the meaning of social action.
(b) We should not apply natural science methods to social science research.
(c) Research conducted within the British empire was biased and unreliable.
(d) Knowledge, in the form of 'facts', should be gained through sensory experience.

30. How does quantification help the qualitative researcher avoid being accused of anecdotalism?
(a) By providing a structure to an otherwise unstructured dataset.
(b) By allowing them to focus on extreme examples in the data and ignore the rest.
(c) By providing some idea of the prevalence of an usual or striking response.
(d) By making it more likely that official statistics will be included in their report.

31. The 'grey goo problem' refers to
(a) clouds of toxic smoke particles emitted from high density urban areas.
(b) the effects of oil spillages upon wild birds in areas of isolated coast.
(c) the polluting effects caused by detergents and domestic waste.
(d) the possibility of nano-size particles self-replicating uncontrollably.

32. Frank (1967) made the claim that 'underdeveloped' societies were
(a) reluctant to surrender their traditional ways of life.
(b) insufficiently involved in the international capitalist economy.
(c) the 'metropoles' to which 'satellite' countries were attached.
(d) economically dependent on the wealthy countries that exploited them.

33. Government has a significant role in an industrial society why?
(a) To protect the industries.
(b) To look after the welfare of the technocrats.
(c) To control the risings of working class.
(d) Top take care of trade and a strategical complexities.

34. Among the simple societies, agriculture is the
(a) fourth level of development.
(b) first level of development.
(c) second level of development.
(d) third level of development.

35. Smith and Tomlinson argued that
(a) racism in schools undermined the move towards equality of opportunity for children from ethnic minorities.
(b) differences in ethnic background were more significant than class or gender in predicting educational achievement.
(c) gender differences in educational achievement could be attributed to inequalities of class.
(d) school character far outweighed ethnic background in determining educational success.

36. In Vedic Sociology, which among the following conclusions, you think, is not correct?

(a) The arrangement was more structural than social.
(b) That nothing was left to accidents, and change in structuring the society.
(c) The Vedic social structure took care both of individual and society.
(d) Education was given the highest importance.

37. Of the following sets of sociologists, one does not fit with the rest. Which one is it?
(a) E. Durkheim, Evans-Pritchard, S.F. Nadel, C. Levi-Strauss.
(b) A. Comte, H. Spencer, L.H. Morgan.
(c) E. Durkheim, B. Malinowski, A.R. Radcliffe Brown, K. Davis.
(d) R. Linton, M. Banton, R. Merton, T. Parsons.

38. Margaret Mead suggested that
(a) gender roles in three New Guinea societies were identical and so must be biologically determined.
(b) adolescence and gender roles varied between societies and so were culturally determined.
(c) anthropological fieldwork can be problematic because the researcher's values affect the way they interpret their observations.
(d) adolescence in the USA is a time of relative calm compared to the experience in Japan and Europe.

39. The case of the former Soviet Union supports Kerr *et al.'s* (1960) claim that
(a) democratic governments serve the interests of a ruling elite.
(b) totalitarian regimes are incompatible with the requirements of advanced industrial technology.
(c) communist societies disperse power between various political parties.
(d) advanced industrial technology strengthens the power of totalitarian regimes.

40. The questionnaire method of data collection is not applicable if there is
(a) a big area.
(b) a heterogeneous area.
(c) an illiteracy.
(d) an overpopulation.

41. Where X means original scores, N means the number of persons in the group and M means the actual means of the scores, the formula for the calculation of the standard deviation would be

(a) $\sqrt{\frac{\sum X^2}{N}+M^2}$ (b) $\sqrt{\frac{\sum X^2 - M^2}{N}}$

(c) $\sqrt{\frac{\sum m^2}{N}-X^2}$ (d) $\sqrt{\frac{\sum X^2}{N}-M^2}$

42. According to Marx, capitalism is driven by
(a) the pursuit of profit.
(b) the ideology of mass consumption.
(c) the megalomania of the ruling-class.
(d) fluctuations in the market.

43. Which among the following is not correct?
(a) Social strata cannot be easily observed and distributed.
(b) Strata in the earth crust cannot be directly observed and described.
(c) Strata in the earth crust can be directly observed and described.
(d) Social stratification is more complex.

44. Who holds this view: "The continuity between natural history and human history may allow numerical concepts to be introduced into the latter. Historical changes can be judged by the extent to which they have helped our species to survive and multiply?

(a) E. Durkheim
(b) Hobhouse L.T.
(c) MacIver and Page
(d) V. Gordon Childe

45. "The state or process of adjustment to a conflict situation in which overt expressions of hostility are avoided and certain compensatory advantages, economic, social or psychological, are gained by both sides, while leaving the source of conflict unresolved and allowing the structural inequalities giving rise to minority subordination to persist." This is the definition of
(a) Cooperation
(b) Accommodation
(c) Assimilation
(d) Both (a) and (c)

46. A survey should avoid asking
(a) short questions
(b) fixed-choice questions
(c) funnelled questions
(d) leading questions

47. Baudrillard argues that increasingly events such as wars and criminal trials are thoroughly media events, not events in the world that are simply reported by the media. What term does he use to describe this?
(a) Hegemonya (b) Simulacra
(c) Ideology (d) Hyperreality

48. Three paths to a definition of sociology described by Alex lnkels does not include
(a) the critical path
(b) the analytical path
(c) the historical path
(d) the empirical path

49. Select the way in which work in early industrial capitalism conventionally differed from work in pre-modern societies.
(a) It was technologically simple.
(b) It was seasonal.
(c) It was carried on at home.
(d) It was waged.

50. Sociological concept which is most closely related to social inequality is
(a) social categorization
(b) social stratification
(c) social classification
(d) social differentiation

ANSWER SHEET

PAPER—I

1. (c)	2. (c)	3. (a)	4. (d)	5. (d)
6. (a)	7. (d)	8. (b)	9. (c)	10. (b)
11. (d)	12. (a)	13. (c)	14. (c)	15. (a)
16. (c)	17. (a)	18. (b)	19. (a)	20. (c)
21. (d)	22. (a)	23. (c)	24. (a)	25. (b)
26. (b)	27. (b)	28. (c)	29. (d)	30. (b)
31. (b)	32. (c)	33. (a)	34. (c)	35. (b)
36. (b)	37. (a)	38. (b)	39. (d)	40. (a)
41. (d)	42. (c)	43. (a)	44. (b)	45. (c)
46. (b)	47. (d)	48. (b)	49. (c)	50. (c)

PAPER—II

1. (a)	2. (b)	3. (c)	4. (c)	5. (c)
6. (d)	7. (a)	8. (d)	9. (b)	10. (c)
11. (b)	12. (b)	13. (a)	14. (b)	15. (d)
16. (a)	17. (b)	18. (a)	19. (a)	20. (b)
21. (a)	22. (c)	23. (d)	24. (c)	25. (b)
26. (a)	27. (b)	28. (b)	29. (d)	30. (c)
31. (a)	32. (c)	33. (a)	34. (a)	35. (a)
36. (d)	37. (c)	38. (c)	39. (a)	40. (d)
41. (c)	42. (a)	43. (a)	44. (c)	45. (c)
46. (c)	47. (c)	48. (d)	49. (a)	50. (d)

PAPER—III

1. (c)	2. (a)	3. (b)	4. (b)	5. (b)
6. (b)	7. (d)	8. (b)	9. (d)	10. (c)
11. (d)	12. (d)	13. (b)	14. (a)	15. (c)
16. (a)	17. (b)	18. (c)	19. (d)	20. (c)
21. (d)	22. (a)	23. (b)	24. (a)	25. (c)
26. (c)	27. (d)	28. (d)	29. (d)	30. (c)
31. (d)	32. (d)	33. (d)	34. (a)	35. (d)
36. (a)	37. (b)	38. (b)	39. (b)	40. (c)
41. (d)	42. (a)	43. (b)	44. (c)	45. (b)
46. (c)	47. (d)	48. (a)	49. (c)	50. (c)

MOCK TEST–2
PAPER–I

1. Minimum program of guidance includes
   (a) occupational information service
   (b) data collector service
   (c) counselling service
   (d) All of the above
2. If majority of students in a class is weak, a teacher should
   (a) not care about intelligent students
   (b) keep his speed of teaching fast so that students comprehension level may increase
   (c) keep his teaching slow which can also be helpful-to bright students
   (d) keep his teaching slow along with some extra guidance to bright students
3. If the principal of your institution is not satisfied with your performance and charge you with the act of negligence of duties, how would you behave with him?
   (a) You would neglect him
   (b) You would take revenge by giving physical and mental agony to him
   (c) You would keep yourself alert and make his efforts unfruitful
   (d) You would take a tough stand against the charges
4. What makes people to undertake research?
   (a) Desire to get intellectual joy of doing some creative work
   (b) Desire to get a research degree along with its consequential benefits
   (c) Desire to face the challenge in solving the unsolved problems
   (d) All of the above
5. Which of the following aims at probing into the phenomenon to formulate a more precise research problem or to develop a new hypothesis?
   (a) Descriptive research
   (b) Conclusive research
   (c) Diagnostic research
   (d) Exploratory research
6. Which of the following is not instructional material?
   (a) Transparency
   (b) Overhead projector
   (c) Printed material
   (d) Audio cassette
7. Of great importance in determining the amount of transference that occurs in the process of learning is the
   (a) knowledge of the teacher
   (b) IQ of the teacher
   (c) presence of identical elements
   (d) use of appropriate elements
8. The characteristic(s) of hypothesis is/are:
   I. It can be tested.
   II. It must consists of known facts.
   III. It must be objective and specific.

(a) I and III (b) I and II
(c) Only I (d) All of these

9. The guide for the research requires which of the following qualities?
(a) Interdisciplinary expertise
(b) Subject matter expertise
(c) Methodological expertise
(d) All of the above

10. Which of the following indicates evaluation?
(a) Seema got 195 marks out of 200
(b) Sapna got 72 percent marks in English
(c) Asha got First Division in final examination
(d) All of the above

Direction: (11-16) Study the following passage and give answer to the questions based on it.

Much of the theoretical literature of archeology in the 1980s devotes considerable energy to bashing the 1970s, and the target often turns out to be the so-called New or Processual Archeology. While many of the attacks come from recent theorists who are attempting to replace it with post-processual archeology, some criticism comes from within what was New Archeology even from the hand of its original champion, Lewis Binford. If scholars from both outside and inside the theoretical developments of the 1970s are rejecting the New Archeology, why am I defending its importance to us today? The answer is very simple...for better or worse, it is us! As Alison Whylie has recently said the New Archeology of the 1960s quickly became everybody's archeology in the 1970s. Most of today's faculty members and senior archeologists were the people who, in one way or another, adopted the teachings of New Archeology. Although most archeologists did not claim to agree with all aspects of New Archeology nor could more than two or three people agree on what it was, virtually one rejected it outright. Typically, each one presented her or his version, often using a New Archeology text as a starting point for pedagogical purposes. Few wanted to be left out of the exciting new theoretical movement of those years, and New Archeology was passed on to the succeeding generation of students who reached maturity in the 1980s and are today's young professionals.

Criticisms now leveled against the New Archeology of the seventies do have merit, but by discounting that era as misguided, critics have overlooked its crucial importance. New Archeology has an important historical role in the developments of the field we have today and it has continuing importance because it is still guiding archeology's trajectory into the future. Equally troubling is that some critics ask us to reject the basic tenets of New Archeology and to replace them with a system often called post processualist archeology. I believe this is rhetoric that not only misrepresents the achievements of the New Archeology of the seventies, but also does not successfully articulate the potential contributions of its own position.

To put the New Archeology of the seventies into perspective, it is important to review the decades leading up to its development. In the first years following World War II, archeology was still a small field, but by the fifties and the sixties, it was expanding rapidly and taking itself quite seriously. Since the launching of Sputnik in 1957 there had emerged a frenzy in the United States to make all disciplines more scientific. Great strides were made in bringing science into archeology through new dating techniques a multidisciplinary approach, early experiments with the use of statistics, and devoting substantial attention to increasing the precision of artifact classification. The sixties provided the nation with both the optimistic Kennedy years, with an emphasis on science and the conviction that we were capable of accomplishing wondrous; things, and the cynical Vietnam era. Coming on the heels of a decade of civil rights unrest, the widespread dissatisfaction with the Vietnam conflict in the late sixties molded a generation of young Americans who were distrustful of established authority. In academic life, there was an increasing emphasis on environment, other cultures, and people oriented disciplines. Anthropology and archeology grew markedly because of these trends. Archeologists were urged to become concerned with sociological issues—the people behind the artifacts.

It was during these decades of rapid change that many of the core concepts of the New Archeology entered the literature. However, they were not, at first, assembled into a program for action that attracted a solid following. Water Taylor advocated the conjuctive approach with little effect, while Leslie White's evolutionism and Julian Styeward's cultural ecology attracted some attention, but largely among cultural anthropologists. Albert Spaulding led a one-man campaign to bring science and statistics into archeology. But the individual whose work catalyzed the New Archeology movement was Lewis Binford, who incorporated these earlier lines of thinking together with an explicit concern for scientific methods and field research designs. Much of Binford's thinking probably crystallised while he was at the University of Michigan, but was during his relatively few years at the University of Chicago that he changed the direction of modern archeology.

11. New Archeology refers to
    (a) newer techniques used in Archeology
    (b) newer inventions used in Archeology
    (c) newer theoretical foundations in Archeology
    (d) None of the above

12. The author defends the Archeology of the 1970's because
    (a) he has a nostalgic feeling about it
    (b) it has research value
    (c) it paved way for newer traditions
    (d) it has historical value

13. The author suggests that
    (a) We should respect new Archeology as a movement in Archeology
    (b) We should go back to the tenets of processual Archeology
    (c) We should treat tenets of new Archeology with respect
    (d) All of the above

14. The importance of Archeology arose from
    (a) the end of World War II
    (b) an increasing scientific outlook
    (c) the launch of Sputnik in 1957
    (d) All of the above

15. Which one of the following is not an area of focus for archeologist?
    (a) Study the interaction of people of small group
    (b) Studying cultures of other people
    (c) Study the social structure of the past societies
    (d) Study the man-environment relationship in the past

16. An archeologist is concerned with
    (a) classification of artefacts
    (b) maintenance of museums
    (c) digging of ancient cities
    (d) All of the above

17. Rhetorics means
    (a) study of the technique and rules for using language effectively
    (b) using language effectively to please or persuade
    (c) excessive use of verbal ornamentation
    (d) All of the above

18. If a receiver replying on 'hmm-mm' or 'Isee'. This type of reply is known as
    (a) positive feedback
    (b) ambiguous feedback

(c) negative feedback
(d) None of these

19. Which of the following FM radio stations is owned by the *Times of India* group?
(a) AIR (b) Radio Rainbow
(c) Radio Mirchi (d) Red FM

20. Find the next number in the following sequence:
9, 8, 25, 12, 49, 18, 121, 26, ?, ?
(a) 142, 36 (b) 169, 36
(c) 225, 36 (d) 196, 36

21. **Statement:** Should there be complete ban on pouched tobacco products (like Gutka) in India?
Arguments:
(i) Yes, it is the most important cause of mouth cancer and mouth ulcer in our country.
(ii) No, there are many people employed in this industry right from manufacturing to retailing. This ban will hamper their livelihood.
Codes:
(a) Only argument (i) is strong
(b) Only argument (ii) is strong
(c) Both the arguments (i) and (ii) are strong
(d) Neither (i) nor (ii) is strong

22. The relationship between Animal, Cows, Dogs can be shown by

(a) 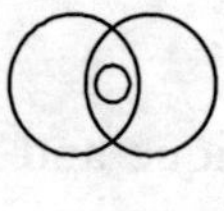 (b) 

(c) 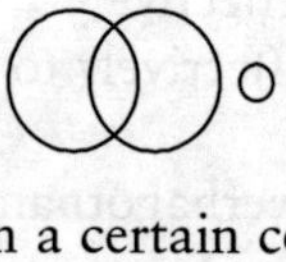 (d) 

23. If in a certain code:
'nso prt kli chn' means 'sharma gets marriage gift'. 'pit lnm wop chn' means 'wife gives marriage gift'. 'tti wop nhi' means 'he gives nothing'. What would mean 'gives'?
(a) kli (b) tti
(c) wop (d) lnm

24. Characteristics of all informal and formal communications are
(a) Same
(b) Structured
(c) Different
(d) None of these

25. Three of the following four are alike in a certain way and so form a group. Find the one which doesn't belong to that group?
(a) Dog (b) Tiger
(c) Horse (d) Lion

26. What is research design?
(a) The methods used in analysis and finding the final conclusion is known as research design.
(b) A researcher needs to prepare a plan of action for his study which is known as research design.
(c) The presentation of final data is known as research design.
(d) None of the above.

27. Recording a television program on a Set Top Box is an example of
(a) content reference
(b) time-shifting
(c) media synchronisation
(d) mechanical clarity

28. Which of the following statements say the same thing?
(i) "I am a teacher" (said by Arvind)
(ii) "I am a teacher" (said by Binod)
(iii) "My son is a teacher" (said by Binod's father)
(iv) "My brother is a teacher" (said by Binod's sister)
(v) "My brother is a teacher" (said by Binod's only sister)
(vi) "My sole enemy is a teacher" (said by Binod's only enemy)

Choose the correct answer from the codes given below:

Codes:

(a) (v) and (vi)
(b) (i) and (ii)
(c) (ii) and (vi)
(d) (ii), (iii), (iv) and (v)

29. In this question there are two statements followed by four conclusions numbered I, II, III and IV.

Statements:

A. All books are trees.
B. All trees are lions.

Conclusions:

I. All books are lions.
II. All lions are books.
III. All trees are books.
IV. Some lions are books.

Choose the correct answer.

(a) Only I and IV follow
(b) Only II and III follow
(c) None of conclusions follow
(d) All conclusion follows

Directions: (30-34) Answer the questions based on following table.

Machines X and Y can independently produce either product P or product Q. The time taken by machines X and Y (in minutes) to produce one unit of product P and Q are given in the table below. (Each machine works 8 hours per day.)

Product	X	Y
P	10	8
Q	6	6

30. If the number of units of P is to be three times that of Q, what is the maximum idle time to maximise total units manufactured?
(a) 8 minutes (b) 0 minute
(c) 12 minutes (d) None of these

31. If X works at half its normal efficiency, what is the maximum number of units produced, if at least one unit of each must be produced?
(a) 119 (b) 135
(c) 127 (d) 136

32. What is the maximum number of units that can be manufactured in one day?
(a) 250 (b) 160
(c) 270 (d) 195

33. If equal quantities of both are to be produced, then out of four choice given below the least efficient way would be
(a) 59 of each with 8 min. idle
(b) 71 of each with 9 min. idle
(c) 53 of each with 10 min. idle
(d) 48 of each with 4 min. idle

34. What is the least number of machine hours required to produce 30 pieces of P and 25 pieces of Q respectively?
(a) 6 hr 30 min. (b) 9 hr 30 min.
(c) 6 hr 40 min. (d) 8 hr 30 min.

35. Telematic is a combination of
(a) Telecommunication and computer
(b) Telecommunication and information
(c) Television and computer
(d) All of the above

36. Following is a part of balance sheet of Timas Pvt. Ltd. Study the table and give answer to the question given below:

(All values in ₹ crore)

Year	Expenditure	Income
1990	3400	4000
1995	3800	4500
2000	4500	5400
2005	6400	8000

Which of the following conclusions is not true?
(a) There has been a steady growth in % profit of the company
(b) There is around 90% increase in expenditure of the firm from 1990 to 2005

(c) Income of the company is doubled in 15 years
(d) Percentage profit in 2000 was 18%

37. If EFGHUK is coded as VUTSRQ then LIMIT can be coded as
(a) KNRNC (b) ORNRG
(c) JKOKG (d) RSTSG

38. The more is 'Resolution Power' of a printer better is its
(a) Speed (b) Colour
(c) Memory (d) Quality

39. Laterite soil develops due to
(a) deposits of alluvial
(b) deposition of loess
(c) leaching
(d) continued vegetation cover

40. Line access and avoidance of collision are the main functions of
(a) network protocols
(b) wide area networks
(c) the CPU
(d) the monitor

41. Communication satellites are placed in
(a) Geostationary Orbit
(b) Polar Orbit
(c) Both (a) and (b)
(d) None of these

42. DDL stands for
(a) Data Deriving Language
(b) Data Definition Language
(c) Data Design Language
(d) All of the above

43. Transistors were first used in
(a) 2nd generation computers
(b) 3rd generation computers
(c) 4th generation computers
(d) None of these

44. Which of the following is not provided in the constitution?
(a) Planning Commission
(b) Election Commission
(c) Finance Commission
(d) Public Service Commission

45. The first satellite launched in space was
(a) Early Bird (b) Sputnik-1
(c) Skylab (d) Aryabhatta-1

46. At what time between 5.30 and 6.00 will the hands of a clock be at right angles?
(a) 45 minutes past 5
(b) $43\frac{5}{11}$ minutes past 5
(c) $43\frac{7}{11}$ minutes past 5
(d) 40 minutes past 5

47. A person can be a member of Council of Ministers without being a member of Parliament for a maximum period of
(a) 45 days (b) 90 days
(c) 180 days (d) One year

48. Many engineers and architects use a different type of pen called a
(a) Pointer pen (b) Computer pen
(c) Light pen (d) Logical pen

49. Which of the following are wrongly matched?

Name of Volcano	Country
(a) Mt. Spur	USA
(b) Mt. Fuego	Guatemala
(c) Mt. Ag'ung	Indonesia
(d) Mt. Lascor	Equador

50. How many types of emergency can be declared by the President of India?
(a) 1 (b) 2
(c) 3 (d) 4

PAPER–II

1. Social planning is a
(a) sporadic effort to bring changes in the economy alone.
(b) effort to bring about educational development.

(c) conscious and a deliberate effort to bring about change.
(d) unconscious and accidental effort to bring about change.

2. Which of the following statements is incorrect?
(a) In the rural areas most of the deliveries are conducted by midwives.
(b) Late marriage leads to more fertility among women.
(c) Early marriages expose women to lengthen child bearing period.
(d) In the context of child bearing the teenaged mothers have more health risk for themselves and children.

3. "Society is held together by the state and if it were not thus held together, it could not exist". In view of this statement, which of the following is correct?
(a) Society and state are identical.
(b) Society is a part of state.
(c) State binds individuals to certain uniform rules of behaviour which are essential for a harmonious and ordered social life.
(d) Society has never existed without state.

4. The term 'emotion work' (Hochschild 1983) refers to
(a) the work done by psychologists, counselors and therapists to help clients with mental and emotional problems.
(b) the techniques used to consciously manage and present emotions that are deemed appropriate for public settings of interaction.
(c) the way in which increasing levels of risk and anxiety have made us think more reflexively about our self-identities.
(d) experiences such as grieving and falling in love, which demand a lot of emotional energy from a person.

5. Which of the following are factors that govern social life in an agrarian society?
1. Persons rather than rules.
2. Kinship rather than formal organisation.
3. Secondary groups rather than neighbourhood.
4. Primary social groups rather than voluntary organizations.

Codes:
(a) 3 and 4 (b) 2 and 4
(c) 1 and 2 (d) 1 and 3

6. Which of the following statements is correct?
(a) Relationship of production is not a cooperative relationship between individuals.
(b) Relationship of production is essentially an exploitative relationship between producers.
(c) Relationship of production is not a human relationship at all.
(d) Relationship of production is not merely the ownership of means of production.

7. Mark out the correct statement.
(a) Estate and caste systems are similar.
(b) Estate system existed in Indian feudal society.
(c) Estate system is a product of feudal Europe.
(d) Estate and class systems are similar.

8. Which among the following is not true regarding value?
(a) Values are unimportant parts of culture.
(b) Values are an important part of every culture.
(c) Values guide a person's behaviour.
(d) Values guide a person's judgment.

9. More than any other Sociologist, has contributed to the codification and systematization of functional analysis.
   (a) H. Spencer
   (b) Emile Durkheim
   (c) T. Parsons
   (d) R.K. Merton

10. It has been said that the one person who most furthered the development of social psychology in North America was Adolf Hitler (Cartwright, 1979). But why?
    (a) World War I created major interest in social psychology, including surveys on the impact of army propaganda films on soldiers.
    (b) He forced a great deal of Jewish academics to emigrate from Germany during World War II, many of whom moved to America to continue their research.
    (c) He encouraged further research into social psychology due to a keen interest in the work of Allport and Sherif.
    (d) None of the above.

11. Match List I (Books) with List II (Authors) and select the correct answer using the codes given below the lists.

List I (Books)

A. *Ideology and Utopia*
B. *Value in Social Theory*
C. *Sociology and Philosophy*
D. *Reason and Revolution*

List II (Authors)

i. E. Durkheim ii. Karl Mannheim
iii. Gunnar Myrdal iv. H. Marcuse

Codes:	A	B	C	D
(a)	iii	ii	i	iv
(b)	ii	iii	i	iv
(c)	ii	iii	iv	i
(d)	iii	ii	iv	i

12. Patriarchal theory has been propounded by
    (a) Morgan (b) Aristotle
    (c) Taylor (d) Henry Maine

13. There is a basic difference between tribe and caste. Mark out the correct statement from among the following:
    (a) Tribe and caste both are complete society.
    (b) Caste is not complete society, tribe is.
    (c) Both tribe and caste are incomplete society.
    (d) Caste is a complete society, tribe is not.

14. In Patterson's study of Brixton, it was found that
    (a) white working class communities resented the arrival of black families.
    (b) black and white residents competed for economic resources.
    (c) African-Caribbean migrants were concentrated in the poorest and most expensive housing.
    (d) All of the above.

15. Which one of the following combinations is true regarding modernization in India?
    (a) Evolution and diffusion
    (b) Evolution and regeneration
    (c) Diffusion and acculturation
    (d) Evolution and acculturation

16. Which of the following is not a consequence of global tourism?
    (a) Developing countries can depend on it as a crucial source of income
    (b) Decreased rates of prostitution and sex tourism
    (c) We have become more aware of 'other' societies and ways of living
    (d) The exploitation of cheap, unregulated labour in poor countries

17. Which of the following is consistent with results of current research conducted in the area of gender roles and the workplace?

(a) Most women believe that there is equal opportunity today between men and women in career choice, advancement, and income.
(b) In about a quarter of households with children, men stay home with the children so their wives can work.
(c) Most men married to working women do not share housework and childcare obligations equally with their working wives.
(d) Most men believe that women should be homemakers because men earn more money.

18. The difference between the frequency polygon and the histogram is that
(a) the frequency polygon represents all the measures of an interval while the histogram shows the curve joining all midpoint of an interval.
(b) the frequency polygon represents the percentile ranks while the histogram represents the measures in an interval in the form of rectangles.
(c) in a histogram the measures internal are represented by a rectangle whereas in a frequency polygon all the measures are represented by the mid-point of the internal.
(d) the histogram represents cumulative frequencies of measures whereas the frequency polygon represents the percentile ranks of measures.

19. **Assertion (A):** In competition, two or more persons/groups are seen vying with one another for a job, reward, profit, etc., and use, non-violent methods to achieve their goal.
Reason (R): Competition in any society focuses attention of people on alternatives and it provides wide range of choices and stimulates new wants and sets of items.
Codes:
(a) Both (A) and (R) are true and (R) is the correct explanation for (A).
(b) Both (A) and (R) are true, but (R) is not the correct explanation for (A).
(c) (A) is true, but (R) is false.
(d) (A) is false, but (R) is true.

20. One strength of ethnography is that
(a) it usually generates richer and more in-depth information than other methods.
(b) the influence of specific variables can be controlled by the investigator.
(c) it can only be used to study relatively small groups or communities.
(d) it is essential when a study is primarily historical or has a historical dimension.

21. The population pyramid of a population that has had a slightly larger birth rate than death rate for several generations will most likely have which of the following shapes?
(a) Wider at the bottom than at the top
(b) Wider at the top than in the middle
(c) Having parallel sides
(d) Bulging in the middle.

22. This diagram best represents

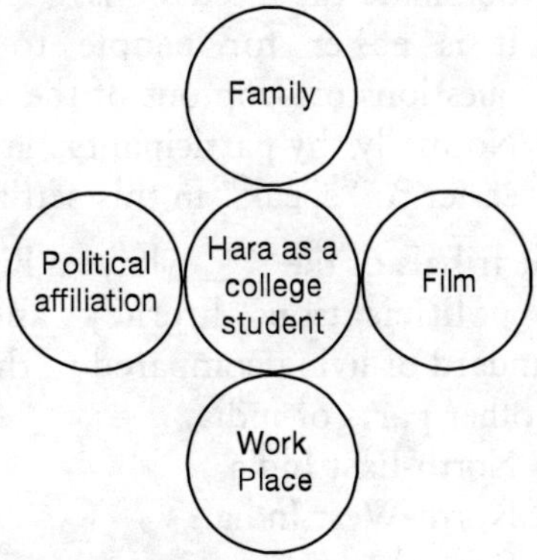

(a) Multiple roles
(b) Role correlation
(c) Statuses
(d) Many roles

23. The qualitative research strategy places a value on
    (a) conducting research that is of a very high quality.
    (b) using numbers, measurements and statistical techniques.
    (c) generating theories through inductive research about social meanings.
    (d) All of the above.
24. In a country, a separatist group has succeeded in seceding from the political union. This has raised the hopes of other centrifugal forces in the country. The possibility of the other centrifugal forces getting active would be the product of the separatist groups.
    (a) Latent dysfunction
    (b) Manifest function
    (c) Manifest dysfunction
    (d) Latent function
25. Which of the following is not a disadvantage of conducting focus groups online?
    (a) It is more difficult to establish rapport without non-verbal cues.
    (b) Those who are fastest at typing may dominate the discussions.
    (c) It is easier for people to ignore questions or drop out of the study.
    (d) Normally shy participants may find it easier to "speak" in this setting.
26. The tribals of the ____ have a high level of politicisation, literacy and high standard of living compared to the tribes in other parts of India.
    (a) North-East India
    (b) North-West India
    (c) Central India
    (d) Southern India
27. Davis and Moore theory can be universally applied to
    (a) Post-industrial society
    (b) Industrial society
    (c) Agricultural society
    (d) Traditional society
28. The flexibility and limited structure of qualitative research designs is an advantage because
    (a) the researcher can adapt their theories and methods as the project unfolds.
    (b) the researcher does not impose any predetermined formats on the social world.
    (c) it allows for unexpected results to emerge from the data.
    (d) All of the above.
29. A basic distinction between culture and civilisation is that
    (a) culture is secondary and civilisation is primary.
    (b) culture is what we are and civilisation is what we have.
    (c) culture is what we have achieved and civilisation is what we aspire to achieve.
    (d) culture is what comes out of intelligence and civilisation is not.
30. Politics and sociology, despite their close relationship do not merge with each other and maintain separate identity. Which of the following does not prove this theory?
    (a) Political science is concerned primarily with institutions and organisations enjoying the approval of the government whereas sociology deals with all types of social institutions approved or unapproved.
    (b) Political science studies all aspects of human beings whereas sociology studies those aspects which are the concern of an individual in society.
    (c) The authority behind political science is that of the state whereas sociology acts from social view point.
    (d) The object of study of political science is the state or political institutions.

31. The capitalistic economy is based on the principle of exacting the maximum from the worker. The misery in which he was left brought into existence the trade unions. These bodies are primarily concerned with the welfare of the workers. To advance and protect their interest they have several means open to them which among the following is not legitimate means available to them.
(a) Going on strike.
(b) Besieging the factory to destroy it since it does not provide the right reliefs.
(c) Collective bargaining for better condition of work.
(d) Submitting the dispute to arbitration.

32. In the 1960s, comprehensive schools did not eradicate class inequalities in education because
(a) selective schools could still 'cream off' the most able pupils, while the comprehensives put children into ability streams.
(b) they tended to recruit pupils from the inner cities and traditionally working class areas.
(c) national testing and league tables made the new schools highly competitive and selective.
(d) teachers in comprehensive schools used the restricted code in the classroom, whereas working class pupils used elaborated codes of speech.

33. Who among the following described, races, "a large, biological, human grouping, with a number of distinctive inherited characteristics which vary within a certain range"?
(a) Fraz Boas (b) Ginsberg
(c) Arnold Green (d) H.T. Mazumdar

34. Consider the following types of power wielders.
1. Religious leaders
2. Military leaders
3. Political leaders
4. Industrial leaders
5. Intellectuals

According to C. Wright Mills, power wielders in American society include.

Codes:
(a) 1, 2, 4 and 5 (b) 1, 3 and 5
(c) 1, 2, 3 and 5 (d) 2, 3 and 4

35. Mark out the incorrect answer. In ancient period cities were
(a) Political centres
(b) Religious centres
(c) Commercial centres
(d) Industrial centres

36. Frazer has distinguished between two types of magic. They are
(a) Black and White.
(b) Homeopathetic and Contagious.
(c) Natural and Psychological.
(d) Real and Pure.

37. Which among the following constitutes a group?
(a) Member of a circus company engaged in performance.
(b) Vegetable sellers following one another into a lane.
(c) Partnership that has failed.
(d) Children running out of the school after it is closed for the day.

38. Caste system in its ideal form, has
(a) education as a means to achieve a higher social position.
(b) marriage as a socially acceptable ways for individual to achieve higher social position for himself/herself.
(c) few socially acceptable ways for individuals to achieve a higher social position.
(d) no socially acceptable ways for individuals to achieve a higher social position.

39. Global economic inequality refers primarily to
    (a) systematic differences in wealth and income within countries.
    (b) systematic differences in wealth and income between global firms.
    (c) systematic differences in wealth and income between poorer countries.
    (d) systematic differences in wealth and income between countries.
40. Weber said that the 'spirit of capitalism' could be traced back to
    (a) inspirational Protestant groups who revived religious ideas.
    (b) the movement towards religious pluralism.
    (c) calvinists who engaged in ascetic practices to gain signs of salvation.
    (d) new religious movements who rejected traditional forms of labour.
41. Why is it important that personal data about research participants are kept within secure, confidential records?
    (a) In case individuals, places or organizations can be harmed through identification or disclosure of personal information.
    (b) So that the participants cannot find out what has been written about them.
    (c) To enable the researcher to track down individuals and find out more about their lives.
    (d) So that government officials, teachers and other people in authority can have easy access to the data.
42. Which one of these is not a version of the sick role as identified by Friedson?
    (a) Unconditionally legitimate
    (b) Conditional
    (c) Illegitimate
    (d) Modified legitimate
43. Which book is considered to be the 'Bible of Sociology'?
    (a) *Mind and Society*
    (b) *Folkways*
    (c) *Masters of Sociology*
    (d) *Sociological Tradition*
44. Social evolution is an example of
    (a) short term, large scale change.
    (b) short term, small scale change.
    (c) long term, large scale change.
    (d) long term, small scale change.
45. ___ is a term used to denote the organic structures as determined by genetic factors and other factors, which will be environmental.
    (a) Phenotype
    (b) Selective breeding
    (c) Genotype
    (d) All of the above
46. Mark out the correct statement among the following
    In rural society.
    (a) There is frequent shifting from one social class to another.
    (b) The class mobility is greater.
    (c) There is no frequent shifting from a social group, or class.
    (d) There is frequent shifting from one place to another.
47. An achieve status is one that is
    (a) derived from abilities and skills.
    (b) depends upon biological condition.
    (c) shared by caste-minded people.
    (d) inherited from parents.
48. He views society as system and argues that any social system has four basic functional prerequisties—adaptation, goal attainment, integration and pattern maintenance. Who is he?
    (a) Robert Merton (b) Marion J. Levy
    (c) Talcott Parsons (d) Edward Shils

49. False consciousness in a class stratification is dysfunctional as it obstructs awareness
(a) about their demands.
(b) of their role in the system.
(c) about themselves.
(d) of their real status.

50. The statement—Sociology has a fourfold origin in political philosophy, the philosophy of history, biological theory of evolution, and the movement for social and political reform, is
(a) False (b) Irrelevant
(c) True (d) Partially true

PAPER–III

1. What make a society?
(a) The interaction of the group.
(b) The system that keeps it together.
(c) The people.
(d) The places of their residence.

2. In sociology, who for the first time emphasised social action as the basis for theory?
(a) Max Weber
(b) Talcott Parsons
(c) R.K. Merton
(d) None of these

3. The term 'Protective Discrimination' is best described as
(a) the provision of better opportunities only for the Scheduled Castes.
(b) encouragement of a spirit of competition among various Scheduled Tribes.
(c) providing only educational facilities in weaker sections.
(d) providing correctional and welfare measures for the weaker sections.

4. To measure the changed purchasing power of currency, the index number that is used is called
(a) Quantity index
(b) Cost of living index
(c) Both (a) and (b)
(d) None of the above

5. Which type of society has more possibility for individual social mobility?
(a) Feudal lord based society
(b) Class based society
(c) Caste based society
(d) Age-grade based society

6. Which among the following is thoroughly ideological revolution?
(a) French Revolution
(b) Industrial Revolution
(c) Renaissance
(d) Reformation

7. The principle or set of principles by which ego's consanguineal relatives are determined is technically known as
(a) Rules of grouping
(b) Rules of lineage
(c) Rules of descent
(d) Rules of kinship

8. The concept of Bureaucratic personality is propounded by
(a) R.K. Merton (b) New Comb
(c) M. Weber (d) Dijlas

9. Of the following, which is a primary group?
(a) School (b) Family
(c) Factory (d) Political group

10. What is one of the main ethical problems associated with conducting a secondary analysis of qualitative data?
(a) Respondents are likely to experience physical harm as a result of the process.
(b) The secondary analyst must adopt a covert role and is at risk of "going native".

(c) It involves deceiving respondents about the nature of the research.
(d) The participants may not have given informed consent to the reuse of their data.

11. The value which cannot be determined graphically is
(a) Mean
(b) Frequency table
(c) Median
(d) None of the above

12. Which of the following is not a feature of all socially stratified systems?
(a) The ranks of different social categories tend to change very slowly over time.
(b) Stratification occurs because of inequalities in assets or property.
(c) People share characteristics without necessarily identifying with each other.
(d) People's life-chances and experiences depend heavily on their social ranking.

13. Which of the following is correct?
(a) Customs as a social discipline is vanishing.
(b) Society depends today more on law than customs.
(c) Laws are the manifestations of the powerful.
(d) Laws may be vindictive.

14. Which among the following is true?
(a) Tonnies saw an evolutionary transition from Gesellschaft to Gemeischaft.
(b) Tonnies saw both Gemeinschaft and Gesellschaft equally important realities of modern age.
(c) Tonnies saw an evolutionary transition from Gemeinschaft to Gesellschaft.
(d) Tonnies saw a cyclical trend from Gemeinschaft to Gesellschaft.

15. Hypothesis cannot be stated in
(a) General terms
(b) Directional terms
(c) Declarative terms
(d) Null and question form terms

16. Bernstein thought that using 'restricted codes' of language disadvantaged pupils at school because
(a) they referred to explicit, context independent meanings.
(b) this pattern of speech made them the target of bullying.
(c) they involved short, simple sentences with a small vocabulary.
(d) they prevented children from communicating outside of their peer groups.

17. *The Material Culture and Social Institutions of the Simpler Peoples*, 1951 is a celebrated book. It is a comparative study of over 400 societies to show that development of social institutions is correlated with changing economic conditions. Identify its authors.
(a) Durkheim and Marcel Mauss
(b) Hobbes, Locke and Rousseau
(c) Hobhouse, Kant and Miller
(d) Hobhouse, Ginsberg and Wheeler

18. The 'Bretton Woods' institutions are
(a) the United Nations and the World Trade Organization.
(b) the International Monetary Fund and the World Bank.
(c) the World Trade Organization and the World Bank.
(d) the International Monetary Fund and the World Health Organization.

19. Which among these is not the 'pattern variables' proposed by Parsons?
(a) Oriental vs Occidental
(b) Specifity vs Diffuseness
(c) Universalism vs Particularism
(d) Achieved vs Ascribed

20. "Health is the greatest gain, contentment is the greatest wealth, faith the best friend and nirvana is the highest happiness." Whose recommendation is this?
(a) *Dhammapada* (b) *Ramayana*
(c) *Bhagavadgita* (d) *Upnishada*

21. What is not the social role in the following?
(a) A lawyer preparing his witness.
(b) An actor involved in act of violence on a screen.
(c) A person announcing programme on TV.
(d) A politician preaching the cult of violence.

22. According to the World Health Organization, which of these is not a main cause of chronic disease and long-term impairments in developing countries?
(a) Poor diet
(b) Poor education
(c) Poor housing
(d) Poor sanitation

23. Social control in the city is different from that of village because
(a) primary groups do not have effective social control in the city.
(b) secondary groups do not enforce particularistic orientation.
(c) the city furnishes anonymity to those who desire it.
(d) the formal social controls are absent in villages.

24. Which Article of the Indian Constitution provides protection to the Scheduled Castes and Scheduled Tribes from social injustice and all forms of exploitation?
(a) Article 46 (b) Article 51
(c) Article 42 (d) Article 45

25. Accommodation is essentially a process of
(a) Group formation (b) Competition
(c) Adjustment (d) Cooperation

26. He in his *Ancient Society*, 1878, developed Bachofen's notions and established an elaborate sequence of family forms from primordial promiscuity to monogamy through which he thought societies must pass. Identify the sociologist.
(a) Henry Maine
(b) Emile Durkheim
(c) E.B. Tylor
(d) L.H. Morgan

27. An 'open' society is one that
(a) does not have any official secrets in its government.
(b) grants every member equal status.
(c) allows people to move between levels of the hierarchy.
(d) has permissive attitudes towards sexual behaviour.

28. Match List I (Name of the Authors) with List II (Title of the Books) and select the correct answer using the codes given below the lists:

List I (Name of the Authors)
A. C.N. Chapekar
B. S.C. Dube
C. D.N. Majumdar
D. T.B. Naik

List II (Title of the Books)
i. *The Kamar*
ii. *The Bhils: A Study*
iii. *Thakurs of Sahyadri*
iv. *The Santal: A Study in Cultural Change*
v. *The Parsees*

Codes:	A	B	C	D
(a)	v	i	iv	ii
(b)	i	iv	ii	v
(c)	iii	ii	v	iv
(d)	iii	i	iv	ii

29. One advantage of using diaries in quantitative research is that
    (a) they are likely to elicit data about sensitive issues or deviant activities.
    (b) they highlight the thoughts, feelings and experiences that are unique to each respondent.
    (c) there is little danger of attrition, as respondents tend to be highly motivated.
    (d) None of the above.
30. While dealing with the problem of social Stratification, M.G. Smith has cautioned sociologists to
    (a) be careful in asserting that simple inequality is inevitable on the grounds of biological differences since these grounds are not by themselves sufficient evidence of stratification.
    (b) ignore the overemphasis sometimes given to the principles by which the distribution of access and opportunities is regulated.
    (c) pay attention to observable inequalities that are uninstitutionalized.
    (d) pay close attention to societies that do not have favoured positions.
31. Who holds that 'culture is the handiwork of man and the medium through which he achieves his/her ends'?
    (a) Kroeber (b) Malinowski
    (c) G.H. Mead (d) F. Boas
32. Who has made distinction between function and dysfunction?
    (a) T. Parsons
    (b) Malinowski
    (c) Radcliffe Brown
    (d) R.K. Merton
33. MacDougall believed that structure and organisation of society is
    (a) different from that of the individual mind.
    (b) at much higher level than the individual mind.
    (c) just the opposite of the individual mind.
    (d) same as that of the individual mind.
34. **Assertion (A):** The policy of protective discrimination adopted by Government of India, after independence, for Scheduled Castes/Tribes has become highly controversial today.
    Reason (R): The reservations SCs/STs in educational institutions and occupational fields have narrowed the gap between these castes on the one hand and higher castes on the other.
    Codes:
    (a) Both (A) and (R) are true and R is the correct explanation for (A).
    (b) Both (A) and (R) are true, but R is not the correct explanation for (A).
    (c) (A) is true, but (R) is false.
    (d) (A) is false, but (R) is true.
35. Which of the following is not a regular national survey carried out by the British government?
    (a) General Household Survey
    (b) Labour Force Survey
    (c) Family Expenditure Survey
    (d) Fashion Sensibility Survey
36. Merton has proposed his theory of role-set in his book
    (a) *Sociological Theories*
    (b) *Social Theory and Social Structure*
    (c) *Challenges Before Sociology*
    (d) *New Trends in Sociology*
37. Which of the following statements are false?
    1. Caste activities have greatly decreased in all villages since development planning has been undertaken.
    2. Industrialisation and expansion of development administration has

stimulated the growth of the middle class.

3. With development planning India has been able to solve its basic problems of unemployment, population growth and poverty.
4. India's development planning has given special focus to integrate women into the development process.

Codes:

(a) 2 and 3 (b) 2 and 4
(c) 1 and 3 (d) 1 and 4

38. The average weekly wages of a group of 50 workers were ₹ 400. It was later discovered that two entries were misread as ₹ 230 and ₹ 140 instead of ₹ 320 and ₹ 410. The correct average is
(a) ₹ 395.6 (b) ₹ 409.7
(c) ₹ 409.3 (d) ₹ 407.2

39. If a study is 'reliable', this means that
(a) The methods are stated clearly enough for the research to be replicated.
(b) It was conducted by a reputable researcher who can be trusted.
(c) The measures devised for concepts are stable on different occasions.
(d) The findings can be generalized to other social settings.

40. Mulholland (1998) argued that privatization changed the relationship between companies and managers in that
(a) the state had greater control than managers over production processes.
(b) flexibility was reduced by the introduction of detailed daily worksheets.
(c) employment depended on performance rather than trust and commitment.
(d) ownership was transferred from small shareholders to senior managers.

41. "Social inequality is a rich source of much that is evil, but also of every thing that is good"—whose view is it?
(a) H. Spencer (b) Kant
(c) Hegel (d) Engels

42. According to Brihaspati
(a) Offspring from three maternal and five paternal generations cannot inter-marry.
(b) Offspring from three paternal and five maternal generations are sapinda and they cannot inter-marry.
(c) Offspring from five maternal generations and seven paternal generations are sapinda and they cannot inter-marry.
(d) Offspring from seven maternal generations and five paternal generations are sapinda and they cannot inter-marry.

43. Who among the following has made important contribution towards developing the idea of reference group?
(a) H. Hyman
(b) R.K. Merton
(c) M. Sheriff
(d) All of the above

44. What major contribution did W.E.B. DuBois make to sociology?
(a) He conducted research on the upper classes of Philadelphia.
(b) He chaired the first department of sociology at the University of Chicago.
(c) He developed a theoretical understanding of racial inequality.
(d) None of the above.

45. What is meant by a 'spurious' relationship between two variables?

(a) A relationship that appears to be true because each variable is related to a third one.
(b) One that is so ridiculously illogical it cannot possibly be true.
(c) One that produces a perfect negative correlation on a scatter diagram.
(d) An apparent relationship that is so curious it demands further attention.

46. Who wanted the Harijans to be integrated into the Hindu society and tried to raise the consciousness of the upper castes through a country wide campaign against untouchability and other constructive work?
(a) Jyotiba Phule
(b) B.R. Ambedkar
(c) E. Ramaswami Naicar
(d) M.K. Gandhi

47. Who among the following has sharply criticised Max Weber for his failure to distinguish legitimacy from legality?
(a) F. Leplay
(b) W.A. Lewis
(c) J. Habernas
(d) C. Levi-Strauss

48. What differentiates an agricultural society from an industrial society?
(a) Social mobility
(b) The environment within which the two societies grow
(c) Mode of occupation
(d) All of the above

49. A woman executive presides over a management board meeting, picks up her daughter from her school and goes to play a game of bridge in the ladies club. She is manifesting
(a) her status set
(b) her elite status
(c) her role set
(d) her style of life

50. Symbolic interactionism is a branch of ______ sociology.
(a) British (b) American
(c) French (d) German

ANSWER SHEET

PAPER—I

1. (d)	2. (d)	3. (c)	4. (d)	5. (d)
6. (a)	7. (b)	8. (d)	9. (d)	10. (d)
11. (d)	12. (c)	13. (c)	14. (b)	15. (a)
16. (d)	17. (d)	18. (b)	19. (c)	20. (b)
21. (a)	22. (b)	23. (c)	24. (c)	25. (c)
26. (b)	27. (b)	28. (c)	29. (b)	30. (b)
31. (a)	32. (b)	33. (c)	34. (a)	35. (b)
36. (d)	37. (b)	38. (d)	39. (c)	40. (a)
41. (a)	42. (b)	43. (a)	44. (a)	45. (b)
46. (c)	47. (c)	48. (c)	49. (d)	50. (c)

PAPER—II

1. (c)	2. (b)	3. (c)	4. (b)	5. (b)
6. (d)	7. (c)	8. (a)	9. (c)	10. (a)
11. (b)	12. (b)	13. (b)	14. (d)	15. (c)
16. (b)	17. (c)	18. (c)	19. (a)	20. (a)
21. (a)	22. (a)	23. (c)	24. (a)	25. (d)
26. (a)	27. (b)	28. (d)	29. (b)	30. (c)
31. (b)	32. (a)	33. (c)	34. (d)	35. (d)
36. (b)	37. (a)	38. (a)	39. (d)	40. (c)
41. (a)	42. (d)	43. (b)	44. (c)	45. (a)
46. (a)	47. (a)	48. (c)	49. (c)	50. (c)

PAPER—III

1. (b)	2. (a)	3. (d)	4. (b)	5. (b)
6. (c)	7. (c)	8. (a)	9. (b)	10. (d)

11. (c)	12. (d)	13. (b)	14. (c)	15. (a)
16. (c)	17. (d)	18. (b)	19. (a)	20. (a)
21. (d)	22. (b)	23. (a)	24. (a)	25. (c)
26. (d)	27. (c)	28. (d)	29. (c)	30. (a)
31. (b)	32. (d)	33. (d)	34. (c)	35. (d)
36. (b)	37. (c)	38. (d)	39. (c)	40. (c)
41. (b)	42. (c)	43. (d)	44. (c)	45. (a)
46. (d)	47. (a)	48. (d)	49. (a)	50. (c)

MOCK TEST–3
PAPER–I

1. In the large group communications, effectively used media is
(a) Radio
(b) Television
(c) Overhead Projector
(d) Computer

2. A child may be suffering from hearing impairment if
(a) he generally says 'please repeat' to the teacher
(b) he speaks loudly unusually
(c) he comes nearer to the speaker during conversation
(d) All of the above

3. If a student is absent from the classes for a long time
(a) Teacher should try to know the cause of his absence
(b) Teacher should try to solve his problems or help him
(c) Teacher should go to his home to meet him
(d) Both (a) and (b)

4. The telecast materials are used to
(a) increases retention power
(b) enhances concentration and learning
(c) reduces the burden of the teacher
(d) All of the above

5. The main function of educational psychology is to provide prospective teacher with
(a) how to deal with students and everyday class situation
(b) research procedures for evaluating current teaching procedure
(c) insight into the needs, problems and styles of behaviour of teacher
(d) insight into various aspects of modern teaching education

6. Which of the following is not a method of research?
(a) Historical (b) Observation
(c) Philosophical (d) Survey

7. The communication which transpires inside a person is known as
(a) group communication
(b) intrapersonal communication
(c) interpersonal communication
(d) mass communication

8. The word research is derived from
(a) Greek word
(b) French word
(c) Spanish word
(d) Latin word

9. Educational quality is
(a) Only a legal right
(b) Fundamental right
(c) Only a customary right
(d) None of the above

10. A good teacher is one who
(a) has genuine interest in his student
(b) is highly intelligent
(c) lives simple life
(d) has mastery over his teaching subject

11. Which of the following institutions is responsible for the implemation of reforms in teaching profession?
(a) National Institute of Educational Planning and Administration
(b) University Grants Commission

(c) National Council for Teacher's Education
(d) National Council for Educational Research and Training

12. The most important characteristic of Open Book Examination system is that
(a) it compels students to think
(b) students become serious
(c) it improves attendance in the classroom
(d) it reduces examination anxiety amongst students

13. Discussion in the class will be more effective if the topic of discussion is
(a) informed to the student well in advance
(b) not introduced
(c) stated before the start of discussion
(d) written on the board without introducing it

14. A person is not a successful communicator
(a) who presents material in a precise and clear way
(b) who sometimes becomes informal before the receiver and developes rapport
(c) who knows a lot but is somewhat reserve in his attitude
(d) who is able to adapt himself according to the language of communication

15. Which of the following provides more freedom for the learners to interact actively?
(a) Small group discussions
(b) Lecture by experts
(c) Viewing of the TV
(d) Use of film projector

16. In this question, four words are given, out of which three are alike in some manner and one is different. Choose the odd one out.
(a) Diamond (b) Graphite
(c) Coal (d) Pearl

17. Two objects or events are related in some way. Pick out that option which has the same type of relationship stated in the given two words:
HANDS : FINGERS :: ?
(a) Competition : Victory
(b) Head : Hair
(c) Skin : Colour
(d) Machine : Tools

18. Human ear is most sensitive to noise in the range
(a) 1-2 kHz (b) 100-500 Hz
(c) 10-12 kHz (d) 13-16 kHz

Direction: (19-23) Study the following passage and give answer to the questions based on it.

A recent report in *News Week* says that in American colleges, students of Asian origin outperform not only the minority group students but the majority Whites as well. Many of these students might be of Indian origin, and their achievement is something that we can be really proud of. It is unlikely that these talented youngsters will come back to India, and that is the familiar brain drain problem. However, recent statements by the nation's policy makers indicate that the perception of this issue is changing. 'Brain Bank' and not the 'Brain Drain' is the more appropriate idea, they suggest that since the expertise of Indians abroad is only deposited in other places and not lost.

This may be so, but this brain bank, like most of other banks, is one that primarily serves customers in its neighbourhood. The skills of Asians now excelling in America's colleges will mainly help the USA. No matter how significant, what non-resident Indians do for India and what their counterparts do for other Asian lands is only a by-product.

But it is also necessary to ask, or be reminded why Indians study more fruitfully when abroad. The Asians whose accomplishments *News Week* records would have probably had a very different fate if they had studied in India. In America, they found an elbow room, books and facilities not available and not likely to be available here. The need to prove themselves in their new country and the competition of an international standard they faced there must have cured mental and physical laziness. But other things helping them in America can be obtained if we achieve a change in social attitudes, especially towards youth.

We need to learn to value individuals and their unique qualities more than conformity and respectability. We need to learn the language of encouragement to add to our skill in flattery. We might also learn to be less liberal with blame and less tight-fisted with appreciation, especially to those showing signs of independence.

19. It is a general believe that the talented young Indians studying in America
   (a) will not return to pursue their careers in India
   (b) have a reputation for being hard-working
   (c) have an opportunity to contribute in India's development
   (d) can solve the brain drain problem because of recent changes in policy
20. Among the many groups of students in American colleges, Asian students
   (a) have only a minority status like the blacks
   (b) are often written about in magazines like *News Week*
   (c) are the most successful academically
   (d) have proved that they are as goods as Whites
21. There is talk of the 'Brain Bank', this idea
   (a) is based on plan to utilise foreign exchange remittances to stimulate research and development
   (b) is a solution to the brain drain problem
   (c) is a new problem caused partly by the brain drain
   (d) is a new way of looking at the role of qualified Indians living abroad
22. The students of Asian origin in America include
   (a) Indians who are the most hard-working of all
   (b) a fair number from India
   (c) a small group from India
   (d) persons from India who are very proud
23. Which of the following most appropriately sums up the intent of the author?
   (a) USA has excelled just because of the contributions from talented immigrants
   (b) We need to look at 'Brain Drain' in a positive way as 'Brain Bank'
   (c) Indians should take pride in the fact that fellow Indians have excelled in foreign lands against all odds
   (d) We need to think of the ways to help grow and retain the talent of our land
24. What should come in place of the question mark (?) in the following series?
   102, 99, 104, 97, 106, ?
   (a) 106 (b) 59
   (c) 95 (d) 64
25. **Statement:** Let us increase the taxes to cover the deficit.
   Conclusions:
   I. If the taxes are not increased, the deficit cannot be met.
   II. The present taxes are very low.
   III. Deficit in the budget are not desirable.

Choose the correct option.
(a) II and III are implicit
(b) I and III are implicit
(c) I and II are implicit
(d) All are implicit

26. **Statements:**
A. Some dogs are cats.
B. None of the cats is a cow.
Conclusins:
I. Some cats are not dogs.
II. Some cats are dogs.
III. Some cows are dogs.
IV. No dog is a cow.
Choose the correct option.
(a) Only II follows
(b) Only III follows
(c) I and III follow
(d) Only IV follows

Directions: (27-30) Using the following table answer the questions given below:

Yearly income (in ₹ '000)

Name/Year	2008	2009	2010	2011
Mahesh	1200	1600	2000	2400
Suresh	1000	1400	1600	2000
Ganesh	900	1200	1500	2000
Seema	2000	2500	3000	3700
Sapna	1200	1200	1500	1700

27. Whose average income for all the four years is ₹ 1400000?
(a) Mahesh alone
(b) Ganesh and Sapna
(c) Mahesh and Suresh
(d) Sapna alone

28. How high is the total average income for four years of men as compared to that of women?
(a) 2133340 (b) 3500440
(c) 4320540 (d) 5440820

29. What is the round figure, the ratio between the total income of men and that of women for all years?
(a) 16:14 (b) 14:15
(c) 15:16 (d) 23:21

30. Can we say women earn more than men?
(a) No
(b) Yes
(c) Not sure
(d) Difference is not so significant

Directions: (31-35) Using the following graph answer the questions given below.

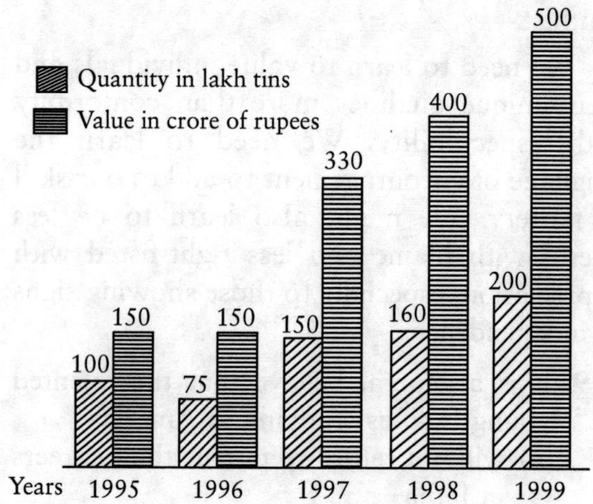

31. What was the approximate percentage increase in export value from 1995 to 1999?
(a) 435 (b) 395.5
(c) 422.8 (d) None of these

32. If in 1998, the tins were exported at the same rate per tin as that in 1997, what would be the value (in ₹ crores) of export in 1998?
(a) 375 (b) 352
(c) 395 (d) 392

33. In which year the value per tin was minimum?
(a) 1996 (b) 1998
(c) 1995 (d) 1999

34. What was the percentage drop in export quantity from 1995 to 1996?
(a) 25 (b) 46
(c) 52 (d) None of these

35. What was the difference between the tins exported in 1997 and 1998?
(a) 10 (b) 1000
(c) 100000 (d) 1000000

36. Which of the following statements is/are true about ozone layer?
(a) It is depleting due to human activities
(b) It is found in upper atmosphere, which absorbs UV rays
(c) It causes skin cancer and genetic disorder
(d) Both (a) and (b)

37. Study the figure and find the region which represents the students who study Physics and Chemistry but not Mathematics.

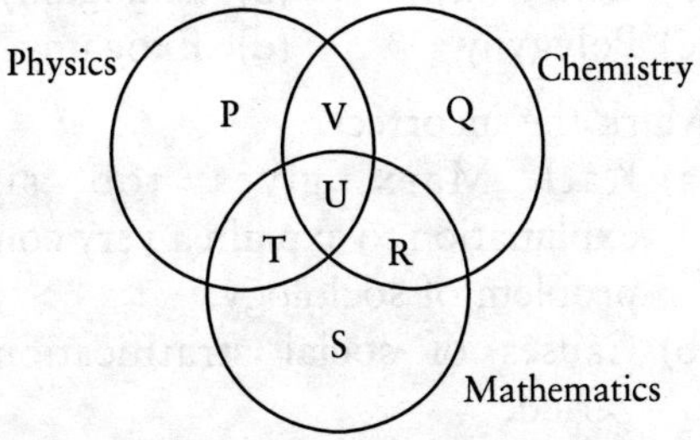

(a) P + T + S + R + U + V
(b) T
(c) P + T + S
(d) V

38. Which of the following is a non-point source of water pollution?
(a) Factories (b) Lawn
(c) Coal mines (d) None of these

39. The depletion of ozone layer causes
I. Skin cancer.
II. Damage to our immune system.
III. Damage to our eyes.
(a) Only III (b) I and II
(c) I and III (d) All of the above

40. Which of the following are associated with the strategic gender concerns? Select the correct answer from the codes given below:
(i) Food security
(ii) Consciousness raising
(iii) Education
(iv) Income generation programmes
(v) Political empowerment
Codes:
(a) (i), (ii), (iv) (b) (ii), (iii), (v)
(c) (iii), (iv), (v) (d) (v), (i), (iv)

41. Web designer is also known as
(a) Web maintainer (b) Web editor
(c) Web master (d) Web author

42. Which of the following schedule of our constitution is related to languages?
(a) Sixth (b) Eighth
(c) Seventh (d) Tenth

43. In the hypermedia database, information bits are stored in the form of
(a) Symbols (b) Signals
(c) Cubes (d) Nodes

44. Explosive volcanic eruption is caused by
(a) High water content in ground
(b) Low viscosity of magma
(c) High viscosity of magma
(d) None of these

45. The VIRUS is a
(a) Device
(b) Software program
(c) Hardware
(d) anti-piracy software

46. Appropriation Act of the General Budget is
(a) a Constitution Amendment Bill
(b) a Finance Bill
(c) a Money Bill
(d) an Ordinary Bill

47. If in a certain language, GERMANY is coded as HGUQFTF then how will you code NEOMAN?

(a) OFQQFT (b) OFQPES
(c) OGRQFT (d) None of these

48. Which of the following is biggest fresh-water lake in India?
(a) Loktak (b) Dal
(c) Sukhna (d) None of these

49. Different memories can be classified according to the concept of
(a) Transfer Rate
(b) Access mode/capacity
(c) Access Time
(d) All of the above

50. Which of the following diagrams represents the relation between red, clothes and roses most appropriately?

(a)  (b) 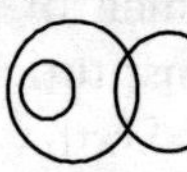

(c) 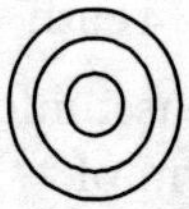 (d) 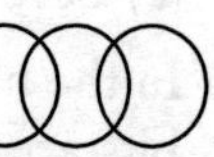

PAPER–II

1. Which among the following is not one of the 'modes of individual adaptation' proposed by Merton?
(a) Rebellion (b) Ritualism
(c) Innovation (c) Association

2. Those kins who branch out from the main group like uncles and cousins are called
(a) Separate kin (b) Lateral kin
(c) Sub-kin (d) Collateral kin

3. Who said this: "Status is the rank-order position assigned by a group to a role or to a set of roles"?
(a) Kingsley Davis (b) Ogburn
(c) Lundberg (d) MacIver

4. A social group, usually with a definite area, dialect, cultural homogeneity, and unifying social organisation is termed as
(a) Peasantry (b) A caste
(c) A tribe (d) A class

5. A social movement based on the expectation of a sudden transformation of society through the intervention of the super natural is
(a) Milienarian movement
(b) Vitalistic movement
(c) Revitalization movement
(d) Nativistic movement

6. Who for the first time used the concept of social structure in sociology?
(a) Spencer (b) Durkheim
(c) Marx (d) Weber

7. Which term is equivalent to group marriage?
(a) Cenogamy (b) Endogamy
(c) Polygyny (d) Exogamy

8. Mark the incorrect.
(a) Karl Marx gives too simple explanation to explain a very complex problem of sociology.
(b) Causes of social stratification are varied.
(c) Distinction is based on birth.
(d) Class distinction is not necessarily based on possession of property.

9. Who among the following gave the example of the invention of self-starter for automobiles as the reason for early women's liberation in the West?
(a) W.F. Ogburn (b) W.G. Summer
(c) W.J. Goode (d) W.E. Moor

10. Which of the following is not a limitation of the focus group method?
(a) It produces a large volume of data that can be difficult to analyse.

(b) The researcher has little control over how the discussion proceeds.
(c) People in groups tend to agree and express socially desirable views.
(d) It reveals the way social meanings are jointly constructed.

11. _____ defined competition as the most elementary type of the four major forms of interaction. It is an aspect of human struggle which is universal, continuous and impersonal.
(a) Ross
(b) Albion Small
(c) Park and Burgress
(d) Saint Simon

12. Traditional working class identity was based around
(a) the class consciousness of members of the proletariat.
(b) shared working conditions in the manufacturing industry.
(c) collective aspirations to move into the middle class.
(d) local communities, extended kinship networks and shared leisure pursuits.

13. *Group Mind* was written by
(a) Spencer (b) Hegel
(c) Bonsanquest (d) MacDougall

14. In the 1990 reform of the National Health Service, hospitals became
(a) state-controlled providers, dependent on funding from the central government.
(b) self-governing trusts competing for purchasing contracts from health authorities.
(c) less inclined to run themselves efficiently, as demand for health care was falling.
(d) increasingly detached from health authorities and providers of private health care.

15. Match List I with List II and select the correct answer using the codes given below the lists:

List I
A. Robert K. Merton
B. Emile Durkheim
C. Talcott Parsons
D. Radcliffe Brown
E. Marion J. Levy

List II
i. The Structure of Society
ii. The Rules of Sociological Method
iii. Social Theory and Social Structure
iv. The Structure of Social Action
v. Structure and Function in Primitive Society

Codes:	A	B	C	D	E
(a)	ii	iv	iii	i	v
(b)	iii	ii	iv	v	i
(c)	i	iii	v	ii	iv
(d)	iv	v	i	ii	iii

16. A crowd is distinguished by its nature
(a) Stable (b) Permanent
(c) Continuous (d) Transitory

17. Global warming can most accurately be defined as
(a) the devastating environmental consequences of climate change.
(b) the build-up of heat-trapping gases within the earth's atmosphere.
(c) the generation of by-products such as chlorofluorocarbons (CFCs).
(d) the chemically induced rise in the earth's average temperature.

18. 'Social change' refers to change in
(a) Food habits
(b) Habitation pattern
(c) Value system
(d) Dress

19. What among the following have not contributed to the social mobility?

(a) The development and expansion of civilization.
(b) The growth of large towns and pilgrim centres.
(c) Orthodoxy and superstition.
(d) Famines and economic changes.

20. **Assertion (A):** Traditionally, a lower caste adopted the lifestyle of the dominant caste in the process of sanskritization.
Reason (R): Adoption of the lifestyle of the dominant caste usually symbolized a case of upward mobility within the caste system.
Codes:
(a) Both (A) and (R) are true and (R) is the correct explanation for (A).
(b) Both (A) and (R) are true, but (R) is not the correct explanation for (A).
(c) (A) is true, but (R) is false.
(d) (A) is false, but (R) is true.

21. The characteristic setting within which intimate, spontaneous, person-to-person interaction takes place is called
(a) A model group
(b) A reference group
(c) A co-operative group
(d) A primary group

22. A society which is characterised by secondary rather than primary group interaction, marked by anomie, and generally characterised by a dulling homogeneity with respect to lifestyles is called
(a) Peasant society
(b) Agrarian society
(c) Mass society
(d) Folk society

23. How is it argued that qualitative research can have "empiricist overtones"?
(a) There is an emphasis on direct observation of people and social settings.
(b) Semi-structured interview schedules are used to quantify behaviour.
(c) It typically involves testing a clearly defined hypothesis.
(d) Qualitative researchers prefer to conduct statistical analyses of their data.

24. Structural-functionalists describe society as
(a) a source of conflict, inequality, and alienation.
(b) a complex network of interaction at a micro-level.
(c) a normative framework of roles and institutions.
(d) an unstable structure of social relations.

25. Some researches have revealed that the headmasters of schools really do not like the parents to come to school and talk to them what would be your assumption about this attitude?
(a) They fear that parents come always with complaints against the schools, etc.
(b) They feel inferior to parents and want to avoid them.
(c) They feel it a waste of time to talk to parents.
(d) They feel at a disturbance in their work.

26. Dual organisation as a functional stratification is prevalent among
(a) Ethclass (b) Tribes
(c) Castes (d) Class

27. The characteristics of peasant societies outlined by Theodore Shanin are
1. The peasant family farm is the basic unit of a multi-dimensional social organisation.
2. Land husbandry is the main means of livelihood, directly providing the major part of the consumption needs.

3. Specific traditional culture is related to the way of life of small communities.
4. The peasants have the underdog position-domination of peasants by others.

Codes:

(a) 1, 2 and 3 (b) 1, 2, 3 and 4
(c) 1 only (d) 1 and 2

28. The death of children below one year of life is known as
(a) Neo-natal mortality
(b) Infant mortality
(c) Child mortality
(d) Intra-uterine mortality

29. 'Pattern variables' are _____ in number.
(a) five (b) three
(c) six (d) four

30. State is "a special repressive force for the suppression of the proletariat by the bourgeois, of millions of tillers by handful of rich". Who said so?
(a) Marx (b) Engels
(c) Lenin (d) MacIver

31. Demographic transition theory is a way of conceptualizing the changes in population which accompanied industrialisation, seeing in these changes a transformation from a system with high birth rate balanced by high death rates to one with low death rates balanced by low
(a) Fecundity (b) Fertility
(c) Death rate (d) Birth rate

32. The book *Folkways* was written by
(a) MacIver (b) Sumner
(c) F.G. Bailey (d) B. Malinowski

33. There are several speculative theories as to the origin of caste system. Which among the following answers as to its origin is the best?
(a) It is a the product of known and unknown causes. It is the handiwork of time.
(b) It is Scheme of the Division of Labour.
(c) It was introduced with the intention to maintain the Brahmanic Supremacy.
(d) The system was used to maintain the racial purity of the dominant race.

34. Which among the following is correct. An entrepreneur is
(a) An innovator
(b) Merely a capitalist
(c) A person with style
(d) A public servant

35. The term 'Historical Sociology' is applied to those sociological phenomena which
(a) are more than a decade old.
(b) are more than aeons old.
(c) are more than a century old.
(d) are more than fifty years old.

36. This diagram best represents

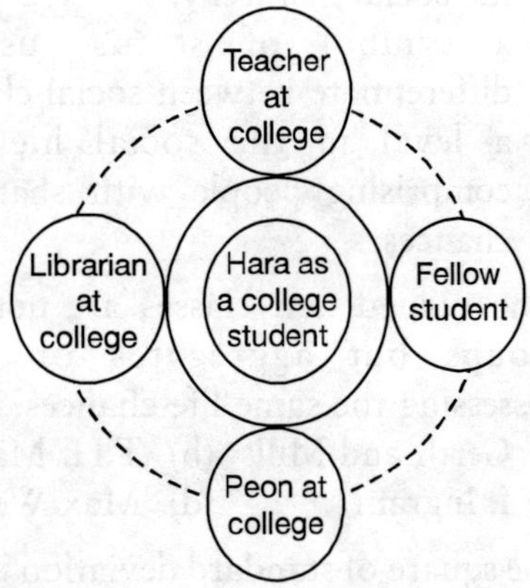

(a) Role set (b) Status set
(c) Statuses (d) Many roles

37. Which of the following pair(s) is/are correctly matched?
1. Variation in mortality with age represents a 'J' shaped curve – Characteristic of developed countries

2. Concept of proximate variables of fertility	– Contribution of K. Davis and Judith Blake
3. Variation in mortality represents 'U' shaped curve	– Characteristic of under developed countries
4. Net reproduction rate (NRR) is equal to one	– A stagnant population

Codes:

(a) 1, 2 and 4 (b) 4 only
(c) 2 and 3 (d) 1 and 3

38. George Simmel's classification of group is based on
(a) Interaction (b) Size
(c) Group dynamism (d) Relation

39. A social stratum is
(a) a methodological tool used to identify a person's social class.
(b) the boundary between two levels of the social hierarchy.
(c) a symbol of status, used to differentiate between social classes.
(d) a level in the social hierarchy, comprising people with shared life chances.

40. Who opined that classes are not social groups but aggregates of people possessing the same life-chances?
(a) Gerth and Mills (b) T.H. Marshall
(c) I. Ingram (d) Max Weber

41. The square of standard deviation is called
(a) Percentage
(b) Variance
(c) Co-efficient
(d) None of the above

42. Politics and sociology despite their close relationship do not merge with each other and maintain separate identity, which of the following does not prove this theory?
(a) Political science studies all aspects of human beings whereas sociology studies those aspects which are the concern of an individual in society.
(b) Political science is concerned primarily with institutions and organisations enjoying the approval of the government whereas sociology-deals with all types of social institutions approved or unapproved.
(c) The object of study of political science is the state or political institutions.
(d) The authority behind political science is that of the state whereas sociology acts from social view point.

43. Microliths are associated with
(a) Neolithic age (b) Chalcolithic age
(c) Mesolithic age (d) Iron age

44. The fact that institutions require specific association to sustain them is of importance for
(a) the institutions of religions only.
(b) determining size of association.
(c) understanding the basic distinction between institutions and other norms.
(d) complex societies only.

45. Why do you need to review the existing literature?
(a) Because without it, you could never reach the required word-count.
(b) To make sure you have a long list of references.
(c) To help in your general studying.
(d) To find out what is already known about your area of interest.

46. Which one of the following statements you think is not correct?
(a) Wars are destructive of all good.
(b) Wars have brought men closer.
(c) Wars have contributed to the development of civilizations.
(d) War is a part of man's heritage.

47. The Bombay prevention of Hindu Bigamous Marriage Act 1947 enforced
    (a) Monogamy among Parsis of Bombay
    (b) Polygamy in the Bombay state
    (c) Monogamy in the Bombay state
    (d) Monogamy in India
48. What is 'biogrammar'?
    (a) It is a genetically based programme which predisposes mankind to behave in certain ways.
    (b) Movements of body that communicate with others, such as raising of eye brows, frowning, etc.
    (c) Grammar of any language concerning different bodily parts.
    (d) It is a programme deviced by genetic engineers to monitor body movements.
49. The most notable contribution to the study of Social Stratification has been given by
    (a) T. Parsons and Marx
    (b) Karl Marx and Max Weber
    (c) Max Weber
    (d) Kingsley Davis and T. Parsons
50. A society's resistance to social change is likely to be negatively related to its
    (a) Integration
    (b) Culture
    (c) Isolation
    (d) Emphasis on conformity

PAPER–III

1. Concept of 'symmetrical family' was propounded by
    (a) Davis and Moore
    (b) Robin Fox
    (c) T. Parsons
    (d) Young and Willmott
2. In a family the grandfather was a farmer in a village and the father taught in a school in a town and now the son is an industrial engineer in a multi-national corporation. This is an illustration of
    (a) horizontal mobility.
    (b) inter-generational mobility.
    (c) cultural mobility.
    (d) intra-generational mobility.
3. Ethnography refers to the descriptive account 5 of the way of life of a particular society. What is ethnology?
    (a) Comparative study of cultural elements in a range of societies.
    (b) Study of a culture.
    (c) A detailed account of specific cultural elements in a society.
    (d) None of the above.
4. Which among the following statements are true?
    1. Structural strain is caused when the norms and values of a society disappear suddenly.
    2. The leadership of social movement plays an important role in achieving its objectives.
    3. Ideology gives always a political slant to movement.
    4. Ideology helps in distinguishing between movements with similar objectives.

    Codes:

(a) 1, 2 and 3	(b) 1, 2, 3 and 4
(c) 2 and 4	(d) 2, 3 and 4
5. Which among the following covers the study of population and social structure including social groups and institutions according to Ginsberg?
    (a) Social anatomy
    (b) Social processes
    (c) Social institutions
    (d) Social morphology

6. Max Weber divided the modes of the legitimation of authority into traditional, rational legal and charismatic. The authority of Nelson Mandela, in the present context, represents which among these?
   (a) Traditional
   (b) Rational legal
   (c) Charismatic
   (d) Both (a) and (c)
7. Educational technology is a process concerned with
   (a) improving the schools through implementation of science and technological subjects.
   (b) using the modern methods of technologies in teaching and learning in schools.
   (c) equipping the technical institutions for better methods of instructions.
   (d) explains the progress of technology through education.
8. Which of the following is not an advantage of using CAQDAS in social research?
   (a) It is faster and efficient than analyzing by hand.
   (b) It makes the process of qualitative data analysis more transparent.
   (c) It helps you to map out the relations between ideas and themes in the data.
   (d) It involves learning skills that are specific to each program.
9. Which among the following is not true regarding 'Okka parage marriage'?
   (a) It is performed to bring another wife as there is tradition of polygyny in okka.
   (b) Husband acquires membership of his wife okka.
   (c) It is 12 pieces of gold transfered from the man's okka to wife's okka.
   (d) It is performed when a okka does not have son to continue the line.
10. Match List I (Concepts) with List II (Features) and select the correct answer using the codes given below the lists:

List I (Concepts)
A. Mechanical solidarity
B. Primary group
C. Little community
D. Kula

List II (Features)
i. Face-to-face relationship
ii. Social similarities
iii. Interdependence
iv. Gift exchange
v. Homogeneity

Codes:	**A**	**B**	**C**	**D**
(a)	i	ii	v	iii
(b)	v	i	ii	iv
(c)	ii	i	v	iv
(d)	ii	iii	i	v

11. Why has the secondary analysis of official statistics been seen as an 'unobtrusive' method?
   (a) The data were originally collected for the same purposes as those of the current researcher.
   (b) It increases the risk of "reactive effects" from participants.
   (c) They do not intrude too much into the researcher's spare time.
   (d) The researcher is removed from the social settings that they are investigating.
12. When accessing the internet, which of these steps is the most essential?
   (a) Recording the full URL.
   (b) Noting the access dates.
   (c) Downloading material to be referenced.
   (d) All of the above are equally important.

13. Which of the following are true regarding the relation between fact and value?
   1. Individuals show greater awareness to facts which support their values.
   2. Individuals tend to be blind to the facts which do not support their values.
   3. Values are not social facts.

   Codes:

   (a) 2 and 3 (b) 1, 2 and 3
   (c) 1 and 2 (d) 1 and 3

14. **Assertion (A):** There is an increasing trend among educated women to get employment as an assertion of their new identity and to provide economic support to the family.

   Reason (R): Employment of women leads to more stress and strain between job roles and family roles resulting in role-conflict.

   Codes:

   (a) Both (A) and (R) are true and (R) is the correct explanation for (A).
   (b) Both (A) and (R) are true, but (R) is not the correct explanation for (A).
   (c) (A) is true, but (R) is false.
   (d) (A) is false, but (R) is true.

15. Who was of the opinion that social investigator should be trained properly?
   (a) Max Weber (b) Margret Mead
   (c) G.H. Mead (d) W.F. Whyte

16. Insects warming around an outdoor light is an example of
   (a) Aggregation (b) Gathering
   (c) Congregation (d) Group

17. For Durkheim, the division of labour is the result of
   (a) economic development.
   (b) increase in population density.
   (c) moral development.
   (d) technological development.

18. Seven people standing silently while waiting for a bus at a bus stop is an example of which of the following?
   (a) A secondary group
   (b) A primary group
   (c) A social category
   (d) An aggregate

19. Which of the following is not a basis of difference between primary groups and secondary groups?
   (a) Breadth of relationships
   (b) Ethnicity of relationships
   (c) Quality of relationships
   (d) Duration of relationships

20. Malinowski's study of the Trobriand Island clearly shows that the prestige and power are related to the
   (a) mastery over boat making.
   (b) good at fishing.
   (c) redistribution of wealth.
   (d) dissemination of knowledge.

21. Age specific birth rate is marked by
   (a) the number of children born per thousand women in specific age class, say 30-34 years of age.
   (b) children of a particular age group say 5-9 or 9-14 years.
   (c) the number of births annually per thousand persons of total population.
   (d) the number of births annually per thousand in the 15-49 child bearing ages.

22. Reflexive role-taking is defined by
   (a) M. Mead (b) R. Linton
   (c) C.H. Cooley (d) G.H. Mead

23. The 'nuclear family' means
   (a) a network of relatives extended within or between generations.
   (b) a group of people sharing living accommodation and meals.

(c) a two generation unit of parents and their children.
(d) the new family created when an adult leaves home and gets married.

24. The great transformation refers to
(a) the changes that led to feudalism.
b) the changes that led to postmodernity.
(c) the changes that led to the dark ages.
(d) the changes that led to modernity.

25. The iron law of oligarchy refers to
(a) the exclusion of women from the highest levels of politics.
(b) regimes that use repression against their populations.
(c) the legal system of the former communist countries.
(d) the tendency for power inevitably to flow towards the top.

26. The antecedents of functional orientations in sociology, it is said, are illustrated by a dictum of Voltaire, to the effect that if there were no God it would be necessary for man shared system of communication, and methods of assigning individual to roles can be referred to as to invent one; meaning that Voltaire regarded belief in God as functionally indispensable to man. Who according to you provided a real impetus to functionalism in sociology?
(a) Parsons and Shils
(b) Comte and Spencer
(c) Marx and Weber
(d) None of the above

27. Mass-society theory suggests that
(a) the subordinate classes are dominated by the ideology of the ruling class.
(b) the content of the media is determined by market forces.
(c) audiences make selective interpretations of media messages.
(d) the media manipulate 'the masses' as vulnerable, passive consumers.

28. The social construction of childhood can be traced back to
(a) increasingly emotional ties between parents and children.
(b) new consumer goods for children, such as clothes, toys and books.
(c) the introduction of compulsory education.
(d) All of the above.

29. Those aspects of social life that have to do with order, stability, and social organization that allow societies and groups to hold together and endure are called
(a) social dynamics
(b) social statics
(c) constructed reality
(d) social absolutes

30. The term "secondary analysis" refers to the technique of
(a) Analysing your own data in two different ways.
(b) Conducting a study of seconds, minutes and other measures of time.
(c) Working part time on a project alongside other responsibilities.
(d) Analysing existing data that have been collected by another person or organization.

31. Why might you tell SPSS to represent the 'slices' of a pie chart in different patterns?
(a) If you do not have a colour printer, it makes the differences between slices clearer.
(b) In order to make full use of the facilities that SPSS can offer.
(c) Because the patterns form symbolic visual images of different social groups.
(d) Because the program tends to crash if you ask it to use colour.

32. It is useful to have a diversity of theories in sociology because
    (a) sociologists can choose the theory that best fits the data they have collected.
    (b) human behaviour is so complicated that no single theory would be adequate.
    (c) innumerable theories have been developed in the many fields of sociology.
    (d) it removes the need to assess a theory according to the empirical evidence.
33. According to Marx Weber
    (a) historically, only the Western societies have been divided on class lines.
    (b) historically, all known societies have been divided on class lines.
    (c) historically, only the agrarian societies are divided on class lines.
    (d) historically, only the capitalist societies are divided on class lines.
34. Ram is working as an accountant's assistant. He is pursuing a course on business management with a hope to become a marketing manager. This process is called?
    (a) Social inequality
    (b) Socialisation
    (c) Educational difference
    (d) Educational mobility
35. Which of the following according to MacIver has no direct relevance with society?
    (a) Procedures (b) Authority
    (c) Force (d) Usages
36. According to Sassen, which of these is not a necessary trait of a global city?
    (a) They are visited by large numbers of tourists from across the world.
    (b) They are centres of direction and policy-making for the global economy.
    (c) They are markets for the exchange of the products of financial services.
    (d) They are the key locations for financial and specialized service firms.
37. The term 'collective consumption' (Castells 1977) refers to
    (a) the provision of health, housing, and education services by the state.
    (b) the privatization of public services by the conservative government.
    (c) the lifestyle practice of shopping in peer groups.
    (d) the form of tuberculosis suffered by those who collect stamps.
38. The principle that a culture must be understood and judged on its own terms without reference to the values of another culture is known as
    (a) cultural relativism
    (b) cultural hegemony
    (c) cultural pluralism
    (d) cultural specificity
39. The response set of 'acquiescence' can be a problem in that
    (a) researchers who wear very strong perfume will distract their respondents.
    (b) some people consistently agree or disagree with a set of questions or items.
    (c) respondents tend to give answers that they think are socially desirable.
    (d) the structured interview is so conducive to reciprocity that male respondents find it hard to stop talking.
40. Change is "an incidental consequence of the fortuitous inter-action of number of people who have become desocialized-that is, stripped of their normal social characteristics—through participation in mass willing." Who among the following is the author of this observation?

(a) Richard T. Lapiere
(b) Karl Marx
(c) MacIver
(d) J.C. Russell

41. Who were of the opinion that every individual has certain rights which cannot be taken away by any authority?
(a) Hobbes (b) Montesquieu
(c) Locke (d) Rousseau

42. Telework is a form of employment that involves
(a) combining non-manual work with the leisure activity of watching television.
(b) running one's own business through telephone helplines or hotlines.
(c) working at home for an outside employer, using information technology.
(d) babysitting and other jobs within a local network, through the informal economy.

43. Who among the following was of the view that it would be inappropriate to look at the joint family system as a collection of nuclear families?
(a) P.N. Prabhu
(b) Pauline Kolenda
(c) I. Karve
(d) M.S. Gore

44. Normative culture is that subdivision of non-material culture that consists of
(a) Mores (b) Standard way
(c) Norms (d) Values

45. In plotting a frequency polygon, it is important to see that
(a) the mid-point of an interval is always taken to represent the entire interval.
(b) each chass interval is represented by a separate rectangle.
(c) mid point of all class intervals are joined together.
(d) None of the above.

46. For him societies were moral systems and it was pertinent to examine symbols and their meaning to people. In this he helped to direct the interest of social anthropologists into a new direction. Who was he?
(a) B. Malinowski
(b) Radcliffe Brown
(c) M. Gluckman
(d) Evans Pritchard

47. The British conceded political representation of the untouchables by the communal award. Gandhi undertook a fast unto death against this award which ultimately led to the withdrawal of the award under
(a) Lahore Pact
(b) Bombay declaration
(c) Shimla Agreement
(d) Poona Pact

48. Which of the following positions is not associated with the hyperglobalizers?
(a) Globalization needs to happen much more quickly.
(b) Citizens lose faith in existing systems of governance.
(c) Regional institutions are becoming as powerful as nation-states.
(d) Individual countries no longer control their own economies.

49. Why did the upper castes have a better education during colonial period?
(a) Because of their racial superiority over the backward sections.
(b) Because of their psychological and mental superiority.
(c) Because of the fact that they were better of in all fields including caste hierarchy and property relations.
(d) Because they were ritually superior to other castes.

50. The Hindu Adoption and Maintenance Act, 1956 is also applicable to
(a) Buddhists, Jains, Muslims, Sikhs
(b) Buddhists, Sikhs, Christians
(c) Buddhists, Jains, Sikhs
(d) Muslims, Christians, Jains

ANSWERS SHEET

PAPER—I

1. (d)	2. (d)	3. (c)	4. (d)	5. (d)
6. (a)	7. (b)	8. (d)	9. (d)	10. (d)
11. (d)	12. (c)	13. (c)	14. (b)	15. (a)
16. (d)	17. (d)	18. (b)	19. (c)	20. (b)
21. (a)	22. (b)	23. (c)	24. (c)	25. (c)
26. (b)	27. (b)	28. (c)	29. (b)	30. (b)
31. (a)	32. (b)	33. (c)	34. (a)	35. (b)
36. (d)	37. (d)	38. (d)	39. (c)	40. (b)
41. (a)	42. (b)	43. (a)	44. (a)	45. (b)
46. (c)	47. (c)	48. (c)	49. (d)	50. (c)

PAPER—II

1. (c)	2. (d)	3. (a)	4. (c)	5. (a)
6. (a)	7. (a)	8. (c)	9. (c)	10. (d)
11. (c)	12. (d)	13. (d)	14. (b)	15. (b)
16. (d)	17. (d)	18. (c)	19. (c)	20. (b)
21. (a)	22. (c)	23. (a)	24. (c)	25. (a)
26. (c)	27. (b)	28. (b)	29. (a)	30. (c)
31. (d)	32. (b)	33. (a)	34. (a)	35. (d)
36. (a)	37. (c)	38. (b)	39. (d)	40. (d)
41. (b)	42. (a)	43. (c)	44. (d)	45. (d)
46. (a)	47. (c)	48. (d)	49. (b)	50. (c)

PAPER—III

1. (d)	2. (b)	3. (d)	4. (c)	5. (d)
6. (b)	7. (b)	8. (d)	9. (a)	10. (c)
11. (d)	12. (d)	13. (c)	14. (b)	15. (b)
16. (a)	17. (a)	18. (d)	19. (a)	20. (c)
21. (a)	22. (d)	23. (c)	24. (d)	25. (d)
26. (b)	27. (d)	28. (d)	29. (b)	30. (d)
31. (a)	32. (b)	33. (b)	34. (d)	35. (c)
36. (a)	37. (a)	38. (a)	39. (b)	40. (a)
41. (c)	42. (c)	43. (d)	44. (c)	45. (c)
46. (a)	47. (d)	48. (a)	49. (c)	50. (c)

MOCK TEST–4
PAPER–I

1. Dewry defines education as a
(a) theoretical need
(b) social need
(c) personal need
(d) psychological need

2. All of the following statements about a teacher are correct except the one.
(a) A teacher changes his/her attitudes and behaviour according to the need of the society
(b) A teacher is a friend, guide and philosopher
(c) A teacher distinguishes between students
(d) A teacher is the leader in the class

3. A person cannot be an effective teacher if he
(a) teaches moral values
(b) is a strict disciplinarian
(c) knows his subject well
(d) has no interest in teaching

4. The most important single factor in underlying the success of a teacher is
   (a) organisational ability
   (b) scholarship
   (c) communicative ability
   (d) personality and his ability to relate to the class and to the pupils
5. If you are irritated and show rashness because of the inadequate behaviour of another teachers, what do you think about your own behaviour?
   (a) Your behaviour is also a sign of maladjustment and so try to control yourself when you are maltreated.
   (b) It is justified because behaviours are choice.
   (c) Your behaviour is not good because elders have the right to behave you in this way.
   (d) All of the above.
6. The term 'SITE' stands for
   (a) Satellite Instructional Teachers Education
   (b) Satellite International Television Experiment
   (c) Satellite Instructional Television Experiment
   (d) Satellite Indian Television Experiment
7. Team teaching has the potential to develop
   (a) highlighting the gaps in each other's teaching
   (b) competitive spirit
   (c) cooperation
   (d) the habit of supplementing the teaching of each other
8. In any research one should
   (a) not try out anything blindly but wait until a sudden flash appears in his mind
   (b) know everything in the area without bothering to learn the details of any
   (c) know more and more about less and less in certain specific sub area
   (d) None of the above
9. Determine the nature of the following definition:
   'Poor' means having an annual income of ₹ 10,000.
   (a) Lexical (b) Persuasive
   (c) Precising (d) Stipulative
10. Which of the following methods implies the collection of information by way of investigators own examination without interviewing the respondents?
    (a) Random probability sampling
    (b) Observation
    (c) Posting questionnaire
    (d) Schedule method
11. Why do teachers use teaching aid?
    (a) For students' attention
    (b) To make teaching fun-filled
    (c) To make students attentive
    (d) To teach within understanding level of students
12. On which of the following statements there is consensus among educators?
    (a) Disciplinary cases should be totally neglected in the class
    (b) Disciplinary cases should be sent to the principal only when other means have failed
    (c) Disciplinary cases should never be sent to principal's office
    (d) None of the above
13. Good evaluation of written material should not be based on
    (a) Logical presentation
    (b) Comprehension of subject
    (c) Linguistic expression
    (d) Ability to reproduce whatever is read

14. A good researcher lays his hands on
   (a) any area as long as manpower and fundings are available in plenty
   (b) a specific area and tries to understand in minute details
   (c) several areas and tries to understand them at fundamental level
   (d) None of the above

15. The basis on which assumptions are formulated
   (a) Universities
   (b) Cultural background of the country
   (c) Specific characteristics of the castes
   (d) All of the above

Read the following passage and answer the questions 16 to 20:

India is dedicated to free institutions and principles of democracy. We are striving to give everyone an opportunity and raise the standard of living for all. A democracy is one where people have the right to live their own lives and develop themselves in their own way under the guidance of their chosen representatives. If our political democracy is to succeed, it is essential that it be buttressed by steps towards economic equality or what has been referred to as the 'socialistic pattern of society'. Poverty and unemployment hold the biggest threat to the successful working of our democratic system.

16. One may infer from the paragraph that in a socialistic pattern of society
   (a) to provide employment to all is the greatest problem
   (b) the socialist party dominates
   (c) all the inhabitants are treated equal
   (d) None of the above

17. The successful working of Indian democratic system is under a threat of
   (a) economic inequality
   (b) poverty
   (c) unemployment
   (d) All of the above

18. In a democratic system
   (a) commodities are freely bought and sold
   (b) government serves the people
   (c) the government is run by the people themselves
   (d) people do not have political freedom

19. The word buttressed in the paragraph means
   (a) Supported (b) Dictating
   (c) Declared (d) Guided

20. Democracy can fail if there is
   (a) opportunity for development
   (b) a weak government
   (c) economic inequality
   (d) unemployment

21. Aspect ratio of TV Screen is
   (a) 4:3 (b) 3:4
   (c) 2:3 (d) 2:4

22. Which of the following is not a product of learning?
   (a) Knowledge (b) Attitudes
   (c) Maturation (d) Concepts

23. The first paper for the human beings was developed by
   (a) The Aryans
   (b) The Babilonians
   (c) The Chinese
   (d) The Sumerians

24. Which sequence in turn will lead one to face the west direction from which one starts turning?
   (a) Right, right, left, right, left, right
   (b) Left, right, left, left, right, right
   (c) Right, right left, left, right, right
   (d) Left, left, right, left, right, left

25. Fill in the blank with the most appropriate choice:

_____ is the supreme medium to express yesterday, today and tomorrow with its own unique language.
(a) Television (b) Cinema
(c) Radio (d) Newspaper

26. In which language the newspapers have highest circulation?
(a) Tamil (b) English
(c) Bengali (d) Hindi

27. Amit is the son of Rahul. Sarika, Rahul's sister has a son Sonu and a daughter Rita. Raja is the maternal uncle of Sonu. How is Rita related to Raja.
(a) Aunt (b) Sister
(c) Daughter (d) Niece

28. **Statements:** A man must be wise to be a good wrangler. Good wrangler's are all talkative and boring.
Conclusions:
I. All the wise persons are boring.
II. All the wise persons are good wranglers.
Choose the correct option.
(a) Only conclusion I follows
(b) Only conclusion II follows
(c) Both I and II follow
(d) None of the above

29. What is the number that comes next in the sequence?
2, 5, 9, 19, 37, ...
(a) 74 (b) 75
(c) 76 (d) 78

30. Match List I with List II and select the correct answer using the codes given below:
List I
(A) Pandit Jasraj
(B) Kishan Maharaj
(C) Ravi Shankar
(D) Udai Shankar

List II
(i) Hindustani vocalist
(ii) Sitar
(iii) Tabla
(iv) Dance

Codes:	**A**	**B**	**C**	**D**
(a)	(i)	(ii)	(iii)	(iv)
(b)	(i)	(iii)	(iv)	(ii)
(c)	(i)	(iii)	(ii)	(iv)
(d)	(iii)	(ii)	(i)	(iv)

31. Who developed the ability to speak?
(a) Aryans (b) Neanderthal
(c) Cro-Magnon (d) Dravidians

32. In what way does communication in small group differ from that in the large group?
(a) Large group communication provides better feedback
(b) Small group provides far more interaction among the participants
(c) Interaction in small group is more restrictive
(d) Small group takes less time to convey the message

33. What is the main aim and objective of provision for feedback in communication system?
(a) Understand more about the content
(b) To make communication better by adjusting at both ends of Encoder and Decoder
(c) Identify the defect of communication
(d) Make necessary modification in communication system

34. Communications bandwidth that has the highest capacity and is used by microwave, cable and fibre optics lines is known as
(a) Carrier wave (b) Hyper-link
(c) Broadband (d) Bus width

35. In a certain code, CLOCK is written as KCOLC. How would STEPS be written in that code?
(a) SPETS (b) SPEST
(c) SPSET (d) SEPTS

36. Which one of the following is not an argument?
(a) Ram is not at home, so he must have gone to town
(b) Ram insulted me so I punched him in the nose
(c) If today is Tuesday, tomorrow will be Wednesday
(d) Since today is Tuesday, tomorrow will be Wednesday.

Direction: (37-41) Study the following pie chart and answer the questions based on it. Following pie chart represents the investment done by Timas Finance Ltd. in the various sectors. (All investments are in ₹ crores)

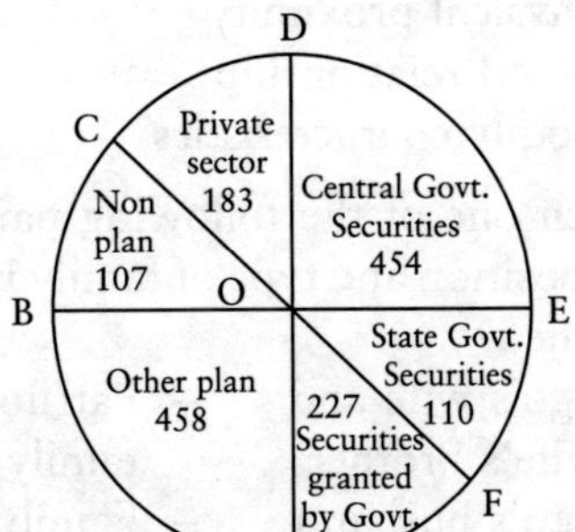

37. The percentage or gross investment in state government securities is nearly
(a) 7.1% (b) 9.2%
(c) 8.6% (d) 7.8%

38. The investment in plan and non-plan sector together is more or less than the investment in government securities (Central and State) by
(a) less, 106 crores
(b) more, 4 crores
(c) more, 1 crores
(d) more, 111 crores

39. The magnitude of ∠AOC is nearly
(a) 132° (b) 123°
(c) 126° (d) 115°

40. The ratio of area of the circle above ∠COF to the area of the circle below it is about
(a) 1 (b) 0.92
(c) 0.94 (d) 0.96

41. The investment in private sector is nearly what percent higher than the investment in State Government Security?
(a) 44% (b) 66%
(c) 54% (d) 46%

42. How many numbers between 100 and 300 begin or end with 2?
(a) 120 (b) 110
(c) 100 (d) 180

43. Which of the following operating system is used on mobile phones?
(a) Windows XP
(b) Windows Vista
(c) Android
(d) All of the above

44. Structure of logical argument is based on
(a) Linguistic expression
(b) Material truth
(c) Formal validity
(d) Aptness of examples

45. HTML is used to create
(a) machine language program
(b) high level program
(c) web page
(d) web server

46. Which of the following pollutants affects the respiratory tract in humans?
(a) Aerosols
(b) Sulphur dioxide
(c) Nitric oxide
(d) Carbon monoxide

47. Which of the following sources of energy has the maximum potential in India?

(a) Wind energy
(b) Solar energy
(c) Ocean thermal energy
(d) Tidal energy

48. In a deductive argument conclusion is
(a) Additional to the premises
(b) Entailed by the premises
(c) Summing up of the premises
(d) Not necessarily based on premises

49. What is the range of the numbers which can be stored in an eight bit register?
(a) –127 to +128 (b) –127 to +127
(c) –128 to +128 (d) –128 to +127

50. Universal Product Code (UPC), a pattern of bars printed on merchandise can be read by
(a) Product Code Reader
(b) Bar Code Reader
(c) Code Reader
(d) Card Reader

PAPER–II

1. The term assimilation is defined
(a) qualitatively with respect to structural or functional differentiation.
(b) by reference to some other object or system, to their compatibility within a common process.
(c) qualitatively with respect to its conformity to a standard of value.
(d) qualitatively with respect to the size of groups and its norms.

2. Which among the following terms is used to denote a social father?
(a) Godfather (b) Genitrix
(c) Genitor (d) Pater

3. Sociologists are primarily interested in
(a) the individual since he is convinced that there really is no such thing as group.
(b) the similarities between human behaviour and the behaviour of other animals.
(c) anything which is related in a causal way to the behaviour of man.
(d) the way in which human beings mutually influences each other.

4. Who was of the view that "Social Stratification is a process by which individuals and groups are ranked in a more or less enduring hierarchy of status"?
(a) Ogburn and Nimkoff
(b) T. Parsons
(c) H. Maine
(d) Baden Powell

5. Which among the following is not the classification of group done by Lewis Gillin Philips Gillin?
(a) Economic conditions
(b) Physical proximity
(c) Blood relationship
(d) Bodily characteristics

6. Which one of the following pairs of kin composition and type of family is corretly matched?
(a) Ego's wife and wife's brother – Patrilocal family
(b) Ego's husband and children – Family of orientation
(c) Ego's mother, father and siblings – Family of procreation
(d) Ego's brothers, sisters and mother – Matrilineal family

7. Who has not attempted a systematic classification of societies nor examine in detail any specific process of social change?
(a) Comte (b) K. Marx
(c) Hobhouse (d) H. Spencer

8. The extended family is the opposite of nuclear family. It does not exist in

(a) India (b) U.S.A.
(c) China (d) Japan

9. **Assertion (A):** It cannot be claimed that the incidents of atrocities on and oppression of Harijans have been totally eliminated, but these have gone down substantially as compared to those in the past.

Reason (R): For ensuring justice to Harijans, strict orders were given to the district authorities to take immediate action against those indulging atrocities on Harijans.

Codes:

(a) Both (A) and (R) are true and (R) is the correct explanation for (A).
(b) Both (A) and (R) are true, but (R) is not the correct explanation for (A).
(c) (A) is true, but (R) is false.
(d) (A) is false, but (R) is true.

10. 'Uncle' is an example of
(a) Discriptive term
(b) Classificatory term
(c) Role relation
(d) Expected behaviour

11. What is meta analysis?
(a) A process of secondary data gathering to assemble all the possibilities for a variable's effects.
(b) A technique of correcting for the errors in individual studies within a survey of a large number of studies, to demonstrate the effect of a particular variable.
(c) A specialized step in a computer software program (SPSS e.g.).
(d) A substitute for original research, which is justified by constraints of time or money.

12. Match List I (Movements) with List II (Periods) and select the correct answer using the codes given below the lists:

List I (Movements)
A. Rajbansi Kshatriya Sabha Movement
B. Naxalite Movement
C. New Cinema Movement
D. Shri Narain Dharma Paripalana Movement

List II (Periods)
i. Nineteenth century
ii. First quarter of 20th century
iii. 1968 onwards
iv. 1960s

Codes:	**A**	**B**	**C**	**D**
(a)	ii	iv	i	iii
(b)	ii	iii	iv	i
(c)	i	iii	ii	iv
(d)	iii	ii	iv	i

13. The form of authority enjoyed by Gandhi, Hitler, Lenin, Martin Luther King could be termed as
(a) a blend of charismatic and rational legal.
(b) a blend of charismatic and traditional.
(c) traditional.
(d) charismatic.

14. Calculus was developed by
(a) Leibnitz (b) Descartes
(c) Francis Bacon (d) Spinoza

15. The Indian society has been described static. Do you agree?
(a) No
(b) Yes
(c) Classes did exist in the Indian society.
(d) The development of castes and sub-castes hindered.

16. Which term describes a society in which women can marry more than one husband at a time but men may marry only one wife at a time?
(a) Polygyny (b) Polyandry
(c) Monogamy (d) Polygam

17. Social distance is often associated with a scaling technique developed by

(a) Moreno (b) Bogardus
(c) Thurstone (d) Likert

18. Who among the following has thought of a large population as a source of political, economic and military power?
(a) Megasthenese
(b) Hiuen-Tsang
(c) Abul Fazal
(d) Kautilya

19. Which concept may explain the process of westernization in India?
(a) Reference group
(b) Accommodation
(c) Acculturation
(d) Assimilation

20. Sociology
(a) is the scientific study of social interaction and organization.
(b) has been used to study social interaction for over 500 years.
(c) is most useful when applied to abstract as opposed to practical-matters.
(d) has little bearing on public policy.

21. Who distinguished two patterns of speech naming them elaborated and restricted codes?
(a) Johnson (b) B. Bernstein
(c) MacIver (d) None of these

22. Nuclear family in its volarized form consists of the
(a) Parents of the same children and children of the different parents.
(b) Parents of the same children and children of the ame parents.
(c) Parents of the different children and children of the same parent.
(d) None of the above mentioned relation exists in nuclear family.

23. The detachment of the performer from the role he/she is playing/performing may be categorised as
(a) Role-distance (b) Distant role
(c) Role detachment (d) Aloofness

24. *Mind and Society* is the work of
(a) Bottomore (b) Alex Inkles
(c) Pareto (d) Harlambos

25. Which among the following is not true regarding Max Weber?
(a) Classes depend on the production of goods and services.
(b) Status group depends on the consumption of goods and services.
(c) When the basis for production of goods and services is stable stratification by class become important.
(d) When the basis for production of goods and services is stable stratification by status group become important.

26. The following measure of central tendency cannot be represented graphically.
(a) Median (b) Quartile
(c) Arithmetic mean (d) Mode

27. Which of the following statements are correct?
1. Urbanisation is a product of industrialisation.
2. Diversity of occupations is a characteristic of urban life.
3. Rural urban migration continues to contribute a major part to the growth of urban population.
4. Owing to urbanization and industrialization the population is highly complex in cities.

Codes:
(a) 1, 2 and 4 (b) 1, 2 and 3
(c) 2, 3 and 4 (d) 1, 3 and 4

28. A view of sociology which emphasises the importance of the analysis of the form of a social relationship and the

comparative study of cases which differ whilst the form remains constant is
(a) Symbolic interactionism
(b) Formalism
(c) Synthetic view of sociology
(d) Comparative sociology

29. 'Man is a social animal.' Who said this?
(a) MacIver (b) Rousseau
(c) Aristotle (d) Freud

30. Which theory holds that population must grow upto certain desired level after which further growth is harmful?
(a) Zero population theory
(b) Optimum population theory
(c) Balance population theory
(d) Maximum population theory

31. One of the potential pitfalls in devising a coding scheme is that
(a) you might run out of photocopier paper.
(b) it can be difficult to obtain a random sample of newspapers.
(c) the unit of analysis is too clearly defined.
(d) the categories may not be mutually exclusive.

32. Mark out the first instrument of exchange that was known in the country and is still in use?
(a) Hundi (b) Letters of credit
(c) Bill of exchange (d) Cheque

33. A man who compares the social significance of tribal rituals in two pre-literate societies is most likely a
(a) Social Anthropologist
(b) Ethnologist
(c) Sociologist
(d) Archaeologist

34. "How expected behaviour is created and modified in interaction" is described by
(a) Role making (b) Role labelling
(c) Role taking (d) Role allotment

35. Customs are powerful in regulating the conduct of people in
(a) Urban societies
(b) Industrialised societies
(c) Simple societies
(d) Modern societies

36. Reservation for scheduled castes is provided in relation to their
(a) Low ritual positions
(b) Population
(c) Social backwardness
(d) Economic backwardness

37. The view that social stratification has beneficial consequences for the operation of a society, is given by
(a) Davis and Moore
(b) Karl Marx
(c) Max Weber
(d) MacIver and Page

38. The movement of people from central cities to smaller communities in the surrounding area is known as
(a) Over-urbanisation
(b) Urbanisation
(c) Suburbanisation
(d) Under-urbanisation

39. Society has been defined as a "web of social relationships" by
(a) R.M. MacIver
(b) R.K. Merton
(c) Talcott Parsons
(d) Emile Durkheim

40. Whom of the following wrote the book *Principles of Population Studies*?
(a) Leela Dubey
(b) Bhende and Kanitkar
(c) Jagannath Pathy
(d) Yogendra Singh

41. The entrance tests for admission to education, is intended to
    (a) find out if the candidates remember what they have learnt in their first degree.
    (b) know whether they can quickly guide and decide about their desire to work as teachers.
    (c) test the scholastic abilities of the candidates.
    (d) how if the candidates remember what they have learnt in their first degree.
42. "Sociology of Values" is developed in India by
    (a) Karl Marx
    (b) Lenin
    (c) Max Waber
    (d) Radha Kamal Mukherji
43. Which among the following features of family acts as a means of social control?
    (a) Social regulation
    (b) Nuclear position
    (c) Sense of responsibility
    (d) Educative role
44. The concept of role and status were first systematically developed by
    (a) Ralph Linton (b) Parsons
    (c) Malinowski (d) Robert Redfield
45. From a sociological perspective, what was a significant cause of BSE?
    (a) Unhygienic farming practices
    (b) New variant CJD
    (c) Changes in food processing regulations
    (d) Cows themselves
46. The average annual growth rate for 1981-91 of Indian population is
    (a) 2.11 per cent (b) 3.25 per cent
    (c) 7 per cent (d) 4.27 per cent
47. Quantitative social researchers rarely claim to have established causality because
    (a) they do not believe that this is an appropriate goal to be striving for.
    (b) they are more concerned with publishing the results of their reliability tests.
    (c) they tend to use cross-sectional designs, which produce only correlations.
    (d) they keep forgetting which of the variables they have manipulated.
48. For Weber, all human action is directed by
    (a) Meaning and motive
    (b) Society
    (c) Individual
    (d) Rationality
49. There are two types of marriage among Muslims. Identify them.
    (a) Monogamy and Polygamy
    (b) Polyandry and Polygyny
    (c) Beena and Muta
    (d) Beena and Meen
50. Who wrote *The Poverty of Historicism* (1957)?
    (a) Karl Marx (b) Karl Manheim
    (c) William Dilthey (d) Karl Popper

PAPER–III

1. Which one of the following is not a point of dissimilarity between human and animal society?
    (a) Both differ in mode of living
    (b) Both differ in character
    (c) Both differ in desire for self-preservation
    (d) Both differ in consciousness

2. The classification of societies into 'Sacrecl' society and 'Secular' society is given by
(a) Emile Durkheim
(b) Faradinand Tonnies
(c) Howard Becker
(d) Herbert Spencer

3. According to Karl Marx there was communal ownership of land in the
(a) capitalist mode of production.
(b) asiatic mode of production.
(c) ancient mode of production.
(d) feudal mode of production.

4. Which of the following is not an expression used for scheduled castes?
(a) Untouchables
(b) Interior castes
(c) Depressed classes
(d) Exterior castes

5. Despite the introduction of a national curriculum in 1988, girls continued to face disadvantages in education because
(a) the hidden curriculum ensures that subjects like science are taught in gendered styles
(b) subject choice remained gendered at a level and in higher education
(c) boys received more attention from teachers in the classroom
(d) All of the above

6. *Sociology: A Multiple Paradigm Science* book is written by
(a) Anthony Giddens
(b) George Ritzer
(c) Thomas Kuhn
(d) Herbert Blume

7. Mythical ancestors are common in
(a) Clans and lineage
(b) Phratries and lineage
(c) Clans and phratries
(d) Clans and joint family

8. Which of the following is a general rule of thumb for designing questions?
(a) Always use vignettes rather than open questions.
(b) Always bear in mind your research questions.
(c) Use ambiguous terms to put respondents at ease.
(d) Never ask a closed question.

9. The term 'virilocal' residence refers to the establishement of their residence by a newly married couple
(a) with the bridegroom's parents.
(b) with the bride's parents.
(c) with the mother's brother of the bride.
(d) independently.

10. The Roman law regards a family as a group that comprised of
(a) parents, children and slaves.
(b) husband, wife and slaves.
(c) parents and children only.
(d) parents, children, servants, slaves, and other common descent.

11. **Assertion (A):** Emphasis on conjugal ties is supposed to weaken the stability of the joint family.
Reason (R): The father-son relationship and the relationship between brothers are more crucial for the joint family system than the conjugal relationship.
Codes:
(a) Both (A) and (R) are true and (R) is the correct explanation for (A).
(b) Both (A) and (R) are true, but (R) is not the correct explanation for (A).
(c) (A) is true, but (R) is false.
(d) (A) is false, but (R) is true.

12. Who is known as the French Sorokin?
(a) W.W. Rostow
(b) Morris Ginsberg
(c) Emile Durkheim
(d) Georges Gurvitch

13. Patriarchal and matriarchal theories about the origin of society believe that society emerged as a result of

(a) evolution of several factors combined together.
(b) use of brute force.
(c) social contract.
(d) expansion of family.

14. Who among the following launched educational reform movements among Muslims in India?
1. Sir Syed Ahmed Khan
2. Sir W.W. Hunters
3. Shah Waliullah
4. Zakir Hussain

Codes:
(a) 2, 3 and 4 (b) 3 and 4
(c) 1 and 4 (d) 1 and 3

15. The children of the siblings of the opposite sex is called
(a) Parallel cousin (b) Cross-cousin
(c) Kin (d) Sister's son

16. Based on the 1981-91 decennial growth rate of population, states with the highest and the lowest growth rates are respectively
(a) Rajasthan and Tamil Nadu
(b) Arunachal Pradesh and Kerala
(c) Nagaland and Kerala
(d) Arunachal Pradesh and Goa

17. Industrial revolution is
(a) a unique occurrence.
(b) a process illustrates a pattern of change that has taken place in the past and is likely to be repeated in future in other societies.
(c) an unique phenomenon.
(d) a process by which drastic change has occurred in the European societies.

18. Match List I (Concepts of structural functional theory) with List II (Scholars associated with concepts) and select the correct answer using the codes given below the lists.

List I (Concepts of structural functional theory)
A. Functional imperative
B. Net balance of functional consequences
C. Universal functionalism
D. Postivistic organicism

List II (Scholars associated with concepts)
i. R.K. Merton
ii. B. Malinowski
iii. August Comte
iv. T. Parsons
v. Marion J. Levy

Codes:	**A**	**B**	**C**	**D**
(a)	iv	i	v	iii
(b)	i	iii	v	iv
(c)	ii	iv	v	i
(d)	iv	i	ii	iii

19. Social Stratification
(a) causes social disintegration.
(b) gives support to untouchability.
(c) is an unavoidable phenomenon.
(d) weakens existing social structure.

20. According to R.K. Merton, a role set is
(a) an array of associated roles related to particular social status.
(b) a set of roles performed by the members in any group.
(c) an array of roles hierarchically ordered in any group.
(d) a set of roles of equal statuses in any group.

21. When cohabition with any male is exclusive over a period of time although that women is still regarded as married to someone, this condition may be discribed as
(a) Exclusive marriage
(b) Secondary marriage
(c) Extended marriage
(d) Primary marriage

22. 'Ambil-anak' marriage is found in
(a) Fiji (b) New Zealand
(c) Australia (d) Indonesia

23. The book *Primitive Polynesian Economy* was written by
(a) R. Thurnwald (b) Malinowski
(c) R. Firth (d) Nadel

24. Parsons argued that the two main functions of the modern family were
(a) emotional support and sexual gratification.
(b) secondary socialization and strict discipline.
(c) oppressing women and reproducing the labour force.
(d) primary socialization and personality stabilization.

25. The president can appoint a commission to investigate the difficulties under which the socially and educationally backward classes of the citizens and to make recommendations to remove such difficulties. This comes under Article
(a) 340 (b) 339
(c) 341 (d) 338

26. There exist three features which distinguish youth culture. Which among the following is not a feature?
(a) Social relationships are organised around the peer groups, not families.
(b) Youth groups are particularly interested in style.
(c) It is a culture of leisure than work.
(d) It is a culture of comfort than pain.

27. Feminist perspectives are distinctive in sociology because
(a) other theoretical perspectives have not researched women.
(b) only women can write from a feminist perspective.
(c) men and women view the world in different ways.
(d) they emphasize the centrality of gender in social analysis.

28. Who describes the new global economy as the 'automaton'?
(a) Jean Baudrillard
(b) Michel Foucault
(c) Manuel Castells
(d) Ulrich Beck

29. A social movement based on the expectation of a sudden transformation of society through the intervention of the super natural is
(a) Milenarian movement
(b) Vitalistic movement
(c) Revitalization movement
(d) Nativistic movement

30. With whom do you associate the concept of social fact?
(a) M. Mauss (b) Max Weber
(c) Emile Durkheim (d) Karl Marx

31. In most societies, urbanization has
(a) discouraged economic growth.
(b) strengthened the influence of extended family system.
(c) promoted collectivism.
(d) weakened traditional values and life patterns.

32. Which is the cause for much pain in divorce proceedings?
(a) Allegations at each other
(b) Custody of the children
(c) Separation between wife and husband
(d) Loss of money.

33. Microliths are associated with
(a) Neolithic Age (b) Iron Age
(c) Mesolithic Age (d) Chalcolithic Age

34. Who has stated that since elites amongst the backward classes are educated and therefore comparatively more enlightened than the rest of the community, they are better able to foresee social change?

(a) Jyotiba Phule
(b) B.R. Ambedkar
(c) Sachchidananda
(d) M.K. Gandhi

35. Who defined family as a "group of persons whose relations to one another are based upon consanguinity and who are therefore kin to one another"?
(a) L.H. Morgan
(b) Kingsley Davis
(c) J. Goody
(d) MacIver and Page

36. Why is it helpful to prepare an interview guide before conducting semi-structured interviews?
(a) In order to allow participants complete control over the topics they discuss.
(b) So that the data from different interviewees will be comparable and relevant to your research questions.
(c) To make the sample more representative.
(d) So that you can calculate the statistical significance of the results.

37. With industrial capitalism, leisure emerged as a concept that meant
(a) the growth of civic, municipal culture through public libraries, museums and art galleries.
(b) distinct periods of non-work and relaxation.
(c) regulated and organized activities to reduce social disorder.
(d) All of the above.

38. The chief vehicle of culture is language. It enables one.
(a) To learn
(b) To acquire and to transmit idea and experiences
(c) To study
(d) To read

39. According to Hindu Succession Act passed in the year _____, the daughter is also given equal rights of inheritance in the property of the father, along with the son. The women get right of the use, sale and mortgage of the property received through inheritance.
(a) 1929 (b) 1955
(c) 1956 (d) 1954

40. Which one of the following statements about sanskritization is correct?
(a) It is an exogenous source of change.
(b) It is a process of positional change.
(c) It is a process of structural change.
(d) It started with the advent of British rule in India.

41. Who among the following had recommended that birth control services should be provided for the promotion of the health of mothers and children?
(a) V. Elwin
(b) G.S. Ghurye
(c) Jawaharlal Nehru
(d) Sir Joseph Bhore

42. The pragmatist philosophy used in symbolic interactionist theory teaches that
(a) we can find true, objective knowledge of the world through our senses.
(b) theory must be augmented by straightforward, plausible methods.
(c) the best social theory was developed in Prague.
(d) knowledge is produced in everyday, practical situations.

43. What do discourse analysts study?
(a) The way discourses 'frame' our understanding of the social world.
(b) The rhetorical styles used in written and oral communication.
(c) Forms of communication other than talk.
(d) All of the above.

44. "Social control explanation" of child abuse is given by
(a) William Goode
(b) Gelles
(c) Kempe
(d) Burges

45. **Assertion (A):** Village Panchayat is quite different from the recent legislative use of the term Panchayat.
Reason (R): The recent usage refers to a statutory local body, formed through elections.
Codes:
(a) Both (A) and (R) are true and (R) is the correct explanation for (A).
(b) Both (A) and (R) are true, but (R) is not the correct explanation for (A).
(c) (A) is true, but (R) is false.
(d) (A) is false, but (R) is true.

46. Which of the following best describes the definition of poverty used by the United States government?
(a) It is based on the concept of relative deprivation, and the poverty line changes as the distribution of income changes.
(b) It is based on the concept of lifestyle, and the poverty line varies according to the needs of the individual.
(c) It specifies the poverty line at a level set in the 1960s and adjusted since to reflect inflation.
(d) It includes the value of government services, such as Medicaid or public housing, when setting the poverty line.

47. Patriarchal theory has been propounded by
(a) Morgan (b) Aristotle
(c) Taylor (d) Henry Maine

48. Society cannot be studied in the same way as the natural world because
(a) it is difficult for sociologists to gain access to a research laboratory.
(b) human behaviour is meaningful, and varies between individuals and cultures.
(c) we cannot collect empirical data about social life.
(d) sociologists are not rational or critical enough in their approach.

49. What is repugnant to the Gandhian State?
(a) Not to accept the supremacy of State
(b) To follow the laws
(c) To submit to the bad laws
(d) Not to follow the laws.

50. The Constitution of India (Article 35) provides for the appointment of a minister for Tribal Welfare in the States of
(a) Bihar, Madhya Pradesh and Uttar Pradesh.
(b) Bihar, Madhya Pradesh and Orissa.
(c) Bihar, Orissa and West Bangal.
(d) None of the above.

ANSWER SHEET

PAPER—I

1. (b)	2. (c)	3. (d)	4. (d)	5. (a)
6. (c)	7. (d)	8. (c)	9. (c)	10. (b)
11. (b)	12. (b)	13. (a)	14. (b)	15. (b)
16. (c)	17. (d)	18. (b)	19. (a)	20. (c)
21. (a)	22. (c)	23. (c)	24. (b)	25. (b)
26. (b)	27. (d)	28. (d)	29. (b)	30. (c)
31. (c)	32. (b)	33. (b)	34. (c)	35. (a)
36. (b)	37. (a)	38. (c)	39. (a)	40. (c)
41. (b)	42. (b)	43. (c)	44. (b)	45. (c)
46. (c)	47. (b)	48. (b)	49. (d)	50. (b)

PAPER—II

1. (b)	2. (d)	3. (d)	4. (a)	5. (a)
6. (d)	7. (c)	8. (b)	9. (b)	10. (b)
11. (b)	12. (b)	13. (d)	14. (a)	15. (a)
16. (a)	17. (b)	18. (d)	19. (a)	20. (a)
21. (b)	22. (b)	23. (a)	24. (c)	25. (c)
26. (c)	27. (c)	28. (b)	29. (c)	30. (b)
31. (b)	32. (a)	33. (a)	34. (a)	35. (c)
36. (b)	37. (a)	38. (c)	39. (a)	40. (b)
41. (c)	42. (d)	43. (a)	44. (a)	45. (c)
46. (a)	47. (c)	48. (a)	49. (c)	50. (d)

PAPER—III

1. (b)	2. (c)	3. (b)	4. (b)	5. (d)
6. (a)	7. (c)	8. (b)	9. (a)	10. (d)
11. (a)	12. (d)	13. (d)	14. (c)	15. (b)
16. (b)	17. (b)	18. (a)	19. (a)	20. (a)
21. (b)	22. (d)	23. (c)	24. (d)	25. (a)
26. (d)	27. (d)	28. (c)	29. (a)	30. (c)
31. (d)	32. (b)	33. (a)	34. (c)	35. (b)
36. (b)	37. (d)	38. (b)	39. (c)	40. (b)
41. (d)	42. (d)	43. (d)	44. (b)	45. (a)
46. (c)	47. (b)	48. (b)	49. (c)	50. (a)

MOCK TEST–5
PAPER–I

1. Which among the following gives more freedom to the learner to interact?
   (a) Small group discussion
   (b) Lectures by experts
   (c) Use of film
   (d) Viewing country-wide classroom program on TV

2. While designing communication strategy feed-forward studies are conducted by
   (a) Media (b) Audience
   (c) Communicator (d) Satellite

3. A theory is correct because
   (a) its derivations match with most observations
   (b) its advocate has written a big volume to establish it
   (c) it is supported by a large number of scholars
   (d) it has a large number of followers

4. Which of the following are true about the concepts?
   I. Concepts have different meanings in different contents.
   II. Concepts are the blocks from which theories are built.
   III. Concepts are ideas, abstractions, that do not have meaning in themselves.
   (a) Only II (b) I and III
   (c) I and II (d) All of these

5. The most sensible idea about teaching and research is that
   (a) they interfere with each other
   (b) they are two entirely different kinds of activities
   (c) they cannot go together
   (d) they are two sides of the same coin

6. Which of the following is quality of a teacher?
   (a) He should know the child psychology
   (b) He should evoke curiosity of the pupils by presenting the subject matter in an effective manner with clear explaining leading to better understanding of the matter
   (c) He should be trained in various teaching methodologies
   (d) All of the above

7. Which of the following is/are true about research?

(i) Gives emphasis to the development of theories, principles and generalisation, which are very helpful in accurate prediction regarding the variable understudy.
(ii) It is always directed towards the solution of a problem.
(iii) It is always based upon empirical or observable evidences.
(a) Both (i) and (ii)
(b) Both (i) and (iii)
(c) Both (ii) and (iii)
(d) All of the above

8. Which of the following methods of teaching encourages the use of maximum senses?
(a) Team teaching method
(b) Problem-solving method
(c) Laboratory method
(d) Self-study method

9. A non-fictional literary composition that forms an independent part of a publication, as a newspaper or magazine is known as
(a) Symposium (b) Paper
(c) Article (d) None of these

10. Photo bleeding means
(a) Photo placement
(b) Photo cropping
(c) Photo colour adjustment
(d) Photo cutting

11. Attitudes, concepts, skills and knowledge are products of
(a) Explanation (b) Learning
(c) Research (d) Heredity

12. To study the relationship of family size with income a researcher classifies his population into different income slabs and then takes a random sample from each slab. Which technique of sampling does he adopt?
(a) Systematic Sampling
(b) Random Sampling
(c) Stratified Random Sampling
(d) Cluster Sampling

13. In business communication, the major obstacles arise because of the
(a) psychological barriers
(b) physical barriers
(c) organisational barriers
(d) mechanical barriers

14. The most important question that a researcher is interested to use statistical techniques in his problem then he has to see
(a) whether worthwhile inferences could be drawn
(b) whether the data could be quantified
(c) whether appropriate statistical techniques are available
(d) whether analysis of data would be possible

15. How can the objectivity of the research be enhanced?
(a) Through its validity
(b) Through its impartiality
(c) Through its reliability
(d) All of the above

16. Which one of the following is not correct? A belief becomes a scientific truth when it
(a) can be replicated
(b) is established experimentally
(c) is arrived by logically
(d) is accepted by many people

17. **Statements:** All cars are ducks.
All ducks are birds.
Conclusions:
(i) All birds are cars.
(ii) All cars are birds.
Choose the correct one.
(a) Only (i) follows
(b) Only (ii) follows

(c) Both (i) and (ii) follows
(d) Neither (i) nor (ii) follows

18. Research can be conducted by a person who
(a) is a hard worker
(b) has studied research methodology
(c) holds a postgraduate degree
(d) possesses thinking and reasoning ability

19. Action-research is
(a) A longitudinal research
(b) An applied research
(c) A research carried out to solve immediate problems
(d) All of the above

Read the following passage and answer the questions from 20 to 24:

The genesis of service tax emanates from the ongoing structural transformation of the Indian economy, whereby presently more than one-half of GDP originates from the services sector. Despite the growing presence of the services sector in the Indian economy it remained out of the tax net prior to 1994-95, leading to a steady deterioration in tax-GDP ratio. The service tax was introduced in 1994-95 on a select category of services at a low rate of five per cent. While the service tax rate and the coverage of services being taxed have increased ever since, the combined tax-GDP ratio of the Centre and States, nevertheless, deteriorated from 16.4 per cent in 1985-86 to 14.1 per cent in 1999-2000. It may be noted that between 1990-91 and 1998-99, the share of industrial sector in GDP dropped by 6.4 percentage points whereas almost 64 per cent of the tax revenue was generated by indirect taxes for which industrial sector continues to be the principal tax base. On the other hand, during the same period, the share of services sector in GDP has increased by 10 percentage points and this sector has still remained poorly taxed.

The rationale for service tax, therefore, lies not only in arresting the falling tax-GDP ratio but also in *ipso facto* improving allocative efficiency in the economy as well as promoting equity. Against this backdrop, the service tax needs to be designed taking into account the fact that (i) the share of services in GDP is expanding; (ii) failure to tax services distorts consumer choices and encourages spending on services at the expense of goods; (iii) untaxed service traders are unable to claim Value Added Tax (VAT) on service inputs, which encourages businesses to develop in-house services, creating further distortions; and (iv) most services that are likely to become taxable are positively correlated with expenditure of high-income households and, therefore, service tax improves equity.

In the Indian context, taxation of services assumes importance in the wake of the need for improving the revenue system, ensuring a measure of neutrality in taxation between goods and services and eventually helping to evolve an efficient system of domestic trade taxes, both at the Central and the State levels.

20. What, according to the passage, was the impact of exclusion of service tax till the first half of the last decade of the past century?
(a) Service sector used to flourish exorbitantly
(b) There was no impact as there was no service tax
(c) There was a steady deterioration in the GDP
(d) Tax-GDP ratio had steadily and gradually aggravated

21. Levying service tax is most likely to achieve which of the following?
    (i) Promoting equity.
    (ii) Check on reducing tax-GDP ratio.
    (iii) Enhancement in allocative efficiency.
    (a) (ii) and (iii)
    (b) (i) and (iii)
    (c) (i) and (ii)
    (d) All of the above
22. The origin of service tax is attributed to
    (a) metamorphosis of our country's economy
    (b) increase in Gross Domestic Product (GDP)
    (c) existence of service sector
    (d) tax of the future
23. Which of the following factors helps service tax to improve fairness across different economic strata of society?
    (a) It improves revenue system
    (b) Taxable services are mostly those that are utilised by the rich
    (c) Untaxed service traders are prevented from claiming value added tax
    (d) Encouragement to in-house services is effected
24. Which of the following is most likely to provide neutrality to various economic activities?
    (a) Consistency in tax structure and revenue buoyancy
    (b) Increase in revenue buoyancy
    (c) Fairness in tax administration
    (d) Equity and efficiency in various activities
25. Which of the following is classified in the category of the developmental research?
    (a) Descriptive research
    (b) Philosophical research
    (c) Action research
    (d) All of the above
26. The education aims at the fullest realisation of all the potentialities of children. It implies that
    I. it is necessary that their attitudes are helpful, encouraging and sympathetic.
    II. teacher and parents must know what children are capable of and what potentialities they possess.
    III. they should provide suitable opportunities and favourable environmental facilities which are conducive to the maximum growth of children.

    Choose the correct one.
    (a) II and III (b) I and III
    (c) I and II (d) All of them
27. How many times has the preamble of Indian constitution been amended so far?
    (a) Once (b) Twice
    (c) Thrice (d) Never
28. The relationship between earth, mountains and forests can be represented as

    (a) 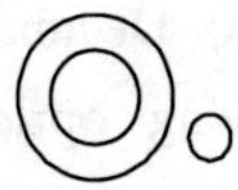 (b) 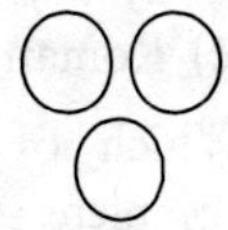

    (c)  (d) 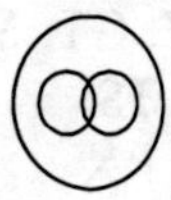
29. Central Fuel Research Institute is situated in
    (a) Pune (b) Jadugoda
    (c) Lucknow (d) Kolkata
30. The letters in the first set have certain relationship. On the basis of this relationship what is the right choice for the second set?

    AST : BRU :: NQV : ?
    (a) OPW (b) ORW
    (c) MPU (d) MRW

31. The number of students in four classes A, B, C, D and their respective mean marks obtained by each of the class are given below:

	Class A	Class B	Class C	Class D
Number of students	10	40	30	20
Arithmetic mean	20	30	50	15

The combined mean of the marks of four classes together will be
(a) 15 (b) 32
(c) 50 (d) 20

32. Communication with oneself is known as
(a) Organisational communication
(b) Interpersonal communication
(c) Intrapersonal communication
(d) Grapewine communication

33. The number system which is not a positional notation system is
(a) Binary (b) Octal
(c) Roman (d) Decimal

34. Which of the following options will complete the series?
AZ, GT, MN, ?, YB.
(a) TS (b) KF
(c) RX (d) SH

35. If '367' means 'I am happy'; '748' means 'You are sad' and '469' means 'Happy and sad' in a given code, then which of the following represents 'and' in that code?
(a) 4 (b) 6
(c) 3 (d) 9

36. What is the excess 3 code?
(a) self-algebraic code
(b) cyclic complimenting code
(c) cyclic algebraic code
(d) self-complimenting code

37. Which of the following is not created by the Act of Parliament?
(a) Railway Board
(b) Atomic Energy Commission
(c) Backward Class Commission
(d) University Grants Commission

38. Which of the following is radioactive pollutant?
(a) Nickel (b) Iron
(c) Chlorine (d) Thorium

39. The first Indian experimental geostationary communication satellite was
(a) Skylab (b) Apple
(c) INSAT-1A (d) INSAT-1B

40. Which one of the following is a research tool?
(a) Diagram (b) Questionnaire
(c) Graph (d) Illustration

41. Which article of the constitution provides safeguards to Naga Customary and their social practices against any act of Parliament?
(a) Article 371 B (b) Article 371 A
(c) Article 263 (d) Article 371 C

42. **Statement:** Although the city was under kneedeep water for a week in this monsoon, there is no outbreak of any water borne disease.
Assumptions:
(i) Waterborne disease usually spreads in monsoon.
(ii) Water concentration at a place leads to waterborne disease.

Choose the correct option.
(a) Only assumption (i) is implicit
(b) Only assumption (ii) is implicit
(c) Both (i) and (ii) are implicit
(d) Neither (i) nor (ii) is implicit

43. Books and records are the primary sources of data in
(a) laboratory research
(b) historical research
(c) participatory research
(d) clinical research

44. The Kothari Commission's report was entitled on
   (a) Learning to be adventure
   (b) Education and National Development
   (c) Education and socialisation in democracy
   (d) Diversification of Education

45. What is the term used for a half byte?
   (a) word (b) bit
   (c) nibble (d) bug

46. C-band transponder in satellites uses the frequency range
   (a) 12 GHz to 14 GHz
   (b) 4 GHz to 6 GHz
   (c) 2 GHz to 4 GHz
   (d) None of these.

47. Which of the following water pollutants is the cause of sterility in human beings?
   (a) Manganese (b) Mercury
   (c) Arsenic (d) None of these

48. Controlled group condition is applied in
   (a) Descriptive Research
   (b) Survey Research
   (c) Experimental Research
   (d) Historical Research

49. Match List I with List II and select the correct answer using the codes given below.

List I (Institutes)
(A) Central Arid Zone Institute
(B) Space Application Centre
(C) Indian Institute of Public Administration
(D) Headquarters of Indian Science Congress

List II (Cities)
(1) Kolkata (2) New Delhi
(3) Ahmedabad (4) Jodhpur

Codes:	**A**	**B**	**C**	**D**
(a)	4	3	2	1
(b)	4	2	1	3
(c)	3	1	2	4
(d)	1	2	4	3

The total CO_2 emissions from various sectors are 5 mmt. In the Pie Chart given below, the percentage contribution to CO_2 emissions from various sectors is indicated.

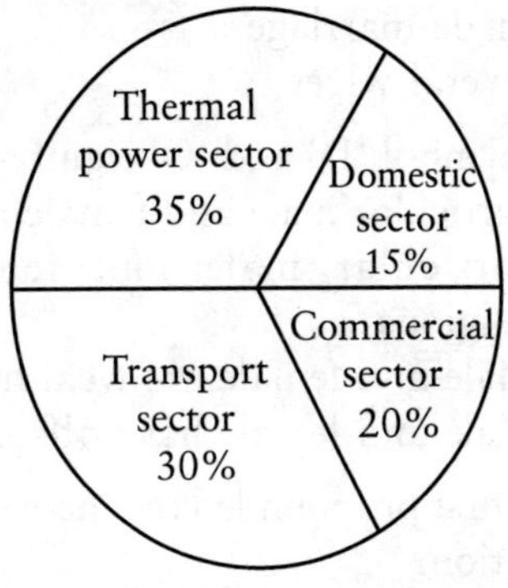

50. What is the absolute CO_2 emission from domestic sector?
   (a) 1.75 mmt (b) 0.75 mmt
   (c) 1.5 mmt (d) 2.5 mmt

PAPER–II

1. Social psychology is most concerned with
   (a) the diagnosis and treatment of developmental, emotional, and behavioural problems in children and teenagers.
   (b) how the thoughts, feelings and behaviours of individuals are influenced by the actual, imagined or implied presence of other human beings.
   (c) the examination of internal mental processes such as problem solving, memory, and language.
   (d) the nature and development of behaviour, thoughts and feelings associated with distress or impaired functioning.

2. The number of individual responses to anomie given by Robert Merton is
   (a) Three (b) One
   (c) Five (d) Four
3. Polygamy means
   (a) several marriages
   (b) several husbands
   (c) single marriage
   (d) several wives
4. The symbol 'D' and 'O' signify
   (a) Particular male and female are dead
   (b) Particular male and female are religious
   (c) Male and female are wealthy
   (d) Male and female have offspring
5. Who first propounded the theory of social evolution?
   (a) Wallace and Darwin
   (b) Herbert Spencer
   (c) Montesquieu
   (d) Aristotle
6. In the traditional hierarchy of status and precedence, which of these members of the upper class are in the right order (from highest to lowest status)?
   (a) Marquesses of England, Earls of Great Britain, King's Brothers.
   (b) Prime Minister, Archbishop of York, Viscounts of England.
   (c) King's Grandsons, Lord High Treasurer, Companions of the Bath.
   (d) Esquires, Serjeants of Law, Dukes' Eldest Sons.
7. Man always strived to arrive at an optimum population. Man took all the factors including environment, skill, customs, etc., into account to attain this number. The optimum number is not fixed for all times. It depends upon the changes that occur in a given country or context. Whose view is this?
   (a) D. Ricardo
   (b) Herbert Spencer
   (c) Alexander Morris Carr-Saunders
   (d) Adam Smith
8. Who said, "Property is to be conceived in terms of control of man over things"?
   (a) R.H. Lowie (b) L.H. Morgan
   (c) T. Veblen (d) L.T. Hobhouse
9. Which of the following are characteristics of the Bureaucratic model?
   1. Distinction between office and person
   2. Legitimization of authority by technical competence
   3. Recognition of informal groups in official scheme
   4. Encouragement of career and differentiated rewards

   Codes:
   (a) 1, 3 and 4 (b) 2, 3 and 4
   (c) 1, 2 and 3 (d) 1, 2 and 4
10. According to whom "sociology is a pure or theoretical science and not an applied science"?
   (a) R. Bierstedt (b) Kingsley Davis
   (c) MacIver and Page (d) Karl Marx
11. When Comte wrote of sociology as a positive science, he meant
   (a) that it should attempt to appeal to as many people as possible.
   (b) that it should show people in the best possible light.
   (c) that it should progress by positing new concepts and theories.
   (d) that it should apply the same methods as physics or chemistry.
12. The philosophy of history as a distinct branch of speculation is a creation of
   (a) Twentieth century
   (b) Thirteenth century
   (c) Eighteenth century
   (d) Nineteenth century

13. The organised forms of social behaviour and their repetition are called
   (a) Customs (b) Norms
   (c) Culture (d) Value

14. Who has written the book *Women and Society in India*?
   (a) Leela Gulati and Leela Kasturi
   (b) Leela Dubey and Pauline Kolenda
   (c) Neera Desai and Maithreyi Krishna Raj
   (d) Leela Kasturi and Leela Dubey.

15. In order to ensure moral freedom in the younger generation the social culture must
   (a) not be a binding chart, but on ladder on which they may climb.
   (b) be binding on students so that they should be within its limits.
   (c) ensure that children avoid abuse of authority and stick to it.
   (d) not allow deviations from the legitimate restrictions of the authority.

16. Match List I with List II and select the correct answer using the codes given below the lists.

   List I
   A. The concentric zone theory
   B. The central place location theory
   C. The sector theory
   D. The multiple nuclei theory

   List II
   i. Ernest Burgess
   ii. Chrystaller
   iii. Homer Hoyt
   iv. Harris and Ullman

Codes:	A	B	C	D
(a)	i	ii	iv	iii
(b)	ii	i	iii	iv
(c)	ii	i	iv	iii
(d)	i	ii	iii	iv

17. Who founded the Sociology Society of London?
   (a) Herbert Spencer
   (b) Victor Branford
   (c) Radcliffe Brown
   (d) Patrick Geddes

18. Sullivan's (2000) study suggested that the proportion of housework men did was greatest when
   (a) their wives were at home and nagged them all the time.
   (b) they had rediscovered themselves as 'new men'.
   (c) they were unemployed or both partners worked full time.
   (d) exciting gadgets like the hoover and electric iron were invented.

19. The integrated project for development and empowerment of women is
   (a) Swashakti (b) Swayamsidha
   (c) Swawalamban (d) Swadhar

20. What is one of the advantages that official statistics have over structured interview data?
   (a) They are completely objective and reliable.
   (b) The researcher can conduct natural experiments in the field.
   (c) They allow the researcher to identify social trends over time.
   (d) They have greater measurement validity.

21. The term 'manufactured risk' refers to
   (a) risks associated with the activities of manufacturing industries.
   (b) risks which result from human interaction with the natural world.
   (c) risks that only affect advanced industrial economies.
   (d) risks that have been exaggerated by the output of the media.

22. **Assertion (A):** In order to survive, an authoritarian state resorts to repression, permanent mobilisation and manipulation.

Reason (R): In an authoritarian state, the bureaucratic apparatus becomes responsive to the needs of the masses.

Codes:

(a) Both (A) and (R) are true and (R) is the correct explanation for (A).
(b) Both (A) and (R) are true, but (R) is not the correct explanation for (A).
(c) (A) is true, but (R) is false.
(d) (A) is false, but (R) is true.

23. Following Marx, there was a spurt in research on the concept of alienation. From where did Marx borrow this concept?
(a) Seeman (b) Spencer
(c) Hegel (d) None of these

24. Which of these is not a feminist criticism of traditional approaches to social class?
(a) The assumption that the class position of women reflects that of men.
(b) The assumption that the man is head of household.
(c) The assumption that men and women both take responsibility for childcare.
(d) The assumption that class is more important than gender.

25. The four ideal types of social action that Weber identified were as follows: instrumentally-rational, value-rational, traditional, and
(a) Effective (b) Infected
(c) Affectual (d) Affective

26. French philosopher, moralist and sociologist, he collaborated with Saint Simon from 1817 to 1823 and corresponded with J.S. Mill. He divided sociology into social statics and social dynamics and elaborated the law of the three stages of human thought theological, metaphysical and positive. Can you identify who among the following matches the above description?
(a) A.N. Whitehead (b) Montesquieu
(c) Herbert Spencer (d) August Comte

27. The crux of the population policy is
(a) to reduce the sex-ratio.
(b) to increase the number of women.
(c) settlement of more people in urban areas.
(d) reduction of the national birth rate.

28. In the industrial society, agriculture is
(a) non-existent
(b) of least consequence
(c) way of life
(d) an another industry

29. Charles Cooley's theory of the looking-glass self emphasizes
(a) the difficulty one experiences in seeing oneself as others do.
(b) the manner in which young children come to a realization that they have a separate identity.
(c) how one's self-concept is heavily influenced by one's physical appearance.
(d) how one's self-concept is based on one's perception of how others see one.

30. *Street Corner Society* is work of
(a) R.E. Park (b) Morgan
(c) Robert Redfield (d) W.F. Whyte

31. During Vedic period the ownership of land rested with
(a) It was considered as the property of God.
(b) Community.
(c) Cultivator.
(d) King.

32. The initiation ceremonies in primitive societies are functional because they are
(a) a traditional and religious expression of the supreme power and value of tradition.

(b) a superstitious and kinship expression of the supreme power and value of tradition.
(c) a ritual and dramatic expression of the supreme power and value of tradition.
(d) a customary and folk expression of the supreme power and value of tradition.

33. The term 'reverse operationism' means that
(a) the measurements we devise can sometimes help to develop a theory.
(b) the theories we devise will often hinder our attempts to measure concepts.
(c) driving instructors always make you practice the most difficult manoeuvre.
(d) techniques such as factor analysis have no place in social research.

34. A social theory which starts from a conception of society and postulates ways in which society influences the individual is a
(a) Microscopic theory
(b) Productive theory
(c) Macroscopic theory
(d) Katascopic theory

35. Sociology can be considered a social science because
(a) sociologists collect data in a relatively objective and systematic way.
(b) ideas and research findings are scrutinized by other sociologists.
(c) its theories are logical, explicit and supported by empirical evidence.
(d) All of the above.

36. Pronatalism refers to the
(a) strong positive value a society places on having children.
(b) view that vitality of the family depends upon the strong physique of the child.
(c) view that a person should not have as many children as possible.
(d) view that only the child can provide sustenance and salvation to the family.

37. Match List I with List II and select the correct answer using the codes given below the lists.

List I
A. People with similar physical characteristics.
B. People with similar cultural characteristics.
C. People with similar age.
D. People sharing similar social happenings.

List II
i. Cohort ii. Ethnic
iii. Race iv. Peer

Codes:	A	B	C	D
(a)	ii	iii	iv	i
(b)	iii	ii	iv	i
(c)	iii	ii	i	iv
(d)	ii	iii	i	iv

38. What is behaviour towards a group or individual which treats them differently from other groups or individuals called?
(a) Racism (b) Projection
(c) Prejudice (d) Discrimination

39. Little traditions are
(a) the traditions which are written.
(b) the traditions of little communities.
(c) the traditions of backward castes.
(d) the traditions which are unwritten and transmitted orally.

40. A human being deprived of all communication with other humans from birth would lack all but one of the followings.
(a) Language
(b) Rudimentary personality
(c) Self
(d) None of the above

41. 'Cultural relativism' is the idea that societies have to be studied in terms of their

(a) religious and spiritual beliefs.
(b) artistic and literary production.
(c) family and kin relationships.
(d) own meanings and values.

42. Select the correct chronological order of scheduled tribes in India in terms of its numerical strength.
(a) M.P., Orissa, Bihar, Gujarat
(b) Bihar, Gujarat, Assam, Orissa
(c) Bihar, Orissa, Gujarat, Rajasthan
(d) M.P., Orissa, Gujarat, Bihar

43. **Assertion (A):** At the time of the framing of the constitution, reservation of jobs for the scheduled castes and tribes was intended for an unspecified period.
Reason (R): Constitutional provisions in respect of reservation of job for the scheduled castes have not ensured their social and economic upliftment within the period specified.
Codes:
(a) Both (A) and (R) are true and (R) is the correct explanation for (A).
(b) Both (A) and (R) are true, but (R) is not the correct explanation for (A).
(c) (A) is true, but (R) is false.
(d) (A) is false, but (R) is true.

44. Why are Coffey and Atkinson critical of the way coding fragments qualitative data?
(a) Because it results in a loss of context and narrative flow.
(b) Because this is incompatible with the principles of feminist research.
(c) Because they invented the life history interview and want to promote it.
(d) Because they think it should fragment quantitative data instead.

45. The relationship between fire and smoke is not a social one as the very relationship is not in any away determined by
(a) Integration
(b) Mutual awareness
(c) Social compulsion
(d) Co-operation

46. What fundamental value does Ronald Dworkin argue is shared by the deeply opposed 'pro-choice' and 'pro-life' positions in the abortion debates?
(a) The centrality of the family
(b) The primacy of spirituality
(c) The sanctity of human life
(d) The freedom of the individual

47. What differentiates an agricultural society from an industrial society?
(a) Mode of occupation
(b) Social mobility
(c) The environment within which the two societies grow
(d) All of the above

48. Those aspects of social life that have to do with order, stability, and social organization that allow societies and groups to hold together and endure are called
(a) social dynamics
(b) social statics
(c) constructed reality
(d) social absolutes

49. "Pollution when unchecked increases in a geometrical ratio. Subsistence increase in arithmetical ratio." Who said so?
(a) Freud (b) Malthus
(c) MacIver (d) K. Davis

50. Group Mind theory believes that society
(a) and individuals have no relations.
(b) is below the individual.
(c) is above the individual.
(d) comes along with the individuals.

PAPER–III

1. A person with whom a person interacts while performing a role is known as
(a) Role strain (b) Role other
(c) Role replacing (d) Role taking

2. Which of the following are likely to happen if a situation is characterised by ethnocentrism?
1. Everything will be measured in terms of one's own cultural standard and found wanting.
2. Indigenous goods will be regarded as somehow defective.
3. Members of other cultures will be less acceptable.
4. The traditional beliefs and characteristics of other culture will be ridiculed.

Codes:
(a) 1, 3 and 4 (b) 1, 2 and 4
(c) 1, 2 and 3 (d) 2, 3 and 4

3. 'The Russian Mir' is the name of a
(a) Very large family turns into a big community
(b) Very small family living in villages
(c) Very small family living in towns
(d) None of the above

4. Contemporary sociology includes
(a) liberal feminism and explicit examination of women's social roles and experiences.
(b) evolutionary relativism.
(c) a combination of biological theory, conflict theory, and evolutionary theory.
(d) postmodernism, feminism, and critical theory.

5. When was the World Wide Web invented at a Swiss physics laboratory?
(a) 1990 (b) 1995
(c) 1980 (d) 1985

6. According to Max Weber, ideal types are
(a) pure types (b) normative types
(c) general types (d) average types

7. Which among the following phenomena explain the significant rituals and social role of the mother's brother in the lives of their sister's children?
(a) Social role of maternal uncle
(b) Mutual role relation
(c) Sibling filiation
(d) Complementary filiation

8. Who among the following is of the view that social structure is an abstract construction of social reality and has nothing to do with the existing reality?
(a) Brown (b) Leach
(c) Levi-Strauss (d) Spencer

9. Which one of the following is not a characteristic of kinship?
(a) It has no affinity between two related persons
(b) It is related and based on sex
(c) In some cases it is specific while in others it is not
(d) It usually indicates generation gap

10. The distribution of power in society is a concern for
(a) Ethnomethodology
(b) Macrosociology
(c) Interactionism
(d) Microsociology

11. "If a determinate human superior, not in the habit of obedience to like superior, receives habitual obedience from the bulk of a given society, that determinate superior is the sovereign in that society, and the society including the superior is political and independent. This view of sovereignty is
(a) Pluralistic (b) Historical
(c) Sociological (d) Legalistic

12. According to Piaget, the phase at which children master abstract, logical notions are able to grasp causality and can recognize false reasoning is the
(a) preoperational stage
(b) sensorimotor stage
(c) formal operational stage
(d) concrete operational phase

13. According to Marshall McLuhan, which of the following is being created by the electronic media?
(a) Global flows (b) Global cities
(c) Global village (d) Global network

14. The PSE survey showed that, between 1983 and 1999, the proportion of people above the poverty threshold
(a) rose from 15% to 19%
(b) rose from 4% to 8%
(c) fell from 24% to 21%
(d) rose from 14% to 24%

15. Which of the following is not associated with late Stone age?
(a) Jalahaili (b) Soan Valley
(c) Bandarawela (d) Birdhanpur

16. Open system of social stratification is
(a) society which allows mobility of caste.
(b) society which allows mobility of individual or groups.
(c) society which allows mobility of groups.
(d) society which allows mobility of individuals.

17. The effect of the Internet upon the public sphere has been to
(a) revive it, by reaffirming a commitment to freedom of speech.
(b) repress it, by promoting only the interests of elite groups.
(c) replace it with a superior form of communication.
(d) reproduce it, by emphasizing face-to-face contact with peer groups.

18. Recent writer on methodology among the following is
(a) Quetlet (b) Saint Simon
(c) Hobhouse (d) J.S. Mills

19. Rural Society though "lacks the integration of the more highly differentiated urban society" is based on:
(a) Danger of natural calamities
(b) Similarities
(c) Mutual interdependence
(d) All of the above

20. **Assertion (A):** At the time of the framing of the Constitution reservation of jobs for the Scheduled Castes was intended for an unspecified period.
Reason (R): Constitutional provisions in respect of reservation of jobs for the Scheduled Castes have not ensured their social and economic upliftment within the period specified.
Codes:
(a) Both (A) and (R) are true and (R) is the correct explanation for (A).
(b) Both (A) and (R) are true, but (R) is not the correct explanation for (A).
(c) (A) is true, but (R) is false.
(d) (A) is false, but (R) is true.

21. Development of industry has greatly contributed to urban growth. Which among the following does denote this?
(a) Concentration of population
(b) Multiplicity of non-agricultural occupations
(c) Specialisation of jobs
(d) All of the above

22. The period comprised by the last quarter of the eighteenth century and the first half of the nineteenth century is richest period from the point of view of:
(a) Social-psychological thought.
(b) European thought.

(c) Sociological thought.
(d) Social thought.

23. The problem of pollution is becoming increasingly acute with the rise of urbanisation on account of which of these following reasons.
    1. Indiscriminate growth of industrial and chemical plants inspite of the efforts through legal measure to check such growth.
    2. Pre-industrial structure of cities with narrow streets and roads, which, have become defective and inefficient in regulating traffic.
    3. Lack of effective and systematic use pattern on account of scarce land and its commercial speculation.
    4. High rise buildings, representing vertical growth of cities, ultimately causing high density of population, congestion on roads and pollution.

    Codes:
    (a) 1 and 4 (b) 1, 2, 3 and 4
    (c) 1, 3 and 4 (d) 3 and 4

24. The key advantage of structured observation over survey research is that
    (a) the researcher is immersed as a participant in the field they are studying.
    (b) it does not rely on the researcher's ability to take notes.
    (c) it allows you to observe people's behaviour directly.
    (d) it does not impose any expectations of behaviour on the respondents.

25. Which one of the following, according to Selig Perlman, accounts for the rise of trade unions?
    (a) Need for identity
    (b) Job scarcity
    (c) Exploitation
    (d) Need for solidarity

26. Like Saint Simon, he also distinguished 3 stages—theological, metaphysical and scientific—and argued that all societies pass through them. Identify the person being referred to
    (a) Herbert Spencer
    (b) Auguste Comte
    (c) Montesquieu
    (d) Malinowski

27. Mark out the primary group among the following.
    (a) Student of history
    (b) The social workers
    (c) Members of a trade union
    (d) Family

28. India has embarked on the process of a
    (a) totally capitalist path of economy development.
    (b) bureaucratic path of economic development.
    (c) socialist path emphasising on mixed economy.
    (d) communist path of economic development.

29. Social stratification means
    (a) existence of group and inner group, the product of economic, social and all other forces
    (b) classification based on power
    (c) classification based on economic conditions
    (d) classification of society into castes

30. To whom will you attribute the following. "Nirvan has been used to indicate the state of perfection in Buddism".
    (a) Dr. S. Radhakrishanan
    (b) Upanishada
    (c) Dharmapada
    (d) The Bhagavdgita

31. Whose definition about society is this: "a complex of forms or processes each of

which is living and growing by interaction with the others, the whole being so unified that with what takes place in one part affects all the rest?"
(a) W.I. Thomas
(b) Charles H. Cooley
(c) MacIver and Page
(d) J.F. Cuber

32. Which one of these is not a dimension of social divisions?
(a) Looks (b) Wealth
(c) Power (d) Status

33. Match List I (Concepts) with List II (Features) and select the correct answer using the codes given below the lists.

List I (Concepts)
A. Mechanical Solidarity
B. Primary Group
C. Little Community
D. Kula

List II (Features)
i. Face-to-face relationship
ii. Social similarities
iii. Interdependence
iv. Gift exchange
v. Homogeneity

Codes:	A	B	C	D
(a)	ii	i	v	iv
(b)	ii	iii	i	v
(c)	i	ii	v	iii
(d)	v	i	ii	iv

34. Who views society as a relation among personal ideas?
(a) Herskowits (b) C.H. Cooley
(c) Mannheim (d) Hegel

35. Classical sociology was concerned with
(a) the emergence and legitimacy of the nation-state.
(b) the emergence of global industrialisation.
(c) the impact of the feminist and environmental movements.
(d) the compression of time and space.

36. Mark out correct statement
(a) Bureaucracy is found only in public organizations.
(b) Bureaucracy is found in both public and private organizations.
(c) Bureaucracy is found only in private organizations.
(d) All of the above.

37. Main objective of 'Nikah' among Muslims is
(a) finding groom for daughter/sister
(b) to purify the bride and groom
(c) religious sanctification of marriage
(d) procreation and legalisation of children

38. In idealized views of science, the experimental method is said to involve
(a) isolating and measuring the effect of one variable upon another.
(b) testing out new research methods to see which one works best.
(c) interpreting data subjectively, drawing on theoretical paradigms.
(d) using personal beliefs and values to decide what to study.

39. Social institutions exist or continue on account of
(a) Differences (b) Likeness
(c) Common history (d) Common origin

40. The system of production for exchange supports the system of
(a) post-industrial economics.
(b) capitalist economics.
(c) socialist economics.
(d) feudal economics.

41. The concepts of "Mechanical Solidarity" and "Organic Solidarity" were developed by

(a) C. Levi-Strauss
(b) H. Spencer
(c) E. Durkheim
(d) A.R. Radcliffe-Brown

42. Which among the following statements is not correct?
(a) No community can be self sufficient these days.
(b) In past communities used to be self sufficient, politically, socially or economically.
(c) The term community denotes almost uniformly and permanently shared lives of people over a definite range.
(d) Every community is self sufficient these days.

43. The aim behind the sacrimental marriage is to
(a) follow the ancient tradition.
(b) facilitate the emotional adjustment.
(c) make the new relationship permanent.
(d) enter upon the new relationship in witness to God.

44. Who was the first Chairman of the 'Backward Classes Commission' in India?
(a) Kaka Kalelkar (b) M.K. Gandhi
(c) B.P. Mandal (d) B.R. Ambedkar

45. How the development of transport and communication helped the growth of cities? Mark out the correct answers.
(a) It connected the city with the different parts of the country.
(b) The local transport added to the population of the city by extending its boundaries.
(c) It connected different parts of the city.
(d) All of the above.

46. "The Mahar were the first people to serve the British officers and their wives as butlers, butchers and ayah and being a beef-eating group, the Mahar did not mind working for the foreign, beef eating master."
Who has observed this?
(a) Irawati Karve
(b) Pauline Kolenda
(c) Sunanda Patwardhan
(d) M.N. Srinivas

47. According to Max Weber, the 'ideal type' refers to
(a) a perspective emphasizing the primacy of ideas.
(b) the best possible outcome available.
(c) the social agenda of political idealists.
(d) a model based on certain features of a phenomenon.

48. What is meant by the term "grounded theory"?
(a) Theories should be grounded in political values and biases.
(b) Theoretical ideas and concepts should emerge from the data.
(c) Theories should be tested by rigorous scientific experiments.
(d) As a social researcher, it is important to keep your feet on the ground.

49. Culture may be defined as the
(a) uncodified ideology of people.
(b) typical habit patterns of people.
(c) pattern of arrangements, material and behavioural adopted by a society.
(d) sum total of collective behaviour.

50. Which of these is not an example of social exclusion?
(a) Homelessness
(b) Tax avoidance
(c) Gated communities
(d) None of the above

ANSWER SHEET

PAPER—I

1. (a) 2. (c) 3. (a) 4. (d) 5. (d)
6. (d) 7. (d) 8. (c) 9. (b) 10. (c)
11. (b) 12. (c) 13. (c) 14. (b) 15. (d)
16. (b) 17. (a) 18. (d) 19. (c) 20. (d)
21. (d) 22. (a) 23. (b) 24. (a) 25. (d)
26. (d) 27. (a) 28. (d) 29. (b) 30. (a)
31. (b) 32. (c) 33. (c) 34. (d) 35. (d)
36. (d) 37. (a) 38. (d) 39. (b) 40. (b)
41. (b) 42. (c) 43. (b) 44. (b) 45. (c)
46. (b) 47. (a) 48. (c) 49. (a) 50. (b)

PAPER—II

1. (b) 2. (c) 3. (a) 4. (a) 5. (b)
6. (c) 7. (c) 8. (d) 9. (d) 10. (a)
11. (a) 12. (c) 13. (a) 14. (c) 15. (a)
16. (d) 17. (d) 18. (c) 19. (b) 20. (c)
21. (b) 22. (b) 23. (c) 24. (c) 25. (c)
26. (c) 27. (d) 28. (d) 29. (d) 30. (d)
31. (b) 32. (c) 33. (a) 34. (c) 35. (d)
36. (a) 37. (b) 38. (d) 39. (b) 40. (c)
41. (d) 42. (a) 43. (d) 44. (a) 45. (a)
46. (b) 47. (d) 48. (b) 49. (b) 50. (a)

PAPER—III

1. (b) 2. (a) 3. (a) 4. (d) 5. (a)
6. (a) 7. (d) 8. (c) 9. (b) 10. (b)
11. (d) 12. (d) 13. (c) 14. (d) 15. (b)
16. (b) 17. (a) 18. (d) 19. (b) 20. (d)
21. (d) 22. (d) 23. (b) 24. (c) 25. (c)
26. (d) 27. (d) 28. (c) 29. (a) 30. (a)
31. (b) 32. (a) 33. (a) 34. (b) 35. (a)
36. (b) 37. (d) 38. (a) 39. (b) 40. (b)
41. (c) 42. (b) 43. (b) 44. (a) 45. (d)
46. (a) 47. (d) 48. (b) 49. (b) 50. (d)